EDUCATION AND SOCIAL CHANGE
IN GHANA

EDUCATION
AND
SOCIAL CHANGE
IN GHANA

by
PHILIP FOSTER

THE UNIVERSITY OF CHICAGO PRESS

This book, one in a series of publications on various
aspects of social, political, and economic change in
the new states of Asia and Africa, is issued under
the joint sponsorship of the Committee for Comparative Study of New Nations and the Comparative Education Center at the University of Chicago.

Library of Congress Catalog Card Number: 65-12040

THE UNIVERSITY OF CHICAGO PRESS, CHICAGO 60637
Routledge and Kegan Paul Ltd.

TO MY FATHER AND MOTHER

PREFACE

AS the first of the newly independent nations of Africa, Ghana has received fulsome attention from scholars in many fields. Yet I make no apology for adding to the library of books on social and political changes in that country, for education has been a Cinderella topic among writers on the new states. Numerous writers do accord the schools a central part in the processes of modernization, but few have perceived the diffusion of formal, western education as one of the basic contributors to the very emergence of the 'new nations'. There is over much of the world a disconcerting gap between the volume and the quality of discussion on educational changes as compared with the treatment of economic and political matters. However, Ghana has been better served than many African countries and I am much indebted to the earlier work of F. L. Bartels, F. H. Hilliard, W. E. F. Ward, H. O. A. McWilliam, C. G. Wise, and more recently David Kimble.

I was drawn to Ghana as a suitable area for an intensive case study in educational development by two principal considerations. The documentary materials relating to the earlier history of the Gold Coast and adjacent areas were unusually extensive and well organized. Then, Ghana has in many respects been a bell-wether for many of the other emerging African states, and not least so in the area of educational development. It now possesses the most elaborated school system in sub-Saharan Africa. But the expansion of this system has given rise to many perplexing problems and revealed many unexpected consequences, and I suggest that similar experiences will be the lot of many other countries, even outside Africa. I hope the reader will not regard this work as a study of Ghanaian education alone but view it rather as a case study wherein some of the basic processes underlying educational growth in states newly emerging from colonial rule are delineated.

I shall be criticized rightly for a rather cavalier treatment of some themes by writers particularly concerned with Ghanaian historiography. On the other hand, readers with principally comparative interests will criticize my neglecting to develop more fully many central themes in a broader context. I hope both sorts of readers will

vii

acknowledge that I have provided a serviceable framework within which educational development in Africa can be related meaningfully to other aspects of social and political change.

Clearly, this work could never have been completed without the counsel and support of many individuals. First, I must acknowledge a great debt to my associates at the Comparative Education Center and notably to C. Arnold Anderson, a colleague and friend since I joined the University of Chicago. I have benefited greatly from the advice of numerous members of the Committee for the Comparative Study of the New Nations, particularly Edward Shils, Clifford Geertz and Lloyd Fallers. We at the Comparative Education Center are grateful to the Ford Foundation for its continued support of our programme while fruitful discussion at the Committee for the Comparative Study of the New Nations has been made possible only through the assistance of the Carnegie Corporation.

It would be impossible to list those individuals in Ghana who have rendered me notable assistance but I must particularly mention the names of Andrew Taylor, Adam Curle, Paul Baxter and David Brokensha, all former faculty members of the University of Ghana. I also acknowledge a considerable debt to those numerous officials at the Ministry of Education who gave freely of their time and who permitted me to undertake the survey of secondary-school pupils reported in this volume. Many secondary-school principals kindly allowed me to conduct my research in their schools and welcomed me with warmth and hospitality. That the survey was effectively completed was in no small measure due to the patience, enterprise and good humour of my research assistant and good friend R. B. Sevor. A great debt of gratitude is also due to my wife. It was her greater knowledge of African ethnography that enabled me to develop a framework of investigation and her extensive fieldwork experience was of inestimable help in our survey of a Fanti fishing village.

I am obliged to the editors of the Sociology of Education, the Harvard Educational Review, the Comparative Education Review and the School Review for permission to reproduce certain materials previously published in their journals.

Finally, I must thank those many Ghanaian young people who assisted me in my work patiently and with good humour. I hope that this volume will constitute in some measure an appreciation of the debt that I owe them.

CONTENTS

Contents

x

MAPS AND FIGURES

TABLES

xi

Tables

I took various opportunities of ascertaining from working men themselves, their opinion as to the value of education. When I asked them whether education was of any use to their children, they seemed to doubt whether I was serious; or if they supposed that I was, they seemed to consider the question rather insulting.

An Irishman whom I met driving a cart summed up the case in favour of education, thus: 'Do you think reading and writing is of any use to people like yourself?' I asked. 'To be sure I do, sir,' the man answered with a strong brogue, 'and do you think that if I could read and write I would be shoved into every dirty job as I am now? No, sir! Instead of driving this horse I'd be riding him.'

MR. CUMIN
testifying before the Newcastle Commission of 1861

INTRODUCTION

STIMULATED by one of the most dramatic political revolutions of this century, the material on social, economic, and political change in contemporary Africa has grown both in volume and quality. Yet studies on education have tended to lag behind research in other fields. Although most social scientists are willing to accord central importance to Western education as an instrument of 'modernization', their examination of the topic is usually marginal or incidental to their major themes.

And, while there is increasing discussion of current educational programmes and policies in the new African states, there is a relative lack of research dealing with the impact of Western-type schools on African societies and the actual role such schools have played in transforming the continent. To be sure, a limited number of sound historical studies exist on the growth of Western education in Africa, but most authors have rarely gone beyond descriptive accounts of the growth in educational provision.[1] The institutional matrix in which the schools function has been given but fleeting attention.

Our task in this study is a little more ambitious. We have attempted to assess the economic, political, and social consequences of a process of transfer of formal educational institutions from the metropole to colonial dependencies. This task involves not only an examination of the structural characteristics of metropolitan education itself but necessitates an investigation of the shifts in function it undergoes to become meaningfully related to a totally new milieu.

It should be said at the outset that there is nothing unique about educational transfer itself. Few systems of formal education in the modern world are local products. Most of them have been diffused in one form or another from a few seminal centres—sometimes with wholesale borrowing and sometimes with only selective transfer of structural features. Ghana is no exception to this rule, and its contemporary educational system still shows relatively little divergence from that of the former metropole. Indeed, most observers have readily pointed out the marked structural similarities between English and Ghanaian education. Characteristically, direct state intervention in the development of a national education system was rather late.

1

The emergence of a dual system of control follows, in many respects, English precedent. Further, as in England, there has been the gradual development of a highly selective educational system largely dominated by the academic secondary school. There has also been a clear tendency until very recently for metropolitan-type curriculums to persist in the schools, particularly at the secondary level. It is possible to multiply examples of such formal similarities.

Observers have not, however, been so ready to indicate the profound functional transformation that the schools have undergone as a result of the process of transfer. There may be, to be sure, a replication of metropolitan models at the structural level but formal education must be incorporated in a 'meaningful' way into the local society—that is, it must be perceived as something which meets the desires and aspirations of indigenous social groups, whether these aspirations are couched in terms of social prestige, economic wealth, or a range of alternative desired ends. This is by far the most important aspect of the entire transfer process, since, as educational assimilation or incorporation proceeds, educational institutions undergo a subtle shift in the nature of their primary functions.

In short, we are attempting to discern the impact of formal education on a group of traditional social and economic structures and, conversely, to assess the effects of those structures upon the functions of the schools. Such an approach takes us far beyond the study of education as narrowly defined. The delineation of the complex relationships between the schools and other aspects of social life entails drawing heavily upon the major social disciplines.

Ghana represents one of the most fruitful areas in Africa for the examination of the process of transfer, since a long history of Afro-European contact enabled Western schools to establish themselves over a considerable period. A point of equal importance, however, is that this new nation is composed of a cluster of neo-traditional social structures, similar in some respects but different in others, which have been exposed in a markedly variable degree to the forces of Westernization. Such a situation provides an opportunity for comparative research in assessing internal variations in the reaction of different social subgroups to a uniform set of educational institutions. Further, although in one sense the Ghanaian case is 'unique', certain aspects of the transfer process have been repeated and are repeating themselves in other areas of Africa. As Ghana has probably the most developed educational system in sub-Saharan Africa outside the Union, events there indicate future trends and problems in other areas of the continent. Prediction is a risky and often unrewarding procedure, yet the factoring-out of what may be regarded as 'constants' in the process of transfer may give some partial insight into future educational trends in other territories recently emerging from colonial overrule, particularly those formerly associated with the United Kingdom.

The Nature of the 'Colonial Situation'

Since institutional transfer takes place within the context of a pattern of relationships which we can term the 'colonial situation', we will briefly examine the salient features of colonialism as they are relevant to our particular study.

Colonialism in Africa obviously involved the establishment of political hegemony over groups of peoples whose social structures and cultures were radically different from that of the metropolitan power. Almost invariably, this process resulted in the absorption into artificial polities of diverse ethnic groups who did not recognize the idea of common nationality or origin and whose primary loyalties were directed to clan, lineage, or tribe.

Concomitant with the establishment of political control was the transfer of metropolitan institutions, whether political, social, or economic, to the colonial territory. The degree to which conscious attempts were made to modify transferred institutions varied from territory to territory and from colonial power to colonial power. French policy, for example, has been characterized as essentially assimilationist in aim, involving the wholesale export of metropolitan culture and institutions to the colonial area, while the British, it is often asserted, did make attempts to adapt exported institutions to what they conceived to be indigenous society, i.e. indirect rule. The characterization of colonial policies as 'assimilationist' or 'adaptive', however, creates a rather artificial dichotomy. Neither the French nor the British were consistent in their policies and the consequences of colonial overrule in the two cases (as we will show later) have not been totally dissimilar.

One crucial element in the whole transfer process has been economic. Invariably the activities of the colonial powers led to the development of an exchange economy which interpenetrated with traditional subsistence activities. Such development was the result of the introduction of cash crops and the growth of extractive enterprises or other commercial activities. It led to the creation of a European-dominated occupational structure of far greater complexity than the largely undifferentiated activities associated with subsistence economies. Further, the absolute size and relative complexity of this structure was augmented by new occupational roles created by administrative necessity. In most cases, though not all, there was a concomitant growth of urban centres, largely involved with the exchange economy and containing populations of heterogeneous ethnic origin. As we shall indicate, these changes in the nature of the economy have been of profound importance for educational development.

It is important to note that the colonial situation had some of the characteristics of a 'caste' society. Representatives of the colonial power formed a tiny proportion of the total population in most areas; they were largely endogamous and their superior social status was symbolized in terms of their observed physical characteristics. Such status had its occupational correlates, and, although Africans might in a few cases achieve occupational parity, they could not by definition aspire to full 'caste' membership. Endogamy, occupation, political and social superordination were indeed reinforced in some cases by almost ritualistic adherence to certain avoidance norms. Such behavioural extremes, however, have not been so marked in West Africa as they have been in other parts of the continent.

From still another viewpoint, representatives of the colonial power were an elite possessing certain caste-like attributes. Most studies dealing with elites, usually political elites, have stressed the dynamic aspects of elite membership. They have concentrated upon the decision-making abilities of elites and their exercise of power. Nadel, however, has drawn particular attention to the importance of elites as normative reference groups, a point of particular importance in this study.[2] His conception of 'elite groups' provides a useful framework on which to build our analysis.

(*a*) Initially the concept relates to a group of persons enjoying a position of general pre-eminence. Yet an elite is not synonymous with any group of individuals enjoying high status within a community. All elites enjoy high status, but not all high status groups constitute elites. Elites must exhibit 'some degree of corporateness, group character and exclusiveness'.[3]

(*b*) The superiority of an elite must be of a general kind rather than derived from limited superiority in terms of certain specific skills or abilities. Thus, although the European minority in the colonial situation enjoyed manifest superiority in terms of certain technical skills, their elite characteristics stemmed from a notion of generalized superiority extending into other aspects of social life.

(*c*) The perceived superiority of an elite must be attainable by others at least in part; the qualities deemed desirable by the indigenous population must be judged imitable and hence worth imitating. 'Thus the elite, by its very manner of acting and thinking, sets the standards for the whole society, its influence or power being that of a model accepted and considered worth following.'[4]

In essence, therefore, an 'elite' may be regarded as a generalized reference group with a capacity for setting standards over a whole range of behaviour beyond those in which the elite may enjoy manifest superiority by virtue of the possession of specific skills.

Generally speaking, the representatives of the colonial power did meet these criteria of an elite, but it is necessary to enter a caveat here in the case of Ghana. European penetration in a commercial sense long preceded the establishment of political control, and, as the following chapters will attempt to indicate, the mere presence of Europeans in no sense gave them elite status. It was not until comparatively late and after the establishment of political overrule that the European minority could be legitimately regarded as an elite. Also, it seems equally apparent that the European 'image' was differential in its effect. It was most powerful in the southern half of the country, particularly in the urban areas, but until the end of the colonial period this could hardly be said to be the case in the North; the mere establishment of political overrule there did not in itself guarantee the emergence of the European minority as an imitable elite.

For our purposes we should regard two characteristics of this colonial elite as particularly pertinent. The first was its virtual monopoly of formal education of a particular type which gave rise to an increasing demand among Africans for educational parity in terms of that *type* of education. Second, the elite itself confined its activities mainly to a relatively narrow range of occupations of an administrative variety. Furthermore, it was internally stratified on the basis of primarily occupational and formal educational criteria. The notion of status as a partial derivative of occupation was largely alien to the traditional society, and it was precisely this reference group function of the colonial elite that provided alternative status models for the indigenous population. One of the results of European penetration was the creation of a more complex occupational structure not only in the sense of sheer occupational differentiation but because new roles, ranked on the basis of prestige and income, provided the basis of the European system of stratification. Needless to say, access by Africans to prestigeful and well-paid occupations was largely effected through formal education. It is therefore the analysis of the relationships between education, occupation, income, and social status that provides us with the significant factors determining the nature of educational development in Ghana.

The Functional Consequences of Educational Transfer

In most societies educational institutions whether formal or informal, have a dual function; they are both homogenizing and differentiating agencies. In the broadest sense they are concerned with the inculcation of values and appropriate modes of behaviour and the teaching of skills which prepare the individual to participate effectively as an adult member of a community. In this respect education can be viewed largely as contributing to social consensus and cohesion in so far as all members of a society are exposed to and internalize the basic elements of a general or common culture. Understandably, anthropological fieldworkers have tended to stress this homogenizing aspect of the educational process. In the case of most African traditional societies, education was conducted largely through the medium of informal agencies and, generally speaking, was undifferentiated in its basic content except by sex. In this context, to view education as primarily a homogenizing process is quite appropriate. It is this preoccupation with the consensual aspects of education that has led to a fruitful body of research concerned with child development and socialization in Africa.[5]

However, such an approach ignores the fact that educational institutions are also differentiating agencies. It is probably true that in societies where education is largely informal the homogenizing function predominates. And, where formal educational institutions begin to appear, it is likely that they operate no less as differentiating institutions. Clearly, this distinction between homogenizing and differentiating functions is not identical with the distinction between formal and informal educational processes. The balance between functions tends to shift as formal patterns of education begin to emerge. As Floud and Halsey observe:

> . . . a fresh set of purely sociological problems is created as soon as educational tasks are performed by specialized agencies, since the possibility then arises that these may behave as relatively independent variables in the functioning of the social system, promoting or impeding change and producing unintended as well as intended and dysfunctional as well as functional consequences.[6]

The function of highly complex institutions of formal education cannot be understood from the point of view of the socialization process any more than the functioning of complex political institutions can be adequately delineated by personality studies of leading politicians. The emphasis of study shifts from individual socialization studies to structural-functional analysis of formal educational institutions in their relationship to processes of elite formation, social differentiation, and the distribution of political and economic status.

The kind of traditional societies that we shall discuss had not developed formal schools; education was generally diffused and undifferentiated, and, as a result, it was irrelevant to processes of social differentiation. With the acceptance of Western-type schools formal education *necessarily* became a significant dimension of social status in a number of emergent social structures.

In this context a great deal of the discussion regarding the possibility of 'adapting' the school to traditional social structures is quite meaningless. Western education was dysfunctional for traditional social structures and systems of status differentiation, in large degree irrespective of what the schools taught, since formal education constituted a new dimension of social structure. As we shall indicate, the idea of the 'cultural adaptation' of schools to traditional society is basically a contradiction in terms; indeed it suffers from the same inconsistencies as the theory of indirect rule. The confusion over adaptation has arisen, however, largely because of a failure to discern the significant differences between education as a homogenizing factor and schools as agencies of social differentiation.

In this study of educational transfer, an attempt will be made to indicate that the major consequences of the transfer of Western schooling to traditional Ghanaian societies were virtually all unanticipated and unintended. A great deal has been made of variations in the educational policies of the different colonial powers, but the kind of educational system which developed in Ghana frequently ran counter to the objectives of the colonial rulers. As the schools, the transferred institutions, began to relate themselves to a new institutional milieu they took on a number of different and frequently latent functions which corresponded in no way with the expectations of colonial educationists. In essence, we are here concerned with the 'serendipity' aspects of educational transfer.

As in most colonial areas, the transfer of educational institutions from the metropole to Ghana occurred with minimal changes in structure but maximal shifts in social function. In the metropole itself formal schools were generally functional in terms of the maintenance of a traditional system of social stratification and diverse patterns of behaviour in various aspects of life. They facilitated social mobility for certain groups and individuals and yet at the same time controlled mobility in such a manner as to maintain the viability of the system. These same institutions were dysfunctional in terms of the *particular type* of social structure found in Ghana. This suggests that the consequences of educational assimilation depend not only upon the nature, duration, and intensity of Afro-European contact but also upon the characteristics of indigenous social structures. In order to stress the significance of this factor we shall in later pages contrast the Ghanaian case with that of Buganda in British East Africa, where Western formal education is not dysfunctional to the traditional Kiganda status system.

The most significant latent function of Western formal education was to foster nascent conceptions of social status which diverged from the traditional model. It is impossible wholly to disentangle the effects of Western education *per se* from other consequences of European overrule including the development of a more complex occupational and economic structure. Clearly, however, emergent conceptions of social status were partially the result of reference group characteristics of the European minority itself in that it provided models for status acquisition based on education and occupation. This is not to suggest that social structures in contemporary Ghana are duplicates of European models; they are, in fact, hybrid systems composed of 'traditional' and 'modern' components. These emergent conceptions of status depend to an increasing extent upon educational and occupational criteria, particularly in urban areas where there is an approximation to Western patterns of social stratification.

Further, early demand for Western education arose from particular groups in Ghanaian society who also demanded a very specific form of academic education. In practice this demand was a reasonable reflection of the economic and political conditions created by Europeans, and attempts to modify the educational system by colonial educationists in the direction of vocational, technical, or agricultural education were largely failures—for three reasons. First, government and missions alike ignored some of the realities of the occupational structure in colonial times. Second, they misapprehended some of the objective social functions of the schools and the purposes for which they were being utilized by Africans. Third, they underestimated their own significance as a normative reference group. For the colonial power the problem of the 'content of education' was important, but the African was seeking 'educational parity' with the elite. There was, in fact, a considerable divergence in the expectations of Africans and Europeans as to the function of formal education.

The development of schools, however, has led in Ghana to the growth of another unanticipated phenomenon, mass unemployment among school-leavers.[7] Though this has been an old problem, dating even from the middle of the last century, it has reached alarming proportions in the last decade. This unemployment raises questions about the degree to which an educational system can be allowed to operate in a quasi-autonomous manner in an 'underdeveloped' economy. As we shall argue, unemployment among school-leavers has not arisen because the schools have employed 'the wrong kind of curriculum' and thus created groups of individuals merely interested in 'white collar' employment. It is rather the consequence of disparities between the rising output of the schools and a low rate of expansion in the exchange sector of the economy. The schools alone can do little about this problem.

Closely intertwined with the problem of unemployment is the development of the Nationalist movement itself. During the nineteenth and the early twentieth centuries, Western education produced a relatively small group of Nationalists coming from a minority who had acquired higher formal education and who gave early nationalism a distinctly intellectual character. However, by the mid-twentieth century, nationalism changed its characteristics and drew mass support, principally from the urban areas, as a direct consequence of unemployment among school-leavers. This relationship between education and political nationalism has fascinated many observers of the Ghanaian scene. We wish, however, to place the problem in a somewhat broader perspective by stressing the continuing relations between political development and education in the post-colonial period.

Since independence many of the educational problems associated with the early period of colonial overrule have been exacerbated. Perhaps in contradistinction to events in the political arena, there has been until recently in education no radical attempt at a break with the colonial past. Indeed, in some respects the educational system has become even more like the metropolitan model. The most signal achievement of the period since 1951 has been a dramatic expansion in the provision of education at lower levels without any marked shifts in the basic character of the system. However, the wider diffusion of primary- and middle-school education has directly enhanced the value of selective secondary schooling as an effective instrument of mobility. In this sense the secondary schools have assumed a particularly 'strategic' position. For this reason we have included within the scope of this study some of the results of a detailed empirical investigation of the contemporary Ghanaian system of secondary schools in order to shed more light on our historical materials and confirm some of the conclusions drawn from them.

Fortunately, available historical materials on education in Ghana are more substantial than those for most parts of Africa. Though no claim can be made that any startling new individual facts have emerged from our study of these sources, there has been a reinterpretation of the facts. They have been placed in a meaningful and systematic context, supplemented where possible by freshly gathered empirical materials. In this context old facts take on new meanings and many of the 'new problems' of contemporary Africa turn out to possess a lengthy ancestry.

REFERENCES

1. The three historical works with material most relevant to the development of formal education in Ghana are F. H. Hilliard, *A Short History of Education in British West Africa* (London: Thomas Nelson and Sons Ltd., 1957); H. O. A. McWilliam, *The Development of Education in Ghana* (London: Longmans, Green, 1959); and Colin G. Wise, *A History of Education in British West Africa* (London: Longmans, Green, 1956). The scope of these studies is, however, explicitly limited to purely 'educational' matters.

2. S. F. Nadel, 'The Concept of Social Elites', *International Social Science Bulletin*, VIII, No. 3 (1956), 413–24.

3. *Ibid.*, p. 415.

4. *Ibid.*, p. 418.

5. Notable among these studies are Otto Raum, *Chagga Childhood* (Oxford: Oxford University Press, 1940); M. Fortes, *Social and Psychological Aspects of Education in Taleland* (Oxford: Oxford University Press, 1938); M. Read, *Children of Their Fathers* (New Haven: Yale University Press, 1959); and Barrington Kaye, *Bringing Up Children in Ghana* (London: George Allen & Unwin, 1962). These works are markedly variable in quality but show a common interest in socialization processes. They are all, in fact, studies in 'culture and personality'.

6. J. E. Floud and A. H. Halsey, 'The Sociology of Education', *Current Sociology*, VII, No. 3 (London: Basil Blackwell, 1958), 168.

7. The use of this term may create some confusion. We refer here specifically to students who have completed a given stage of education, not to school dropouts.

PART ONE

The Historical Background

I

SOME DIMENSIONS OF TRADITIONAL SOCIAL STRUCTURE

ANY examination of the impact of Western educational institutions on African societies presupposes an analysis of traditional social structures. This is a task which the educational sociologist approaches with some diffidence, since even the smallest contemporary African political units constitute a bewildering cultural and linguistic mixture. Nonetheless, such an examination is essential as a starting point for analysis. The functional incorporation of western institutions can only be understood in terms of their effect upon traditional concepts of status and social differentiation and other aspects of social structure. The following discussion will largely ignore indigenous processes of education since they are only of limited importance in examining the roles of western schools. The primary task is to indicate the basic uniformities underlying the varying types of political and social structure which existed in Ghana before the extension of effective European control. In 'traditional society' in this part of Africa it is possible to point to certain structural uniformities which underlay most indigenous social systems without attempting a total ethnographic summary of each group.

The Physical Environment

Contemporary Ghana, although one of the smaller West African nations covering an area of some 93,000 square miles, exhibits a degree of cultural and linguistic heterogeneity that is typical of the new African nations. This heterogeneity is partly a consequence of the creation of artificial national boundaries while the juxtaposition of culturally distinct groupings is explainable if the topographical features of the country are examined.

From the point of view of relief (see Fig. 1) the average height of

13

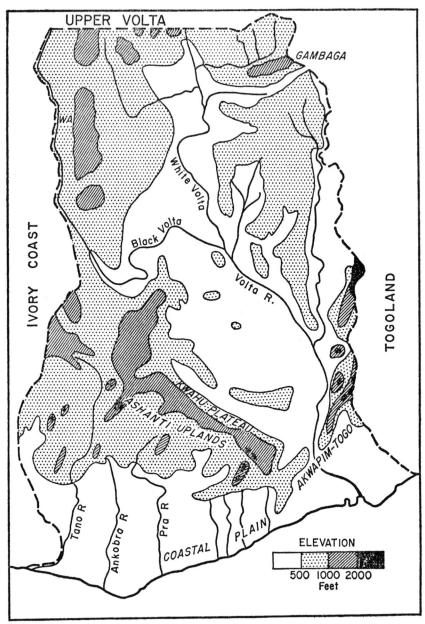

Fig. 1. Ghana: Relief and Principal Drainage.

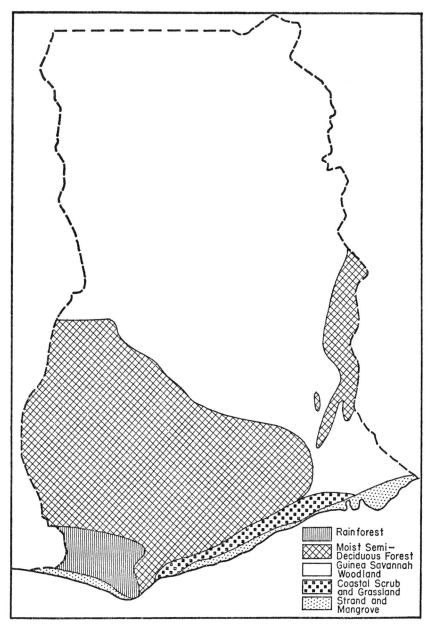

Fig. 2. Ghana: Vegetation.

the area is only some 1,500 feet, although a few isolated peaks may reach 3,000 feet in elevation. Behind a narrow coastal plain rise the Southern Ashanti Uplands and the Kwahu Plateau, while farther to the east the Akwapim-Togo range extends into former French West Africa. The central region of Ghana comprises a low-lying and thinly populated area, drained by the valleys of the Black and White Volta. To the north a gradual ascent occurs, culminating at its highest points in the Gambaga scarp to the north-east and the area around Wa to the west. In general, the relief of Ghana is distinguished by relatively limited variation, and, with the possible exception of parts of the Volta Region, topographical variation has not hindered the traditional migration of peoples.[1]

Climatic and vegetational zones show more marked variation (Fig. 2). The coastal strip is predominantly one of scrub and grassland, with the exception of the southwestern corner of the country around Axim, where a rainfall of over 70 inches per annum has produced dense rain forest. North of the coastal plain, however, increased rainfall has created a broad belt of deciduous forest land covering southern and central Ashanti and Akim. This forest zone may be regarded as the agricultural and economic heart of Ghana, producing as it does the major proportion of the country's agricultural and mineral exports. To the north a progressive diminution of rainfall leads the forest zone to give way to an increasingly park-like, open savannah which covers an area of some 65,000 square miles comprising the Northern Region and a proportion of northern Ashanti.[2]

Since neither topographical nor vegetational variation hindered the movement of African peoples, Ghana has been subject to successive waves of migration from an early period which involved the frequent absorption of autochthonous inhabitants by newer invaders. The larger political aggregations were in intermittent contact with each other before the coming of the Europeans, and Akan influence was particularly felt by the majority of other cultural and linguistic groups.

The Principal Ethnic Groupings

Although linguistic classifications have undergone considerable amendment in recent years, the people of Ghana may be divided into five principal groupings distinguished not only by linguistic affinities but also by the possession of common cultural attributes and, to some extent, by common myths of origin. These are the Akan, the Ga-Adangme, the Ewe, the Guan, and the Gur-speaking peoples (Fig. 3).[3]

Numerically the Akan form the predominant linguistic and cultural

16

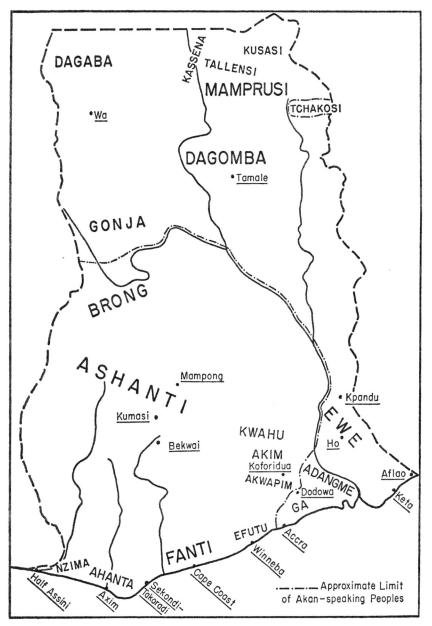

Fig. 3. Ghana: Principal Tribal Divisions.

group within Ghana and in 1948 constituted approximately 44 per cent of the total population.[4] Linguistically the Akan are themselves divisible into two major subclassifications, the Anyi-Baule and Twi speakers. So far as Ghana is concerned, the latter is the considerably larger of the two and includes within it two major groupings, the Ashanti and the Fanti, who together comprise over one-half of the total Akan population. It seems probable that the Fanti constituted the first wave of Akan migration, reaching the coastal zone from the north about the thirteenth century, followed soon after by the ancestors of the present Ashanti, who occupied mainly the forested zone north of the coastal plain.[5] For the most part, the Akan peoples have occupied the central and southern forested areas of Ghana, though the Fanti are primarily coastal dwellers. Fragmentary groups (notably the Tchakosi) are to be found in pockets among the predominantly Gur-speaking population of the northern savannah belt.[6]

The Ga-Adangme peoples who constitute some 9 per cent of the Ghanaian population moved along a westerly route, probably from Dahomey, during the sixteenth century or earlier and settled sections of the eastern littoral.[7] The Ga created a series of small independent townships along the coast, including that of Accra, the present capital city. They were by no means a homogeneous group in terms of origin or social organization and would appear to comprise both migratory and autochthonous elements, the latter having certainly acquired the Ga language.[8] The Adangme, a people closely related to the Ga both culturally and linguistically, were somewhat later settlers who occupied an area east of the Ga and nearer to the west bank of the lower Volta. A most significant difference between the Akan and Ga-Adangme lies in the matrilineal organization of the former and the patrilineally based structure of the latter peoples.

The Ewe exhibit sufficient cultural and linguistic uniformity to be classified as a distinct grouping, although, once again, there are local variations in language and political and social structure.[9] The origins of the group lie probably in the area east of the Niger, and it appears likely that their arrival within the boundaries of modern Ghana roughly coincided with the period of Ga migration. They occupy the southeastern segment of Ghana, east of the lower Volta extending from the coast in the area of Keta-Ada to about 80 miles inland. The Ewe number approximately 13 per cent of the total Ghanaian population and like the Ga-Adangme are a patrilineal people; indeed, in spite of distinct differences between these two groups certain basic elements of social structure appear to be common to both Ga and Ewe.

The Guan-speaking peoples form an interesting, if for our investi-

18

gation, somewhat unimportant minority. It is probable that they were among the earliest migrants into present-day Ghana, preceding the later Akan movements.[10] At present, Guan speakers constitute about 1 per cent of the total population and are principally to be found in scattered pockets among the Akan, the largest southern group being the Efutu around the immediate area of Winneba. There are also scattered Guan communities along the Akwapim Ridge while the Gonja (*Gbanya*) of the Northern Region are Guan speakers.[11] It seems probable that many Guan groupings have been absorbed linguistically and culturally into larger Akan aggregations, but in some cases relatively small groups have preserved elements of linguistic and cultural autonomy, notably in some of the small towns on the Akwapim Ridge.

The peoples who occupy what is now the Northern Region of Ghana remained something of an ethnographic mystery for some period, since there initially appeared to be a remarkable heterogeneity in language and social organization within the area. As a result of the work of Rattray and others it is now clear that apparent variations masked a considerable degree of cultural and linguistic uniformity over the whole region.[12] Virtually all the Northern peoples, constituting over 30 per cent of the total population, belong to one of four subdivisions of the Gur-speaking peoples: the Mole-Dagbani, Grusi, Gurma, and Senufo.[13] Within this Gur-speaking area are to be found some Guan speakers (the Gbanya, Nchambulung, and Nawuri) and one Mande-speaking people (the Bussansi).[14] It is appropriate to treat the Northern Region as one distinct cultural and linguistic area, though in the case of some of the larger political units some Akan influence is evident.[15]

This fivefold classification will serve as an adequate basis for the following general discussion of indigenous social structures. It should be pointed out, however, that since the main cultural belts of West Africa follow an east to west direction, the superimposition of recent national boundaries has led to the fragmentation of culturally allied groups. The Akan, for example, are separated from their relatives the Anyi of the Ivory Coast; the majority of the Ewe are to be found in former French Togoland; the northern peoples are separated from similar groupings in the northern Ivory Coast, Upper Volta, and northern Togoland. Furthermore, all these peoples have been exposed in the past to markedly different degrees of European contact and influence. Fanti contact with European representatives dates from the end of the fifteenth century, as does that of the Ga, while direct intercourse with the Ashanti was virtually non-existent until the nineteenth century and even then only intensively after 1874. The extension of European control over the northern peoples was not established until early in the twentieth century. As we shall indicate in later chapters the differential degree of European contact has been of profound significance for educational development.

Traditional Society among the Akan

Our discussion of traditional social structures must devote quite disproportionate attention to the Akan group. Not only do they constitute the largest linguistic and cultural aggregation but they have played a crucial role in the development of modern Ghana. Most documentary evidence relating to early educational developments concerns the Fanti areas, while in a more negative sense the intermittent conflict between the Fanti and their British allies and the expanding power of the Ashanti Confederation remained a dominant issue throughout the nineteenth century. It was, in fact, among the coastal Akan that the most significant political, social, and educational developments first occurred and to some extent social change in other areas paralleled earlier Akan patterns of change. In our portrayal of Akan structure as it probably was at the period of initial European contact the use of the past tense should not be taken to imply that, at present, traditional elements do not coexist alongside emergent or modern ones. An outstanding feature of Akan society has been the considerable vitality of traditional cultural elements which maintain themselves in spite of profound changes in economic and political organization.

Although politically fragmented, all Akan recognized their common origin through membership in seven major, exogamous, non-localized matriclans (*Ebusuakuw*).[16] These major clans each traced descent to a common putative female ancestor but, in fact, did not constitute functional or corporate units, and among the Fanti, at least, it would appear that the rules of clan exogamy were not always strictly enforced.[17] In practice, the core of Akan social and political organization was the localized corporate lineage (*Ebusua*) composed of all descendants of a common female ancestor traced through the maternal line to a depth of some four or five generations. The use of similar terminology to describe both the non-localized matriclans and the localized segmentary matrilineage is initially confusing, but, to the Akan, membership of the latter determined an individual's rights and duties while responsibilities to one's matriclan were very loosely defined.[18]

All Akan recognized a dual principle of descent. Blood (*mogya*) was inherited through the mother and determined lineage membership, succession, and inheritance. The male principle or spirit (*ntoro*) transmitted through the paternal line regulated certain unions of sexes.[19] In effect, the latter had relatively limited implications for social structure, and it was essentially the maternal line which was socially significant.[20] Alongside the basic unilineal descent group existed a nuclear territorial unit, the village, which usually consisted of an aggregation of several different lineages, themselves divided into predominantly patrilocal extended households.[21] Within such territorial units a division between lineages occurred which constituted a basic dimension in the stratification of Akan society; one lineage was regarded as 'royal' in opposition to all the remaining 'commoner' lineages in the village, and it was from the former that the village headman (*Odikro*) was chosen.

Although it has been frequently observed that Akan social and political institutions were among the most complex in Africa, it is important to stress that their hierarchical social and political organization was based on the essentially simple principle of the unilateral matrilineage and the territorial unit of the nucleated village. In practice, the higher levels of organization were functional duplications of the lower, the lower being microcosms of the whole structure.[22] Rattray has described in considerable detail how successive migrations from older and larger villages to new settlements elevated the status of the headmen of the former to that of subchiefs having jurisdiction over divisional clusters of villages. The continuance of this process led to the emergence of large-scale territorial state units (*Aman*) headed by paramount chiefs (*Amanhene*) to whom village headmen were responsible through the subchiefs. Akan structure may therefore be described as a series of successive aggregations giving rise to a hierarchical organization based on the duplication of common structural elements at different levels.[23]

The ultimate size of such aggregations varied considerably among the Akan. The Fanti remained fragmented among a number of independent political units. Only among the Ashanti did a process of almost continual conquest during the eighteenth century lead to the creation of a more general confederacy wherein the great *Amanhene* of previously independent political units became tributary to a common ruler (*Asantehene*). Among the Ashanti particularly, the development of political organization led to the emergence of an indigenous bureaucracy and the proliferation of specific offices concerned with military and political functions.[24] Recruitment to such offices, however, was primarily on the basis of descent. This brings us to the core of our discussion, an examination of the nature of stratification, recruitment, and social mobility within Akan social structure.

It has already been indicated that a fundamental distinction existed between royal and commoner lineages and that recruitment to political office from the village to the state level could only be through membership in the former. Another principle of stratification was the division between commoners and slaves. In effect, it is possible to speak of Akan society as having a tripartite system of stratification based on descent.[25] Formally, at least, recruitment to office was on the basis of ascriptive criteria; significant social and political roles were open to only limited numbers of individuals on the basis of age, sex, and lineage membership. However, characterization of these three groups as strata or classes may be misleading if they are regarded as the principal dimensions of Akan social structure, or if it is assumed that they were significantly related to marked occupational differences or inequalities in wealth.

The essence of Western systems of stratification is that social strata are associated, for the most part, with distinct differences in wealth and occupation and that social classes emerge as distinctive subcultures. In the case of the Akan the criterion of descent was crucial and the differentiation of strata on the basis of wealth and occupation was minimal. Slaves were expected to perform many of the heavy manual tasks, but frequently slave activities were not unlike those of free members of society. Although differences in wealth did occur in Akan society, slaves could acquire substantial possessions and even carry out certain political functions.[26] Similarly it would appear inappropriate to characterize these strata as possessing distinctive subcultural traits. In spite of the hierarchical appearance of Akan units, one is impressed rather by the considerable cultural homogeneity of the population and the lack of any complex system of social differentiation.[27]

As in most African societies, the division of labour was very limited. Most individuals whether slave or free, royal or commoner, were subsistence agriculturists and in these circumstances a status hierarchy essentially based on occupational criteria was manifestly impossible.[28] There were, however, a few occupational specialists to whom special respect was accorded, such as goldsmiths, weavers, wood-carvers, and specialist religious functionaries. Recruitment into these occupations was the result of prolonged training, though primarily based on descent. In this sense these small occupational groupings, sometimes organized on a guild basis, differed radically from modern Western occupational clusters. As a consequence of limited specialization, Akan structure did not necessitate the development of specialized formal educational institutions for the prolonged training of immature members of the society. The latter function remained primarily a parental responsibility and was usually carried on within the informal situations of everyday life.[29] The education of youth did not vary significantly between segments of society and, as such, could not function as a basis of status differentiation. From a sociological viewpoint, a great deal of the significance of formal educational institutions lies in their differentiation of function and the extent to which varying groups obtain access to one or another of them. It was precisely this factor which enhanced the importance of Western educational institutions at a later date. Where educational institutions remain informal, generalized, and undifferentiated they cannot operate as criteria of status differentiation but only of cultural transmission. In practice few roles were closed to an Akan by virtue of lack of specialized training, except, perhaps, certain specific functions associated with the royal court of Ashanti for which special training of youth did occur.

Recruitment to office, then, was based principally upon ascriptive criteria of age, sex, and lineage. All chiefs and most 'bureaucratic' officials were recruited from designated lineages and, theoretically at least, from the senior lines of those lineages.[30] Inheritance of both property and office was to younger maternal brothers and thence to the male offspring of the senior siblings. However, to draw a formal picture of Akan laws of inheritance and mode of recruitment would emphasize what may be termed the 'monolithic' aspects of Akan society. A formal structural analysis would give an impression of a social system in which mobility existed only as a result of the aging process. To be born a slave, to be born a commoner was to be deprived of opportunities to enter more desirable positions in society, while to be born a younger son or maternal nephew was to have a restricted chance to occupy significant offices. However, in practice, the opportunities for mobility within the social system were greater than might be supposed.

In regard to recruitment to significant offices, the principles of primogeniture were frequently ignored and although officeholders were usually from the eldest branch of the female line they were not necessarily the eldest sons of that line.[31] Further, a clear 'jump' was sometimes made by selecting functionaries from junior lineages. There was a great deal more 'unorthodoxy' in the system than would appear at first sight, and it was possible for junior scions of junior lineages to achieve positions of eminence. In effect, there was always a practical compromise between purely ascriptive criteria of recruitment and an assessment of personal 'fitness' for the job.[32] Personal qualities of tact, leadership, intelligence, and knowledge of lineage affairs often assumed considerable importance; senior claimants to

23

office were frequently passed over with not only the approval of members of the lineage but also, in the case of royal lineages, with the tacit consent of commoner lineages.[33]

Not only would there appear to be fluidity within lineages themselves, but some mobility occurred between the principal 'strata' of Akan society. Slaves could amass wealth and achieve a measure of personal power and were, in the vast majority of cases, adopted into full membership of free lineages; their descendants would so intermarry with the kin of their former owners that the slave origins of certain lineages were known to only a few.[34] It is probable that a very substantial proportion of the Ashanti were of slave origin, and the general Akan reluctance to speak of one's own or others' antecedents would indicate that the incorporation of slave elements into commoner or royal lineages was by no means restricted to Ashanti alone.[35] Similarly, though this is by no means generally demonstrable, there is some evidence that commoner lineages did achieve royal status and that royal lineages did lapse into commoner status.[36]

We are stressing here that change did occur within traditional society quite apart from group mobility due to warfare. Social mobility, though necessarily limited, was a reality. One very significant divergence from Western patterns must be noted, however. Within contemporary Western societies social mobility is not only accepted but, to a greater or lesser extent, has become an element of formal ideology. Within Akan structure its reality was accepted but not specifically approved as an element of formal ideology.

The process of individual or group mobility was legitimated by the creation of fictional or quasi-fictional lines of descent. In this context, one of the principal functions of Western educational institutions was not only to create new criteria of status but to allow individuals to bypass traditional modes of social mobility and substitute legitimation by achievement for legitimation through reconstruction of the genealogical past. The following chapters on the historical development of education in Ghana will attempt to elaborate on how this process occurred.

Another crucial feature of Akan structure lay in the internal distribution and exercise of power and authority itself. The hierarchical nature of political and social organization gave a superficial impression of autocratic control with the apparent ability of chiefs to exercise a wide degree of discretionary or arbitrary power. Nothing could be further from the truth. In practice, officeholders from the *Asantehene* himself down to the level of the village headman were unable to exercise anything but the most limited authority without the approval of counsellors or lineage heads.[37] Village headmen were obliged to consult the heads of commoner lineages and, as Rattray has demonstrated, the commands of the great *Amanhene* and the *Asantehene* himself were the result of previous consultation—their very maintenance in office depended upon the extent to which they acknowledged the right of state councils to determine policy. Even the inauguration of chiefs could not take place without a general consensus of the commoner lineages that the candidate was acceptable. Akan society had a built-in system of elaborate 'checks and balances' at every level which successfully curtailed the exercise of arbitrary or despotic power. There was no clearly marked chain of command; decisions could not be effectively enforced from the top of the hierarchy without the concurrence of the lower levels of the political structure.[38]

Furthermore, all chiefs and lineage heads combined political office with specific ritual and religious functions upon which the continuance and prosperity of the community was believed to depend.[39] Ritual functions strengthened the image of the chief, not as an innovator but rather as a conserver of tradition, a living link with the ancestors. This coalescence of political and religious roles strengthened the essentially conservative nature of Akan institutions.

A like principle operated with regard to traditional land tenure. Although land was commonly regarded as belonging to the 'stool', the chief's role in land allocation was essentially one of a mediator between the ancestors, the real owners of the land, and the living.[40] A chief or lineage head was in no position to permanently alienate any land. Traditional tenure may be defined as a communality of ownership with a permitted, though limited, degree of individuality of usufruct.[41] Indeed, chiefs formerly could not even own private property, what they possessed belonging to the office and not to the individual. Although chiefs received tribute, their continuance in office depended largely on their disbursement of wealth and not on its accretion.[42]

These very real limitations upon the exercise of arbitrary power and the prescriptions of roles that chiefs and lineage heads were obliged to play as conservers of tradition will prove to be important when we come to discuss the transfer and incorporation of Western institutions. Even after a lengthy period of contact with European groups, the Akan were reluctant to accept those twin forerunners of Western penetration, the school and the church. Tentatively it might be hypothesized that social structures of the Akan type have an initially high resistance to innovating forces originating outside of them. In this context a fruitful comparison can be made between the Ashanti Confederacy and the East African kingdom of Buganda.

25

A Comparison of Buganda and Ashanti

Both states appear at first sight to exhibit similar structural features; a hierarchical political organization with a systematic gradation of territorial chiefs headed by a single monarch. Beyond this, however, the parallel breaks down. The principal chiefs and functionaries of Ashanti held office primarily by virtue of lineage membership. The major territorial chiefs and political functionaries of Buganda were personal appointees of the monarch (*Kabaka*) and depended for their continuance in office upon his personal assessment of their loyalty and of their discharge of delegated functions.[43] In such a system personal patronage was of profound importance. A chief's role was not that of a conserver of tradition but that of a purely political officeholder whose continuance in office was subject to the personal whims of an arbitrary and often despotic monarch.[44] In return for their absolute allegiance to the *Kabaka*, favourites were rewarded by suzerainty over land tracts or the right to exploit new areas acquired as a result of Kiganda territorial expansion. The idea of absolute obedience to a highly personalized power extolled by the Baganda was totally alien to Ashanti society in spite of the ritual stress on the power of the *Asantehene*. Furthermore, unlike the *Asantehene*, the *Kabaka* was pre-eminently a political functionary with few religious and ritual roles.[45] In consequence the *Kabaka* could act not only as a conserver of social traditions but as an innovator and source of social change.

As a result of this complex of features one would expect the degree of social mobility to have been higher in Buganda than in Ashanti. Indeed, Kiganda social structure contained *traditional* factors which made it particularly susceptible to innovation and which favoured the rapid incorporation of Western institutions after only a short period of contact. Buganda, in fact, represented a political kingdom where the classical notion of the 'downward filtration' of European influence and institutions was possible. This was not due simply to the existence of a hierarchical political system, since Ashanti exhibited the same structural feature, but happened because authority was concentrated at the apex of the political system and flowed from top to bottom, untrammelled by the checks and balances of Akan structure. The nature of chiefly authority was therefore one of the primary factors in determining the comparative assimilative capacities of the two cultures.

Christianity and Western education made more progress within a quarter of a century in Buganda than they had in virtually three hundred years of European contact with the coastal Akan.[46] Signifi-

26

cant differences occurred not only in the rate of proselytization and educational enrolment but also in the groups that made use of the new institutions. In Buganda, Christianity soon became the religion of the dominant elite who were the first to send their children to formal Western schools. Both in Ashanti and the other Akan areas the development of formal schools was initially regarded with some suspicion by the traditional elite.[47] The education of the heirs of chiefs—a recurrent theme in both French and British policy which regarded the chiefs as the foci of development and change—could meet with success in a structure such as that of Buganda but met with lengthy initial failure among the Akan.

Elaboration of these comparative remarks would seem beyond the scope of this chapter and would unduly tread on the field of the specialist in comparative politics, but the implications of these political diversities for the student of educational development are profound.[48] The incorporation of Western institutions would appear to be dependent not only upon the nature, duration, and intensity of European contact but also upon the inherent assimilative capacities of diverse indigenous social structures. Buganda, perhaps with the addition of Dahomey, seems to be an unusual political and social structure in Africa. Most other areas in that continent where centralized political structures existed seemed to approximate more to the Akan model. Indeed, the process of assimilation of formal educational institutions has been described as typically involving an initial period of indifference or even hostility on the part of local populations, followed by a trickle and belatedly with mass demand for Western education.[49] We shall examine this pattern in greater detail in later chapters.

Other Ethnic Groups

In the light of our preceding discussion of the rudiments of Akan political and social structure, a more cursory examination can be made of the other principal Ghanaian groups. In spite of distinct differences in language and culture, certain Akan-type elements appear in the social structures of these people and, particularly in the case of the Ewe, there appears to have been marked borrowing from the Akan. With the exception of the Ga, however, contact with the British was minimal until the late nineteenth and twentieth century, while the vast majority of the Ewe people remained under German administration until 1914.

The Ga. While the Akan had developed a complex hierarchical poli-

27

tical structure based ultimately on the segmentary lineage with the concurrent development of an indigenous bureaucracy, the Ga-Adangme stood at the other end of the continuum and remained fragmented into a number of small political units without the development of the chiefly office or a clearly defined political hierarchy.[50] The migrating Ga moved into their present coastal area probably around the fifteenth century and ultimately merged with an autochthonous group, the *Kpeshi*, who, while they survived, were still regarded as the owners of the land.[51]

The Ga settled into six coastal townships which remained totally independent of each other and which were, in fact, aggregations of segmentary patrilineages grouped together for purposes of common defence. Tema, for example, was composed of several 'houses' each tracing descent through the male line to a common ancestor. Older and larger houses frequently segmented into subhouses.[52] Outside the principal towns, which were originally little more than small fishing settlements, expansion took the form of development of small villages initially consisting of a man with his wife and children who had established the new unit. As these villages grew they retained initial ties with the parent settlement and were regarded as subordinate units of the town of origin.

The Ga do not appear to have developed royal lineages and the government of the autonomous towns was largely in the hands of a council of lineage heads, or *Wulomei* (singular: *Wulomo*), representing the great houses of the town.[53] Ga political institutions have been described as a 'democratic gerontocracy' because there was not only equality between the *Wulomei* of distinct lineages but their appointment as lineage heads was subject to the consent of other lineages within the town as well as general approval by their own lineages.[54] *Wulomei* were responsible for the control of the internal affairs of their own lineages and combined only for purposes which affected the well-being and safety of the whole community. Indeed the Ga word for town (*Mang*) really means a military confederation and stresses the looseness of Ga political and social organization.[55]

Recruitment to office on the basis of lineage seniority was strongly affected by consideration of personal qualities, and formal rules of descent and inheritance were frequently set aside in accord with the general principle that 'all succession is a question of election by relatives not of inherent right'.[56] Though recruitment to office was perhaps freer than among the Akan, the position of Ga *Wulomei* duplicated that of the Akan lineage heads (*Ebusuapanyin*) in many respects. They were not only political but religious and ritual functionaries and served as intermediaries between the ancestors and the

28

living. Within Ga society the slave class could achieve significant office, and cases occurred in which they were actually obliged to assume the onerous duties of a *Wulomo* and their descendants became *Wulomei* after them.[57]

These parallels with Akan organization must not be overstressed, since the Ga never developed a clear hierarchical organization and attempts at confederacy among the Ga townships in the face of Akan military pressure were usually short-lived. At the lower levels of sociopolitical organization, however, the resemblance between Akan and Ga structure is striking despite differences of descent line (patrilineal and matrilineal).

The Ewe. The Ewe were an intermediate group lying between the more politically centralized chiefdoms of the Akan and the more dispersed organization of the Ga, sharing some of the characteristics of each group. Like the Ga, the Ewe did not develop any large-scale political units; up to the end of the nineteenth century they remained fragmented into more than 120 'subtribes' (*duwo*, singular *du*) varying considerably in size and often with linguistic and cultural differences.[58] As with the Akan and Ga the basic territorial unit was the village, a cluster in this case of segmentary localized patrilineages (*fome*). (Some groups notably the *Anlo* recognized the existence of larger non-localized patriclans (*hlo*) similar in nature to the Akan *ebusuakuw*.)[59] However, the localized patrilineage formed the basis of political and social structure and a familiar pattern of division of lineages between 'commoners' and 'royals' paralleled Akan structure.[60] As with the Akan, royal status was claimed on the basis of primacy of occupation of a village area. Indeed, Manoukian's careful summary of existing ethnographic material on the Ewe would indicate that in spite of patrilineal descent, the basic structure of the Ewe nuclear village was similar to that of the groups previously discussed.

The Ewe *duwo*, as a result of the emergence of royal lineages, did develop the chiefly office, and chiefdoms usually consisted of a capital town with a number of subsidiary villages; only in very few cases was there a development of territorial organization at the subchief level.[61] There is a strong presumption that the development of royal lineages among the Ewe was the result of Akan influence, since the Ewe themselves still regard the institution of kingship as an innovation and state that at the time of the initial migration they had no kings but only elders.[62] The position of chiefs or lineage heads was very similar to that among the Akan. The exercise of power appears to have been uniformly checked by the action of counsellors and the chief's position depended upon a general consensus.[63] Indeed, the

29

office was so circumscribed that individuals often chose to avoid it. Once again, the Ewe chiefs and lineage heads combined political and ritual functions and acted in special relationship to the ancestors. Where special officials existed as they did in the larger chiefdoms, they usually bore variants of Akan titles.[64]

Ewe sociopolitical institutions were not basically dissimilar from those of the Akan, although Ewe units never reached the size of Akan aggregations. The Ewe system of checks and balances may be viewed as an intermediate form of organization—in the early period, perhaps, like that of the Ga, but developing a hierarchical structure largely as the result of Akan influence.

The Northern Peoples. The peoples of what is now the Northern Region of Ghana may be given more summary treatment, since contact with European culture was minimal until the annexation of the area in 1901, and the impact of Western institutions was limited until recently. So far as educational development is concerned the situation even now is quite similar to that in the coastal zones in the early twentieth century.

In one respect the social and political organization of the Northern peoples is unique; it has been the result of the superimposition of a small alien elite of Moshi origin upon a large number of autochthonous peoples who exhibited a high initial degree of linguistic and cultural uniformity.[65] In some cases, though not all, the ruling group still regard themselves as of different origin and have retained many distinctive cultural and linguistic traits.[66] Since intermarriage appears to occur between the two groups it would be improper to regard them as constituting castes, but the term 'quasi-caste' organization might be appropriate in describing some of these structures.

In three cases (Dagomba, Mamprusi, and Gonja) the invaders were able to establish centralized political kingdoms.[67] The ruling class of Dagomba and Mamprusi are possibly from the same line, though the Gonja Kingdom appears to have been founded somewhat later by groups said to have originated in Mande.[68] Outside these three kingdoms there appears to have been no overriding central authority and the internal political system has been described as 'acephalous and segmentary'.[69] Even within the three political kingdoms the structure was loose, and divisional chiefs were virtually independent of the central authority except for the provision of annual gifts and tribute.

Most northern peoples recognized both patrilineal and matrilineal descent, though almost without exception the patrilineal line appeared to provide the basis of social organization while matrilineal descent conferred spiritual attributes.[70] This represents a complete reversal of the Akan position regarding *mogya* and *ntoro*. The base of all northern social organization was the localized segmentary patrilineage. However, the basic territorial unit was not the village but rather the 'homestead', consisting of two or more close agnates with their wives, children, and other dependents. The pattern of northern settlements shows an even distribution of small residential units contrasting with the nucleated settlements of the south.[71]

Where the chiefly office existed, as for example in Dagomba, there was a division between royal lineages (*Nabihi*) and commoner groups (*Dagban-Daba*), though here the principle of division was not on the basis of primacy of occupation but stemmed from the division between the 'people of the land', the autochthons, and the chiefly class of invaders.[72] In other areas, however, no division of lineage types along these lines is apparent and most northern peoples represented extreme cases of acephalous segmentary groupings. Once again, however, we observe the coalescence of political and religious functions in chiefs in the centralized kingdoms and in lineage heads in all areas.

One significant difference does emerge, however. The important function of 'land trustee' performed by the southern chiefs was here carried out by a specific office, that of the earth priest (*Tend'ana*). Special functions relating to land allocation were reserved to these priests who were in most, though not all, cases representatives of the autochthonous groupings.[73] This dualism appears to be specific to the north, but it would be inappropriate to regard the chiefs as purely secular since most of them did have significant ritual functions particularly connected with the ancestral cult.[74]

Although certain structural elements existing in southern societies were duplicated in the north, it is not our aim to give an impression of general uniformity but rather to stress the similarity of certain nuclear units of social structure. In practice there was a vast difference between the elaborate Akan structure and the simple segmentary lineages of the north. Even where political kingdoms existed in the north they owed something to Akan influence.[75]

Some Generalizations concerning Traditional Society

This very general survey of the principal traditional structures of Ghana has been vastly oversimplified and particular stress has been given to delineating some of the structural uniformities and repetitive elements to be found among the various groupings. Detailed studies of structural variation are of great importance, but the level of generality at which our discussion has been pursued is appropriate to the purpose in this particular study. There is some merit in an attempt to draw together a mass of heterogeneous ethnographic data in order to examine what we mean by 'traditional society' in these areas. Without developing rigid classificatory criteria, the following paragraphs will isolate those characteristics that appear relevant to an analysis of education.

The basis of political and social organization in all cases was the unilateral descent group or lineage. Even where a centralized, hierarchical political organization utilizing territorial divisions existed, as among the Akan, the structure was built upon the nuclear unit of the lineage. Since the presence of this basic unit has been noted in all the societies discussed, we may view the range of social structures as existing on a continuum with the loose acephalous groupings of some of the northern peoples providing one pole and the more centralized and hierarchical structures of the Akan the other.

Status within all these societies rested to a varying degree upon ascriptive criteria of sex, age, and lineage origin. An individual's future political and social roles were determined to a great extent by the accident of birth. Those traits contributed a static element to the structures. In practice, however, nearly all groups demonstrated a capacity to compromise between purely ascriptive criteria of recruitment and achievement criteria of personal fitness for the role. Strict rules of inheritance and succession could be set aside, though the degree to which this compromise was effected appeared to vary considerably. For example, compromise appeared to be common among the Akan, but in the appointment of senior chiefs among the Dagomba and Mamprusi, stricter principles of primogeniture and seniority were followed.[76] Just as Western societies exhibit a mixture of both achievement and ascriptive criteria of recruitment, these traditional societies were not 'pure types'. However, the difference between traditional societies of this type and those of the West lay in ideological differences also. To a greater or lesser degree achievement recruitment has received an explicit ideological charter in the Western world, a factor that was virtually absent in traditional society.

In all these traditional societies it is possible to speak of 'social strata', but this term must be used with considerable reservation. 'Strata' could be defined by reference to objective criteria of descent and people classified as royal or commoner, slave or free, but none of these groups constituted distinct subcultures to nearly the same degree as the classes of Western society. One is impressed, in fact, by the general cultural homogeneity of the populations and the relative lack of a complex system of behavioural differentiation between 'strata'. In effect, if one wishes to examine the nature of traditional structure, one looks at lineage organization not at stratification;

although strata existed, they did not constitute the most significant or meaningful dimensions of social structure.

In this context it is important to note that studies in Western communities have focused primarily on the examination of social class based largely upon difference of occupation and wealth, with an unfortunate tendency to regard this as synonymous with the study of social structure. In practice Western societies incorporate several dimensions of status not necessarily based on class affiliation. And concentration by social scientists upon the dimension of stratification is justified because this is often the most significant variable in predicting behavioural differentiation and role. Similarly, in traditional Ghanaian societies the lineage dimension was all important in predicting the roles or behaviour of each individual, while the dimension of stratification was of very limited value in understanding how the structures actually functioned. The notion of 'social strata' is, therefore, of very limited use in societies such as these, even though individuals did move between them. In most cases, however, such movement was authenticated by the creation of fictional lines of descent or a reconstruction of the past. Thus an apparent continuity of structure was preserved in all these societies.

The economic basis of these societies in Ghana was sedentary agriculture or fishing, and the populations were composed overwhelmingly of subsistence farmers. Occupational specialists formed a tiny minority even within Akan society, and specialist occupational roles were usually combined with subsistence farming. Deference was given to special abilities and training but, in the circumstances, occupational criteria could not become the basis of a major system of status differentiation.

In turn, the relative absence of a complex system of division of labour or function implied the absence of formal educational institutions. The pre-eminent function of the informal pattern of indigenous education was the transmission of an essentially common culture and the maintenance of social cohesion. Education performed a homogenizing and conservative function, while the alternating function of educational institutions in creating a criterion of social differentiation was non-existent or minimal.

The most significant area in which specialized roles occurred was in the political structure of some of these peoples. However, as this structure rested on the lineage organization, a system of built-in checks and balances placed effective restraint upon the exercise of despotic power or arbitrary privilege and to some extent limited the significance of officeholders as innovators. The conservative outlook of the traditional elite was further enhanced by the fact that they were

33

also religious functionaries and intermediaries between the living and the ancestors. The limitation of the powers of the chief or lineage heads was illustrated nowhere more dramatically than in the case of traditional land-tenure systems where absolute rights of alienation were specifically denied. This 'conservative' type of social structure was initially highly resistant, to Western penetration in contradistinction to an alternative model, that of Buganda.

None of these societies, as the preceding discussion has implied, gave rise to essentially urban groupings in the sense of large-scale nucleated aggregations of ethnically heterogeneous groups involved in complex activities of production and exchange. Even among the southern groups where nucleated settlement was general, such villages seldom exceeded a few hundred farmers or fishermen, and these were generally linked by a network of lineage and affinal ties. Even the great Ashanti capital of Kumasi had no more than a few thousand inhabitants in the middle of the last century.[77] Within such aggregations traditional status systems could maintain themselves and allow the absorption into the traditional structure of limited numbers of migrants. The significance of the later growth of large conurbations of heterogenous ethnic origin lies essentially in the fact that the maintenance of traditional status systems based on real or putative descent became an impossibility.

Finally, these societies were all characterized by a high level of structural-functional integration consequent upon a limited degree of institutional differentiation and the relative cultural homogeneity of their populations. This does not imply that they existed in a state of structural-functional equilibrium or that each cultural element served some vital function. The idea of a holistic interdependence or complete functional unity of the social structure may be a useful heuristic device, but it is not demonstrable empirically. The occurrence of war, migration, and absorption of minorities taken alone would indicate that these groups did not exist in a state of static equilibrium or consensus. However, the general level of functional integration was undoubtedly far higher than that in Western societies in which extreme institutional differentiation has brought a correspondingly looser integration and leeway for institutions to function in a quasi-autonomous manner within the social matrix.[78] This looser type of structure permits uneven development of institutions and consequent lags between them.

The concept of structural-functional integration is crucial to this study; it implies that institutional transfer will have significant effects on most aspects of social organization. Western educational institutions were ultimately meaningfully incorporated by local populations into their way of life, but the consequences for the integration of the traditional social structure were profound. Such incorporation was not an additive process but involved the continued restructuring and realignment of traditional social organization. It is this process of meaningful integration and institutional realignment that subsequent chapters will examine.

REFERENCES

1. E. A. Boateng, *A Geography of Ghana* (Cambridge: Cambridge University Press, 1959), pp. 12–21.

2. C. J. Taylor, *The Vegetation Zones of the Gold Coast* (Accra: Government Printer, 1953).

3. W. E. F. Ward, *A History of Ghana* (London: George Allen & Unwin Ltd., 1958), pp. 37–40.

4. The following percentages relating to the principal linguistic groupings of contemporary Ghana have been computed from The Gold Coast *Census of Population 1948* (Accra: Government Printer, 1950).

5. Ward, *op. cit.*, p. 43.

6. M. Manoukian, *Tribes of the Northern Territories of the Gold Coast* (London: International African Institute, 1952), p. 7.

7. M. J. Field, *Social Organisation of the Ga People* (London: Crown Agents for the Colonies, 1940), p. 83.

8. *Ibid.*

9. M. Manoukian, *The Ewe-Speaking People of Togoland and the Gold Coast* (London: International African Institute, 1952), p. 9.

10. Ward, *op. cit.*, p. 39. There is some confusion regarding the Guan since they are occasionally regarded as constituting the first wave of Akan migration. See D. E. Apter, *The Gold Coast in Transition* (Princeton: Princeton University Press, 1955), p. 22. However, the Guan do not speak an Akan dialect, and, where they have retained their cultural autonomy, they are a patrilineal people quite distinct in their organization from the matrilineal Akan.

11. Manoukian, *Tribes of the Northern Territories*, p. 6. It would probably be more accurate to say that the Gonja language and the dialects of the southern Guan stem from a common proto-Guan dialect.

12. R. S. Rattray, *The Tribes of the Ashanti Hinterland* (2 vols.; Oxford: Clarendon Press, 1932), I, pp. ix–xiii.

13. D. Westermann, *Some Notes on the Foregoing Linguistic Material*; Rattray, *op. cit.*, I, 122–29.

14. Manoukian, *Tribes of the Northern Territories*, p. 7.

15. Rattray, *op. cit.*, II, 565–69.

16. J. B. Christensen, *Double Descent among the Fanti* (New Haven: Human Relations Area Files, 1954), pp. 19–21.

17. Child Development Research Unit, *Preliminary Report of a Social Survey of Egya I* (Legon: University College of Ghana, 1960), p. 60.

18. *Ibid.*, p. 53.

19. R. S. Rattray, *Ashanti* (Oxford: Clarendon Press, 1923), p. 78.

20. *Ibid.*

21. R. S. Rattray, *Ashanti Law and Constitution* (Oxford: Clarendon Press, 1929), p. 4.

22. *Ibid.*, p. 74.

D

23. *Ibid.*, p. 404.

24. *Ibid.*, p. 77.

25. S. Polger, 'Akan Clerks' (Ph.D. dissertation, Department of Anthropology, University of Chicago, 1957), p. 10. The author attempts, however, to distinguish four major strata: chiefs and elders, royal lineage members, commoners, and slaves. There is a confusion here between the concept of strata based on descent and 'officeholders'. Clearly, it was possible for officeholders to be at the same time members of the royal or commoner lineages and the system was, in fact, tripartite.

26. Rattray, *Ashanti Law*, p. 40.

27. Apter, *op. cit.*, p. 97.

28. *Ibid.*

29. Rattray, *Ashanti Law*, pp. 9–10.

30. *Ibid.*, p. 4.

31. *Ibid.*, p. 81.

32. Child Development Research Unit, *op. cit.*, p. 56.

33. Rattray, *Ashanti Law*, p. 82.

34. *Ibid.*, p. 40.

35. Child Development Research Unit, *op. cit.*, p. 55.

36. Apter, *op. cit.*, p. 266.

37. Rattray, *Ashanti Law*, p. 82.

38. *Ibid.*

39. Detailed descriptions of the ritual and religious functions of the chief are to be found in Rattray, *Ashanti*, pp. 92–202.

40. Rattray, *Ashanti Law*, p. 344.

41. K. A. Busia, *The Position of the Chief in the Modern Political System of Ashanti* (London: International African Institute, Oxford University Press, 1951), p. 199.

42. As we shall indicate in later pages, chiefs frequently did alienate land, in fact, particularly after the introduction of cocoa as a cash crop.

43. L. A. Fallers, 'Despotism, Status Culture and Social Mobility in an African Kingdom', *Comparative Studies in Society and History*, II, No. 1 (October 1959), 18–20.

44. *Ibid.*, p. 21.

45. D. A. Low, *Religion and Society in Buganda 1875–1900* (East African Studies No. 8; Kampala: East African Institute of Social Research, n.d.), p. 4.

46. In 1922 Buganda, with an estimated population of 786,000 had a school enrolment of over 58,000 pupils, less than fifty years after the first European contact. The whole of the Gold Coast Colony in 1920 had a population of over one million with just over 25,000 enrolled pupils. The 'Colony' here refers to the maximum areas of European contact and excludes both Ashanti and the Northern Territories. These statistics have been computed from Gold Coast Colony, *Education Report for the Year 1920* (Accra: Government Printer, 1920), and the Uganda Protectorate, *Blue Book 1922* (Entebbe: Government Printer, 1922).

47. Fallers, *op. cit.*, p. 28.

48. See, however, Apter's discussion of the contrast between 'pyramidal-consummatory' and 'hierarchical-instrumental' systems of authority. D. E. Apter, *The Political Kingdom in Uganda* (Princeton: Princeton University Press, 1961), pp. 84–107.

49. Roland Oliver, *The Missionary Factor in East Africa* (London: Longmans, Green, 1952), p. 172.

50. Field, *op. cit.*, p. 72.

51. *Ibid.*, p. 83.
52. *Ibid.*, p. 12.
53. *Ibid.*, p. 15.
54. *Ibid.*, p. 72.
55. *Ibid.*
56. *Ibid.*, p. 46.
57. *Ibid.*, p. 153.
58. Manoukian, *The Ewe-Speaking People*, p. 30.
59. *Ibid.*, p. 22.
60. *Ibid.*, p. 31.
61. *Ibid.*
62. *Ibid.*, pp. 30–31.
63. *Ibid.*, p. 32.
64. *Ibid.*, p. 33.
65. A. W. Cardinall, *The Natives of the Northern Territories of the Gold Coast* (London: George Routledge & Sons Ltd., n.d.), p. 16, and Rattray, *The Tribes of the Ashanti Hinterland*, I, ix–xiii.
66. Manoukian, *Tribes of the Northern Territories*, p. 3.
67. *Ibid.*, p. 47.
68. *Ibid.*, p. 14.
69. *Ibid.*, p. 47.
70. *Ibid.*, p. 25.
71. M. Fortes, *The Web of Kinship among the Tallensi* (London: International African Institute, Oxford University Press, 1949), p. 44.
72. Manoukian, *Tribes of the Northern Territories*, p. 28.
73. Rattray, *Tribes of the Ashanti Hinterland*, I, 257.
74. Manoukian, *Tribes of the Northern Territories*, p. 50.
75. Rattray, *Tribes of the Ashanti Hinterland*, II, 565–79.
76. Apter, *op. cit.*, p. 115.
77. T. E. Bowdich, *Mission from Cape Coast to Ashantee* (London: John Murray, 1819), p. 324.
78. A short but excellent discussion of this concept is contained in M. Fortes, 'The Ashanti Social Survey: A Preliminary Report', *Rhodes-Livingstone Journal*, No. 6 (London: Oxford University Press, 1948), p. 3.

II

THE GROWTH OF EUROPEAN
INFLUENCE UNTIL 1850

WE have suggested in previous pages that the incorporation of Western institutions would be slow during the earlier phases of Afro-European contact. This was particularly the case with the schools, and initial demand for formal education was limited to very specific groups. Interest in Western education was closely correlated with two other aspects of European influence; these were the extension of an exchange economy and the gradual extension of European political control. The association of these factors was not fortuitous, since we regard the growth of early educational demand as *necessarily* correlated with economic change and shifts in political control. Stated briefly, the effect of these two factors was to introduce a number of European-type functions and roles which operated independently of the traditional status structure. Only within such a changing social framework could the demand for formal education begin to be manifest at all. To state the hypothesis alternatively: although formal education has come to operate as a significant factor in affecting the distribution of power and status within African society, in the initial phases of contact at least there will be virtually no demand for formal education unless some changes have *already* occurred in the traditional structures. If, for example, there had been an attempt to offer Western education *in vacuo*, and if it had not been associated with significant changes in the economy or the system of political control, it is likely that educational demand would have remained minimal; educational institutions *by themselves* would not have constituted powerful factors in social change.

In this context, it is unprofitable to isolate the functional implications of educational transfer from other correlative changes in social structure. Although historians have recently undertaken the task of tracing the growth of formal education on the Gold Coast, there has been little attempt to examine this process in the light of economic and political change nor has there been any effort by them to assess its significance for traditional social structures. This chapter will in part re-examine the fragmentary materials on early education in the light of more general sociological concepts. In this context we have regarded 1850 as the watershed for educational development; up to this date educational demand was limited and, although significant economic change was taking place, the second of our two factors, the extension of European political control, was minimal. Together with the analysis of the functional significance of Western education we must undertake some examination of the formal educational structures themselves. Was this a process of simple transference of educational institutions and curriculums, or was there evidence, indeed, that European educationists were conscious, at this early period, of the need to make significant changes in educational practice in the light of African conditions?

Early European Settlements

In spite of French claims to have reached the Gold Coast as early as the mid-fourteenth century, the establishment of a Portuguese fort at Elmina in 1482 marked the beginning of recorded European contact with the area. By 1500 the Portuguese had created a Guinea Company for trade with the coast and had established additional posts at Axim, Shama, and Christianborg, but their monopoly of a profitable trade was soon challenged.[1] By the mid-sixteenth century their trade was intermittently interfered with by the activities of English interlopers who met with limited success, while in 1589 the establishment by the Dutch of a lodge at Moree followed an initial, successful voyage of three years earlier.[2]

The beginning of the seventeenth century saw a renewal of competition between the trading representatives of a succession of European powers. Abortive attempts were made by the British to establish trading companies to the Guinea coast in 1618 and 1631, and soon after the latter date the first British fort was established at Kormantin.[3] The declining power of Portugal could not check the depredations of her aggressive rivals, and after an initially unsuccessful attempt ten years earlier, the Dutch captured the Elmina fort in 1637. Five years later the Portuguese were obliged to cede all their bases on the coast to the Dutch West India Company in return for Holland's renunciation of claims to Brazil. The Portuguese had, in fact, 'served for setting dogs to spring the game, which, as soon as they had done, was seized by others'.[4]

British and Dutch were joined by the Danes, and by the mid-seventeenth century a chain of eleven small trading posts and forts extended along the coast from Axim to Christianborg. The seven Dutch forts in the western and central coastal zones overlapped the two British posts at Cape Coast and Anashan, while Danish activity was greater in the eastern areas. Maximal contact was, therefore, with the coastal Akan, notably the Fanti, while, to a lesser extent, trading contacts had been made with the coastal Ga groups.

Bosman, in his survey of the European trading stations at the commencement of the seventeenth century, drew attention to the generally precarious position of these settlements. The forts were almost uniformly undermanned and their state of readiness was rarely sufficient to guarantee effective defence against attack by the African coastal states. The land upon which the forts stood was subject to the payment of ground rents to local chiefs on the basis of the signing of notes of agreement. Further, the trading activities of the European companies were in no way accompanied by any form of jurisdiction or control over local populations. Indeed, the policy of the companies appeared to be based upon the idea of detachment from all local affairs outside the necessities of trade. European inhabitants of the forts generally perceived it to be to their advantage to refrain from interference in the activities of local rulers. The Europeans were in no position to interfere, since the ability of the Africans to cut off supplies of foodstuffs to the forts and control all trade outlets frequently reduced them to the status of suppliants. Bosman observes:

> From what I have said, you may be informed what places the English and we possess in Fantyn, both of us having an equal power, that is, none at all. For when these people are inclined to it, they shut up all the passes so close that not one merchant can possibly come from the in-land country to trade with us, and sometimes, not content with this, they prevent the bringing provisions to us, till we have made peace with them.[5]

Commenting upon the relations between the Europeans and the Fanti, he remarks:

> This land is so populous, it is very rich in gold, slaves, and all sorts of necessaries of life; but more especially corn, which they sell in large quantities to English ships. This great opulency has rendered them so arrogant and haughty, that an European who would traffic with them is obliged to stand bare to them.[6]

The unexpected skill of Africans in trade combined with their strong position vis-à-vis the European led to their being characterized as 'crafty, villainous . . . and fraudulent'; these sentiments were paralleled by Fanti disdain for the inhabitants of the forts who, for the most part, were too weak to defend themselves.[7] Indeed, Christianborg was easily captured in 1693 and not returned to the Danes until the following year. Relations between the coastal peoples and the Europeans were therefore entirely governed by the requirements of a mutually lucrative trade. The balance of power lay essentially with the African political units. In this context, a striking difference emerges between early European contact on the West Coast of Africa and the expansion into eastern Africa in the last quarter of the nineteenth century. In the latter case the activities of the great charter companies were associated with the rapid extension of administrative control of the areas in which they operated. This early demonstration of military superiority combined with the rapid growth of European political authority finds no parallel in early Gold Coast development.

The precarious position of the European companies was exacerbated by the depredations of interlopers. Bosman computed the coastal trade as worth 7,000 marks (£220,000) per annum in the early eighteenth century with the Dutch controlling the larger share, but the activities of Dutch and British interlopers accounted for well over a third of this amount.[8] The Dutch and Danes were not seriously affected, since their companies were government organizations. A series of English chartered companies receiving no government subsidy or support were forced to withdraw from the coast until, in 1712, a direct grant of £10,000 per annum was made by Parliament to the Royal Africa Company for the upkeep of the coastal trade, subject to its being thrown open freely to all English ships.[9] This general arrangement of a parliamentary grant was renewed in 1750 when the successor to the Royal Africa Company, the African Company of Merchants, was established with a grant of between £10,000 and £15,000 per annum from Parliament with all British merchants eligible to join on the payment of a fee of £2 per annum.[10] This relationship between the trading company and Parliament remained substantially unchanged until 1821. The arrangement implied that although parliamentary interest was peripheral, the company's activities were subject to periodic scrutiny. From this tenuous association was to later emerge the direct control of the coastal areas by the Crown.

The Development of the Ashanti Confederacy

While the precarious establishment of European trading places was taking place on the coast, a series of events of equal significance was occurring in the interior. Towards the close of the seventeenth century

41

the paramount chief of Kumasi overthrew the power of Denkyera, to which he was formerly tributary, and entered upon a period of conquest and expansion which was to end in the creation of the great Ashanti Confederacy. Kwahu and Assin were quickly reduced to tributary status, while by the mid-eighteenth century, the areas of Brong, Dagomba, and Gonja were obliged to accept the suzerainty of Kumasi.[11] This marked the limit of Ashanti expansion to the north. But in the south, Akim, Akwapim, and Banda were defeated and recognized the overrule of the former chief of Kumasi, now the *Asantehene*. Between the coastal ports and this new empire lay nothing more than the fragmented political units of the Fanti and other coastal groups. Indeed, Ashanti pressure began to be felt from the mid-eighteenth century onwards, though there is no record of any direct contact between the British and the Ashanti court until 1792.[12] The great struggle between the coastal Fanti with their British allies and the Ashanti, which was to form the backdrop to political, economic, and educational development through the whole nineteenth century, had not yet begun.

Some Consequences of European Contact

Although we have indicated that European political influence was negligible until the end of the eighteenth century, three significant and closely associated developments had already taken place. Even by the beginning of the eighteenth century the first growth of coastal urban centres was already marked. The gradually more heterogeneous populations of these towns were primarily involved in a growing exchange economy based upon the European trade rather than with traditional subsistence activities:

> The seabord was still divided into practically the same kingdoms as those that existed when the Portuguese settled on the Coast; but two centuries of trade with Europeans had increased the importance of the Coast towns and raised them from the position of tiny fishing villages to that of populous trading centres, which either became the capital of their respective kingdoms or rivalled the capitals in importance.[13]

This process continued throughout the eighteenth century and was associated with a second feature of special significance. The Fanti, particularly, were able to assume effective control over the coastal trade with the interior and more than any other group became associated with European influence. Ashanti expansion towards the coast was motivated primarily by a desire for direct trade with European entrepreneurs in guns, powder, cloth, and rum in exchange for slave surpluses. Free access to the coast became a cardinal factor in Ashanti policy, while Fanti middlemen virtually monopolized the channels of trade and became everywhere the mediating link between the European and the interior.[14]

Third, as a corollary to the process of coastal urbanization and trade, the first signs of a wealthy merchant class were already appearing. Even in the early eighteenth century Bosman mentions a class of Africans who 'have acquired a great reputation for their riches, either devolved on them by inheritance or trade'.[15] Whether the coastal chiefs were the primary beneficiaries of trading activities is not clear, but Bosman's remark signified that a new dimension of social status had begun to emerge. Differences of wealth were minimal within traditional societies and what differences there were could be regarded as the concomitant of social status rather than its determinant. The inevitable effect of the coastal trade was to create a cluster of new roles associated with commercial activities and a group whose interests were closely linked with those activities. Even though Europeans remained the insecure tenants of coastal chiefs and made no attempt to interfere with local jurisdiction, their presence had created the conditions which ultimately led to the transformation of traditional status systems. The extension of political control was to come much later, as was the influence of the Christian missions, but the effect of trade and urbanization alone was to have a series of repercussions on traditional societies; the influence of educational institutions was, in fact, intimately connected with these processes.

Educational Developments before 1800

Recent research has indicated that the Portuguese undertook the earliest educational experiments on the Gold Coast. In a series of instructions to the captain at 'Edina' (Elmina) King Joao III advised his representatives to 'take special care to command that the sons of the Negroes living in the village learn how to read and write, how to sing and pray while ministering in church'.[16] The mode of payment to the schoolmaster was indicated, based upon the number of pupils in attendance to a maximum of fifteen. The school was required to conduct regular catechetical instruction and lessons on how to read. The school was certainly still in existence in 1572 but the general extent of Portuguese educational efforts is unknown, and they were terminated with the abandonment of their coastal possessions in 1644.[17] Sporadic Catholic efforts at proselytization continued until the early eighteenth century but no real renewal of Catholic educational activities was to occur until 1880.

Other European groups, however, were to continue with their own educational activities with one feature that appears to be virtually unique to the Gold Coast. In most areas in Africa, early educational enterprise was closely associated with the activities of organized missionary bodies. In the Gold Coast it became, for a time, a subsidiary function of the great merchant companies, whose activities preceded the advent of real missionary endeavour by over one hundred years. This is not to suggest that the early schools provided a secular education; such a development would have been unthinkable in the light of contemporary European practice. Teaching duties were closely associated with castle chaplaincies in most cases; an examination of curriculums indicates the considerable significance attached to religious instruction. These schools were remarkably similar to the English charity schools of the same period. There is no indication that these institutions were primarily regarded by their founders as training institutions for the supply of clerical subordinates in company activities, though this development, as we shall see, was largely inevitable.

The Dutch were responsible for the foundation of a school at Elmina in 1644[18] which survived for virtually two hundred years; a similar establishment was begun by the Danes in Christianborg in 1722.[19] The first unequivocal evidence of educational activities in British forts is provided by the arrival of Thomas Thompson, a missionary of the Society for the Propagation of the Gospel in Foreign Parts, who arrived from New Jersey in 1751 and established a school at Cape Coast Castle.[20] That institution commenced, therefore, as the enterprise of an individual missionary, but Thompson was obliged to return to England because of ill-health in 1756, and the future development of the school was closely associated with the Company. Thompson was responsible for sending three Africans to England for an education in 1754 and while two died there, the third, Philip Quaque was ordained and returned to the coast in 1765 as 'Missionary, schoolmaster and Catechist to the Negroes on the Gold Coast'.[21] The vicissitudes of Quaque's subsequent career are well documented elsewhere—it is to the nature of this early school and its clientele that we must direct attention.[22]

The school suffered during its chequered early career not only from the general indifference of the Africans but from the very lukewarm support afforded to it by the company and its officials. By the 1780's the school had been reduced to a 'pitiable condition' and survived only as a result of timely aid from the Torridzonian Society—a group of officials who had formed themselves into a dining club.[23] The society provided funds for the education, clothing, and feeding of twelve mulatto children in 1788. In the same year, an instruction to the resident officers of the company to attend church indicated that fines for non-attendance 'be appropriated to the benefit of the Charity School for Mulattoe Children kept in this Castle'.[24] At the same period, the committee of the Company of Merchants, meeting in London, viewed the existence of the school with satisfaction and discussed the issue of uniforms and books to the scholars, the latter 'consisting of Primers, Spelling Books, Testaments and Bibles, of a common Edition'.[25]

After this temporary enthusiasm the fortunes of the school once again languished until the second decade of the nineteenth century, a record of disappointments and setbacks that was paralleled by the experience of the Dutch school at Elmina and the Danish institution at Christianborg. Generally speaking, the curriculums of these early schools were similar; reading, writing, with the occasional addition of arithmetic, and the inevitable core of biblical instruction consti- tuted the sum total of knowledge that they dispensed.[26] In effect, the curriculums of the schools offered the same content as those European institutions catering for the education of the 'poorer classes' at this period.

We have indicated that the demand by Africans for European education was at this time extremely limited, if it existed at all. This raises the crucial question, Who were the pupils of the early schools? Although there is some slight evidence that the Dutch school at Elmina might have recruited on a wider basis, there is little doubt that the pupils were largely recruited from castle mulattoes. Unlike Sierra Leone, the Gold Coast never contained any proportion of transplanted slaves, and school enrolment consisted largely of the offspring of European garrisons and the local population. These recruits were supplemented by the children of some of the wealthier African traders in the urban centres, but there is no indication that the schools were successful in obtaining pupils from any wider seg- ment of African society or that local chiefs were particularly inter- ested in sending children to school.[27] The pattern of initial demand was by no means random, and, as our previous hypothesis suggests, it seemed to come precisely from those groups who were to some extent peripheral to African traditional society—from mulattoes and from the children of African traders who were intimately involved with the emergent coastal economy. The comparative examination of pupils in early African schools has yet to be undertaken, but (with the notable exception of Buganda) we may tentatively suggest that early demand arose in very limited groups who were already marginal or peripheral to traditional status structures. The growth of a mass

45

demand is a far later phenomenon. Certainly, at the end of the eighteenth century the continued existence of the schools was a matter of as much doubt as the permanency of the coastal forts themselves.

Political and Economic Change, 1800–1850

The first half of the nineteenth century can be said to have been dominated by two significant political developments. The first was the continued expansion of the Ashanti towards the coast, an expansion which was to bring them into direct conflict with British and Fanti interests. The second was the slow, almost imperceptible extension of British control over the coastal region in spite of a vacillating and usually inept policy regarding relations with the Fanti.

By the end of the eighteenth century the Ashanti had completed the process of conquest over the peripheral Akan groups and faced only the numerous Fanti states, which were themselves expanding slowly to the north. In 1803, a dispute over the return of two chiefs who had sought refuge with the Fanti prompted the first hostilities, and a large-scale invasion of Fanti territory was undertaken by the Ashanti in 1806.[28] The British decision to afford protection to Fanti refugees within the fort at Anomabu, and to defend it in the face of an intense Ashanti assault, was of vital importance. The policy of non-intervention in the internal affairs of native states had been, in effect, abandoned and the British were committed irretrievably to the support of the coastal peoples against the Ashanti. Such a result was not of Ashanti seeking, and, to a great extent, what followed was largely due to a British policy which at best could be described as inconsistent—at worst as dishonest. The consequences, however, were quite clear; for virtually seventy years the British were pinned to the coast by a highly successful military power, and the Ashanti were to remain largely insulated from those very factors which were already making for marked social change in the coastal zone. Paradoxically, the very military success of the Ashanti was to be ultimately disastrous to them. During the major part of the nineteenth century, the militarily weak Fanti states were to associate themselves with growing British influence while the Ashanti remained virtually insulated from it. While the Ashanti remained resolutely opposed to the spread of Christianity or formal education, the Fanti were increasingly accepting both. Consequently, when the Ashanti were finally incorporated into a wider political unit under British hegemony, they were for a period virtually excluded from access to new-type roles associated with it. Above all, these political factors were to give rise to marked inequalities in educational provision as between Fanti and Ashanti that persisted until the middle of this century.

The First Ashanti War was followed by additional conflicts in 1808 and 1813 and led to the signing of treaties with the inland power in both 1817 and 1820.[29] However, the conditions of the former were later broken by the British while the latter, negotiated by J. Dupuis acting as consul, was repudiated by the governor and council at Cape Coast. The seriousness of the British position on the coast was recognized, however, when Parliament abolished the African Company of Merchants and transferred the administration of the coastal forts directly to the Crown represented by the governor of Sierra Leone. No doubt such action was partially a result of the loss of the profitable slave trade which had accounted for nine-tenths of the value of coastal exports during the early part of the century and which was abolished in 1807, to the sorrow of British and African traders alike.[30]

Disaster was to follow in 1824, during the Fourth Ashanti War, when the British were crushed at Insanmankow and the governor, Sir Charles McCarthy, killed in action. As a result, the British government decided to withdraw from all coastal settlements in 1829 and was only prevented from so doing by the opposition of the London merchants. A compromise was reached by which the effective control of the coastal forts was to remain in the hands of a committee of merchants, appointed by the British government, who were to receive an annual subvention of £4,000 per annum for the upkeep of the forts. The arrangement of 1829 allowed the administration of British law within the forts only; it expressly forbade the exercise of any authority or jurisdiction over the districts outside them or over Africans living under their 'protection'. In effect, it is difficult to see what protection the forts were able to afford, and the defeat at Insanmankow had done much to lower what little prestige the British enjoyed on the coast.[31]

The appointment of George Maclean as the first governor of the forts under the London committee proved to be the turning point in the extension of British political control. From 1830 onwards, largely as a result of Maclean's energy and personal reputation with the coastal chiefs, a form of limited authority began to be exercised among them with respect to matters of criminal jurisdiction. In 1842 the Select Committee of the House reporting on conditions on the West Coast of Africa was obliged to comment that in spite of the limits of jurisdiction imposed by the 1829 agreement, 'a kind of irregular jurisdiction has grown up, extending itself far beyond the limits of the Forts by the voluntary submission of the Natives themselves whether Chiefs or Traders, to British Equity'.[32]

47

The committee, appointed as a result of endemic British doubts regarding the feasibility of continuing the forts on the Gold Coast, recommended (largely as a result of Maclean's urgings) that the government of the Gold Coast settlements once more be undertaken directly by the Crown. This was with the understanding that the dominions of Her Majesty should extend only to the forts themselves while outside them no attempt should be made to prevent undesirable usages such as slavery, except by 'persuasion, or other peaceful means'.[33] At that date the total British possession on the coast numbered four forts, at Dixcove, Cape Coast, Anomabu, and British Accra.[34] The status of the forts had changed, since, as a result of a British and allied victory over the Ashanti at Dodowa in 1824, the sites upon which they stood had become the absolute property of the British. This was a consequence of the capture of 'notes' promising the payment of ground rents to the Fanti from whom these documents had been previously captured by the Ashanti. British possession of the notes implied that the sites of the forts were now their absolute property and all payment of ground rent ceased.[35]

In 1843, therefore, control of the forts was once more vested in the Crown represented by the governor of Sierra Leone. In spite of intentions to limit British jurisdiction, the famous 'Bond' of 1844, signed by the chiefs of Denkyera, Abrah, Assin, Donadie, Domminassie, Anomabu, and Cape Coast, marked a further regularization of British authority. Although this treaty conferred no new territorial rights, it legalized the previous jurisdiction in criminal matters that had been particularly exercised by Maclean. Although these groups were in no sense British subjects, the voluntary acceptance of such jurisdiction marked the real beginning of British hegemony and control; the way was now open for direct British intervention in the internal affairs of the native states.[36]

The Expansion of Educational Facilities, 1800–1850

The most outstanding feature in educational expansion during the first half of the nineteenth century was the re-emergence of the missions. After the cessation of Catholic efforts in the seventeenth century the Moravian Brethren made a series of unsuccessful attempts to establish themselves between 1737 and 1771. After this date the field was to remain fallow, except for the occasional efforts of castle chaplains, until the great growth of European missionary societies towards the end of the eighteenth century.[37] Two of these, the Wesleyan Methodist Missionary Society and the Basel Society, were to

48

play a crucial role in the expansion of educational facilities, and, more important from our point of view, they were to proceed with radically different assumptions about the type of education to be provided for Africans.

The Gold Coast, as we have indicated, was virtually unique in Africa in that the early growth of schools was not associated with mission activity, and the early nineteenth century was to show a continued interest by the African Company of Merchants and later the Crown in the development of education. Not only was this to be a rare feature in British Africa but it was a radical departure from early English educational practice. In England itself, it was only in 1833 that an Education Committee of the Privy Council was empowered to administer grants-in-aid to voluntary schools, and before 1870 no public bodies existed for the direct provision of schools. Although we have implied that educational practice in British Africa paralleled but lagged behind English experiments, the Gold Coast witnessed a unique development when the Crown authorities after 1821 aimed at the provision of not one but a chain of government schools directly financed from public funds, this preceding missionary endeavours by a decade. Certainly by 1841 these government schools were still in existence, paralleled by a growing chain of mission institutions which later absorbed them. In effect the 'dual' system of control existed in the Gold Coast almost thirty years before its emergence in England itself.

The Cape Coast School, which had managed to survive since 1800, receives mention in contemporary records once again when a Reverend William Phillip was appointed as chaplain and schoolmaster in 1815 with explicit instructions from the Committee of the Company to 'render himself sufficiently master of the Madras system, to be able to remedy any defects in their school'.[38] Not only was the curriculum of the school to follow the European pattern but the reference to monitorial teaching methods shows an attempt to transfer directly an element which had already become the standard method for the instruction of the poor in England. The school remained the nucleus for future government expansion and, by 1822, had two schoolmasters and three African teachers attached to the establishment with a pupil enrolment of over seventy, a figure that was unchanged by 1830.[39] Also, between 1821 and 1840 additional government schools were created at Dixcove and James Fort (British Accra) and, most surprisingly, a separate school for girls was established at Cape Coast—an indication that the provision of clerical assistants was not, as is sometimes supposed, the sole aim of the Crown in creating these institutions.[40] Though these schools were supported largely from

49

Crown funds, some aid was forthcoming from local African traders and merchants.[41]

With the advent of the missions, a new phase of expansion was to begin in the third decade of the century. The first Basel missionaries arrived at Christianborg in 1828 at the invitation of the Danish governor, de Richelieu, but early efforts were disastrous. Loss of life was appalling and, by 1840, out of nine missionaries sent out, only one had survived and not one baptized convert had been made.[42] The initial experience of the Wesleyans was hardly more encouraging; their first representative, Joseph Dunwell, arrived in 1835 at the invitation of the Fanti Bible Group, a small band of literate Africans who had formerly been associated with the Cape Coast School. Dunwell died six months later, and between 1835 and 1844, out of a total of thirty-four missionaries sent to the area, fifteen died while the remainder, with the exception of four, were forced to leave the coast within two years because of ill health.[43] Indeed, the continuance of the mission was almost entirely due to the efforts of one man, Thomas Birch Freeman, who arrived on the coast in 1838 and was to remain there for fifty-two years.[44]

By 1841 the Wesleyans had been able to make substantial progress in terms of the number of schools under their control although some doubt may be expressed as to the quality of education given in them. The report of the Commissioner to the Select Committee of the House prepared in that year gives a reasonably detailed picture of the state of educational facilities at that time; nothing could be clearer than that the missions were not 'paving the way', since a substantial proportion of scholars were in government, not mission institutions. The school at Cape Coast appeared to be in flourishing condition with an enrolment of 165 pupils and a staff of six, while the Jamestown school claimed forty or fifty children 'in a forward state of progress'. There were also government institutions at Anomabu, Dixcove, and Elmina, the latter with seventy boys and girls.[45]

The Commissioner reported at the same time that there were eleven missionary schools in the whole of the 'colony' with over three hundred pupils 'of which two are partially supported by government'. J. B. Freeman's evidence indicated the existence of nine Wesleyan institutions at Cape Coast, Anomabu, Accra, Winnebah, Mansue, Salt Pond, Kommenda, Dominasi, and Ahassa.[46] Two significant features emerge. First, Wesleyan educational activities were confined overwhelmingly to the Fanti coastal towns and trading stations, a pattern that was to persist. Second, although the later Education Ordinance of 1882 has sometimes been regarded as constituting the beginning of government aid to voluntary schools, the evidence

50

points to a precedent for such action existing since 1841 when some government support was actually being given.[47] This step was being taken only eight years after the first parliamentary grants to education in England. The government institutions on the Gold Coast were absorbed by the missions with no renewal of direct government ownership of any schools until very late in the century. Instead, a more typically English structure emerged, the expansion of the school systems by voluntary agencies assisted by limited government grants-in-aid.

By 1841, owing to the mortality rate among missionaries in Accra, no schools had been begun by the Basel Mission, and the decision was made to shift the focus of missionary activities away from the coastal zone to the healthier Akwapim Ridge. The mission headquarters were thus transferred from Accra to Akropong in 1835 by the lone surviving missionary. A boys' school was commenced in Akropong in 1843 and in 1847 an establishment for girls was begun.[48] The decision of the Basel Mission that 'the sphere of work in an African tribe offered more hope than the sophisticated and demoralized population of a coast town' was of profound importance.[49] There was no doubt that the healthier Akropong area was more conducive to missionary survival, but whether it was a more fruitful area for missionary activity is a matter of some doubt. The urban areas with their development of an indigenous merchant class, with their heterogeneous populations predominantly dependent on an exchange economy, and with a nucleus of literate inhabitants were far more likely to have proved a profitable sector for proselytization. The Wesleyans working in these coastal towns were able to develop a system of day schools with English as a medium of instruction.[50] They were able to take advantage of an already growing urban demand, a demand that was closely associated with the occupational structure of the towns and where, as we shall indicate, the vocational implications of formal education were already apparent. The Basel Mission's decision implied that they were obliged to undertake a 'frontal assault' on traditional society where the conditions for the rapid incorporation of educational institutions did not exist. As a result, the mission was to stress a policy of detachment of individuals from the traditional milieu by a concentration upon boarding institutions. Moreover, the basis of instruction necessarily became the vernacular.[51] Later pages will elaborate on this distinction and attempt to conclude whether different educational and social consequences flowed from the adoption of divergent mission policies.

The Missions in Ashanti

Both missions were, however, attracted by the prospect of proselytization in Ashanti. Freeman was first able to reach Kumasi in January
1839, where he was met with considerable suspicion. It appears that
although the Ashanti were not strongly opposed to the preaching of
the gospel they strongly resisted the idea of the foundation of a
school which they feared could lead to rebellion and political unrest.[52]
A shrewder perception of the possible consequences of Western education is difficult to imagine. The most powerful, perhaps the only
effective, instrument at this time for proselytization was the school.
From the Ashanti viewpoint the preaching of the gospel might be
harmless enough and was probably likely to have little effect, but to
select children for specific training in a specialized institution was a
very different matter, the implications of which were not lost on them.
Freeman was able to undertake a second visit to Kumasi in 1841, in
connection with the return of two 'princes' who had been educated
in England. On this occasion, no doubt partly as a result of the return
of the young men, the reception was somewhat more favourable and
a small grant of land was made to build a mission which progressed
very slowly in the ensuing years and ended with the later renewal of
hostilities with the coast.[53] That the Ashanti were resolutely opposed
to the creation of schools is evident from the reply given to those
Wesleyans who had hoped in 1876 to resume the mission after the
Sixth Ashanti War, 'We will accept the mission if you act as Mr.
Freeman did to help the peace of the nation and the prosperity of
trade, but you must understand that we will not select children for
education, for the Ashanti children have better work to do than to sit
down all day idly to learn "Hoy! Hoy! Hoy!".'[54] Wesleyan lack of
success was paralleled by Basel experience, and a visit by a single
missionary in 1839 met with an indifferent reception while the representative himself was held in Kumasi for over a year.[55] The development of education in Ashanti was not to occur until after the Sixth
Ashanti War in 1874, and even then progress was minimal until the
first decade of the twentieth century.

The Curriculums of the Early Schools

It would appear that no marked changes had occurred in the school
curriculums since the close of the eighteenth century. Both the Cape
Coast school and the Wesleyan institutions employed the 'British and
Foreign' system of monitorial instruction. The core of the work was
reading, writing, and religious instruction, supplemented by arith-

metic and geography for the more advanced pupils at Cape Coast, while history was included on the curriculum of the Wesleyan institutions. A contemporary observer remarked that generally 'reading, writing, and arithmetic, with a very imperfect acquaintance with the principles of the Christian religion, constituted the full extent of the school education'.[56]

Criticism of the limitations of the curriculum were supplemented by harsher observations on the methods of instruction and the prevalence of rote learning. The Commissioner for the Select Committee in his observations remarked:

> There is too much time employed in the school in the mere exercise of memory, too much of a mere teaching of words, and neglect of the knowledge of things, and too little employment of the faculty of thinking and of instruction in the habits of industry.[57]

One is impressed, in fact, by the remarkable parallels in curriculum and instruction that existed between these schools and their contemporary counterparts in English elementary education. Indeed, it is probable that the institution at Cape Coast compared not unfavourably in standards with the charity schools of England.[58] These parallels have often been indicated but, unfortunately, analysis by educational historians has rarely gone further than this. The structural similarities between the systems were manifest but failure to examine the very different functions performed by these educational institutions and the motivations which led people to enter them has resulted in a series of errors in interpretation. For example, since early education was manifestly academic in nature, it has been assumed that there was an indifference on the part of Europeans to the development of trade and agricultural institutions. It is said that an academic system which had developed in response to European social and economic conditions was 'imposed' on African populations. Further analysis reveals that the reverse was the case. European educators were very much concerned with the development of alternative forms of educational institution while African demand, limited as it was, took the form of pressure for academic instruction.

It is incorrect to suppose that careful consideration was not being given by local teachers to the question of the 'suitability' of the curriculum or that the desirability of technical, vocational, or agricultural institutes had been overlooked. There is ample evidence to suggest that educationists both in the Gold Coast and Britain were very concerned with the lines along which colonial schools were developing—and the discussion in the 1840's led off a century of similar examination of the problem.

The investigating Commissioner for the Select Committee was concerned to discover, in both the Gold Coast and Sierra Leone, whether model farms (attached to each school) had been developed and if trade training was being undertaken at any institution.[59] At this date no such activities had been begun, but all witnesses, and these included Maclean and Freeman, were enthusiastic over the development of such centres.[60] A Wesleyan project for the creation of a model farm school at Dominasi was already under consideration, and, as we shall see, trade and agricultural training was to become a crucial branch of the Basel curriculum. The Commissioner supplemented his remarks with the proposal to establish a model farm in each settlement and 'in the towns, to afford the masters the facilities of having every child taught some trade or calling at the same time that he is sent to school to read and write'.[61]

Writing only five years later, Lieutenant Governor Winniett was to observe:

Connected with the general branches of education, Model schools for the instruction and training of boys in the knowledge of various useful mechanical arts are most important desiderata; at present there is no employment for educated boys, except as teachers in schools, and clerks in government and mercantile establishments and hence the results of education, pleasing as they may be, are not so healthy, vigorous, and permanent as they would be if they were associated with various branches of useful mechanical knowledge. These desiderata are greatly worthy of the attention of an enlightened government.[62]

The literature of this period contains many references to the 'bookish' nature of African education[63] and to the necessity for trade and agricultural training. But the most remarkable and systematic expression of views on this subject is contained in a report by the Education Committee of the Privy Council to the Colonial Office dated 1847 which was described as

a short and simple account of the mode in which the Committee of the Council on Education considers that industrial schools for the coloured races may be conducted in the colonies and to render the labour of the children available towards meeting some part of the expenses of their education.[64]

The significance of the document lies not only in its content but in its being the first general statement of British educational policy in colonial areas; it was not until 1925 that further considered opinion was available from the Colonial Office. The opinions of the Committee of the Privy Council, in suitably modified form, are enjoying more than current popularity in connection with educational planning in underdeveloped areas and it is appropriate to examine the document in some detail. In the view of the Committee the principal objects of education for the coloured races could be summarized as follows:

1. To inculcate the principles and promote the influences of Christianity by such instruction as can be given in elementary schools.
2. To accustom the children of these races to habits of self-control and moral discipline.
3. To diffuse a grammatical knowledge of the English language as the most important agent of civilization.
4. To make the school the means of improving the condition of the peasantry by teaching them how health may be preserved by a proper diet, cleanliness, ventilation and clothing, and by the structure of their dwellings.
5. To give practical training in household economy and in the cultivation of the cottage garden as well as in those common handicrafts by which a labourer may improve his domestic comfort.
6. To communicate such a knowledge of writing and arithmetic and of their application to his wants and duties as may enable a peasant to economize his means, and give the small farmer the power to enter into calculations and agreements.
7. Improved agriculture is required to replace the system of exhausting the virgin soils, and then leaving to natural influences alone the work of reparation. The education of the coloured races would, therefore, not be complete for the children of small farmers, unless it included this object.
8. Lesson books should teach the mutual interests of the mother country, and her dependencies, the natural basis of this connection and the domestic and social duties of the coloured races.
9. Lesson books should also set forth simply the relation of wages, capital, and labour, and the influence of local and general government on personal security, independence, and order.

The committee, however, was not content to state objectives alone, but developed a series of suggestions regarding the actual structure and organization of the schools. Four types of institutions were to be created. Elementary schools were to aim at the inculcation of basic skills but were to be followed by two alternative types of institutions. 'Day Schools of Industry' were to cater for both boys and girls between the ages of thirteen and nineteen and these were conceived as partially self-supporting institutions. Boys were to be organized into working parties connected with trades, agriculture, and gardening, while girls were to be instructed in all practical branches of housewifery. The general aim was the development of 'habits of

55

steady industry' leading to a 'settled and thriving peasantry'.

Parallel with such institutions, model farms would be created, giving systematic instruction in agriculture between the ages of fourteen and nineteen; a series of normal schools were to be established for the training of teachers. In this latter case the curriculum once more reflected the agricultural pre-occupations of the framers of the proposals. Courses for future teachers were to include—in addition to biblical instruction—chemistry and its application to agriculture, the theory of natural phenomena in relation to agriculture, land surveying and practical mensuration, the theory and practice of agriculture and gardening, and the management of farm stock (including the treatment of disease).

The committee further indicated that its proposals could not be indiscriminately applied, and it would be necessary to know more details of the cultures of the various colonies in order to effect a closer adaptation of the plans of the schools to the wants of the inhabitants.

It is a sobering fact, indeed, to realize that not only in content but in the use of phraseology this document was hardly improved upon for over a hundred years. Contemporary discussion virtually duplicates the views of the committee. To quote two examples:

> A problem facing the educational authorities is to devise a curriculum which will meet the needs not only of a small minority who will engage in non-agricultural pursuits but the bulk of the population, in order that they may be able to lead a better richer life in a rural environment.[65]

Or alternatively, a recent study by the United Nations proceeds precisely on the lines indicated by this early report. A general series of criticisms of the academic high school is followed by a number of recommendations requiring 'the creation of a fully integrated system of agricultural education within the general framework of technical and vocational education'.[66] We shall return in later pages to an examination of the assumptions which underlie this general approach.

In general, the examination of contemporary nineteenth-century sources would indicate a climate of opinion that was very favourable to new educational experiments in the area of technical and agricultural education, combined with considerable doubts regarding the suitability of academic forms of instruction. In view of this, it is initially difficult to explain the developments that followed; the emergence of a highly academic system of education with very limited provision of alternative forms of instruction. A later observer was to remark regarding the views of the early committee that it was 'sad to think that eighty years ago there was in circulation a document which might and ought to have inspired those who were responsible for the administration of the Empire, to do something which was, in effect, begun half a century later'.[67] This stricture cannot be accepted without reservation, since attempts were made, both in the Gold Coast and other African territories to develop agricultural and technical schools, with generally disappointing results. The failure of these schemes is to be interpreted not as the result of an unwillingness of educationists to try them but is explainable by a series of factors operating outside the schools themselves.[68]

Having indicated that European opinion and policy was by no means dominated by an intention to reproduce European academic education on the Gold Coast, it seems appropriate to examine whether the academic systems which existed were 'imposed' upon traditional cultures, a view which appears to command considerable support. Earlier discussion has indicated that since the extent of British control over the coastal region was only peripheral at this stage, there was no question of compelling children to enter school or of enforcing regular attendance even in those areas directly contiguous to the forts. Maclean was obliged to use persuasion in seeking pupils for the school at Cape Coast, and the precarious position of the early missions made it impossible for them to exert any strong pressures on local populations. Compulsory attendance laws were quite out of the question, but even if the British had been in position to legislate rules of attendance of any sort they certainly could never have been enforced. Such legislation is only practicable where an overwhelming proportion of eligible children are already attending school on a voluntary basis, and this is not likely to occur until the bulk of the population is already convinced of the tangible advantages likely to accrue from formal education. Such conditions did not exist at this period and in parts of Africa, including the present Northern Region of Ghana, they do not exist today.

The missions particularly were obliged to use every device to attract children into the schools, and Raum's description of their difficulties during the pioneer phase seems to have parallels throughout Africa:

> The difficulties experienced by early missionaries in attracting buyers for their educational wares is shown in the desperate attempts made by them to induce children to attend. Bribes in the form of food, clothes, even money payments, were common; chiefs had to be persuaded to accept education for children.[69]

This situation was certainly typical of the inland areas in which the Basel Mission was working, and progress in the first ten years was negligible while bribes were frequently used to induce attendance.[70]

However, the Wesleyans operating primarily in the coastal towns could take advantage of a limited support for the schools. But, in general, neither mission nor government was in a position to create a demand for education directly, and the principal way by which children could be attracted to school was by providing a form of education for which a limited demand *already* existed. As we shall indicate, this existing demand was essentially for an academic education. The notion that academic types of instruction on a European pattern could be imposed distorts the facts of the situation. It may even be regarded as a convenient fiction to explain the success of academic schools as opposed to the relative failure of agricultural and trade-training institutions. If 'academic' systems were demonstrably not imposed and if there was considerable enthusiasm among educationists for alternative types of curriculum, why was it that these academic systems survived and grew while divergent experiments withered? The answer to this question is to be found in an examination of the orientations of Africans themselves towards schooling.

African Attitudes to Western Education

The apparent attractiveness of the proposals of the Education Committee of the Privy Council concealed several assumptions regarding the function of educational institutions that it was not justified in making in view of the actual economic and social conditions on the coast at that period. The proposals constituted one of the earliest attempts to consciously adapt the schools to perform one primary function: the development of a thriving agricultural economy. Certainly some of the stated objectives were religious and political in nature; but the core of the proposals was economic in its orientation and, as it turned out, the committee was correct in assuming that the tropical colonies would remain essentially agricultural communities. What could appear more reasonable than to consciously utilize the schools in carrying out a programme of economic development, by creating a prosperous and 'thriving peasantry'?

The initial assumption was that the creation of schools and curriculums designed for this purpose would generate a demand for such an education among the 'coloured races'. The second assumption, closely related to the first, was that African expectations regarding the potential functions of educational institutions were congruent with those of Europeans, or could be made so. Although reference was made to the 'wants' of the coloured races this assessment was based upon an examination of the colonial economies, and a judgment was made regarding the type of education deemed appropriate

58

for development. The 'wants' were purely putative in nature and no attempt was made to examine the crucial variables in the situation: what was the extent of educational demand and why was it so limited; what groups were, in fact, using the schools and to what uses were existing Western educational institutions being put? Had the proponents of such schemes of educational reform been prepared to examine African expectations regarding the role and function of the schools, the failure of the schemes might have been predicted. The discrepancy between stated policies or objectives and the actual developments that were to take place was not due to the resistance of the 'conservative educator' but was a result of African unwillingness to accept educational alternatives.

Initially, what was the overall state of demand for educational facilities during this period? It has been indicated that until the end of the eighteenth century demand was very limited and confined to particular groups in the coastal towns; during the first half of the nineteenth century, although broadening of demand was to occur, there was no dramatic increase in popular enthusiasm for the schools. Speaking of the coastal towns in 1841, Maclean observed that many parents were evincing great anxiety to send their children to school, but comments by C. H. Bartels and T. B. Freeman were far more guarded. Bartels remarked that the population did 'not embrace the advantages offered to them so readily as they should', while Freeman merely observed that parents were a 'little less reluctant to send children to school than they had been two or three years before'.[71] Brodie Cruikshank writing a few years later drew attention to the widespread prejudice against European education and remarked that most Africans had come to the conclusion that 'the school was a very good thing for white men, but not for black'.[72]

Early demand for education was primarily associated with the towns, thus accounting for the different early experience of the Basel and Wesleyan institutions. Since demand was by no means universal, even in the urban milieu, however, it is appropriate to consider the nature of the early clientele of the schools in more detail. In the eighteenth century the 'castle schools' had recruited pupils who were, to some extent, marginal to traditional African society: they were castle mulattoes or the children of African traders who were involved in the exchange economy of the coastal region. During the early nineteenth century was there any evidence of a widening of the basis of recruitment? And, most significant, was it found possible to recruit individuals who were eligible for significant high-status roles within traditional society itself?

There is no doubt that from an early date British policy, if it could

59

be described as such, had aimed at the enrolment of the sons of chiefs into the schools with the idea of attaching them to the British interest. Thus Article 9 of the Treaty of 1817 signed by the kings of Ashanti and Juaben required that:

> The kings agree to commit their children to the care of the Governor-in-Chief for education at Cape Coast Castle, in full confidence of the good intentions of the British Government and of the benefits to be derived therefrom.[73]

The proposal met with considerable opposition from the officials of the Court of the *Asantehene* and there is no evidence to suggest that these terms of the treaty were carried out.[74] Indeed, some doubt is attached to this version of the document since a copy of the treaty produced for Dupuis by the *Asantehene* on the occasion of the former's visit to Kumasi in 1820 did not specify whose children were to be sent. Dupuis was later to observe that 'the article No. 9, showing the King's disposition to send his own children to Cape Coast for education is falsely inserted'.[75]

Maclean, pursuing a more energetic policy, was to meet with greater success; he concluded a treaty with the *Asantehene* in 1831 which resulted in two young Ashanti 'princes' (Ansa, the son of the former *Asantehene* [Tutu Kwamina] and Inkwantabissa, the son of the incumbent [Okutu]) being sent to England for education.[76] They returned to Kumasi in 1841, accompanied by Freeman, but it is significant that neither remained at the court of Ashanti but they settled permanently in Cape Coast on British government pensions.[77] Their anticipated role as educated chiefs, acting as intermediaries between the British and the Ashanti, never developed, for reasons that will be indicated in later paragraphs.

Maclean was also active in persuading each of the principal Fanti chiefs to send one of his sons to school, and the policy would appear to have met with some success. Maclean's efforts were re-echoed in the proposals of the Commissioner for the Select Committee of 1842 when he recommended:

> ... the encouragement to schools of a higher class than any of which there are at present; to which, amongst others, the neighbouring Chiefs should be invited to send their sons to receive an education which might fit them to be of benefit to their own people directly, if they returned to their families, or indirectly, if they remained, by entering into connection with British interests.[78]

The idea of creating a hierarchy of institutions to be associated with differential criteria of recruitment finds its parallel in English policy at this period; both the Newcastle and Taunton reports were to make it the basis for the development of the English secondary-school system throughout the nineteenth century.[79] The policy of 'aristocratic' recruitment into special institutions was not confined to British territories alone. Faidherbe on his appointment as governor of Senegal in 1854 created an 'Ecole des Hôtages' for the sons of chiefs.[80] The enthusiasm of the latter for the policy seems evident from its title and, generally speaking, the reaction of the chiefly group to such efforts seemed to be unfavourable over most of Africa. Where the chiefs could be persuaded to send sons at all, those sent were not infrequently the most stupid children of junior wives, while even the chiefs who were enthusiastic about the creation of a new school withdrew their support when it was suggested that their own children should attend.[81] The application of the same policy in British India during the first half of the nineteenth century met with similar resistance from traditional rulers.[82]

In view of these comments it would seem that Maclean's policy had met with remarkable success, since chiefs did occasionally make requests for schools to be established in their area. It was known that 'many of the chiefs had a secretary in constant attendance upon them, frequently their own sons, who have received their education in the schools'.[83] There was certainly evidence that the chiefly group valued literacy as an important adjunct to their dealings with the British and each other, but in spite of this, Maclean's policy, apparently successful, had its limitations.

Our previous discussion of traditional social structure among the Akan and other groups has indicated that continuance in the chiefly office was dependent to a great extent on the meticulous discharge of traditional functions, the role of conserver rather than innovator. It has been indicated that individuals eligible for significant traditional roles would not be likely to enter the schools and European education might in this light be viewed not as a qualification but as a potential disqualification for traditional office.[84] Most Europeans seemed not to have been conscious of the fact that matrilineal inheritance among the Akan automatically excluded the sons of chiefs from the assumption of chiefly office.[85] Sons were not members of the royal lineages of their father and the mere fact of paternal relationship was of no political significance to the Akan except that fathers were responsible for the training of their children.

In this context the fact that the two Ashanti 'Princes' returned to Cape Coast is not surprising; they were simply not eligible to perform politically significant functions in traditional society. Similarly, the practice of coastal chiefs in sending their sons to school in order to assume later secretarial duties would imply that efforts were being made to provide alternative roles for them, even though access to traditionally significant status was closed. In practice, the traditional status structure remained unaffected by the policy of 'aristocratic recruitment'; instead of attracting to the schools a group whose high prestige in traditional society might be reinforced by European education, the British were probably gaining the attendance of precisely those groups who were barred from access to traditionally important roles. A further indirect comment on the success of Maclean's policy concerns the level of literacy among Fanti chiefs who ratified the articles of the Fanti Confederacy in 1871; virtually all of these chiefs were illiterate.[86]

What evidence exists on this early period would tend to show that the pattern of recruitment into the schools, although somewhat broader than in the eighteenth century, had not changed significantly since then. Although no specific mention is made of the mulatto group, it is apparent that a high proportion of students were the sons of coastal traders and the wealthier merchants of the urban areas, supplemented by the children of clerks in government employment.[87] The fortunes of these groups were closely associated with the exchange economy and the continued success of European commercial enterprises.

These remarks go some way to explain the apparently contradictory conclusions that recent students have reached regarding recruitment into early African schools. It has been stated that as a result of European attempts to recruit 'sons of noble houses' into the schools, early students continued to be preponderantly from 'socially superior backgrounds'.[88] Another observer, referring to the west coast in general, expresses the view that the early generations of educated Africans were of 'lowly origin'.[89] The inadequacy of these judgments lies in their ambiguity and failure to differentiate clearly between indigenous status systems and the cluster of occupational roles that had emerged as a result of European contact. It is not sufficient to indicate that sons of chiefs attended school unless it is made clear whether they were eligible for recruitment into traditionally significant roles. Bearing the previous discussion on traditional society in mind, it seems particularly inappropriate to use the term 'socially superior background' since it carries with it the idea of traditional social strata which were associated with distinct differences in subculture, a factor which we regarded as not apparent in traditional social structure. A similar criticism might be made of the use of the term 'lowly'. Both analyses, in fact, represent attempts to utilize terminology that might be appropriate to describe the relationships between educational recruitment and social class in the Western world but which is inadequate with reference to traditional groupings of this type. The crucial dimensions here are the degree to which individuals were *primarily* associated with activities in the traditional sector and whether they were 'eligible' for traditional positions of leadership on the basis of primarily ascriptive criteria. In this sense early recruitment into the schools was from groups who were not primarily associated with traditional activities but were rather connected with the exchange economy and European-type functions; it would also appear that most of them were not eligible for traditionally prestigeful office. In functional terms, the schools by operating increasingly as the gateway to new occupational categories constituted an alternative avenue of mobility operating independently of traditional modes of status acquisition.

It might be tentatively suggested that where Western educational institutions have been transferred to traditional societies of this type (bearing in mind the very divergent model of Buganda) members eligible for chiefly or other traditional office will be reluctant to use these institutions until such time as extended European political control exerts direct pressure on modes of traditional recruitment. By this we mean that continuance in office becomes dependent not only upon the discharge of traditional functions but also upon the capacity of the chiefs to maintain satisfactory relations with the European administration. In this connection, Fortes was to remark of Ashanti over one hundred years after the period under discussion, that literacy was valued among candidates for chiefships only in that it enabled relationships with the European administration to be maintained; it was not regarded as relevant in the discharge of functions relative to the chiefdom itself. The acquisition of European education, in fact, was 'as much a self-protective reaction . . . as a "progressive" move.'[90]

This tentative hypothesis would tend to find support in Indian experience; just as Maclean's 'aristocratic' policy seems to have failed in the Gold Coast, British educational policy in India was to meet with similar setbacks. Regarding the clientele of the early Indian schools it has been remarked that 'the educated class sprang from a fairly distinct economic and social stratum of the native population. This grouping, however, did not correspond to the aristocratic pattern which had been in the mind of those who shaped official policy in the early part of the century'.[91]

The use of the term 'stratum' in this context refers to the commercial groups of nineteenth-century India and, as we have indicated, it was these groups who were also supplying a large proportion of recruits to the early Gold Coast schools. The position of traditional elites in the Gold Coast was progressively weakened by their inability to perceive the necessity for European education. For, once European political control became effective, there was always the possibility that the locus of power would shift from the chiefs in favour of alternative groups who had earlier recognized the potential significance of schooling. However, it needs to be stressed, because the distinction has not always been made apparent, that this problem was not to arise until the second half of the nineteenth century. Since European political control was almost non-existent until 1850, the growth of the early schools was of little political significance at this stage. In practice, at this period the crucial variable in the situation was an economic one arising from the close relationship between the schools and the occupational structure of the urban areas.

The Schools and the Occupational Structure

It has been indicated that alongside traditional social structures, urban coastal centres were developing with heterogeneous ethnic populations and an increasingly differentiated occupational structure connected with the European trade. This structure was by no means complex, comprising as it did occupations of a primarily clerical nature, both in the administration of the forts and commercial enterprises, with a limited possibility for individuals to become self-employed merchants.[92] The total number of personnel at the forts at this period amounted to only a few hundred, and vocational outlets for the products of the schools were few. It seems clear, however, that African aspirations were essentially oriented to clerical occupations in commerce or government and, most particularly, to the financial rewards accruing to such occupations. The products of the schools were unwilling to engage in any 'industrious manual occupation while commerce alone was therefore regarded as an eligible road to a position in society'.[93]

Education, in practice, was valued for its cash return, and it remained virtually the only mode by which individuals could partially dissociate themselves from traditional society and enter the small but relatively lucrative number of posts then open to Africans. Generally speaking, the student was guided 'by what appeared most advantageous for his temporal advancement',[94] but it is difficult to see how else European education could have been viewed at this period. It is interesting to note that European comment regarding the 'sordid' motivations of Africans entering the schools at this and later periods is paralleled by precisely the same attitude regarding the motivations of the contemporary English labouring classes to education. The

Census of Great Britain of 1851 was to contain the remark that the type of education given at this period in England was regulated more by a consideration of its material advantage rather than by any appreciation of the benefits of knowledge in itself.[95] In the context of Indian education it was likewise to be shrewdly observed that English education was valued not for its power of 'searching purification' but because of the money to be achieved by means of it.[96]

In view of the similarity of these observations it seems surprising that educationists have not paid more attention to the close relationship existing between the differential rewards of the occupational structure and the educational systems of colonial areas. European education appeared initially to enjoy little prestige for its own sake and the relative success of academic education lay not in its power as an 'educational tradition' but rather in its overwhelmingly vocational nature:

> It enabled young men to keep memoranda, copy papers and accounts, to superintend the discharging of cargo from vessels, oversee out-of-doors work, and such simple employments; but it did not qualify them for conducting a merchant's business, although . . . several acquired a sufficient knowledge of book-keeping to become, at first, factors and clerks to the merchants; and finally, to carry out business on their own account.[97]

From this viewpoint, the type of education provided might be criticized in terms of its depth or adequacy but not with respect to its general content; it was closely geared, in fact, to the vocational aspirations of those African parents who considered it desirable to send their children to school. Governor Winniett's remarks regarding the limited opportunities open to Africans in trade, merchant offices, and school-teaching were substantially correct; the implications which he drew regarding the desirability of trade and agricultural institutions were more suspect.[98] Our examination of the groups using the schools and the vocational aspirations of the African clientele would indicate that the latter type of education was not being demanded.

However, two alternative explanations for the phenomenon might be advanced. First, it is possible to argue that a potential demand for trade and agricultural training existed among other African groups and that efforts to create such training would have met with success. Second, it could be hypothesized that the vocational aspirations of Africans were themselves largely determined by the type of education given and that alternative forms of curriculum would have led to shifts in the vocational aspirations of the clientele of the schools.[99]

The following chapter will indicate that these explanations are hardly adequate, since alternative types of schooling were tried and were generally unsuccessful. Moreover, African preferences for clerical employment remained unchanged even where pupils were persuaded to undertake trade or industrial training. In this case, the vocational aspirations of Africans had little to do with the schools themselves but were a direct reflection of the actual vocational opportunities open to them. It seems that they were a result of African perceptions of the differential rewards accruing to different types of occupation. In fact, they reflected the evaluation of various types of jobs by the Europeans themselves. In situations like this, where vocational opportunities in the European sector are limited and only a small proportion of the local population enter the schools, it is probable that vocational aspirations will be highly specific and, in consequence, alternative types of schooling will be rejected. In situations where an overwhelming proportion of the eligible child population is in school, motivation to enter the schools may be less precise and be dominated by the idea that 'everybody goes'. In early African situations this was not the case. Where education is viewed as a potentially profitable investment, educational demand will be more specific and closely related to African perceptions of the differential rewards of the occupational structure. It seems fairly clear that both in the early Gold Coast and in most parts of Africa, parents did not send their children to school so that they could return to subsistence agricultural activities, even if the schools provided courses of agricultural training. Education meant one thing above all, the opportunity to enter more highly paid posts within the exchange sector of the economy.[100]

In indicating the close nexus between the schools and the occupational structure, it is not implied that government or missions established the early schools with the principal aim of providing recruits to the lower echelons of government or commercial service; such an attribution is a gross oversimplification of motive. With the missions, and to some extent with government institutions, the curriculum was particularly geared to instruction in Christian doctrine. As we have indicated, where the vocational implications of education were mentioned at all, it was in the context of trade and agricultural training. For the missions the extension of the formal schools was purely subordinate to the primary aim of proselytization, and the schools were effective instruments in carrying out this purpose. In order to attract pupils the missions were obliged to provide the kind of education demanded by Africans. As a result not of deliberate intent but of the vocational aspirations of Africans themselves, the schools necessarily became closely associated with the occupational structure. If the missions had not perceived the trend of African demand and attempted to provide courses with negligible vocational implications, the work of conversion would have been retarded. The missions were essentially in the position of salesmen attempting to distribute a product for which the demand was limited and where the problem of modifying the nature of the product in the light of consumer preferences was all important.[101] Even at this early stage, African expectations were playing a far larger part in shaping the nature of the educational system than is commonly supposed.

Early Dysfunctional Consequences of Western Education

In spite of the close association between the educational system and the occupational structure, there were already indications by 1850 that the supply of literates was already exceeding the demand for their services.[102] Within traditional society the possibility of dysfunctional relationships between educational institutions and the economy did not exist; the educational process was generalized and undifferentiated and associated with a largely undifferentiated occupational structure. However, when educational development took place concurrently with the growth of a European dominated occupational structure, then dysfunctional consequences were likely to follow. Opportunities within the exchange sector, as distinct from the subsistence sector, of the economy were very limited and at the same time no direct control was exerted to check the output of the schools, the graduates of which anticipated employment within the exchange sector. The development of highly specialized institutions such as schools and the parallel growth of an exchange economy enormously increases the possibility of disequilibrium between these institutions. There are no guarantees that the products of an educational system can automatically find employment.

Such dysfunctionalities were clearly apparent in the early Gold Coast. Since early vocational expectations were relatively rigid and vocational opportunities few, unemployment did occur among those who were not prepared to accept a return to subsistence activities as the reward of formal education. This problem has long been recognized in many underdeveloped areas and, indeed, the disparity between vocational expectations and the limited future roles open to the products of the schools has been regarded as a contributory factor to the growth of nationalist movements in both India and Africa. It is interesting to note that such a position was already in evidence before the middle of the nineteenth century on the Gold Coast, where many coming from schools 'for want of any adequate employment . . . sank to the level of the uninstructed natives and lost, in a great measure, even the traces of their early education'.[103] As an indirect comment on the views of Africans regarding the purpose of education, the remark is enlightening, but it led to the characterization of the unemployed products of the schools as dishonest, unwilling to undertake employment, and willing to live by their wits at the expense of their illiterate brethren.[104] European criticism during the latter half of the nineteenth century was to be directed neither at traditional African leadership nor at the wealthier merchant group but rather at these unfortunate 'in betweens' of the educational system.

The Nature of the Educated Group

There has been a tendency to regard the educated members of nineteenth-century Gold Coast coastal society as relatively homogeneous and as enjoying some form of collective status vis-à-vis both Europeans and the remainder of the African population; this was not the case, and there was considerable heterogeneity within the educated group itself. At one extreme were the wealthy, literate merchants and, at the other, a larger group of semiliterate 'Cape Coast Scholars' able to find only the poorer type of clerical employment or none at all. Since the eighteenth century Gold Coast Africans had been studying in Europe in small numbers; several of the leading Gold Coast merchants had either been educated in England or in the college established at Fourah Bay in 1827.[105] The great merchant families— such as the Smiths, the Hansens, the Brews and the Blanksons among others—constituted a highly educated minority who, to a great extent, identified themselves with and were accepted by Europeans on terms of parity.[106] For example, James Bannerman, a merchant and magistrate, who was to be appointed lieutenant governor of the Gold Coast in 1850–51, was described by his European contemporaries as a 'gentleman in manner and feeling' and was regarded as an Englishman by the European community although he was born in the Gold Coast of mixed ancestry.[107] One is impressed by the fact that racial differences between the European minority and these groups of wealthier indigenous traders were less significant at this period than the fact that they possessed a degree of common culture. The local merchants lived in the same sections of the coastal towns as their European counterparts and built European houses.[108] The adoption of European dress and the use of the English language and English names indicated that this group identified with the European minority and certainly did not regard themselves as 'natives'. If our previous remarks regarding the homogeneity of African traditional society are borne in mind, it is significant that the educated group was not only differentiated from the traditional sector by the pursuit of new occupations, but it was beginning to constitute a minority with a distinct culture of its own, modelled largely on European behaviour, and only in this sense could it be designated a 'social class'.

At the other extreme were the 'Cape Coast Scholars', poorly educated and regarded with disdain both by the Europeans and the more highly educated Africans. There is a curious ambivalence, in fact, about the whole European attitude towards the lesser products of the schools. Urged to emulate European behaviour, they were, at the same time, an object of derision for attempting to do so and Europeans were particularly critical of the results of a process which they themselves were responsible for setting in motion.[109] Indeed, European attitudes towards the 'Cape Coast Scholar' seem to have their parallels in most parts of the Empire.

The Position of the European Minority

Having indicated the heterogeneous nature of the indigenous educated group, we must finally examine the position of the Europeans themselves. So far as traditional society was concerned, it would be inappropriate to regard them as either a high or a low status group; more accurately they had *no* status in traditional terms, and their impingement upon traditional culture was peripheral and minimal. They did not enjoy a position of general pre-eminence, nor indeed were they regarded as possessing qualities that were considered worth imitating by any but a tiny minority of Africans. Bearing Nadel's criteria of an elite in mind, it is clear that the European minority at this period had few of the characteristics of a colonial elite and their capacity for setting *generalized* standards was negligible except in the towns.[110] Indeed, during the 1820's a vacillating political policy coupled with military defeat led to European prestige reaching an all time low. Apart from a very limited role in directly influencing the cultural behaviour of an African minority within the towns, Europeans were not a generalized reference group upon which African aspirations were modelled.

In consequence, the demand for Western education did not arise as a result of its 'prestige' or the prestige of European cultural attributes in general. Similarly, the strength of the academic curriculum had little to do with its traditionally high evaluation in European culture. Wherever demand occurred it was associated essentially with the vocational opportunities open to Africans, and in consequence it was initially confined to the towns where an economic environment existed in which formal education could be effectively utilized. Outside the towns, therefore, European education remained meaningless; since it could not be utilized in seeking lucrative employment it had no status implications whatsoever. Indeed, not only was European education non-functional in the traditional context, it could prove dysfunctional for potential traditional officeholders where continuance in office depended upon the meticulous discharge of traditional functions.

In the first half of the nineteenth century, therefore, although European education was becoming a significant factor in social change, in so far as it was creating an educated class who constituted at the same time a distinct cultural group, it seems equally clear that Western education would have made little progress at all unless significant change had already occurred as a result of the development of a coastal exchange economy. As we have indicated the growth of European education had little to do with the 'prestige' of European culture, but during the second half of the century continued economic development and radical changes in the political role of the British were to have considerable effects on educational expansion.

REFERENCES

1. W. W. Claridge, *A History of the Gold Coast and Ashanti* (2 vols.; London: John Murray, 1915) I, 55.

2. *Ibid.*, p. 84.

3. *Ibid.*, p. 90.

4. W. Bosman, *A New and Accurate Description of the Coast of Guinea*, Vol. XVI of a 'General Collection of the Best and Most Interesting Voyages in All Parts of the World', ed. John Pinkerton (17 vols.; London: Longman, Hurst, Reas, and Orme, 1808–14), p. 340.

5. *Ibid.*, p. 363.

6. *Ibid.*, p. 362.

7. *Ibid.*, p. 386.

8. *Ibid.*, p. 375.

9. Claridge, *op. cit.*, I, 207.

10. *Ibid.*, p. 214.

11. *Ibid.*, p. 193.

12. *Ibid.*, p. 293.

13. *Ibid.*, p. 155.

14. *Ibid.*, II, 5.

15. Bosman, *op. cit.*, p. 392.

16. R. M. Wiltgren, *Gold Coast Mission History 1471–1880* (Techny, Ill.: Divine Word Publications, 1956), p. 21.

17. *Ibid.*, p. 92.

18. J. S. Wartemberg, *Sao Jorge D'El Mina. Premier West African European Settlement: Its Traditions and Customs* (Ilfracombe, North Devon, Elms Court, Torrs Park: Arthur H. Stockwell Ltd., 1950), p. 140.

19. C. G. Wise, *A History of Education in British West Africa* (London: Longmans, Green, 1956), p. 31.

20. S. R. B. Attoh-Ahuma, *Memoirs of West African Celebrities* (Liverpool: Phillips, 1905), p. 46. There is some slight evidence, however, that educational facilities may have existed at Cape Coast before this date. See F. Wolfson, *The Pageant of Ghana* (Oxford: Oxford University Press, 1958), p. 91.

21. Attoh-Ahuma, *op. cit.*, pp. 49–50.

22. F. L. Bartels, 'Philip Quaque, 1741–1816', *Transactions of the Gold Coast and Togoland Historical Society*, Vol. I, Part V (1955), pp. 153–71.

23. *Ibid.*, pp. 161–62.

24. J. J. Crooks, *Records Relating to the Gold Coast of Africa* (Dublin: Browne & Nolan Ltd., 1923), p. 75.

25. *Ibid.*, p. 77.

26. Brodie Cruikshank, *Eighteen Years on the Gold Coast* (2 vols.; London: Hurst & Blackett, 1853), II, 60.

27. Wise, *op. cit.*, p. 4.

28. Claridge, *op. cit.*, I, 228–50.

29. A full account of the signing of these treaties is to be found in T. E. Bowdich, *Mission from Cape Coast Castle to Ashantee* (London: John Murray, 1819), and J. Dupuis, *Journal of a Residence in Ashantee* (London: H. Colburn, 1824).

30. Although the over-all total of slave exports from the Gold Coast was not high compared with the amount for the whole Guinea Coast, slaves from this area were regarded as the most valuable since they made the best labourers—though 'they were of a more impatient and mutinous disposition than those obtained from other parts of Guinea'. Claridge, *op. cit.*, I, 172.

31. *Ibid.*, pp. 402–6.

32. Great Britain, *Parliamentary Papers*, Vol. XI, 1842, 'Report of the Committee on the West Coast of Africa', Part I, pp. iv–v.

33. *Ibid.*, Part II, p. 139.

34. Crooks, *op. cit.*, p. 278.

35. Claridge, *op. cit.*, I, 391.

36. *Ibid.*, p. 452.

37. C. P. Groves, *The Planting of Christianity in Africa* (4 vols.; London and Red Hill: Lutterworth Press, 1948), I, 73.

38. Crooks, *op. cit.*, p. 114.

39. *Ibid.*, pp. 145, 261.

40. Great Britain, *Parliamentary Papers*, Vol. XI (Reports), 1842, 'Appendix to the Report of the Committee on the West Coast of Africa', pp. 4, 18, 75, 91.

41. Wise, *op. cit.*, p. 8.

42. Groves, *op. cit.*, I, 301.

43. A. E. Southon, *Gold Coast Methodism: The First Hundred Years, 1835–1935* (London: Cargate Press, 1935), pp. 38–40, 80.

44. *Ibid.*, pp. 54–55.

45. Great Britain, *Parliamentary Papers*, 'Appendix to the Report...', pp. 4–93.

46. *Ibid.*

47. *Ibid.*, p. 88.

48. F. H. Hilliard, *A Short History of Education in British West Africa* (London: Thomas Nelson & Sons Ltd., 1957), p. 64.

49. Groves, *op. cit.*, I, 300.

50. Great Britain, *Parliamentary Papers*, 'Appendix to the Report...', pp. 89–91.

51. A. W. Wilkie, 'An Attempt To Conserve the Work of the Basel Missions on the Gold Coast', *International Review of the Missions*, 1920, pp. 86–94.

52. Southon, *op. cit.*, p. 70.

53. *Ibid.*, pp. 54–55.

54. G. G. Findlay and W. W. Holdsworth, *The History of the Wesleyan Methodist Missionary Society* (5 vols.; London: Edgworth Press, 1921–24), IV, 175. The implication here is that although the Ashanti would not deliberately hinder the activities of the mission they would do nothing to support the development of formal education.

55. Groves, *op. cit.*, I, 300.

56. Cruikshank, *op. cit.*, II, 60.

57. Great Britain, *Parliamentary Papers*, 'Appendix to the Report . . .', p. 19.

58. Great Britain, *Report of the Commissioners Appointed To Inquire into the State of Popular Education in England* (6 vols.; London: George E. Eyre and William Spottiswoode, 1861), I, 133.

59. Great Britain, *Parliamentary Papers*, 'Appendix to the Report . . .', p. 94.

60. *Ibid.*, pp. 89–94.

61. *Ibid.*, p. 19.

62. Crooks, *op. cit.*, p. 308.

63. This type of criticism was by no means confined to conditions on the West Coast of Africa. Similar strictures were directed at the early mission schools on the East Coast. See R. Oliver, *The Missionary Factor in East Africa* (London: Longmans, Green, 1952), p. 19.

64. Great Britain, *Colonial Office Library, Miscellaneous Pamphlets*, Vol. I, No. 1. The full text of the original report is to be found in H. S. Scott, 'The Development of the Education of the African in Relation to Western Contact', *Yearbook of Education*, 1938 (London: Evans Bros., 1938), pp. 693–739.

65. Samuel J. Hurwitz, 'Education in the British Commonwealth and Colonies', in *Comparative Education*, ed. A. H. Moehlmann and Joseph S. Roucek (New York: Dryden Press, 1951), p. 185.

66. United Nations, Committee on Information from Non-Self-Governing Territories, *Special Study on Educational Conditions in Non-Self-Governing Territories* (New York, 1960), p. 8.

67. Scott, *op. cit.*, p. 711.

68. See this chapter below, section on African attitudes.

69. Otto Raum, 'The Demand for and Support of Education in African Tribal Society', *Yearbook of Education*, 1956 (London: Evans Bros., 1956), p. 537.

70. Wise, *op. cit.*, p. 17.

71. Great Britain, *Parliamentary Papers*, 'Appendix to the Report . . .', pp. 89–94, 99.

72. Cruikshank, *op. cit.*, II, 65–68.

73. Claridge, *op. cit.*, I, 297.

74. Bowdich, *op. cit.*, p. 416.

75. Dupuis, *op. cit.*, p. 35.

76. Claridge, *op. cit.*, I, 412.

77. Groves, *op. cit.*, II, 224.

78. Great Britain, *Parliamentary Papers*, 'Appendix to the Report . . .', p. 92.

79. See particularly, Great Britain, *Report of the Schools Inquiry Commission* (21 vols.; London: George E. Eyre and William Spottiswoode, 1868), I, 15.

80. L. L. C. Faidherbe, *Le Sénégal* (Paris, 1889), p. 366.

81. Raum, *op. cit.*, p. 537. For a recent example of this see R. W. Chaundy, 'A School with an Agricultural Bias in a Backward Area', *Oversea Education*, XIX, No. 1 (October 1947), 579–85.

82. Bruce Tiebout McCully, *English Education and the Origins of Indian*

Nationalism (New York: Columbia University Press, 1940), p. 185.

83. Cruikshank, *op. cit.*, II, 113.

84. That this attitude persisted well into the twentieth century is clear from an address by Nana Ayirebi Acquah III. Gold Coast, *Legislative Council Debates, 1927–1928* (Accra: Government Printer, 1928), p. 384.

85. *Ibid.*, p. 377.

86. See the discussion on the Fanti Confederacy in chap. iii.

87. Cruikshank, *op. cit.*, II, 61.

88. Gail Kelly, 'The Ghanaian Intelligentsia' (Ph.D. dissertation, Department of Anthropology, University of Chicago, 1959), p. 59.

89. S. Leith-Ross, 'The Development of a Middle Class in the Federation of Nigeria', *Development of a Middle Class in Tropical and Sub-Tropical Countries* (Brussels: International Institute of Differing Civilizations, 1956), p. 181.

90. M. Fortes, 'The Ashanti Social Survey: A Preliminary Report', *Rhodes-Livingstone Journal*, No. 6 (London: Oxford University Press, 1948), p. 29.

91. McCully, *op. cit.*, p. 185.

92. Cruikshank, *op. cit.*, II, 185.

93. *Ibid.*, p. 65.

94. *Ibid.*, p. 61.

95. Great Britain, Census of Great Britain 1851, *Education: England and Wales, Report and Tables* (London: George E. Eyre and William Spottiswoode, 1854), p. xli.

96. C. C. M., 'A Defence of the Bengali Middle Classes', *National Magazine*, I (1876), 22–23.

97. Cruikshank, *op. cit.*, II, 60.

98. See above, p. 54.

99. Considerable attention will be devoted in later pages to the question as to what degree the academic curriculum was responsible for the vocational aspirations of educated Africans. However, the view that school curriculums play a vital role in determining vocational aspirations is widely held though upon what evidence is not clear. For an excellent discussion of the same problem in a different social setting see Olive Banks, *Parity and Prestige in English Secondary Education* (London: Routledge & Kegan Paul, 1955), p. 10.

100. Gold Coast, *Legislative Assembly Debates, 1953*, II, No. 1 (Accra: Government Printer, 1953), 667.

101. It is interesting to note that the missions were quite unable to compete for the products of their own schools against more lucrative opportunities in commerce. Cruikshank, *op. cit.*, II, 74.

102. Crooks, *op. cit.*, p. 308.

103. Cruikshank, *op. cit.*, II, 64.

104. *Ibid.*

105. For an account of some of these overseas scholars see Attoh-Ahuma, *op. cit.*

106. J. E. Casely-Hayford, *Gold Coast Native Institutions* (London: Sweet & Maxwell, 1903), p. 95.

107. Wolfson, *op. cit.*, pp. 123, 128.

108. *Ibid.*, p. 125.

109. Cruikshank, *op. cit.*, II, 65.

110. See chap. i.

III

THE 'GOLDEN AGE' OF THE
GOLD COAST

DURING the first half of the nineteenth century, rapid social change had been confined to a narrow coastal belt where the development of commercial activities had created a chain of small urban centres. The second half of the century was to witness a dramatic increase in the extent of British political control over not only the coastal towns but the territories of the Ashanti Confederacy and those areas which now comprise the Northern Region of contemporary Ghana. In less than fifty years, peoples whose previous contact with the British had been minimal or non-existent, were to be incorporated into a wider political framework, which also included those coastal groups who had already experienced a prolonged period of culture contact.

Even before 1850 this contact had created an urbanized, Western-educated minority, which consciously modelled much of its social behaviour upon that of the European traders and administrators. Western education was partially responsible for the divergent culture of this minority, but, as we have seen, the initial demand for formal education was closely associated with the vocational opportunities created by European contact. New clerical roles became the basis for a new, distinct occupational structure. With the extension of European political control Western education became more significant. Access to office, even within the traditional sector, became dependent upon not only traditional concepts of legitimacy and function but also upon British acceptance and approval.

We shall indicate here the significance of political developments for education while delineating certain structural characteristics of the educational system. In addition we will consider the characteristics of the educated 'class' in more detail in order to assess to what extent traditional conceptions of status among them had been replaced by more European-type criteria. Some of the educated group were to

74

emerge as significant figures in early Nationalist activities on the Gold Coast. Since these activities were associated with a series of educational proposals, we must also indicate how these proposals differed from the policy of the colonial power and the missions.

The Nature and Consequences of British Expansion

Let us now briefly sketch the process of British expansion. Political control of the coastal zone was extremely tenuous as late as 1850, but in that year the remaining Danish possessions were transferred to the British Crown and, in 1872, after years of indecisive bargaining, a treaty was signed with the Dutch ceding the latter's settlements on the coast to the United Kingdom. Two years later the coastal region south of the Ashanti Confederacy was annexed and declared a Crown Colony. As a result the coastal Akan and Ga peoples acknowledged British jurisdiction, while a series of campaigns during the remainder of the century was to lead to the extension of British authority over the Adangme and a minority of the Ewe people. By 1879 control had been established in a continuous coastal strip between Half Assini in the west and Aflao in the east.

However, the northern boundaries of the Colony were ill-defined and so long as the powerful Ashanti Confederacy lay to the north, British control of the coastal regions was bound to remain insecure. One ineffective campaign had been launched against the Confederacy in 1863 and eleven years later an expedition under Sir Garnet Wolseley captured and destroyed Kumasi, then withdrew to the coast. The Confederacy had never been a stable political unit and, as a result of this defeat, the defection of certain tributary states led to its progressive disintegration. In 1896 a further expedition to Kumasi led to the deportation of the *Asantehene* and many of his court when he refused to accede to a British demand that he accept their protection. Only five years later further hostilities led to the formal annexation of Ashanti and the dissolution of the Confederacy.

British control over the northern peoples was effected with a minimum of military activity. After 1880 British officials penetrated deeply into the Ashanti hinterland in an effort to check the depredations of African slave traders moving into the area from the north while, at the same time, treaties were concluded with several northern chiefs. French and British spheres of influence were delineated by a series of treaties in the eighties, and in 1901 the northern areas were annexed as a protectorate. By that date the boundaries of contemporary Ghana had been substantially defined.[1]

British expansion followed significantly different patterns of penetration from the coast in each of the three areas of the Gold Coast; the Colony, Ashanti, and the Northern Territories. This phenomenon implied very different contact situations between British and Africans in each area. In the Colony itself, a long history of culture contact existed and as a result of outright annexation this contact was to be intensified. Ashanti constituted an intermediate zone where Afro-European contact was less intense, and the social structure of this region was to remain essentially traditionalistic until well into the twentieth century, when the development of a cash-crop economy based on cocoa was to commence a period of more rapid social change. In the Northern Territories the impact of British overrule was minimal and had little direct effect on the lives of the people. Indeed, in this area, traditional social structures were to remain substantially intact right up to the achievement of independence in 1957 and to a large degree thereafter.[2] As we shall indicate, the differing degree of contact and the varying rate of social change in the three areas were reflected in turn in a very uneven development of the educational system. During the period of British hegemony this was not a factor of outstanding importance because of the relatively independent type of administration existing in the three major areas of the Gold Coast. However, the question of inequality of access into the schools became more crucial with the establishment of a unitary form of government after independence.

We must now examine the type of administrative structure created as a result of British expansion. To some extent, the northward movement from the coast was effected with some degree of reluctance and, as late as 1865, a total withdrawal from all territories was being considered as soon as this could be reasonably accomplished.[3] But the process of expansion had gone too far to be halted, and British misgivings were largely reflected in their distaste for imposing a direct type of administration upon newly acquired territories. In most areas an attempt was made to utilize indigenous political structures in the administrative process, subject to residual powers being reserved to the Crown.[4] It was anticipated that such an arrangement would result in the minimum of direct interference by the British in the internal affairs of African states, and the policy adopted was a peculiarly local variant of indirect rule. It could hardly be said that indirect rule on the Gold Coast was applied as consciously and systematically as it was in northern Nigeria, where Lord Lugard's policy involved the transformation of indigenous political units into Native Authorities with clearly defined legislative, fiscal, and judicial powers. A really systematic attempt to create a Native Authorities system in the Gold Coast was never made until well into the twentieth century when there was virtually no chance of its success, and it is appropriate to regard early practice vis-à-vis traditional political structures as one of laissez-faire rather than systematic indirect rule.[5] In practice, a Native Jurisdiction Ordinance of 1883 was to remain substantially the basis of local administration until 1927. The Ordinance, although it recognized the chiefs and gave them restricted legislative and judicial functions, made no provision for the creation of native treasuries nor were powers of local taxation delegated to them. Most important, the powers of chiefs were considered to be derived from the Crown and the government was empowered to suspend or depose chiefs wherever this was considered desirable.

It is sufficient for our purpose to indicate two assumptions that underlay the policy of indirect rule however unsystematically it was applied on the Gold Coast.[6] First, there was a belief that it was possible to utilize traditional political structures in the administrative process. Second, since no colonial power can remain interested solely in the preservation of the *status quo ante*, it was believed that the chiefs could be used as the agents or foci of a moderate degree of controlled social change.[7] Indeed, this attitude, as we have seen, underlay Maclean's much earlier policy of educating the sons of chiefs. Paradoxically, British misunderstanding of the nature of traditional institutions both emphasized and diminished the powers of traditional rulers. First, it was believed that chiefs were autocratic rulers who could exercise a degree of arbitrary authority and hence were in a position to initiate 'social improvements' among their people. Previous discussion has indicated that this was not the case. British support often encouraged rulers to exceed their traditional spheres of jurisdiction. Nowhere was this clearer than in the last quarter of the nineteenth century when chiefs frequently alienated land to mining and timber companies in return for money payments, a direct contradiction of African concepts of land tenure and land trusteeship.[8]

Second, the ultimate authority for continuance in the chiefly office depended upon British approval, and not solely upon the chief's acceptable discharge of traditional functions. Whatever attempt was made to perpetuate the political forms of traditional society, there was no question of where the ultimate authority lay; in effect, chiefs became government agents and were obliged to act out two completely incompatible roles. Traditional concepts of the conservative function of the chiefs were bound to conflict with British ideas of using them as agents of innovation, and they could not carry out the functions expected of them by the British without at the same time imperilling their status with their subjects. A chief considered 'efficient' from the British viewpoint frequently ran the risk of destoolment by his own people, and one deemed acceptable by his subjects was liable to British destoolment. The result was an increased 'turnover' of chiefs during the period of British hegemony.[9]

The concept of indirect rule, whatever form it took, commended itself both upon grounds of expediency and administrative economy as well as for 'continuity' potential even within the colonial situation. Traditional institutions did not however lend themselves to such a process, and there was a basic incompatibility between the colonial situation and the maintenance of traditional institutions. The same incompatibilities were present (as we shall see when we consider British theories of 'cultural adaptation' of the schools) in the sphere of formal education.

Political practice was such that at the same time that the British were attempting to utilize indigenous institutions, the sanctions which underlay them were being swept away in the coastal areas. The slow growth of Christianity was undermining the ritual and religious functions of the chief, while the extension of an exchange economy was seriously effecting his traditional economic functions relating to land trusteeship. With the development of cash crops such as cocoa and the extension of mining and timber enterprises, the nature of traditional tenure was to undergo transformation. Most important, from our point of view, the growth of a Western-educated group, with political ambitions of its own, further undermined chiefly authority. When we examine the functional consequences of the transfer of Western educational institutions in this chapter we shall indicate that the combination of policies of indirect rule and a peculiarly British approach to educational policy was to result in a series of unanticipated consequences for the whole of the traditional structure.

The Development of the Educational System

The growth of British political control was paralleled by a gradual, by no means dramatic, extension of facilities for formal education during the second half of the century.

Statistics relating to the early growth of the schools are inadequate before 1880. In 1856, the Wesleyans claimed a total of twenty-eight schools on the west coast with a total of 1,200 pupils (these returns included institutions in southern Nigeria at Badagry and Abeokuta).[10] It is probable, however, that in the Gold Coast itself, the Wesleyans had some thousand scholars in attendance, since a contemporary observer had remarked that their institutions were producing several hundred scholars per year all 'very tolerably educated'.[11] Basel mission expansion was certainly slower at this period, their first two schools being established in 1843 and 1847 respectively, and their work was primarily in the inland area of Akwapim.

A much clearer picture emerges in the last twenty years of the century. In 1881 there were 139 'assisted' and government controlled schools in the country with a total enrolment of just over 5,000 children.[12] The growth of the system is indicated in Table 1.

TABLE 1

THE GROWTH OF GOVERNMENT AND ASSISTED SCHOOLS 1881–1901*

Controlling Body	1881	1891	1901
Government	3	4	7
Basel Mission	47	27	61
Wesleyan Mission	84	17	49
Bremen Mission	4	2	3
Roman Catholic	1	3	12
Total	139	53	135

* Calculated from F. Wright, 'The System of Education in the Gold Coast Colony', *Special Reports on Educational Subjects* (London: H.M.S.O., 1905), XIII, Part II, 3.

It should be noted that the statistics do not include returns for a large number of 'unassisted' mission schools for which statistics are unavailable but, until well into the twentieth century, unassisted schools far exceeded the state-aided sector in number and enrolment. Hence the table underestimates the extent of educational provision at this early period. The remarkable drop in the number of schools between 1881 and 1891 is not to be interpreted as indicating a real reduction in the overall number of schools but is probably the consequence of the withdrawal of grants from numerous institutions. This pattern of fluctuation was by no means uncommon in British Africa, but it has led observers to underestimate educational provision, and has created apparent anomalies in the upward trend of schools facilities. Last, the entry of the Roman Catholic and Bremen missions into the field should be noted. The latter mainly worked in German Togoland and, with the exception of these few institutions, their schools were largely among the eastern Ewe. A more detailed picture of the growth in educational facilities is available for the period after 1890 (Table 2).

TABLE 2

THE GROWTH OF GOVERNMENT AND ASSISTED SCHOOLS 1890–1902 *

	Schools under Inspection			Number of Scholars on the Roll and in Average Attendance	
Year	Govern- ment	Assisted	Total		
1890–91	5	49	54	5,076	3,641
1891–92	5	69	74	6,666	4,847
1892–93	6	66	72	7,350	5,195
1893–94	5	70	75	7,689	5,828
1894–95	7	93	100	9,954	7,570
1895–96	6	109	115	11,205	8,558
1897	7	111	118	. . . .	8,478
1898	7	112	119	11,181	8,369
1899	7	123	130	12,240	9,239
1900	7	131	138	11,996	8,911

* Computed from Wright, *op. cit.*, p. 8.

The growth of institutions in the aided sector, although steady, was by no means rapid and was subject to considerable fluctuations, while regular attendance was considerably below the total of enrolled scholars. None of the aided schools was in either Ashanti or the Northern Territories. It is also clear that the *direct* role of government in the provision of schools was very limited, and we must consider why this was the case.

Government Educational Policy

During the first half of the century the government had played a far from inactive role in the provision of schools before the advent of mission activity, and as late as 1841 the number of government institutions rivalled that of the Wesleyans. In the early period of Gold Coast history, the extent of direct government activity in education finds no parallel in British experience, but in the second half of the century, development was to be strongly influenced by English practice. Government was to assume a more limited definition of its role in the provision of education although the attempt to reproduce structural characteristics of English education was to lead to very different results from those anticipated.

The year 1852 may be regarded as the high-water mark of projected government activity in the field of education. In that year a meeting of the British governor and the principal chiefs of those territories lying between Ashanti and the coast resolved itself into a Legislative Assembly and authorized the collection of a poll tax of one shilling per capita to be

> devoted to the public good in the education of the people, in the general improvement and extension of the judicial system, in affording greater facilities of internal communication, increased medical aid, and in such other measures of improvement and utility as the state of social progress may render necessary.[13]

The funds were to be utilized in this manner after the payment of stipends to the chiefs and, in 1858, an amendment to the ordinance specified that two-thirds of the residue was to be used solely for the maintenance of schools and hospitals.[14] The ordinance was ineffective largely as a result of the refusal of the coastal population to pay the tax, but it was paralleled by the Education Ordinance of 1852 which provided for an institution for the training of teachers and the establishment of a chain of schools.[15]

Although both the Poll Tax Ordinance and the Education Ordinance of 1852 were unsuccessful, they are significant in that they marked the last systematic attempt of government to enter the educational field directly through the provision of schools. No mention was made of mission institutions in the ordinance and it seems clear that the intention of the government was a systematic and *controlled* development of the educational system. The failure of the ordinances was to lead to a reversal of policy in which government was to interpret its educational role in a more limited fashion.

After 1852, the continued expansion of mission institutions was largely a result of their own efforts, though after 1874 limited grants-in-aid were made to them. It was not until 1882 that a serious attempt was made to make the role of government in educational provision regular and lay down conditions under which government was prepared to make grants-in-aid to mission institutions. The Education ordinances of 1882 and 1887 were primarily attempts to reproduce the structural characteristics of English education which had emerged as a result of the Education Act of 1870 and to control the general nature of the curriculum of the Gold Coast schools so as to conform more closely to that of the metropolitan power.

The 1882 Ordinance, 'for the Promotion and Assistance of Education in the Gold Coast Colony', created a central Board of Education and made provision for the establishment of a series of local boards to assist in the administration of the grants-in-aid system wherever these were deemed advisable. Primary schools were to be divided into two classes: 'government schools', maintained entirely from public sources and 'assisted schools', established by missions or private individuals but aided from government funds. The minimal curricular requirements, upon which grants were to be based, included the provision of instruction in reading, writing, English language, and arithmetic, with needlework for girls; grants could be obtained for optional subjects such as English grammar, history, and geography.[16]

The ordinance clearly attempted to reproduce the system of control which had been characteristic of English education since 1870 and further paralleled English practice in its effort to create *ad hoc* bodies, in the shape of local boards of education, to administer grants-in-aid. As in England between 1870 and 1902, there was a reluctance to incorporate educational administration within the framework of local administration. The motives for the curricular specifications are fairly clear, resting as they did upon the necessity for some basis on which grants-in-aid could be administered. It should be noted in this context that no reference was made for aid to instruction in the vernacular, which, as we shall see, had become the basis for all early teaching in the Basel system.

The 1882 ordinance proved unworkable for fairly obvious reasons. In England the Act of 1870 had led to a dramatic growth of *ad hoc* school boards which numbered over 4,000 by 1895, and had paved the way for the progressive absorption of voluntary agency schools into the public system.[17] On the Gold Coast, where demand for education was limited, there was no likelihood that effective *ad hoc* agencies could be set up and, in practice if not by design, the effect of the ordinance was to place the future development of education more firmly in the hands of the missions. Also, the administration of specific grants to schools required the development of an effective and far-reaching inspectorial system which was inconceivable on the Gold Coast at this period. The ordinance did provide for the appointment of an inspector of schools, but, since his duties were also expected to cover the inspection of schools in Sierra Leone and Lagos, he was only able to visit a small proportion of those on the aided list.

Although amendments to the ordinance were passed in 1882 and 1883, a more substantial effort was made in 1887 to rectify the shortcomings of the earlier enactment.[18] The most notable innovation was the replacement of provisions relating to the establishment of local school boards by the requirement that the administration of all aided schools be placed in the hands of one or more 'managers' with authority to appoint local managers wherever this was deemed expedient.[19] In practice, this amounted to a recognition that responsibility for the schools would remain firmly in mission hands, since no alternative organizations existed which could have carried out the managerial functions effectively.

Provision was made, however, for the creation of a central school board with wide discretionary powers to frame rules for the inspection of schools and the certification of teachers, while the conditions under which the government was prepared to administer grants were fairly generally stated. Two such conditions were that aided schools should be open to all children without distinction of religion or race and that no children should receive any religious instruction objected to by parents or guardians.[20]

Further the ordinance attempted to create a class of industrial schools 'in which a proportion of pupils, to be fixed by the Board of Education, devote not less than ten hours a week to manual labour on a regular or approved plan'. Manual labour was 'understood to mean any kind of handicraft, manufacturing process, or agricultural work, and, in the case of females, household work'.[21]

In practice, the more general provisions of the ordinance received explicit definition in a series of rules framed by the Board of Education to facilitate the administration of grants. Such rules were subject to periodic revision, but before 1900 two trends may be noticed, the first generally salutary in its effect, the second undoubtedly restrictive.

First, there was an attempt to expand the limited curricular proposals of the earlier ordinance and widen the basis upon which grants could be given. In the Rules of the Board of Education for 1898, therefore, drawing, industrial instruction, and physical exercises had been added to the curriculum, while optional subjects for which grants could be earned also, included singing, elementary science, bookkeeping, shorthand, and mensuration.[22] Additional subjects could also be approved provided that a graduated scheme for teaching them was presented. In effect the rules did not impose such a curricular straitjacket upon aided schools as would at first appear, and additional subjects were added to the curriculum.

A more pernicious policy, apparent in the Rules of 1898, was the attempt to administer a proportion of the grants on the basis of 'payment by results' along the lines of Lowe's notorious 'Revised Elementary Code' of 1862.[23] At a period when the provisions of the code were being progressively removed in England there was an effort to enforce similar provisions in most colonial territories. Thus Paragraph 62 of the Rules of 1898 stated that the board would make 'A grant of 6s for each scholar present at the annual inspection who shall pass in reading, writing and arithmetic according to the conditions in Schedule A. Failure in one subject will reduce this grant to 4s, and failure in two subjects will reduce this grant to 2s.'[24]

Elaborate schedules were prepared for the teaching of alternative subjects and grants were approved on the basis of adherence to these schedules. Industrial instruction received a more generous grant of ten shillings per head for more senior pupils and five shillings per head for junior pupils, provided that the general plan of instruction met with the general approval of the board and not less than ten hours a week was devoted to it.[25]

It is now appropriate to examine in more detail the actual consequences of government policy during this period. It is clear that the framers of the original ordinances were heavily influenced by the English Elementary Education Act of 1870 and the provisions of the Revised Code of 1862, but while these structural similarities between the two systems may be noted, it is equally clear that the consequences of these pieces of legislation in the two countries were quite dissimilar.

The result of the 1870 Act in England was a radical expansion of non-denominational schools which by 1900 constituted the bulk of the elementary-school system, both through direct expansion and by the incorporation of many formerly voluntary schools. In this case the growth of *ad hoc* educational bodies had been remarkably effective in supplementing the activity of voluntary agencies. In the Gold Coast, the result of the ordinances of 1882 and 1887 was precisely the opposite. The plan of the 1882 Ordinance to create local school boards was completely stillborn, while the 'managerial' system created by the Ordinance of 1887 constituted a recognition that the future development of the educational system was to remain largely in the hands of the missions. At this period there was no likelihood that educational functions could be devolved upon non-denominational local authorities.

Further, an examination of the ordinances alone would give the impression that a rigid curriculum had been imposed upon the schools and that the overall expansion of the educational system might have been checked by the inability of schools to qualify for grants. However, the significance of the ordinances lay as much in what they did *not* say as in what they did specify. No restrictions were placed upon the opening of schools by any group or individual, and such institutions were not required to comply with the conditions of the ordinances and rules unless they wished specifically to apply for grants. In practice the actual development of the system was to occur to a large degree outside the conditions laid down by ordinances and the pattern of Gold Coast education was not totally circumscribed by grants-in-aid provisions.

The reason for the formidable growth of schools outside the grant-in-aid sector is not difficult to discover. The aim of the government in passing the ordinance was to create a systematic base for the administration of grants-in-aid while at the same time attempting to raise levels of instruction in the schools. Such a policy was bound to conflict with mission aspirations. The missions conceived the schools primarily as powerful instruments for proselytization, and, with few exceptions, maximum expansion was justified by the necessity for 'covering the ground' as rapidly as possible. The typical pattern of education in British Africa well into the twentieth century was a relatively small core of institutions receiving grants-in-aid with the considerable development of an unaided system with extremely variable standards of instruction.[26]

It is possible to argue that had the early ordinances been accompanied by legislation designed to prevent the opening of private mission or proprietary institutions, the government might have been effective in controlling the quantity and quality of mission instruction as they were in some French territories. Even if this had been the case, the system of grants-in-aid for specific subjects required the development of a complex inspectorial system and administrative structure that could not have been effectively created at this early stage. Furthermore, the idea of imposing restrictions upon the creation of independent schools would have been unthinkable in terms of the climate of English opinion at this period.

Further, had it been possible to systematically enforce the provisions of the ordinances in schools it seems equally clear that they would have not taken on the uniform appearance that examination of these pieces of legislation would suggest. Both the Basel Mission and the Wesleyans were in receipt of grants for many of their schools, but, as we shall indicate in examining their systems, they were able to develop totally different school organizations and curriculums even within the framework of the ordinances.[27] This degree of latitude allowed in the interpretation of government provisions would indicate that even grant-aided schools were not subject to such rigid examination as might be supposed.

In indicating the very real limitations upon the effective administration of these early codes one factor of overwhelming importance arises. The overall expansion of the Gold Coast system of education was neither directly in the hands of government nor was it subject to effective government control: education never became a part of a coherent government policy and its development was largely autonomous and uncontrolled. It was not governed by considerations of placement of its graduates into the occupational structure and no successful attempt was made to model curriculums upon the needs of the colonial power. It is *the autonomous development of educational institutions* that is the initial outstanding characteristic of schools development in British Africa. In attempting to account for the growth of academic systems of education in the Gold Coast, the answer is not to be found primarily in the nature of early legislation.

This relatively uncontrolled expansion of the educational system permitted a remarkably uneven pattern of access into the schools as between various sections of the Gold Coast. In examining the more adequate statistics available for the twentieth century in the following chapter we shall have occasion to point out this clear ecological pattern of schools distribution. The reasons for it, however, did not lie in a reluctance on the part of the missions to create schools in response to demand but stemmed from the essentially 'free market' approach to schools so typical of British territories. No restrictions were placed upon the opening of schools, and missions were comparatively free to operate in all areas. In effect, the pattern of distribution of schools closely followed the pattern of differential demand and itself became an indirect index of the extent to which indigenous social structures were already undergoing transformation as a result of European contact. Consequently, school enrolments were far higher in urban areas where traditional status systems could not effectively maintain themselves and were lowest in those areas such as the Northern Territories where such systems were still relatively intact.

The Policy of the Missions

Having examined the limited degree to which government legislation imposed effective checks on schools expansion we now turn to the actual policies of the two principal missions. Previous discussion has indicated that the climate of educational opinion up to the middle of the century was by no means unfavourable to the development of agricultural and industrial institutions while the Ordinance of 1887 provided for grants to be administered to 'Industrial Schools' on the receipt of a satisfactory programme of instruction. An examination must now be made of the extent to which the missions attempted to put such programmes into practice.

The predominantly urban activities of the Wesleyans during the first half of the century had enabled them to develop a system of day schools, utilizing English as the language of instruction and concentrating upon work in reading, writing, and arithmetic, with the occasional addition of history and geography. This type of curriculum was more closely geared to the vocational opportunities existing in the towns, consisting as they did of clerical appointments in commerce or government. The mission did make attempts to undertake alternative experiments in rural areas outside the towns in response to contemporary criticism of their system.

In 1850 at Beulah near Cape Coast, the mission began its first experiment in agricultural education through the creation of a model farm school where work on the land was to be closely related to instruction in the classroom.[28] Similar institutions were created at Dominassie and Napoleon, both in Fanti territory. Experiments were made in the cultivation of crops which might be suitable for production by African farmers: these included coffee, cinnamon, mangoes, ginger, olives, and grapes. In addition, Freeman was particularly active in obtaining supplies of seed and agricultural implements for distribution to local farmers, while giving instruction on methods of cultivation.[29]

In spite of this enthusiastic beginning, within ten years every one of these promising experiments had failed through lack of support, and, so far as the Fanti were concerned, it would appear that agricultural schools were not a satisfactory alternative to the usual academic instruction given in Wesleyan institutions. There is no record of attempts to provide specifically agricultural schools after this date, though the mission was responsible for the creation of a small industrial school at Cape Coast during the eighties where instruction was given in carpentry, blacksmithing, and printing.[30]

The attitude of the Wesleyans to industrial training, however, was by no means one of wholehearted acceptance. The evangelical outcome of education was of overriding importance, and, though the mission was prepared to develop programmes of industrial training, this was undertaken only where it could be proved to be the sole or the best means by which church members might live a consistent Christian life.[31] In the urban areas where the Wesleyans worked, academic programmes were effective in drawing students, and the Wesleyans did not undertake a systematic policy of detachment of the individual from his social milieu, a policy which the Basel mission was to follow.

The decision of the Basel missionaries to operate principally in inland areas led to the development of an educational system resting upon agricultural and industrial training and vernacular instruction. A nineteenth-century representative of the mission was to remark:

> The Basel Mission, recognizing the fact that industrial training is a most important factor in the education of a heathen un-civilised nation, tried to exercise an every-day influence on the people, making the spade and other instruments go hand-in-hand with the Bible.[32]

The system as it developed might be regarded as one of the most remarkable attempts to develop a system of industrial and agricultural training in any colonial territory. The first three years of school included an intensive programme of agricultural and manual instruction with classroom work being given in the vernacular. Older students were gathered in residential, 'higher-central' schools with industrial and agricultural education as the core of the curriculum. Boarding schools were established for girls in which a strong emphasis was given to courses in domestic economy. At Akropong, experimental work in agriculture was undertaken and the results of such research utilized in the schools. Virtually every school in the interior had a small plantation on which coffee, sisal hemp, and later cocoa were cultivated by the students.[33]

Industrial training in the local schools was supplemented by advanced work at a central industrial training institution in Accra, where instruction was given by both European and African staff. This school, created in 1877, offered a three-year course which turned out skilled ironworkers, joiners, and carpenters.[34]

The Basel Mission adhered to the principle that early education should be conducted in the vernacular, and from the first, Ga and Twi were selected as the languages of instruction. An alphabet was developed and graduated primers were produced in these languages. No transition was made to English until sufficient progress had been made in the written African language.[35] This policy of the mission, however, did not reflect any high evaluation of African languages or for that matter of African culture. Vernacular teaching was justified by reference to educational necessity, and, if anything, the Basel missionaries were far less sympathetic to traditional culture than their Wesleyan contemporaries.[36] The aim of Basel industrial and agricultural training combined with residential institutions and the practice of pupils 'boarding in' with the missionaries was aimed at isolating the African Christians from traditional culture and establishing self-supporting Christian communities.[37]

In reviewing both government and mission policy it seems evident that the early development of an 'academic' variety of education on the Gold Coast cannot be fairly ascribed to deliberate policy on the part of either group. Government was not successful in controlling the course of educational events. It is noteworthy that an early ordinance contained provision for per capita pupil grants to industrial programmes, very broadly defined, on a scale considerably higher than those for other subjects. The missions, as we have seen, attempted to promote industrial and agricultural training.[38] If we are to examine the significant determinants of the nature of the schools, we must inquire into the occupational structure created by British expansion and the character of the educated African groups who, for the first time, were making recommendations regarding educational policy.

Education and the Occupational Structure

In contrasting British and French educational policy in Africa, Wallerstein remarks:

> British educational policy was haphazard and neglected placement, in part because it was largely in the hands of the missions, whereas the French educational policy, conducted largely in state schools, was more systematic. The French trained only those for whom they were willing to find a position in the colonial structure. But the British trained without regard for this, and they did not expand the positions available for African placement to meet the expanded supply.[39]

In general, this analysis is correct.[40] Proselytization was a primary motive in schools expansion and consideration of the vocational opportunities open to the African a secondary factor. However, it is, perhaps, inaccurate to describe the growth of the schools as 'haphazard' simply because restrictive policies had not been applied to check their rate of development. In practice, the pattern of expansion essentially reflected the pressures of African demand. There was, in fact, a rough correlation between the number of schools and the vocational opportunities open to Africans within the European controlled economic sector; in consequence, there was a much higher concentration of schools within the urban areas than in rural districts. Nonetheless, an oversupply of graduates became visible from the early 1840's, and the efforts to create agricultural and industrial institutions were a reaction to this situation.[41]

European expansion was not to lead to any dramatic widening in vocational opportunities open to Africans. During the first half of the nineteenth century these had been confined to a few clerical posts with commercial companies or government. The nature of the British administration did not require the creation of a large bureaucratic structure since it was carried out, to a great extent, through indigenous political institutions. Even by 1900 economic development was negligible; the principal exports consisted of palm oil and palm kernels. Cocoa had not yet developed into a cash crop of importance. Although the first attempts to develop gold mining with European capital had been made in 1877, development was extremely slow and production never exceeded 18,000 fine ounces per year.[42] Few industrial establishments of any kind existed.[43]

In view of the nature of the Gold Coast economy at this period the African pressure for clerical forms of employment was a realistic one. The almost complete absence of industrial establishments implied that the demand for skilled artisans was limited; furthermore, an artisan's income was below that received by a clerk.[44] The demands of the missions for artisans were not great, and the Basel Mission was not only able to supply its own needs but up to the end of the century produced sufficient artisans to meet the requirements of both commercial and government enterprise. Indeed, the skilled graduates of the Basel schools were actually to be found working as far as the Congo.[45]

The proponents of industrial and agricultural education who had admired the work of the Basel Mission and roundly condemned the more academic institutions of the Wesleyans had, in fact, totally ignored the implications of the vocational structure created by European contact.[46] Critics of African aspirations for clerical employment ignored the fact that, however limited, the advantages of that type of employment far outweighed any occupational alternatives. In criticizing many of the mission institutions for producing nothing but clerks who could not find employment they seemed unaware that the relatively stagnant Gold Coast economy could not absorb more than a very limited number of artisans. The hope that educated youth would return to the land as farmers or village artisans was naïve since, as we have shown, the aspirations of educated Africans were focused upon the new European-type vocations. Further, African aspirations were not only a realistic reaction to opportunities, but they were reinforced by a growing perception of a hierarchy of occupational prestige for which the Europeans themselves, albeit unconsciously, provided the model.

In stressing that the occupational structure played a far greater role in determining the vocational ambitions of Africans than is often supposed we have implied that the schools themselves were hardly responsible for determining the career preferences of the graduates of the schools.[47] If this were correct then one would expect the aspirations of the pupils in the Basel industrial schools to differ markedly from those in the Wesleyan institutions. One of the earlier Basel missionaries, however, showed a greater perception of the very real limitations of any curriculum in influencing vocational preferences when he remarked:

> How far this manual work will have a lasting influence upon the character of the scholars is difficult to say. The hope which one of the School Inspectors had in proposing technical classes at the Government School at Accra, that such technical instruction would induce scholars who had

passed Standard V to apprentice themselves for a period of three years at least, in order to become workmen in the Public Works Department will, we are afraid, meet with sad disappointment. There is a distaste for anything savouring of labour among upper standard boys who think that to be a scholar is to be a gentleman, and to be a gentleman precludes the possibility of gaining a livelihood except by the pen. Therefore it is and will be always an exception to the rule when a boy who has passed Standard V makes up his mind to learn a handicraft, as smith or carpenter.[48]

This statement, coming from a representative of a mission whose policy stressed industrial training, avers clearly that the curriculum was not the decisive influence upon occupational choice and that the products of the Basel schools were just as inclined to seek clerical employment as their Wesleyan counterparts. The writer probably exaggerated the 'prestige' element in clerical employment, since there were also very real income advantages attaching to it, as against manual occupations. This passage is particularly significant in itself, since it illustrates very clearly that the alien idea of 'gentlemanly' or prestigeful occupations had already taken root.[49] When we examine the nature of the European group and the occupations which they undertook, their effect as a reference group in determining African notions of occupational prestige will be apparent.

The Educated Minority and Traditional Society

So far, our analysis has concentrated upon the relationship between Western education and the relatively narrow range of vocational opportunities created within the European-dominated sector of employment. As a result of the effective establishment of European political control Western education was to have direct consequences for traditional society itself, which led ultimately to the progressive disintegration of indigenous status structures.

It has been previously noted that traditional rulers who adhered to traditional concepts of office were likely to disappoint the colonial administration which undertook to replace them with more pliable individuals. In many cases, individuals chosen by the administration were literates who conformed more readily to European conceptions of 'progressive' and 'efficient' administrators. In preserving the formal characteristics of indigenous political structures while at the same time shifting the criteria of recruitment, the colonial administration had struck a profound blow at traditional conceptions of legitimacy. Although traditional societies tempered ascriptive criteria of recruitment to select suitable individuals for chiefships, the action of the

91

colonial power was to result in a progressive shift from ascriptive to achievement criteria for office. The criteria of selection came to depend increasingly upon European conceptions of efficiency. Thereby an alternative vocational outlet became open to literate individuals within the traditional sector.

In one respect, the situation was less difficult for the administration among the Akan, for they had a manifest chiefly organization, even though the powers exercised by the chiefs were less than supposed. However, in the acephalous political systems the structure of authority was by no means clear, and the reaction of the British was most frequently to appoint candidates to a 'chiefship' of their own invention.

This process is clearly documented for the Ga. As we have seen, Ga political and social structure was based upon the principle of the segmentary lineage with lineage heads (*Wulomei*) exercising strictly circumscribed functions. But most of the Ga towns had developed also the office of *Mantse* associated with specific ritual functions in warfare. The office neither carried with it great prestige nor was it politically significant. British misunderstanding of the role of the *Mantse* led to the assumption that it was the equivalent of the Akan chiefly office with the consequence that the *Mantse* were elevated to the status of chiefs and vested with powers that traditionally could only be exercised by the *Wulomei*. Further the *Mantse* of Accra was elevated to the position of paramount chief of all the Ga. A hierarchical form of organization was imposed upon a formerly acephalous group.[50]

It is most significant that prolonged litigation over the Ga chiefships was begun in nearly every case by literates convincing the administration that the office of *Mantse* was in fact a chiefly office.[51] Further, in most cases the office came to be occupied by literates who had previously been in minor clerical employment and who had received British support in pressing their claims. Though the Ga case is clearer than most, the replacement of traditional rulers by more suitably 'qualified' candidates was widespread and the misunderstanding by the British of traditional political processes led ultimately to literate individuals enjoying opportunities to manipulate the traditional system in their own interest.

This brings us in more general terms to one of the outstanding functional consequences of educational transfer: opposition between the emergent educated minority and the traditional rulers. Indeed, throughout the late nineteenth century and right up to the termination of British rule the differences between the traditional rulers and the educated group were perhaps more salient in the Gold Coast than in any other area in British Africa. Whatever temporary rapprochements were effected between these groups in common opposition to some elements of British policy, there is no doubt that their aims were ultimately incompatible. The educated group aimed at the curtailment of chiefly authority, even when avowedly supporting it, while the chiefs could not regard the aspirations of the educated as constituting anything else but a threat to traditional authority. The conflict between these groups is more apparent when we consider the nature of early Nationalist activities on the Gold Coast.

Western Education and Early Nationalism

It is clear that the first development of nationalism in the Gold Coast was closely associated with the creation of a Western-educated and urbanized minority.[52] Nationalism may be logically regarded as one of the consequences of Western education although an unanticipated one. In no small measure, nationalism was a result of the relatively autonomous development of schools in a situation with a very limited occupational structure. Actual unemployment was present among the more poorly educated graduates of the schools from 1850 onwards, but the greatest tensions were to arise among the more advanced products of Western education. Even in the first half of the nineteenth century a trickle of individuals had been educated at European universities or at Fourah Bay, and it was this minority which resented most strongly the British policy of limiting their access to senior places within the administration.

Indeed British policy seems to have retrograded during the second half of the century. Although individuals such as Bannerman had achieved high office at an earlier period, certainly by the second half of the century only junior administrative posts were open to the most highly educated Africans. Their conditions of service were uniformly inferior to those of personnel recruited in the United Kingdom.[53] As a result this group became less eager to achieve posts within the administration but were attracted to professional private practice in law and medicine—a phenomenon equally apparent in nineteenth-century India.[54] It has been customary to regard African aspirations as directed primarily towards government posts, but this appears to be a later development. Certainly, in the nineteenth century, law offered an extremely lucrative alternative to the more restrictive conditions of government service as a result of the volume of litigation connected with land and property rights.[55] However, such remunerative alternatives did not alter the fact that the most highly educated groups regarded themselves as deprived of access to the most desirable roles monopolized by Europeans. Speaking of the genesis of Nationalist movements in colonial territories, Emerson characterizes the educated groups of the nineteenth century in the following manner:

> Conscious that they no longer fitted into the older society from which they had emerged, they found themselves rejected as equal partners by the dominant Westerners. While many were absorbed into the framework of colonial governments and enterprise, they were denied access to the upper positions of responsibility, command, and wealth. Inevitably they felt the bitter frustration of inability to secure in their own societies positions which corresponded to their expectations and newly acquired knowledge and skills.[56]

Although positions of some wealth were, in effect, open to Africans through trading or the professions, the roots of early nationalism lay in the inadequate channels for mobility within the nascent social structure created by European overrule. The effect of Western education was to socialize individuals to 'anticipate career patterns, which they were not permitted to fulfil'.[57] In British territories the situation was exacerbated, as we have seen, by the reluctance of government to control educational expansion. The characteristic mode of indirect administration through local rulers further limited vocational opportunities and, at a very early stage, created a basic antagonism between the traditionalists and the emergent educated minority.

By the middle of the century there was already evidence that the existence of a Western-educated minority in the urban areas had seriously affected the status of traditional rulers. In that year Brodie Cruikshank and James Bannerman were to observe to Governor Winniett that there had been a systematic encroachment upon the authority of the chiefs 'through the elevation of the lower classes' and 'an extraordinary modification amounting almost to a subversion' of the rights of the chiefs had 'been silently and acquiescently effected'.[58]

Two years later Governor Hill attributed the failure of the Poll Tax Ordinance to the agitation of 'certain educated Natives with no real pretensions to any power' who were 'in the practice of assuming an authority with the people that did not belong to their position', and his remarks indicate the extent to which the educated sections of the population were already constituting an effective opposition to European control and the authority of the chiefs.[59]

The political activities of the educated men were to acquire even greater significance with the formation of the Fanti Confederation in 1868. Originally founded by the principal Fanti chiefs as an organization to resist a proposed exchange of British and Dutch possessions on the coast, the Confederation emerged in 1871 with the more general aims of improving the social conditions of the Fanti peoples while providing a constitutional framework for self-government under the conditions laid down by a select committee of 1863.[60]

The Constitution of the Confederation, to which were appended the names of all the principal Fanti chiefs and educated men, provided for the creation of a legislative assembly with powers of direct taxation.[61] The forty-seven articles of the Constitution included a widespread programme of social improvement including the construction of roads, the development of agriculture and industry, and the exploitation of mineral and other resources of the country. Most significant, the articles contained a series of proposals relating to the provision of educational facilities (to which we shall return later in this chapter). Our present concern must be with the role of the educated minority in the creation and composition of the Confederation. Claridge observes:

> The whole Constitution seems to have been framed by a few educated and semi-educated men, primarily no doubt for the good of their country, but secondarily for the benefit of themselves; and it was alleged that many of the Chiefs whose marks were appended to the documents had no knowledge of their contents and had not even been present at the meetings.[62]

This is a rather harsh judgment and there is evidence that the Articles of the Confederacy were the product of real co-operation between the chiefs and the educated men. However, an examination of the document does indicate that its effect would probably have been to circumscribe the role of the chiefs. Although membership of the executive was to include five chiefs and six educated men, all crucial offices were monopolized by the latter. The office of king-president was to be filled from the chiefly ranks, but Article 15 specified that the vice-presidency should be given to a representative of the educated group with power to preside over the legislative assembly, which could only be summoned by the secretary of the confederation.[63] This post was also reserved for one of the educated. It is difficult to avoid the conclusion that had the Confederation succeeded there would have been a partial transfer of power from the chiefs to the educated minority. The antipathy of the latter to the chiefs indulging in any form of secular politics (on the grounds that such activity would interfere with their discharge of traditional functions) provided a legitimate excuse for the monopolization of political activity by themselves.

The Confederation itself was short-lived due to strong and rather ill-conceived opposition from the colonial regime, and support for the scheme collapsed. The significance of the Confederation lay not in its achievements but in its revelation of the growing importance of Western-educated elements on the coast and the parallel erosion of the traditional authority of the chiefs.

Before the end of the century the educated group was to be more successful in its organization of the 'Aborigines Rights Protection Society' in 1897 with the aim of defeating the Public Lands Bill of that year.[64] This bill would convert to Crown land all unoccupied areas, with the aim of checking the accelerated process of land alienation to European mining and timber companies. Such an action was regarded by chiefs as an unpardonable interference in traditional concepts of 'land trusteeship', and they were joined in their opposition to the act by the Western-educated element (consisting of the more important traders, lawyers, and other professionals). After the formation of the society a deputation was sent to England which resulted in the withdrawal of the Lands Bill. The society itself continued as a Nationalist organization headed by the representatives of a small group of African professional men.

In briefly summarizing the activities of early Nationalists on the Gold Coast we have attempted to examine the role of Western education in producing a group of individuals who first led opposition to the colonial power. More significant, Western education also produced an element in society whose prestige and influence did not derive from traditional concepts of legitimacy and status and for whom formal education had been an instrument of mobility. Whatever temporary alliances existed between the chiefs and the educated minority, the two groups were essentially competitive. While the educated could be regarded as 'upstarts' by the chiefs, the latter were equally criticized for their lack of 'progressiveness' by the educated.[65]

The small group of professional men who headed the early Nationalist reaction on the Gold Coast, however, were characterized as much by their adherence to Western concepts of constitutional action as they were by their opposition to the colonial power. They wished to maintain the British connection and achieve self-government through constitutional means without the development of massive support from the general population.[66] In examining the writings of these early Nationalists one is impressed by the degree to which their programmes had been influenced by British concepts of constitutionality. In addition, an examination of the works of J. E. Casely Hayford and J. M. Sarbah (two of the outstanding Nationalist writers at the end of the century) indicates that the professional classes found it difficult to identify themselves with traditional African culture and

96

had to a degree assimilated the cultural characteristics of the colonial rulers.[67] It is to this question that we must now turn.

The European Prototype and the Educated African

The extent to which the educated minority had absorbed a complex of European behaviour is illustrated by the following description of activities in Cape Coast during the 1890's:

> Everyday life in Cape Coast took on the colour of the Victorian era. The School Assembly Hall would echo one evening to the resolutions passed by the local branch of the Society for the Prevention of Cruelty to Animals; the next it would be filled with an enthusiastic audience treated to a magic lantern lecture on the Stately Homes of England, followed by 'Selections on a patent organ which combines the whole effect of a brass band in itself'. A photographer executed 'portraits on opal mounted on silk plush blocks, also on gilt-edged glasses', Beeton's *Complete Etiquette for English Gentlemen* sold at the Bookshop. English clothing and English names were postulates of the Christian life.[68]

The imitation of Europeans, so amusingly described in this oft-quoted comment by Smith, represented the more visible side of a widely ramifying transformation: the replacement of traditional conceptions of social status and self-respect by criteria reflecting occupation and education. In order to understand this process it is necessary to examine the characteristics of the European minority itself.

These representatives of English society were themselves recruited from a relatively narrow stratum and, in large part, were of middle-class origin. More important, the range of occupations undertaken by them on the Gold Coast in the colonial period was necessarily limited. Their activities were confined to a small number of administrative and supervisory functions none of which involved them in manual activities. In the earliest period European technicians were few and some of these were engaged in teaching duties with the missions. As a result, therefore, African perceptions of European society were derived, for the most part, from observation of a highly selected and unrepresentative group. The acculturative situation under these conditions has been described as one of 'transfrontal learning', where:

> ... the acculturation ... takes place away from the 'place of origin' or from the society which usually 'supports' that culture. .... When knowledge of a culture is brought to some alien spot by a few of its agents, it is unlikely that a representative range of that culture or society will be present.[69]

As a result of European political control, the British now constituted an elite, a generalized reference group upon which the aspirations of some Africans were modelled. Since, however, this group performed such a limited range of functions it was almost inevitable that African ambitions should be directed towards similar types of employment and, as we shall see, to similar types of education. Further, even in later periods when the European colonial elite included a wider range of occupational groups it remained highly stratified and the technician was never accorded parity or prestige with the administrative officer.[70]

The continual criticism by Europeans of the demand among the products of the schools for white collar employment was obtuse since it ignored the fact that these aspirations reflected European evaluations. One observer has remarked:

> If Africans want to be clerks it is surely because they have seen the clerks exalted. . . . What Africans seek today consciously is power, and the symbol of power is a man sitting at a desk covered with bits of paper. The very use of the word secretary . . . is a sign of the dignity with which our society invests the clerkly office. The African has never seen the same dignity attached to the man skilled with his hands, to the artisan or the mechanic. In blaming him, therefore, for his hankering after the black-coated occupations we are blaming him for adopting too closely the values of our own society.[71]

Individuals were ranked increasingly upon the basis of their occupations and the degree to which they had adopted European patterns of living.[72] Since education provided the sole gateway to European-type occupations it necessarily became a criterion of status within the emergent social system of the urban areas.

The work of J. M. Sarbah, a lawyer and one of the early Nationalist leaders, illustrates dramatically how far this process of 'restratification' had gone.[73] In characterizing the structure of urban society at the end of the nineteenth century, Sarbah indicates that in addition to the illiterate masses there were three groups differentiated on the basis of educational and occupational criteria. First, there were those who could barely scrawl their names and who were restricted to a relatively narrow range of menial occupations. Second, there were the 'petty clerks' who despised 'the dignity of labor' and were too idle to improve their stations in life by further education. It is interesting to observe that Sarbah's criticisms of this intermediate group were precisely the same in content as those levelled by contemporary Europeans.[74] Both condemned them for their duplicity and willingness to deceive illiterates and upbraided them for their lack of enterprise in bettering their condition. Sarbah's remarks, in fact, illustrate how completely he had assimilated European attitudes vis-à-vis the lesser products of the educational system. Third, Sarbah describes the class that was 'known and respected of all men'—the professional group. These were the owners of the larger African commercial enterprises. This minority was regarded as exemplifying the benefits of 'higher education'. They were frequently educated abroad and sent their children to England for further studies.

Sarbah's views indicate the degree to which the Western-educated minority had abandoned traditional concepts of status and how explicit occupational and educational criteria were replacing traditional evaluation based on descent. This minority was differentiated from the masses by specific cultural characteristics, by the willingness with which they assimilated European values, and, above all, by their ability to employ the language of the colonial elite which further differentiated them from most traditional rulers.[75]

It would be inaccurate however to typify the most highly educated minority as constituting a 'middle class' in the sense that they occupied an intermediate position within a hierarchy of social classes characterized by differences in occupation and income. They certainly possessed common cultural characteristics derived from European models and in this respect constituted a divergent cultural minority, but at the same time they were partially involved in the traditional status structure and many of the educated men were particularly proud if they could trace their affiliations to 'noble lines'.[76] It is more appropriate to typify this kind of emergent social structure as 'dualistic' in nature and compounded of both traditional and European criteria of status.[77] So far as formal education was concerned, however, there is little doubt that here the European image was particularly powerful, and the educational demands of Africans reflected this model.

The Nationalists and the Schools

In view of the preceding analysis it is not surprising that early educational efforts by Africans should be concerned with the founding and support of *Western-type* schools and that early Nationalist programmes should contain demands for the development of education along essentially metropolitan lines.[78]

Before the last quarter of the century wealthy Fanti traders, in particular, had been responsible for the provision and maintenance of schools and from those institutions 'came a long stream of educated clerks into Government, commercial and Mission work'.[79] It is notable that these early efforts were restricted to the provision of

H   99

elementary day schools on the Wesleyan model. There is not one instance of African funds actually being utilized for the support of industrial or agricultural institutions. It is equally significant that the provision of schools by Africans themselves reflected the 'free market' conditions of early educational enterprise and the absence of restrictions upon the creation of new institutions.

The early educational views of the Nationalists received their clearest exposition in the Articles of the Fanti Confederation of 1871. The provision of formal schools was regarded as an important element in the Confederation's general programme of economic and social development. Article 8, Clause 4 stated that one object was:

> To erect school-houses and establish schools for the education of all children within the Confederation, and to obtain the service of efficient schoolmasters.[80]

Articles 21 to 25 attempted in more detail to outline plans for the construction of schoolhouses and the expansion of the system. The Confederation resolved as follows:

> Article 21. That national schools be established at as early a period as possible in the following districts: Braffoo Country, Abrah, Ayan, Gomewah, Ekumfi, Edgimacoe, Denhia and Assin.
> Article 22. That normal schools be attached to each national school for the express purpose of educating and instructing the scholars as carpenters, masons, sawyers, joiners, agriculturists, smiths, architects, builders, etc.
> Article 23. That schools be also established and schoolmasters procured to train and teach the female sex, and to instruct them in the necessary requisites.
> Article 24. That the expense of erecting each school be defrayed from the national purse, but that each king and chief be requested to render all possible aid to facilitate the movement by supplying men and materials.
> Article 25. That in districts where there are Wesleyan Schools at present established the kings and chiefs be requested to insist on the daily attendance of all children between the ages of eight and fourteen.

It would appear the primary aim of the framers of the articles was to establish national schools directly financed from the revenues of the Confederation in those areas where Wesleyan institutions did not exist; in this respect the policy resembled the contemporary English practice of 'filling in the gaps' in the educational system. There is certainly no indication that the aim of the Confederation was to replace existing institutions or to depart radically from the type of education already being provided.

The creation of normal schools for the provision of trade-training merely echoed the views of successive European educationists and administrators; the use of the term 'normal school' in this context does not imply that these were teacher-training institutions but rather supplementary trade schools. In practice no attempts were made by Africans to establish schools of this nature until late in the first half of the twentieth century.

For the rest, the proposals of the Confederation can be regarded as little more than pious resolutions. At this stage there was not the least likelihood that compulsory attendance could be required in most areas, particularly since the chiefs were to be regarded as the instruments of enforcement, while the creation of girls' schools, in which the missions had not been inactive, was hardly likely to be successful in view of the constant opposition of the local population to enrolling girls.[81] Further, the Confederation might have had considerable difficulty in attempting to raise funds through taxation. British mistakes had contributed to the failure of the Poll Tax Ordinance in 1852 and created a situation of mistrust that might have impeded even the work of the Confederation.

Policy statements alone are hardly satisfactory indications of African motivations regarding Western education. It is profitable to see what educational institutions were *actually* being supported by Africans after 1870. European educators were far from 'imposing' academic institutions upon the African population; they were reluctant to create secondary institutions of an academic nature, while African activity was almost solely centred upon the creation of this type of school. Our analysis must now examine the provision of secondary schools.

The Provision of Secondary Education

Apart from the recommendation by the early commissioner for the Select Committee of 1841 that schools of a higher grade be established for the sons of chiefs, there is no indication that British policy-makers were enthusiastic about the provision of grammar schools. A primary aim of this and the previous chapter has been to indicate that far more enthusiasm was present among educationists regarding the creation of schools for agricultural and trade training. In 1894 a scheme for the establishment of government scholarships for the encouragement of higher education was instituted, but until 1900 no Africans had qualified for these awards.[82] The Rules of 1898 also indicated that grants might be made to 'any High School, Grammar School or Secondary School' at the rate of £1 per head for schools classed as

'Fair' and at £2 per head for schools classed as 'Good', but there is little doubt that government was lukewarm to the provision of such institutions.[83] The Director of Education remarked in 1900:

> Of Higher or Secondary Education there is very little. The training seminaries of the Basel Mission may be said to be the only attempts at an education other than merely elementary. . . . It will be time enough to think of establishing schools for higher education when the Elementary Schools are in a satisfactory condition, and that will largely depend on the success of our endeavors to secure a better class of teachers.[84]

In practice, the pressure for higher education of an academic variety was to come largely from educated Africans, and it is this group who were most active in supporting such ventures. The Wesleyans opened a secondary school for boys at Cape Coast in 1876; the first attempt to provide a more advanced education on the Gold Coast. Active support for this endeavour came from John Sarbah, J. P. Brown, and W. E. Pietersen, all Africans who were among the active early Nationalists.[85] The school was obliged to close in 1889 because of lack of funds and staff but was reopened through public subscription and the aid of Sarbah, Brown, and A. W. de Graft Johnson; J. E. Casely-Hayford was appointed principal of the institution for a short period.[86] The school managed to survive in a precarious condition until 1905; after this date it met with increasing success and was renamed Mfantsipim School, the first successful Gold Coast secondary institution.

The group mentioned above attempted to extend their activities in the provision of secondary education by floating the 'Fanti Public Schools Company and National Education Fund' for the creation of secondary schools in every large town; they were not successful in raising funds for such a project.[87] Some years later a 'Fanti National Education Scheme' proposed by Casely-Hayford also made reference to the necessity for establishing secondary or higher-grade schools and scholarships for students 'in aid of a liberal and professional education'.[88]

By the end of the century there were four schools, three in Cape Coast and one in Accra, that gave all the education which purported to be more than elementary. Though they may have been secondary schools in name only, it is significant that they were totally staffed by Africans and supported by them.[89] Two of these institutions were later to receive more adequate support from the Wesleyan and Anglican missions in the early twentieth century and emerge as Adisadel and Mfantsipim schools, but their origin was largely due to African enterprise.

The motivation among the African leadership for secondary institutions of a Western type is not difficult to perceive. Such institutions potentially constituted gateways into professional occupations and could train students for entry into British universities. Beyond this, however, African aspirations were geared to a far more general concept of 'parity' in educational provision. For those Africans to whom the European minority represented qualities deemed worthy of imitation, Western education became the most obvious tangible symbol of European power. Education was, therefore, synonymous with the type of education provided in the metropolitan country; deviations from that pattern were not acceptable. As we shall see in following pages, European attempts to adapt the schools to African conditions failed to take account of this aspiration. What the schools taught was not so important in itself, provided that their curriculums were similar to those of English institutions at the same level. Whether the colonial elite wished or not, their function as a reference group implied that the nature of schools could not deviate too markedly from the English model.

Some General Conclusions on Early Educational Development

This chapter has served to illustrate the dangers inherent in any attempts to reconstruct the development of an educational system by examining formal policy statements on education alone. Descriptions of educational goals or purposes as expressed by policy-makers are often an unproductive source of information on the processes of educational transfer. In examining salient aspects of early British thought on African education it has been possible to illustrate the disparity between policy pronouncements and actual developments. Although this point has been made by historians, there is a distressing tendency to fall back upon *ad hoc* explanations for what may be regarded as the 'paradoxes' of African educational development. For example, the slow growth of technical facilities has been ascribed to the lack of interest in such institutions by the colonial power, or the relative success of academic institutions has been interpreted as a result of the 'imposition' of such structures on indigenous populations. These views have almost been enshrined as the 'stock-in-trade' of educational observers, but there is little evidence to support such assertions. These dubious judgments have stemmed from an inadequate methodological approach. The primary concern of the analyst must not be with formal policy but rather with the functional consequences of educational transfer. What, in fact, were the objective and frequently unanticipated results of the growth of educational institutions resulting from European overrule? Next, attention must be directed to the purposes for which the schools were being used by their African clientele and to the pattern of expectations generated among those who received formal education. Such an analysis must go far beyond description of the formal school structure and examine the whole range of consequences stemming from the colonial situation.

So far as their aims can be disentangled, missions and government alike stressed the evangelical purpose of the schools. Particular attention was given to providing elementary education with a pronounced industrial and agricultural bias. There is little doubt that both these groups sought to develop education along somewhat different lines from that given in the United Kingdom. This attitude did not apply, however, to the *structural* characteristics of the school system; here there was an attempt to reproduce a pattern of administration that apparently had been successful in England. The consequences of the early education ordinances and rules were quite different, however, from those resulting from English legislation. Far from creating a state system, the future development of the schools was to be associated with the rapid growth of institutions outside the state-aided sector. In practice, the conditions for the effective administration of such a system did not exist on the Gold Coast, but even if they had, there seems reason to doubt whether a centralized structure which imposed a uniform curriculum on the schools would have emerged. It has been indicated that the Basel and Wesleyan missions developed totally different systems of education even within the grant-aided sector. The primary motivation for the framing of the early ordinances stemmed more from a need to develop criteria upon which limited government aid could be given rather than from a desire to create a centralized curriculum. In fact, there was always considerably more latitude given to schools aided by the board than is at first apparent from inspection of the ordinances.

It seems clear, however, that this structural arrangement led to an overexpansion in schools in relation to the very limited vocational opportunities open to Africans within the colonial period. A series of unanticipated and unintended consequences were to stem from this. Certainly Western education was a powerful instrument of social change, but the kind of change produced was certainly not that envisaged by early educationists.

The results of Western education were most manifest within the towns where traditional structures were already undergoing transformation. Within towns there was the growth and increasing influence of a Western-educated group with distinctive cultural characteristics derived from the European model. The urban population was already beginning to be socially differentiated upon the basis of criteria alien to traditional society.[90] Wealth, education, and occupation set certain groups apart from the majority and it was these groups who were particularly active in their opposition to traditional leadership. Education, in practice, constituted an alternative path to social mobility outside the traditional structure, and the creation of this new status hierarchy was bound to lead to tension between the emergent educated groups and traditional units. Besides this incipient opposition, the limitation placed upon access to the highest positions within the European-dominated occupational structure fostered early Nationalist movements which were led and organized by the urbanized, Western-educated elements. So far as the political consequences of Western education are concerned, 'Colonization not only created the social conditions of its demise; it provided also the ideological weapons.'[91]

Outside the towns where education was not widely diffused the process of change was less dramatic, but even here the requirements of the colonial administration necessitated the recruitment of individuals to chiefships on the basis of non-traditional criteria, with the consequence that literates were frequently recruited to roles for which they were not eligible. In Ashanti and the Northern Territories, however, this process was not evident before the twentieth century, and both areas remained strongly traditionalistic.

The economic consequences of Western education were far less satisfactory than the early protagonists of industrial and agricultural education had supposed. Far from giving an impetus to economic growth in industry or agriculture, the schools seemed rather to reflect the bias of the occupational structure towards clerical employment. In practice, African demands for academic education had little to do with the curriculums of the schools but reflected their realistic perception of the differential rewards accorded to individuals within this occupational structure. In spite of attempts to create industrial and agricultural schools, it is apparent that the rationale which underlay the policy was mistaken, since the financial and prestige rewards resulting from such instruction were not commensurate with those derived from academic studies.

In viewing the development of education in terms of the expectations of Africans and the purpose it served for them, rather than from the viewpoint of the colonial power, African pressures for academic forms of education and particularly for academic secondary education are readily understandable. In practice the African clientele of the schools received very much the kind of education that they so reasonably desired. During the nineteenth century most British educationists on the coast had espoused the cause of technical and agricultural education as a key to economic development. African parents, however, like those elsewhere, did not send their children to school to meet the need for economic growth; they sent them there to maximize their children's opportunities within the emergent occupational and prestige structure created by colonial rule.

REFERENCES

1. The most definitive account of the rapid expansion of British political control after 1874 is to be found in Claridge, *A History of the Gold Coast and Ashanti* (London: John Murray, 1915), I, 550 ff.

2. See also D. E. Apter, *The Gold Coast in Transition* (Princeton: Princeton University Press, 1955), p. 37.

3. Claridge, *op. cit.*, I, 536.

4. F. M. Bourret, *The Gold Coast: A Survey of the Gold Coast and British Togoland 1919–1946* (Stanford: Stanford University Press, 1949), pp. 51–60.

5. L. P. Mair, *Native Policies in Africa* (London: G. Routledge & Sons, 1936), p. 158.

6. It should be realized that the concept of indirect rule has been susceptible to a variety of interpretations. See Lord Lugard, *The Dual Mandate in British Tropical Africa* (Edinburgh & London: W. Blackwood & Sons, 1923). Also for a summary of these policies see R. E. Robinson, 'Why "Indirect Rule" Has Been Replaced by "Local Government" in the Nomenclature of British Native Administrations', *Journal of African Administration*, II, No. 3 (October 1955), 12–15. For our purposes, Mair's definition of indirect rule as 'the progressive adaptation of native institutions to modern conditions' is adequate. Mair, *op. cit.*, p. 56. More fully, it is 'an attempt to preserve what can still be preserved of indigenous institutions in a situation in which the radical modification of many of them is assumed as necessary and desirable'. *Ibid.*, p. 269.

7. Apter, *op. cit.*, pp. 124–25.

8. The increasing volume of litigation connected with land-alienation during the colonial period proved a primary source of income for many African lawyers and to some extent was responsible for the popularity of the profession among early educated Africans. It should also be noted that land was not only alienated to European companies but to indigenous migrant cocoa farmers from other areas. Thus, for example, lands in Akim were frequently alienated to individuals coming from Akwapim.

9. Sir Alan Burns, *The Colonial Civil Servant* (London: Allen & Unwin, 1949), *passim*.

10. Rev. J. Leighton Wilson, *Western Africa: Its History, Conditions and Prospects* (New York: Harper & Bros., 1856), p. 493.

11. Brodie Cruikshank, *Eighteen Years on the Gold Coast* (London: Hurst & Blackett, 1853), I, 263.

12. Compiled from A. W. Cardinall, *The Gold Coast 1931* (Accra: Government Printer, 1932), p. 192.

13. Claridge, *op. cit.*, I, 479.

14. J. M. Sarbah, *Fanti Customary Laws* (2nd ed.; London: William Clowes & Sons Ltd., 1904), p. 102.

15. H. O. A. McWilliam, *The Development of Education in Ghana* (London: Longmans, Green, 1960), pp. 27–28.

16. F. H. Hilliard, *A Short History of Education in British West Africa* (London: Thomas Nelson & Sons, 1957), pp. 69–71.

17. Between 1870 and 1884, 4,402 board schools had been created in England and Wales, about one-quarter of which had been transferred by voluntary managers. E. Herbert Lyon, *The Education Commission, 1886–1888: A Summary of the Final Report Containing the Conclusions and Recommendations of the Commissioners* (2nd ed.; London: H.M.S.O., 1888), p. 59.

18. Gold Coast, *The Education Ordinance 1887* (No. 14 of 1887).

19. *Ibid.*, par. 7, sec. 1.

20. *Ibid.*, par. 7, sec. 4 and par. 7, sec. 6.

21 *Ibid.*, par. 12.

22. Gold Coast, *Rules Passed by the Board of Education and Approved by the Governor under Section 4 of the Education Ordinance, 1887* (1898).

23. Lowe's code had originally provided for a payment of ten shillings per subject on every child who passed in the three 'Rs' plus a grant of six shillings on average attendance.

24. Gold Coast, *Rules Passed*, par. 62.

25. *Ibid.*, par. 67.

26. By 1887 government contributed less than 10 per cent of the total cost of education in the Colony, and by 1904 expenditure on education only amounted to 3·6 per cent of total government expenditure. Sarbah, *op. cit.*, p. 244.

27. It has been suggested that school curriculums were carefully controlled by government education officers and 'under colonialism all secondary socializing structures participated in varying degrees in the inculcation of attitudes of conformity and acceptance'. Gabriel A. Almond and James S. Coleman, *The Politics of Developing Areas* (Princeton: Princeton University Press, 1960), p. 334. This is something of an exaggeration and, in practice, there was considerable autonomy in the development of curriculums. The latter were less controlled by government agencies than they were by the entry requirements of higher institutions.

28. Claridge, *op. cit.*, I, 182.

29. A. E. Southon, *Gold Coast Methodism: The First Hundred Years, 1835–1935* (London: Cargate Press, 1934), pp. 74, 87.

30. *Ibid.*, p. 93.

31. *Ibid.*, p. 121.

32. W. J. Rottmann, 'The Educational Work of the Basel Mission on the Gold Coast', Appendix A.I to *Special Reports on Educational Subjects* (London: H.M.S.O., 1905), XIII, Part II, 301.

33. F. Wright, 'The System of Education in the Gold Coast Colony', *Special Reports on Educational Subjects* (London: H.M.S.O., 1905), p. 9.

34. Rottmann, *op. cit.*, p. 297.

35. *Ibid.*, p. 305.

36. Though some assume that the Wesleyans were quite inactive in promoting vernacular studies, this was by no means the case. They were responsible for the preparation of the first Fanti grammar between 1882 and 1887 and, in the following century, were active in the preparation of a whole series of primers and readers in local languages. Southon, *op. cit.*, pp. 136–38.

37. See also McWilliam, *op. cit.*, p. 24.

38. Speaking of Africa in general Read remarks that

another result of recent research has been to establish the intention of the early missionaries to emphasize the training of Africans in agriculture and elementary technical skills. . . . The eventual emphasis on literary skills was largely due to pressure from the Africans themselves.

M. Read, 'Education in Africa: Its Pattern and Role in Social Change', *Annals of the American Academy of Political and Social Science*, CCXCVIII (March 1955), 173.

39. I. M. Wallerstein, *The Emergence of Two West African Nations: Ghana and the Ivory Coast* (New York: Columbia University Press, 1959), p. 59.

40. Hailey also remarks,

The most characteristic features of French educational policy have been: first, the universal use of French as the medium of instruction; second, a general policy of relating the provision of the more advanced type of education to the demand which appears to exist for it; third, the strong emphasis on vocational training as the form which such education should take.

Lord Hailey, *An African Survey* (2nd ed. rev.; Oxford: Oxford University Press, 1957), p. 1197. However, Hailey falls into the error of contrasting 'vocational' and 'academic' education. In practice, academic education has been the most vocational type of education in West Africa.

41. Sumter, one of the earliest inspectors of schools, was to remark of the Gold Coast, 'If any compulsory training is needed here it is industrial.' Quoted by H. S. Scott, 'The Development of the Education of the African in Relation to Western Contact', *Yearbook of Education*, 1938 (London: Evans Bros., 1938), p. 716.

42. W. E. F. Ward, *A History of Ghana* (London: George Allen & Unwin, 1958), p. 396.

43. Bourret, *op. cit.*, p. 26.

44. Wallerstein, *op. cit.*, p. 241.

45. Rottman, *op. cit.*, p. 300.

46. A similar point is made by Wallerstein, *op. cit.*, p. 241, and by W. E. F. Ward, *Educating Young Nations* (London: Allen & Unwin, 1959), p. 120. The situation, however, was by no means unique to British colonial areas. In a recent study in Senegal the vocational aspirations of children were found to be largely oriented to clerical types of employment and the writer concludes, 'moreover the slow pace of economic expansion precludes any big increase in the number of openings for technical workers or in the supervisory grades in industry'. P. Mercier, 'The Evolution of Senegalese Elites', *International Social Science Bulletin*, VIII, No. 3 (1956), 445.

47. It should not be assumed that this type of generalization is applicable only to African territories; it is a view that commends widespread support in the context of English education itself. Referring to English secondary schools, Dent remarks,

They were tied hand and foot to an academic, bookish and sedentary curriculum wholly irrele-vant to the life and needs of any modern civilized society. . . . A tragic but inevitable result of this perverted policy of academization has been the diversion of a very large proportion of the best brains of the country into the black-coated occupations. . . . A complementary and equally deplorable result has been an appalling inversion of values. The clerk who properly should be the amanuensis of the engineer or skilled craftsman, has been falsely elevated to be his social superior and taught to regard him with disdain.

H. C. Dent, *A New Order in English Education* (London: Routledge, Kegan Paul, 1942), p. 28. The statement really implies that the schools have been responsible for the creation of an occupational hierarchy in the United Kingdom, a hierarchy which is the most crucial variable in determining social class affiliation. Such a view exaggerates the impact of the schools on the social system and, in practice, sees the schools as *creating* the status components of the occupational structure.

48. Rottmann, *op. cit.*, p. 300.

49. See chap. i for previous comments on occupational status in traditional society.

50. M. J. Field, *Social Organization of the Ga People* (London: Crown Agents for the Colonies, 1940), p. 117.

51. *Ibid.*, p. 137.

52. Such a statement seems to have more general application than to Africa. See Almond and Coleman, *op. cit.*, p. 336.

53. Claridge, *op. cit.*, I, 631. See also Burns, *op. cit.*, p. 295. It should be noted that this reversal of 'liberal' policy occurred in other parts of the Empire at about the same period, though its causes are by no means clear.

54. Bruce Tiebout McCully, *English Education and the Origins of Indian Nationalism* (New York: Columbia University Press, 1940), p. 191.

55. Gail Margaret Kelly, 'The Ghanaian Intelligentsia' (Ph.D. dissertation, University of Chicago, 1959), p. 48.

56. Rupert Emerson, *From Empire to Nation* (Cambridge: Harvard University Press, 1960), p. 54.

57. Wallerstein, *op. cit.*, p. 58.

58 Contained in a letter dated the 22 August 1850 to Governor Winniett and written by James Bannerman and Brodie Cruikshank. Quoted by Claridge, *op. cit.*, I, 482.

59. *Ibid.*

60. Apter, *op. cit.*, p. 24.

61. The complete text of the Articles of Confederation is to be found in J. Casely-Hayford, *Gold Coast Native Institutions* (London: Sweet & Maxwell, 1903), pp. 327–40.

62. Claridge, *op. cit.*, II, 619.

63. See also J. C. de Graft-Johnson, *African Glory* (London: Watts, 1954), pp. 171–72.

64. The implications of such a bill are well explained by Apter, *op. cit.*, p. 53.

65. The antagonism between chiefs and the intelligentsia runs like a thread throughout later Legislative Council Debates on the Gold Coast. See particularly Gold Coast Government, *Legislative Council Debates* (Accra: Government Printer), 1925–26 and 1926–27. As late as 1927 Nana Ofori Atta saw the delegation of any powers to the educated classes as a matter of 'remote contingency'. *Ibid.*, 1926–27, pp. 255–60. We have already seen that such tension did not initially exist between the educated classes and the chiefs in Buganda. Neither was it apparent in northern Nigeria where the children of chiefs were among the first to attend schools; as a result the traditional social hierarchy remained unaltered in that area. E. R. Yeld, 'Islam and Social Stratification in Northern Nigeria', *British Journal of Sociology*, XI, No. 3 (1960), 112–28. Antagonism between traditional ruler and the Western-educated minority is not, therefore, an inevitable corollary of Western education. In the Gold Coast Western education undermined traditional authority. In Buganda and the northern Nigerian Emirates, in the early stages, it almost certainly reinforced it.

66. Emerson, *op. cit.*, p. 243.

67. Both writers were professionally trained lawyers.

68. Edwin W. Smith, *Aggrey of Africa* (London: Student Christian Movement, 1929), p. 43.

69. Kelly, *op. cit.*, p. 87.

70. So far as the writer is aware no comprehensive studies have yet been made

of the composition of colonial elites, but it seems likely that European colonial society was more rigidly stratified than its counterpart in the metropole.

71. 'Africans Want to be Clerks', *Colonial Review*, VI, No. 5 (March 1950), 137.

72. For similar analyses drawn from distinct parts of Africa see Ellen Hellman, 'The Emerging African Middle Class in South Africa', *Colonial Review*, IX, No. 5 (March 1956), 144, and J. Clyde Mitchell, 'The African Middle Classes in British Central Africa', *Development of a Middle Class in Tropical and Sub-Tropical Areas* (Brussels: International Institute of Differing Civilizations, 1956), pp. 222–32. Also J. Clyde Mitchell and A. L. Epstein, 'Occupational Prestige and Social Status among Urban Africans in Northern Rhodesia', *Africa*, XXIX, No. 1 (January 1959), 22–39.

73. Sarbah, *op. cit.*, p. 246.

74. Compare Sarbah's remarks with Claridge, *op. cit.*, I, 465.

75. See also McCully, *op. cit.*, p. 209, for a similar examination of the situation in nineteenth-century India.

76. For example James Aggrey was particularly proud of his royal line. 'No paramount chief's line on the Gold Coast is higher than mine, and very few are as high as mine.' Smith, *op. cit.*, p. 19.

77. See also Almond and Coleman, *op. cit.*, pp. 21 ff., and Apter, *op. cit.*, p. 156 for succinct accounts of 'dualism' in political structures in the colonial period.

78. The present writer would agree that considerable difference of opinion exists on this matter. Kimble has recently documented the growth of 'cultural nationalism' on the Gold Coast which manifested itself in a partial rejection of European names, dress, behaviour, and values: David Kimble, *A Political History of Ghana, 1850–1928* (Oxford: Clarendon Press, 1963), pp. 506–62. So far as education is concerned, J. E. Casely-Hayford, *Ethiopia Unbound* (London: C. M. Phillips, 1911) contains a plea for the development of a truly 'African' as opposed to a 'European' education. Two points can be made in this connection. First, manifestations of cultural nationalism were associated (as they usually are) with a very small acculturated minority; the very group that was the furthest removed from traditional culture was the most active in asserting its values. Second, there is always an element of contrived artificiality in the efforts of intellectuals, however sincere, to reinterpret traditional culture, and a very great gap exists between an emotional commitment to cultural nationalism and a willingness to see this commitment translated into practical action. The fact is that African intellectuals did very little to 'Africanize' the schools even when they had an opportunity to do so. This reflected their basic emotional ambivalence *vis-à-vis* traditional African culture and their shrewd perception of the realities of the colonial situation.

79. Southon, *op. cit.*, p. 122.

80. Casely-Hayford, *op. cit.*, p. 122.

81. The establishment of girls' schools in the Gold Coast had been attempted from an early period but with little success. For Wesleyan difficulties in this sphere of education see Southon, *op. cit.*, pp. 130–32.

82. Wright, *op. cit.*, p. 9.

83. Gold Coast, *Rules Passed by the Board of Education*, par. 73.

84. Wright, *op. cit.*

85. Southon, *op. cit.*, pp. 126–30.

86. J. C. de Graft-Johnson, *op. cit.*, p. 185.

87. Casely-Hayford, *op. cit.*, p. 341.

88. *Ibid.*

89. Gold Coast Government, *Report of the Committee of Educationalists* (Accra: Government Printer, 1920), p. 24.

90. See also Daniel F. McCall, 'Dynamics of Urbanization in Africa', *Annals of the American Academy of Political and Social Science*, CCXCVIII (March 1955), 151–60.

91. Wallerstein, *op. cit.*, p. 249.

IV

THE DYNAMICS OF EDUCATIONAL GROWTH IN THE LATE COLONIAL PERIOD

BY 1900 the establishment of British overrule had been completed in the Gold Coast. In the Colony itself there had been encroachment upon the powers of traditional rulers, a process that was completed by the outright annexation of the Colony in 1874. In Ashanti the last remnants of revolt against European hegemony had been crushed by military force and the exile of the *Asantehene*. In the Northern Territories, occupation was peacefully effected by the signing of treaties with the chiefs. To the East, penetration had been completed, though not without some military conflict. Henceforth, the Colony, Ashanti, and the Northern Territories were to diverge with respect to the nature and intensity of British control; attempts were made to develop policies of indirect rule in Ashanti and the North far more systematically than had been attempted in the Colony itself. Despite efforts made to preserve indigenous institutions in the political sphere, in the last resort the source of legitimacy of traditional rulers and the ultimate sanctions underlying the system lay with the British colonial administration and not with traditional authorities.

The nature of expansion from the coast had resulted in a markedly uneven pattern of social and economic change. At one extreme were the coastal peoples who had been exposed to over three centuries of European contact, with the concomitant growth of urban centres and an exchange economy; at the other were the northern peoples whose traditional social structures and subsistence economies were barely affected by the imperial power.[1] The consequences of this situation for education were profound, and it is appropriate to consider the overall pattern of educational expansion before examining its political and social implications.

The Dynamics of Educational Growth in the Late Colonial Period

The Growth of the Educational System

The character of European penetration had produced by the end of the nineteenth century, clear inequalities in the provision of educational facilities, a feature that was marked throughout the colonial period. Furthermore, the reluctance of the colonial power to impose controls upon the quality and quantity of educational provision had led to the autonomous growth of an educational structure which lay to a considerable degree outside the system of government or grant-aided schools. This is clearly illustrated in Table 3.

TABLE 3

THE PROVISION OF PRIMARY AND SECONDARY EDUCATION, 1901–50*

Year	Government and Grant-aided Institutions†	Non-Grant-aided Institutions‡	Total Number of Institutions	Enrolment in Grant-aided Institutions†	Enrolment in Non-Grant-aided Institutions‡	Total Enrolment
1901	135	120	255	12,018	Not avail.	—
1911	160	217	377	18,680	Not avail.	—
1920	218	309	527	28,622	13,717	42,339
1925	236	300	536	32,839	Not avail.	—
1930	344	253	597	42,445	11,696	54,151
1935	389	283	672	45,305	17,170	62,475
1940	472	476	948	62,946	28,101	91,047
1945	503	Not avail.	—	74,183	69,129	143,312
1950	1,621	1,378	2,999	209,303	71,717	281,020

* Computed from Gold Coast, *Reports of the Education Department* (Accra: Government Printer, 1901–50); Gold Coast, *Report of the Education Committee 1937–1941* (Accra: Government Printer, 1942), pp. 29–30, and A. W. Cardinall, *The Gold Coast 1931* (Accra: Government Printer, 1932), pp. 194–200.

† This includes institutions totally financed from government sources, government-aided mission institutions, and a small proportion of Native Authority schools. The latter marked an attempt to devolve educational functions upon local authorities on the British model. This was unsuccessful and by 1940 enrolments in Native Authority schools constituted less than 1 per cent of the total.

‡ Figures for non-grant-aided schools include both mission and purely proprietary institutions. The returns for these are, in fact, approximations, and, since the completion of annual returns was not compulsory for these institutions, they are almost certainly an understatement of the extent of the private system.

Certain features are immediately apparent. Throughout most of the period of colonial rule the expansion in educational facilities was by no means dramatic and barely matched the growth in the child population until the post-1940 decade, when a dramatic increase is evident.[2] Further, the extent of the non-aided system is impressive. Even by 1950 the private schools, run largely by missions, accounted for almost half of the total number of institutions and for just over 25 per cent of the total enrolments. Thus non-assisted institutions operated in large numbers in spite of the continual extension of grants-in-aid to new institutions. It is clear that the effect of the Ordinance of 1887 and its successor of 1925 was not to establish a highly centralized educational structure nor to effectively control the curriculums of the schools. Indeed, until 1944 the registration of schools was not required and no attempt was made to exert detailed control even over the activities of grant-aided institutions except for a series of minimal regulations. Also, the number of schools totally financed and administered by government remained small. By 1900 there were only four government institutions of all types and the rate of expansion thereafter was slow (see Table 4).

TABLE 4

NUMBER OF GOVERNMENT PRIMARY AND SECONDARY INSTITUTIONS, 1920-50*

Year	Number of Government Schools	Total Enrolment	Percentage of Total Enrolment
1920	20	4,292	10·2
1930	30	6,524	12·0
1940	25	6,670	7·3
1950	48	8,678	3·0

* Compiled from: Gold Coast, *Reports of the Education Department* (Accra: Government Printer, 1920-50), and Gold Coast, *Report of the Education Committee 1937-41* (Accra: Government Printer, 1942), pp. 29-30.

The system, in fact, substantially represents a 'free market' in schooling. Neither missions nor private entrepreneurs were prevented from entering the market in response to the demand for facilities, and in the case of the former the presence of government operated as a direct stimulus to missionary expansion in the educational field. The missions were aware that if they did not maximize their educational efforts then direct government provision might be extended, denying to them what they realized to be their most potent instrument for proselytization.[3]

The reluctance of government to impose controls on educational expansion is equally apparent from an examination of the secondary-school system over the period. Between 1900 and 1910 only four institutions provided any form of secondary instruction and these schools were largely the result of early African enterprise. Indeed until 1940 the growth of secondary institutions was extremely slow (Table 5).

TABLE 5

GROWTH OF THE SECONDARY SCHOOL SYSTEM, 1920–50*

Year	Type of School	Number of Schools	Enrolment
1920	Government	1	42
	Assisted	1	75
	Non-assisted	1	90
	Total*	3	207
1930	Government	2	162
	Assisted	2	376
	Non-assisted	2	63
	Total	6	601
1940	Government	2	401
	Assisted	3	798
	Non-assisted	12	1,436
	Total	17	2,635
1950	Government	2	857
	Assisted	11	1,919
	Non-assisted	44	3,386
	Total	57	6,162

* Computed from: Gold Coast, *Reports of the Education Department, op. cit.*; Gold Coast, *Report of the Education Committee 1937–1941, op. cit.*; Gold Coast, *Statistical Reports*, Series I, No. 6, 1952–53 (Accra: Government Printer, 1953), p. 1.

British policy regarding the provision of secondary education was extraordinarily cautious during the whole period. Only two government secondary schools existed in 1950, while government aid had only been extended to a further eleven assisted schools. However, after 1940 a remarkable growth is apparent in academic secondary institutions. Even more striking is the fact that most of these schools were not government financed or aided and for the most part they were schools begun on a proprietary basis by Africans and staffed by Africans.[4] What is the outstanding feature of the later colonial period is the vigour of the academic tradition in spite of government caution. In view of a constant volume of criticism that the colonial power was directly responsible for the growth of academic-type institutions there is virtually no evidence to support this contention and in our later discussion on government policy it will be indicated that government was more interested in the growth of technical and agricultural schools than it was in the promotion of academic institutions.

In both primary and secondary education, therefore, the rate of expansion was comparatively slow until the dramatic upsurge in the post-1945 period. Assuming a constant rate of growth similar to that which had occurred in the period 1911 to 1934, it was calculated that it would have taken 600 years before all the child population as shown in the 1931 census would have been enrolled in school.[5] However, such estimates depended upon the assumption that the demand for Western-type education was general throughout the area, and this can be by no means substantiated. Before discussing the differential nature of African demand for education it is appropriate to discuss the most striking feature of Gold Coast education, the disparities in its provision.

Inequalities in Educational Provision

During the nineteenth century schools had been almost totally concentrated in the southern coastal zone, largely as a result of the inability of the missions to expand north in the face of Ashanti hostility. With the opening up of the interior new opportunities presented themselves, and the Catholic missions, particularly, expanded into the Northern Region, opening their first school at Navrongo in 1910. Government was no less active and had opened its first school in Tamale the previous year. It is interesting to note that government was particularly concerned with the Northern Territories in the early stages because of the isolated nature of the area, while Ashanti was left more to the missions. In spite of these activities inequalities in the provision of schools remained very marked until the end of the colonial period (Table 6).

TABLE 6

THE DISTRIBUTION OF PRIMARY AND SECONDARY SCHOOL FACILITIES,
1950*

Area	Number of Schools	Total Enrolment	Estimate† of population (to the nearest thousand)	Per Cent of Total population in School
Colony and Ashanti	2,601	249,376	2,875,000	8·1
Trans-Volta (Southern portion)	315	26,525	273,000	9·6
Northern Territories (including north- ern portion of Trans-Volta)	83	5,059	1,093,000	0·5
Total	2,999	281,020	4,241,000	6·6

* These figures include all schools whether government, grant-aided, or non-assisted.

† These figures are computed from a projection based on an estimated 1·5 per cent increase in population per annum from the Gold Coast, *Census of Population 1948* (Accra: Government Printer, 1950), but should be regarded as crude approximations only. It is fairly certain that the 1948 Census considerably underestimated the size of the population in the Gold Coast.

It is unfortunate that the government practice of grouping statistics for the Colony and Ashanti together make it impossible to indicate the very real differences between Ashanti and the coastal zone. It is possible, however, to plot the distribution of education more accurately by using available statistics on levels of schooling for the total population (Table 7).

117

TABLE 7

PERCENTAGE OF POPULATION WITH SIX YEARS OF EDUCATION
OR MORE IN 1948*

Area	Standard III† and Above	Area	Standard III† and Above
The Gold Coast	4·0	(3) *Northern Territories*	0·21
(1) *The Colony*	5·8	Dagomba	0·36
Accra‡	12·0	Gonja	0·21
Ahanta-Nzima	5·5	Krachi	0·80
Akwapim-New Juaben	11·3	Mamprusi	0·11
Birim	5·5	Wa	0·2
Cape Coast‡	4·5		
Ho§	6·6	(4) *The Larger Towns*	
Keta/Ada	3·3	Accra	17·8
Sefwi	2·8	Kumasi	10·5
Volta River	5·1	Sekondi/Takoradi	15·4
Wasaw-Aowin	4·9	Cape Coast	24·9
(2) *Ashanti*	3·9	Koforidua	14·0
Bekwai	3·8	Winneba	8·7
Kumasi‡	4·7		
Mampong	4·1		
Wenchi	2·1		

* Gold Coast, *Census of Population 1948, op. cit.*
† Standard III represents six years of primary education.
‡ These refer to administrative districts and not to the individual towns.
§ Ho represents the southern portion of Trans-Volta.

The general decline in levels of education from south to north, with Ashanti occupying an intermediate position somewhat below the average, is apparent. Among regions there is in fact a gradation from 5·8 per cent for the Colony to 0·21 per cent in the Northern Territories; district variations range from 12·0 to 0·11.

The most striking feature revealed by the table is the remarkable relationship between education and urbanization.[6] In each of the six largest towns, educational levels are far higher than for the Gold Coast as a whole. Furthermore, if the statistics for Accra Municipality are removed from those for Accra District, the percentage for the latter drops to 3·3 per cent or below the average for the Gold Coast, heightening this relationship. If the figures for Standard VII and above (at least ten years of education) are taken alone, the statistics

118

are 1·6 per cent for the Colony and 0·13 per cent for the Northern Territories, but in the eleven cities which had a population of over 10,000 in 1948 the percentage is 6·2.[7]

In stressing the uneven distribution of schools it has also been implied that during the colonial period there were clear-cut differences in their availability for various ethnic groups. Given such marked disparities, it is pertinent to ask how far they were explainable in terms of the differential rates of urbanization as between major regions.

Fortes has indicated that in 1945 there were close parallels between tribal origin and standard of education within Kumasi Municipality itself.[8] He observed that less than 0·5 per cent of children attending school were of Northern origin though northerners numbered about 5 or 6 per cent of total population. However, a large proportion of the northerners in Kumasi were purely temporary migrants and did not, in fact, constitute what might be termed an urbanized group. Unfortunately, Fortes's conclusions do not indicate whether differential ethnic enrolments were a function of urbanization or were due to ethnic factors *per se*. It would have been advisable to group the sample on the basis of their period of residence in Kumasi to see if apparent ethnic variations were explainable in terms of urbanization alone.

Some additional data are available regarding the tribal composition of the student body in the Accra primary and middle schools in 1954.[9] These statistics made no attempt to relate the tribal distribution in the schools to the distribution of tribal groups in the population of Accra as a whole. This is understandable since no data for this latter distribution are available after 1948 and, as they stand, the data are not very enlightening. However, using the 1948 Census material as a base, a very crude attempt can be made to relate tribal enrolment to tribal proportions in the total Accra population. This type of calculation is precarious and rests on two assumptions: (1) We shall assume that tribal proportions in the Accra population remained substantially unchanged between 1948 and 1954. (2) We shall assume that the proportion of children between six and fifteen (which we shall arbitrarily regard as school-going age) remained unchanged over the period. Taking overall population proportions we could state that in 1954 the Ga represented 51·6 per cent of the total population of the municipality but 73·3 per cent of the school enrolments, while at the other extreme the Kwahu represented 2 per cent of the Accra population but only 0·4 per cent of enrolments. However, such a measure is too crude, since it ignores varying child populations among ethnic groupings, particularly recent immigrants. If allowances are made for

The Historical Background

a varying child population we see the modified results in Table 8.

TABLE 8

DIFFERENTIAL ACCESS TO SCHOOLING BY TRIBE—ACCRA, 1954

Tribe	Percent-age of Accra popula-tion in 1948*	Estimated population in Accra 1954†	Proportion of Children of 6–15 in Group 1948‡	Estimated Child population 6–15 in 1954§	Actual Child population Attending School in 1954**	Percentage of Estimated Child population Attending School in 1954††
Ga	51·6	99,100	22·9	22,700	20,594	91·0
Ewe	11·1	21,300	19·5	4,150	1,656	40·0
Fanti	5·2	9,900	20·8	2,050	1,957	96·0
Nigerian	4·7	9,000	13·4	1,200	769	64·0
Hausa	3·4	6,500	13·1	850	609	72·0
Ashanti	1·7	3,200	18·6	600	436	72·0
Adangme	2·8	5,400	22·0	1,200	1,253	—
Akwapim	2·2	4,200	18·4	750	717	96·0
Kwahu	2·0	3,800	20·9	800	112	14·0
Zabarima	1·8	3,400	5·0	150	Nil	—
Others	13·5	25,900	Not included	—	—	—
Total	100	191,000				

* Computed from Gold Coast, *Census of Population 1948, op. cit.*

† Based on the assumption that population proportions remained constant and using 191,000 as the estimated population for 1954. Calculated to the nearest hundred.

‡ Gold Coast, *Census of Population 1948, op. cit.*

§ Assuming 1948 proportions. Calculated to the nearest fifty.

** Derived from Acquah, *op. cit.*, p. 112.

†† Calculated to the nearest whole number.

In spite of the limitations and crudity of the data it would appear that significant differences do occur among ethnic groups within the urban milieu. We are faced again, however, with the problem that the material is not sufficient for us to examine whether 'apparent' ethnic variations are, in practice, a function of duration of urban contact. As in the case of Fortes' material there must be a strong presumption that this is the case, since the four peoples with over 90 per cent of their child population in school (the Ga, Fanti, Adangme, and Akwa-pim) are from the southern coastal area with its long tradition of European contact where urban centres have existed for over one hundred years. Groups from farther inland with a predominantly rural background are far less represented.

The analysis so far has stressed the degree of regional variation in schools provision throughout the colonial and immediate post-colonial period and indicated that these variations occurred on both an ethnic basis and most strikingly along urban-rural lines. An adequate analysis must attempt to provide not only an *ad hoc* explanation but a more general series of reasons for variations in school enrolments.

Coleman in an analysis of the political consequences of areal variations in the acquisition of Western education in a given territory has seen the uneven distribution of schools facilities in Africa as due to two primary factors.[10] The first is attributable to deliberate government policy, as in Nigeria, where efforts were made to exclude the missions from operating in the northern areas in the belief that mission activities would be disruptive of the political structures of the Emirates. Such policies, however, were not pursued in the Gold Coast. Few efforts were made to limit the activities of the missions, although in the case of the North, some administrators viewed their work with somewhat jaundiced eyes.

Coleman sees the second factor as the accidental character of mission expansion itself, typified in the Gold Coast by missionary inability to move northward until the end of the nineteenth century. It should be conceded that this is in one sense the obvious explanation. The differences between the Colony, Ashanti, and the North could be explained by the fact that mission contact in the latter areas is comparatively recent. Similarly, it could be equally argued that urban-rural differences were due to the fact that it was more convenient to build schools in urban centres where the existence of a large, spatially concentrated child population facilitated educational development.

We should regard these factors as partial but by no means sufficient causes of the phenomenon. It has already been observed that the expansion of education in the Kingdom of Buganda during the late nineteenth and early twentieth centuries was remarkably swift in spite of the fact that this area was geographically less accessible than any part of the Gold Coast and missionaries no more numerous. Second, the Baganda were essentially a rural people and the spread of Western education was not markedly an urban phenomenon as it appeared to have been in the Gold Coast. In the light of these marked divergences from the Gold Coast pattern it seems pertinent to suggest that the accidental nature of mission penetration is one, but only one, of the factors which influence rates of educational assimilation.

Additional arguments have been employed to explain inequalities in access and its closely related phenomenon, 'wastage' at different levels of the school system. It would appear generally to be true that areas with the lowest rates of enrolment are also the areas with the greatest 'wastage'.[11]

First, some would contend that low enrolment in many areas is largely a function of poverty. Kandel observes that 'these difficulties are due to poverty which compels parents to keep their children from school or withdraw them early in order to work'.[12] The argument is by no means a new one and was advanced to explain low enrolments and wastage in nineteenth-century England. The Newcastle Commission observed at that time: 'It appears from our evidence that, though poverty may be at times alleged as a cause of absolute non-attendance it is more commonly an excuse rather than a justification, inasmuch as many parents of the very poorest class send their children to school.'[13] Similarly the census commissioners of 1851 had indicated that there was very little correlation between parental income and school attendance.[14] The absence of adequate data regarding income in the Gold Coast makes such an analysis impossible, but urban-rural differences in enrolments could be explainable on this basis only if rural incomes were uniformly lower than urban incomes, a generalization that is open to some doubt if the extent of cocoa production in some rural areas is borne in mind.

The weakness of the contention lies more in its definition of poverty as an 'absolute' level. People may not send their children to school through apparent inability to pay school expenses, yet, in practice, be prepared to expend considerably larger sums in fulfilment of traditional obligations. In this context educational expenditure is regarded as a less appropriate form of investment. Some fragmentary empirical evidence is available on this point from material collected by the present writer during a social survey of a Fanti fishing village, conducted in 1960. This community has among the lowest school enrolments in any area within the coastal zone in spite of its proximity to a coastal centre with more than adequate school facilities, and parents advanced inability to pay school fees as the principal reason for non-attendance.[15] It was observed, however, during the period of survey, when no less than three funerals took place, that sums far in excess of school fees were rapidly raised by villagers to meet funeral expenses. Second, school attendance on the part of children was not clearly correlated with parental income, since many of the most substantial members of the village community were not active in sending their children to school while others in clearly more humble circumstances made every effort to ensure regular attendance. Although we cannot disregard absolute poverty as a cause of low school enrolment, we consider the low evaluation of educational investment as against the alternative of traditional or other forms of neo-traditional expenditure to be a most significant factor.

A similar argument developed to explain variations in urban/rural enrolments is related to the concept of 'opportunity cost'. It is contended that attendance of children at school leads to the loss by the home of valuable economic services performed by them. The 'cost' of education is high in terms of economic services foregone. Though such a factor cannot be disregarded, particularly in cattle-rearing areas where young boys especially are involved in lengthy herding duties, its significance may easily be overestimated. In interviews with parents and children in this fishing community it was clear that the contribution to the village economy of boys and girls below the age of fifteen was slight. Indeed, some children remarked that they preferred going to school because they had absolutely nothing to do at home. Likewise, in a number of surveys conducted by associate students of the Institute of Education at the University College of Ghana in 1960 it was apparent in both urban and rural areas that non-school-going children, although performing duties at home, did not do so much more than school-going children as would justify their non-attendance at school.[16] This limited empirical evidence would once again throw some doubt on the particular application of the concept of opportunity cost.[17]

The foregoing attempts to explain regional variations suffer from one defect. Whether the explanations are couched in terms of rural poverty, government neglect of certain areas,[18] or opportunity costs, the analyses all tacitly assume that if it were *not* for these factors then the incidence of demand for educational facilities would have been general throughout the colonial period and that sections of the population were being deprived of a Western education through difficult objective circumstances. It is contended here that this was not the case. Even if all the factors listed had been absent, there would still have been considerable variation in the provision of education in response to a highly differentiated demand on the part of Africans themselves—as between north and south and between urban and rural areas. Since there is no indication that the population of the Gold Coast was uniformly convinced of the supposed benefits of Western education, it is appropriate to consider the pattern of local demand and relate it to a more general view of educational assimilation.

The Incidence of Demand for Education

It has been indicated in previous chapters that demand for education within the coastal zone was closely associated with the growth of towns and that the southern rural areas were quite often indifferent to the extension of schools facilities. This was no less true of Ashanti, where the chiefs' opposition to the selection of children for school persisted well into the twentieth century.

In 1901 the Methodist Church in Ashanti could only claim 8 members, and as late as 1934 this number had only increased to 2,000. The expansion of schools was extremely slow; in 1905 the Wesleyans had only seven schools with a total of 219 pupils while the Basel Mission was in roughly the same position with ten schools and 207 pupils.[19] Both government and missions at this time were clearly conscious of the fact that the Ashanti strongly opposed sending children to school.[20] It appeared that the limited support for education in Ashanti was largely restricted to the central and southern areas closer to the coast.

Low demand for schooling was even more true of the Northern Territories, where government had been active from the early twentieth century in the establishment of schools with an agricultural and technical bias.[21] Yet in 1928 the governor of the Gold Coast indicated that the general lack of support for education in the Northern Territories had obliged some schools to be closed while others were far from being filled, in spite of a special policy of free schooling, special courses, and other inducements to persuade people to send their children to school.[22] The missions were no less conscious of the problem: 'Hitherto the people have shown no desire for education and even distrust the government doctors.'[23] Even as late as 1955 resistance to enrolment was regarded as the primary cause of low attendance in the North.[24] Lest it be inferred that low enrolments here were due to the absence of a suitably 'adapted' curriculum it should be noted that in the Northern Territories more than any other, special efforts had been made in the field of agricultural education believed to be appropriate for northern peoples.

It should not be assumed, however, that the relationship between demand and schools distribution was by any means a perfect one since from the 1920's onward it would appear that the increasing demand in the coastal towns could not be met by the efforts of the government and the missions. In 1920 it was noted: 'In Accra and the coast towns generally the demand for admission is very great and this year again the unpleasant duty of refusing admission to hundreds of pupils for whom there was no accommodation, had to be performed.'[25]

In practice, therefore, there were many areas in which the government and missions did not catch up with demand, while in others they had developed more schools than were required. If the development of schools had followed the incidence of demand more closely it is likely that the relative differences between the northern and southern halves of Ghana would have been even greater during the colonial period, as would the difference between urban and rural areas. Government and missions alike were prepared to 'push' education in areas where it was not demanded to the probable detriment of districts where it was.

To demonstrate that there were significant variations in demand, however, is not to explain them. To suggest that demand for education was correlated with the degree and intensity of European contact is a generality that needs further explanation and one that needs some qualification. We must now consider what generated the demand for Western education among the Gold Coast population, why it was so uneven in its incidence and why, when it did arise, it increased so suddenly?

The transfer of educational institutions from the metropolitan power has been described above as a two-part process.[26] It involved not only the transfer of structural elements of the metropolitan system but also the incorporation of Western educational institutions by colonial peoples. The schools had to be perceived as meaningful institutions by the latter and supportive of their own goals. Under what conditions was the incorporation of institutions accomplished in the Gold Coast?

In the earlier analysis of the traditional social structures of Ghana it was observed that most of these showed a high degree of structural-functional integration with a coalescence of political, economic, and religious functions associated with a limited number of differentiated social institutions. In practice, such systems had their own 'built-in' opportunities for mobility, but these were hardly associated with the notion of social strata. Mobility was not mainly dependent on the acquisition of wealth but rather upon the manipulation of lines of descent. Such systems appear to have an initially high resistance to European contact and it would seem generally true that, throughout the Gold Coast, there was initially opposition to the enrolment of children in school. In this context we have advanced the thesis that within traditional societies of the Gold Coast pattern the demand for education will not arise until significant changes have *already* occurred in the social system as a result of European contact. Then and only then will a cumulative pattern of demand emerge. We shall refer to this process as the delayed incorporation of educational institutions (as opposed to the situation in Buganda where incorporation was immediate or certainly less dependent upon marked changes occurring initially). Although it is fair to say that in the Gold Coast the demand for education was related to the duration and intensity of European contact, it appears equally true that as between the Gold Coast and Buganda, the initial assimilative capacities of the two sets of social structures varied.

In the previous chapter we have indicated the factors which preceded the demand for education in the urban areas in the nineteenth century and conceived them to be the progressive substitution of an exchange for a subsistence economy and the creation of a differentiated occupational structure as a result of European contact. In this chapter we may extend this generalization beyond the urban areas and see whether in the rural areas there was a rough correlation between the extension of a cash-crop economy and the incidence of the demand for education.

The Demand for Education in Rural Areas

Throughout the history of the Gold Coast in this century, cocoa has remained the only substantial cash crop and still remains vitally important. Yet the main development of the crop did not take place until after the commencement of the twentieth century. Over the period 1896–1900 exports averaged only 230 tons per year but rose to over 14,000 tons per annum in 1906–19, and by 1930 they exceeded 200,000 tons per year.[27] Cocoa-growing is by no means evenly distributed throughout Ghana. Unsuitable climatic conditions made it impracticable in the Accra plains and the North, and its development was restricted to the forest belt largely in Akim, Akwapim, and Ashanti. Also, the periods at which cocoa-growing spread to the forest areas were markedly different. Production of the crop by local farmers began in the Akwapim-New Juaben areas before the turn of the century, but since then there has been a marked tendency for the centres of cocoa production to move northward and westward into Ashanti—hastened by soil exhaustion and, later, swollen shoot disease in the southeast.[28] Hence, by the end of the colonial period Ashanti constituted the main area of cocoa production. In practice, the demand for education tended to follow this movement of cocoa with increasing educational activity in the Akwapim area quite early in the century but no real evidence of mass demand in Ashanti until the thirties, when cocoa was becoming firmly established.[29]

There is no attempt here to speak in terms of simple cause and effect, but it is suggested that the development of this cash-crop economy created a series of conditions which struck at the heart of traditional society and, at the same time, favoured the acceptance of Western education by introducing a potentially greater fluidity in the traditional structures themselves.

The production of cocoa offered new opportunities for cash income and led to greater inequalities in individual wealth than could be achieved within the traditional structure. Second, the increased value of land as a factor of production within the cash-crop economy caused a gradual transition from lineage to individual claims to land ownership—one cause of the constantly growing amount of land litigation during the colonial period. Particularly among the Akan, there was an increased desire to pass on cocoa lands and income derived from cocoa production to one's own offspring rather than through the matrilineal line.[30] This led to a progressive weakening of traditional lineage ties and, to an increasing desire to avoid traditional kin obligations.[31]

Such changes were bound to weaken the traditional rights and duties of chiefs regarding land trusteeship. Each new opportunity for wealth accretion through cash-cropping opened new channels for acquiring prestige and status outside the traditional modes. The increased fluidity created within traditional structures led at the same time to a greater demand for Western education as an alternative mode of status achievement. It has been observed that a substantial amount of earnings derived from cocoa production were utilized in the education of children 'in such a way as to qualify them for any other occupation than cocoa farming'.[32] The effect therefore was to draw the educated products of the schools into an occupational structure dominated by European concepts of prestige and status.

It would be an oversimplification to regard the increased demand for education as a simple sequel to the spread of a money economy; Western education itself was a powerful force in social change directly responsible for the creation of an educated group generally antagonistic to traditional leadership. It is appropriate, therefore, to regard the extension of Western education and the enlargement of the exchange sector of the economy as mutually reinforcing factors leading to the progressive disintegration of traditional structures and their successive replacement by new concepts of social status and new modes of acquiring it. In the particular case of the Gold Coast, however, it would appear that the extension of cash-cropping was generally antecedent to the growth of a mass demand for education. Southon, in fact, has indicated that the real rise in the demand for education did not occur until after the great cocoa boom of 1907, when the lands in the eastern section of the forest belt were increasingly devoted to cocoa production.[33]

Thus, in attempting to describe the generation of differential demand for Western education in the Gold Coast we have pointed to three general factors of primary importance: (1) The establishment of effective European overrule, which created an administrative structure within which posts were available to educated Africans and which gave opportunities for the latter to displace traditional rulers.[34] (2) The creation of opportunities within an occupational structure dominated by European commercial enterprises, particularly in the coastal area. (3) The enlargement of the exchange sector through the development of cash-crop economies within rural areas which introduced increasing fluidity within traditional structures themselves.

These factors, singly or in combination, provided a social situation in which Western education could 'take'. In this sense it is readily understandable why the demand for education was so uneven and why it grew rapidly after a lengthy period of initial indifference. The contrast between the Gold Coast and Buganda is quite remarkable, since in the latter area the religious conversion of a substantial proportion of the Kiganda population and the development of early schools preceded the effective establishment of European overrule and certainly was antecedent to the development of a cash-crop economy based on cotton. Certainly more work needs to be done before adequate comparisons can be made, but these observations point to a factor of some theoretical importance regarding the assimilative capacities of two radically different types of African social structure.

Education and Urbanization

In spite of the increasing momentum of social change in rural areas, the most intensive demand for Western education occurred in rapidly growing urban centres. Hence it is advisable to examine the process of urbanization itself, since the towns constituted a paradigm for social change and manifested in more dramatic fashion the progressive modification of traditional social structures.

An outstanding feature throughout the colonial period was the dramatic growth in the size and influence of urban areas. The population of Accra rose from 17,892 in 1901 to 135,926 in 1948, a rate of growth that was paralleled in most other urban centres.[35] In 1931 there were nineteen towns in Ghana with a population of between 5,000 and 10,000, while in 1948 there were over fifty towns of this size, mostly in the south. In the same year 12 per cent of the Ghanaian population was to be found in towns with a population of 10,000 and over, and another 3·5 per cent in towns with a population of between 5,000 and 10,000.[36] Since 1948 the process of urbanization has accelerated both in terms of the absolute population of urban areas and as a proportion of the total Ghanaian population.[37]

The absolute size of urban centres is important in itself but perhaps even more significant is their ethnic heterogeneity. Using Accra once more as an example, Table 8 has shown that there were two major tribes represented in the municipality in 1948, but in the 13·6 per cent classified as 'others', there were no less than fifty other distinct tribes plus a section of 'unclassified' groupings.[38] Such heterogeneity is typical of all the larger urban units and indicates the tremendous degree of internal geographical mobility of the population primarily into the urban areas. In 1948, only 47·3 per cent of men enumerated in the larger cities were born there and only 57·5 per cent of the women.[39]

Size and heterogeneity in urban areas are antithetical to the persistence of traditional structures. These structures depend primarily upon concepts of lineage and descent, and political and social cohesion is partly maintained by creating fictional lineage ties. Furthermore, social status is frequently maintained or acquired by a similar process. A structure based upon such principles manifestly could not function effectively under urban conditions. It was in these urban centres that traditional structures were eroded most rapidly and alternative criteria of status emerged.[40]

Within the towns the weakening of 'primal' ties based on lineage, clan, or tribe is reflected in the growth of alternative associations based upon occupational criteria, such as trade unions or commercial associations, and the growth of this type of organization has been documented by Busia in the case of Sekondi-Takoradi and by Acquah in the case of Accra.[41] An additional indirect index of the disintegration of traditional societies is provided by intertribal marriage; Busia estimated that it occurred in over 30 per cent of cases in a sample of 333 families in the Sekondi-Takoradi area.[42] Also, the importance of consanguinity as a determinant of residential patterns is lessened in the light of other factors such as the criterion of ability to pay rent.[43]

Sheer size and ethnic heterogeneity within urban areas are of importance, but a factor of equal significance is the development of more complex occupational structures within them. The types of occupational opportunity open to the urban dweller obviously exceed the narrow range of activities within traditional society and, clearly, different occupations are associated with marked dispersion in levels of income and with differentiated levels of prestige. Of course, the complexity of the occupational structures of West African towns is still relatively limited. Even as late as 1960 only 16 per cent of the adult population of Accra was employed in what might be loosely described as white-collar jobs, while almost one-third of the adult population were small-scale traders and shopkeepers.[44] In addition, there was a very broad base of semiskilled or unskilled labour. Thus what we have is the commitment of virtually the total labour force to the exchange economy but with a very high proportion of 'self-employment' in minor commercial activities. The proportion of the labour force with high-level or even moderate skills is still quite small.[45] However, occupational differentiation is proceeding as can be seen from a comparison of census data for 1948 and 1960. The important thing is that such differentiation is enormously significant for the kind of social organization that is emerging within the towns.

In examining the factors of size, heterogeneity, and occupational differentiation we have indicated those factors that are deemed most likely 'to preclude the functional persistence of tribal organizations as autonomous units in the economic or political sphere'[46] and which can give rise to 'nascent' systems of social differentiation based not on descent but on alternative criteria of occupation and education.

It is unfortunate that neither urban social surveys conducted in the Gold Coast nor government publications present data showing the relationship between level of education and occupation. At certain levels the relationship must exist by definition; for example, clerks must be literate, but the degree of 'looseness' between the variables cannot be assessed. Fortes has drawn attention to a close relationship existing between occupation and education in Kumasi, but here again categories are cut across by ethnic differentials.[47] It seems clear that increasingly throughout the colonial period access to the most lucrative and prestigeful occupations was achieved to a great degree through education.

It may be contended, however, that the progressive dissolution of traditional structures did not *necessarily* imply that education, occupation, or income should become the basis of emergent status systems. This would be to ignore the very significant role of the colonial elite itself which, as we have previously observed, provided the model for emergent African conceptions of status. This appraisal was developed in our analysis of nineteenth-century developments, but it was during the twentieth century that the European minority fully emerged as a 'colonial elite' which operated as a generalized reference group upon which African aspirations were based, particularly in the towns. This elite itself was stratified by occupation and educational background; it is not surprising, therefore, that African perceptions of the occupational hierarchy should be partially based on their experience with the European minority.

It should be recognized, nonetheless, that the emergence of new types of status system during the colonial period does not necessarily posit the development of a class system along essentially European lines. European class structures based primarily on criteria of education and occupation are associated with marked divergences of sub-culture between classes. We have pointed out features in nineteenth-century Gold Coast development which indicated the degree to which the educated minority had assimilated a number of European cultural traits which differentiated it from the uneducated mass. It would be premature, however, to suggest that emergent status systems duplicated European models or that the development of social 'strata', as we understand them, was a consequence of the process. At present in the towns, social structure is a bewildering compendium of status variables based on occupation and education but shot through with ties based on ethnic, clan, and lineage loyalties. All that can be safely said is that education, through its increasingly close association with the process of occupational recruitment, operated throughout the colonial period and continues to operate as an increasingly significant variable in emergent conceptions of social status.

This lengthy analysis of the ecology of schools distribution has attempted to provide a framework by which inequalities in schools provision can be explained without recourse to *ad hoc* arguments. If, as is suggested, the differential demand for education can be basically attributed to an uneven rate of social and economic change in the Gold Coast, it is not unreasonable to suggest that marked ecological variations will similarly occur in any area where different rates of change are occurring.[48] Further, from a purely economic point of view the persistence of such variations is not necessarily to be depre-cated. In the political context the persistence of inequalities in the dis-tribution of schools facilities may be an irritant in the post-colonial period. On economic grounds alone, however, a strong case could have been made out for a policy concentrating educational efforts in areas where demand was manifest instead of one attempting to diffuse education uniformly. It is significant that both the colonial power and its successor have concentrated upon a policy of educating the 'back-ward' areas, in spite of which inequalities are almost as great as ever.[49]

In the last analysis, the basis of initial demand for Western educa-tion was economic and was a response to new opportunities provided by European contact. Busia has observed that this was clearly so in Ashanti, and it was reinforced by the belief that literacy would put the Ashanti in a position to 'compete with literate coast people and no longer remain at the mercy of alien clerks'.[50] Fortes, writing towards the end of the colonial period when the demand for education was accelerating in Ashanti, observed:

The demand for schools is sweeping the country. It is the outstanding instance of a matter on which almost full unanimity is found in every community, for which the people everywhere are prepared to make substantial economic sacrifices, and to promote which they are ready to drop factional differences. . . . It is instructive to ask why this is so. In broad terms it represents an effort to adapt Ashanti social organisation to the ever increasing demands and pressures of the various forces of European civilisation that are transforming the whole society. Thus there is a strong economic element in it, connected with the tendency to seek more satisfying and remunerative occupations than that of farming, with the tendency towards greater urbanisation, and with the ideals of economic achievement in commerce, the civil service, etc., put before young Africans by the representatives of European civilisation in the country. The combination of what appears to be a high and steadily increasing income, security for life and power and prestige which the African believes to be characteristic of the status of the European civil servant and the European business man forms the ideal to which every schoolboy aspires. Failing a 'white collar' job, any job in the European sector of the economy is more desirable than one in the African sector; and for all such jobs it is often essential and always advantageous to be educated. . . . In this the African is behaving like everybody who lives in a differentiated and changing economic system. The same process was occurring in India, Malaya and other far Eastern countries that are emerging from the pre-industrial stage; it has been taking place in England over the past 30 or 40 years. . . . In pre-industrial countries this tendency comes strongly to the fore when the European sector of the economy begins to dominate the whole economic system and thus is associated with a rapidly rising demand for schools and a European type of education. It should be noted that there are sound objective reasons for such a tendency. In a country like the Gold Coast there is and has been, for half a century at least, an increasing demand for clerical service and commerce. There is also an increasing demand for other workers of a skilled and semi-skilled type in the European sector of the economy —in mining, in transport and so on. This demand has stimulated competition to enter schools. And any African who succeeds in gaining entry to the civil service, to commerce or to the higher grades of European economic activity is manifestly better off than the majority of farmers and unskilled producers. Moreover, the demand for better and better trained clerical (and now also technical) workers is bound to increase rather than fall with further economic and social development. The enthusiasm for schools, though it is uncritical and naïve, therefore has a sound economic basis, given the present economic structure of the country.[51]

By stressing the economic basis of demand it is not implied that purely 'prestige' elements were absent. The status of an 'educated man' was important, particularly in the towns, even where it was not linked to direct economic advantages. Nonetheless by indicating that the mainspring was economic in nature we have also implied that demand was most specifically oriented to those types of education which promised the greatest rewards. Educationists have made a great deal of the 'irrational' nature of African demand for white-collar jobs and the unrealistic nature of their ambitions for an academic education. On the contrary, within the framework of colonial society, African aspirations were eminently realistic and geared closely to the realities of the occupational structure. What educationists have often regarded as a 'non-functional' education, whatever the phrase may mean, proved to be an eminently functional one in the light of African expectations and aspirations.

Education and Occupational Opportunities

During the nineteenth century, as we have seen, the occupational structure of the towns was such that in terms of employment opportunities and future income levels there was a realistic desire on the part of Africans for clerical employment. This reflected itself in a demand for an academic type of education. There was an almost total lack of interest in agricultural or technical education, which were markedly inferior substitutes on income criteria alone. The error of most nineteenth-century educators had been to suppose that it was the curriculum of the schools which was responsible for this type of educational demand and not African perceptions of the realities of the occupational structure. Even where agricultural and technical schools had been started they were not successful, and, in terms of our analysis, it could hardly be expected that the curriculums of these types of schools would have had any effect in diverting students back to agricultural or technical pursuits.

The entire later period of colonialism tells the same story. The preceding quotation by Fortes has indicated that the demand for technical workers came very late in the colonial period, but the nature of European overrule and the activities of European controlled commercial enterprises made it inevitable that employment needs be more heavily oriented towards clerical workers to fill the lower echelons of the administration. Access to such remunerative employment was more clearly guaranteed by academic than by technical forms of education.

The demand for technicians and craftsmen was never high. By 1948

133

the category of skilled workers and artisans accounted for less than 10 per cent of the male labour force and this figure included traditional craftsmen.[52] Paradoxically, the efforts of the government to stimulate technical education resulted in actual unemployment among the products of these schools, few of whom attempted to found their own businesses. By the end of the colonial period the products of technical schools were frequently obliged to find employment in the police force.[53] Similar problems were apparent in the propensity of individuals trained in technical, scientific, and professional fields to enter jobs not specifically related to their training.[54]

In addition, the academic sector of the educational system had one pre-eminent advantage over all technical alternatives. By their very nature in colonial times, trade, technical, or agricultural schools were terminal institutions training individuals in specified future economic roles. To be trained as a mechanic meant, for the most part, to remain a mechanic, to be trained as a carpenter was to remain a carpenter— the most glittering prizes of educational mobility were closed to the products of these schools. But the academic system and, above all, the secondary schools provided the intermediate link in a chain of institutions leading to higher instruction and entry into the professions most highly regarded (and incidentally the most lucrative), those of medicine and law.[55] However statistically remote the chances of an individual reaching these levels were, there was at least the opportunity to do so and African students had constantly before them the image of those who had achieved such distinction through the possession of academic qualifications.[56]

Further, the expansion of the bureaucracy had opened a new range of opportunities for the graduates of the secondary schools and now provided an alternative to the 'professional' outlets. It should not be assumed, however, that public services ever absorbed a high proportion of the Gold Coast population. So far as overall opportunities for Africans within public service were concerned, by 1951 people employed on a wage or salaried basis within the public employment sector only accounted for 93 thousand or 7·7 per cent of an estimated labour force of 1·2 million. This public sector did contain 41 per cent of all recorded employees. This is to say, although 82 per cent of the estimated Ghanaian labour force was mainly engaged in subsistence or cocoa-farming and petty trading, of the remaining 18 per cent employed on a wage or salary basis, no less than two-fifths were employed by government.[57] This suggests that although overall employment opportunities were not great for the products of the schools, they were virtually as high in public service as they were in commercial fields, providing a relatively simple explanation of why public employment became a realistic alternative in the colonial period.

At the highest levels of the bureaucratic structure opportunities were extremely limited. By 1939 senior posts in the establishment only numbered 241 and all but 41 of these posts were manned by Europeans. As late as 1952 when these posts numbered 1,918 as a result of post-war expansion, only 42 per cent of them were staffed by Africans. The progressive 'Africanization' of the top levels of the bureaucracy was extremely slow throughout the colonial period and fell far short of the projected estimates of earlier governors.[58]

Notwithstanding these limitations it should be clear that given the occupational structure of Ghana during the colonial period the often criticized tendency for the products of the schools to enter white-collar jobs particularly in government service was actually realistic. Even statistically, opportunities were greater here than in the technical field while the chance to achieve the highest levels, if not great, were probably as good as they were in commerce. Furthermore, government service enjoyed conditions of security and permanence not necessarily duplicated elsewhere.

It is equally clear that entry into these most preferred posts was achieved through the academic secondary school, of which there were relatively few throughout the period. It is unfortunate that little material exists on the occupational destinations of secondary-school-leavers during the early period. In the case of Achimota School, by 1935 over 30 per cent of the graduated student body had entered the civil service, excluding those who would proceed to further studies and then enter the service. Though no data are available for Mfantsipim it is interesting to note that this latter school, as compared with Achimota, has a much greater reputation for meeting the needs of the bureaucracy, and it is possible that far more of its products entered government employment.

In this context, it is easy to see why the most rapidly growing sector of the educational system during the late colonial period was the academic secondary school (Table 5). Given the occupational structure we have described, an academic education was pre-eminently a *vocational* education allowing entry into the most prestigeful and highly paid occupations. The idea that the academic secondary schools were responsible for producing individuals who disdained manual tasks and hence sought clerical employment is a notion that dies hard, and the belief that the curriculum of these schools is responsible for dysfunctionalities in the employment situation is still quite widespread among educationists. This belief is the opposite of the actual relationship between the schools and the occupational structure. White-collar aspirations stemmed from a realistic perception of occupational opportunities and from a recognition that the academic grammar school provided access to them. The African did not enter clerical employment because he had been to an academic secondary school; he went to an academic secondary school because it provided most effective entry into such employment. The prestige of the academic secondary school had perhaps less to do with the courses of study that it provided than with the prestige and income levels of the occupants that it trained for.[59]

Another factor of considerable importance was the quest for 'parity' in education. However benevolent the intentions of the colonial rulers, all colonial societies were 'caste' structures composed of a subordinate indigenous caste and a superimposed endogamous colonial elite. Although Africans could aspire to a limited number of higher occupations, they could not, by definition, be members of the European caste. Similarly, their efforts to obtain parity of conditions with the latter entailed access to educational institutions of an identical character with those of the metropolitan power. Deviations from the metropolitan curriculum, particularly at the secondary level, were, as we shall see in our later comments on Achimota, regarded with the greatest suspicion. Western education, in fact, remained the most visible and tangible manifestation of European power, hence access to that power demanded entry to the type of education provided in the metropole itself.

It seems a valid sociological generalization that subordinate castes will normally attempt to emulate the social characteristics of the dominant caste. In the case of Western education this emulation would appear to have been based on eminently realistic perceptions of the power structure of the colonial period. Where Africans were involved with the European elite in an admittedly unequal competition for the highest rungs of the occupational ladder, access to these posts was determined by their ability to hold equivalent or often superior qualifications and to demonstrate their equality with the elite. Tentatively it might be argued that within caste-type colonial situations where mobility within 'nascent' or 'emergent' social structures provides the basic motivation for education, there will be a tendency for colonial peoples to demand educational equivalence whether the colonial elite deem it educationally wise or not. We shall return to a more careful consideration of African attitudes in a later section on theories of 'cultural adaptation', but the most succinct statement by Africans regarding the advisability of deviations in the curriculum is to be found in pages relating to South Africa. In connection with the establishment of a proposed Inter-State Native College in 1908 it was observed that:

The sound proposition that the college should from the commencement adapt itself to the existing educational needs of the country, and, proceeding where necessary on tentative lines, be developed into a College of University standing, was strongly opposed by certain educated Natives who felt that this was an insidious attempt to repress their people. One of these Natives said that this proposition meant that they were to get a stone instead of bread. They were anxious to get higher education. Where did they see it? They wanted the same education, not a bastard education, not to begin with new experiments. Even if this curriculum was bad, it was not their place to patch it up and correct it. They wanted the same higher education as the white people.[60]

The attitude evinced might not have been desirable in the light of educational theories but it did contain a shrewd appraisal of the social functions of education as an instrument of mobility. Given the unwillingness of the colonial power to exert total control over the quantity and content of African education—as was certainly the case in British territories—the development of education on essentially metropolitan lines was largely inevitable. No other system could have met African aspirations so effectively.

Education and Unemployment

In attempting to indicate the relatively sound economic and social basis upon which African expectations were based in the colonial period it should not be overlooked that serious problems did arise so far as the employment situation for many school graduates was concerned. Attention has already been drawn to the existence of a number of unemployed literates in the coastal towns during the nineteenth century; this remained a chronic feature during colonial times. However, as a result of the quickening expansion of the educational system during the late forties the problem was becoming increasingly acute. Unfortunately, no adequate statistics on unemployment are available for the colonial period, since registration at labour exchanges was voluntary and represented only a tiny proportion of individuals seeking employment.[61] Busia, however, reported as a result of his investigations in 1950 that an extremely serious problem of unemployment had emerged in Sekondi-Takoradi, a situation that was certainly duplicated in other major towns.[62] Legislative Council debates during the period also indicate a growing concern with the incidence of unemployment among school-leavers and showed that government was far from unaware of its extent.

The causes for such unemployment were normally attributed to the academic curriculums of the schools, and 'vocational and agricultural education' was deemed the solution for the problem.[63] Some doubts have been cast upon the validity of this analysis; the writer contends that vocational aspirations were less determined by the educational system than by African perceptions of relative occupational rewards. In practice, the schools played only a modest part in shaping aspirations. Schools by themselves could no more create technologically minded individuals than they could create agriculturally minded individuals.[64] Attempts to solve the unemployment problem by 'vocational' education projects were unlikely to be successful, since the educationists' analysis of the causes of unemployment was based on questionable assumptions.

Nigeria provides an analogous case:

> For half a century commentators on Nigeria have said that school leavers refuse to work with their hands: 'they want white-collar jobs', is an expression still frequently heard. The implication is always that the school leavers are lacking in some undefined morality. The school-leaver turns out, however, to be more perceptive of economic opportunity than the commentator. Naturally the school leaver will make his strongest bid for the class of job with the most appealing net advantages of which money income and its regularity are the principal ingredients. If a school-leaver can win a job as a junior clerk, or as a messenger in a government office, at £100 a year, and if he watches his living costs carefully, very likely he will be better off than his father who is farming in the home village.[65]

In this context it seems clear that the issue of unemployment in this type of economy is not at bottom one of 'functional' or 'nonfunctional' education. Unemployment is not related to the character of the schools *per se* but is rather a dysfunctional consequence of the relationship between a rapidly expanding school output and a virtually stagnant economy. Much has been made of the fact that the schools produced too many clerical aspirants, but the fact that technical employment possibilities were even more limited during the colonial period is conveniently forgotten. The problem was not that schools were producing too many people with a particular type of training while other opportunities were available; whatever training was given, there were insufficient employment opportunities for school-leavers in *any* sector of the exchange economy. It was and remains a problem of general unemployment within the exchange sector, not a 'frictional' form of unemployment due to the maladaptation of an educational system.

The nub of the problem therefore lies in the slowness with which a large subsistence economy is converted to an exchange economy. As late as 1953, just after the effective close of the colonial period, over

50 per cent of the adult Ghanaian population was involved in purely subsistence activity, while another 20 per cent were cocoa farmers.[66] Apart from the individuals involved in petty trading activities, only approximately 8 per cent of the population was employed within the exchange economy, including both commercial and government activities. As has been indicated, however, the products of the schools were motivated by a desire to enter paid employment within this relatively small sector of the economy. It was not that they desired white-collar employment alone but that education implied, for them, a movement from the subsistence sector to jobs within the exchange sector.

Where education is regarded as an investment in future employment opportunities within an existing exchange economy and where return to the land is an admission of failure, then unemployment among school-leavers would appear to be a probable consequence *irrespective* of the type of education given.[67]

The Political Consequences of Educational Expansion

The previous analysis has implied that mounting unemployment before 1951 had little to do with the presence of 'colonialism' *per se*. Indeed, as we hope to show in a later chapter, this feature has been even *more* pronounced since the end of colonial rule. The notion that the presence of representatives of the colonial power deprived most graduates of African schools of positions is manifestly absurd. During the colonial period the number of expatriates never exceeded 6,000, and in most cases the nature of the jobs that they held was such that they did not displace the bulk of school-leavers. Nonetheless, resentment was felt by suitably qualified Africans so far as higher level positions were concerned, where there is little doubt that more effective 'Africanization' could have been accomplished at an earlier date.

The previous chapter has shown how quite early on, Western education was indirectly responsible for creating a group to whom access into the highest levels of the bureaucracy was denied and who constituted the core of the early Nationalist movement on the Gold Coast. It was this minority of professional lawyers and intelligentsia who supplied the leadership of Nationalist activities throughout most of the colonial period. So long as the mass of the population remained unaffected by the lack of opportunity within the occupational structure the Nationalists could not count upon mass support for their activities.

The post-1945 period showed a radical transformation in the nature and personnel of the Nationalist movement. In effect, it represented the development of a mass organization, not controlled by the earlier Nationalists themselves but by a group with less claim to constituting an 'intelligentsia' and deriving their support, principally in the urban areas, from the increasing number of unemployed primary-school-leavers. Apter has indicated convincingly that post-war nationalism, which resulted in the effective transfer of power in 1951, derived its impetus from the increasing number of Standard VII boys who were unable to find employment in a slowly developing economy.[68]

The genesis of post-war nationalism in Ghana has received exhaustive treatment elsewhere, and certainly it must be regarded as the major unanticipated consequence of educational transfer. Just as Western education in the earlier days was to provide the ideological charter for the early Nationalists, it was later to provide the raw material for the development of a mass movement. Though unemployment among the mass of school-leavers was not a result of the colonial situation itself, it was sufficient that the frustrated products of the schools should *believe* it to be so.[69] Whether colonialism had maintained itself or not, it would appear probable that the same situation regarding employment opportunities would have existed, a judgment that would seem amply borne out by events since 1951.

Parallel with the growth of a mass Nationalist movement was an acceleration of a process that had commenced in the previous century: the gradual erosion of the powers of traditional rulers and their replacement by individuals whose self-concepts were more coincident with that of the colonial elite. Underlying the political changes in the Gold Coast there was a latent or active conflict between traditional rulers and the educated group.

British attitudes towards the growing educated segment of the population were, to say the least, ambivalent. Although they were obliged to rely increasingly upon the latter to fulfil administrative functions, particularly in local government, the growing influence of the educated minority was perceived as a direct threat to the maintenance of traditional authority. The later colonial period was marked by a stiffening of attitude on the part of the administration towards the educated group. As a result of the development of theories of indirect rule there was a consistent attempt, beginning in the twenties, to reconstitute traditional authorities. Between the Native Administration Ordinance of 1927 and 1944 efforts were made to strengthen chiefly authority and traditional councils and to incorporate them into a viable Native Authority system.[70] It was not until 1948, in fact, that a lessening of the power of the chiefs was recommended, as a result of a belated recognition of the influence of Western education.[71]

Such attempts to recreate traditional authorities and use them as the basis for development were, as we have seen, largely unworkable. At the same time that the colonial administration was attempting to bolster traditional authority it was obliged to utilize different criteria of recruitment in staffing positions within the local administrations. Long before the British attempted to apply consistent notions of indirect rule, the basis upon which traditional forms of authority had rested had been swept away in the larger towns and was fast being eroded in other areas. It appeared, in fact, that at the same time the administration was working for the strengthening of the system of chiefship, it was also encouraging forces opposed to it.

The most obvious factor leading to the decline of traditional authority was Western education itself. We have drawn attention to its importance in the nineteenth-century Gold Coast, and by 1915 the growing opposition to traditional authority by educated elements was manifest in Ashanti.[72] The administration, although cognizant of the situation, never reconciled itself to the fundamental incompatibility between theories of indirect rule and those forces which had been set in motion by European overrule. Thus the Acting Secretary for Native Affairs, speaking in 1927, observed:

In a country where the overwhelming mass of the inhabitants are illiterate it is but natural that those members of the native community who have received some education should exert a degree of influence disproportionate to their numbers. It is probable that if every chief in the country and every commoner as well, were literate there would be no clash of political aspirations because the people would not tolerate any attack on their political institutions. At present, however, less than a half of the chiefs and but a small fraction of the people are literate and, as only a restricted political career is open to the educated commoner within the compass of a Native State, it sometimes happens that the educated African, attracted by the strange but convenient doctrine of the equality of men, becomes a disciple of the European conception of government through representative institutions and seeks to bring about their introduction into the country. The consummation of such an ideal which would result in reducing the chiefs to the position of mere puppets who would then have no more influence on the government of the Native State (through the ballot box) than the humblest of their subjects, naturally carries with it the destruction of the native system of government.[73]

The governor, commenting on the above remarks, observed that the Constitution had to be founded on chiefly councils which were regarded as the breakwaters defending native institutions against the disintegrating waves of Western civilization.[74] It is surprising that in spite of its early realization of what Western education was doing the administration could never reconcile itself to the progressive weakening of traditional authority or its degeneration into a number of formal structures stripped of their traditional functions and sanctions.

Leading chiefs were no less conscious of the potential effect of Western education upon their office. In 1920 a 'Committee of Educationalists' recommended the creation of a secondary school to be particularly utilized by the heirs of chiefs, an attempt that harked back to Maclean's much earlier policy and which was compatible with current notions of indirect rule.[75] In applauding the suggestions, Nana Ofori Atta, paramount chief of Akim-Abuakwa observed:

> ... If the educated native is going to be trained for him to look down on, or to tell his parents, relatives or chiefs in that sort of sarcastic language to which we have been accustomed 'you are not advanced and skilled as I am, you do not know the tricks of the civilised world, you do not deserve the leadership naturally conferred on you, etc.', and then, without any authority from the right source places himself in a position to which he has no claim, then I fear our path to civilisation will have been badly made. If the educated native is not going to keep within the limit to which his birthright entitles him and if in his desire to help his people and his country, rather than becoming rightly, a member of Advisory Board, he constitute himself, without the necessary mandate, a ruling or legislative body, it would be no wonder if our expensive educational schemes sustained a failure. ...[76]

Notwithstanding the opposition of chiefs and the ambivalent policy of the colonial administration, the spread of Western education implied the almost inevitable dissolution of chiefly authority and made it impossible for the development of traditional institutions to be utilized effectively within the process of social change in the Gold Coast. The reduction of the chiefs to the position of 'puppets' was not effected during the colonial period but was one of the triumphs of nationalism in 1951, a final victory for Western education!

REFERENCES

1. See chap. iii.

2. The overall rate of expansion of the population of the Gold Coast was calculated to be approximately 1·75 per cent per annum in 1948 or between 40,000 and 70,000 per year from 1900. Gold Coast, *Census of Population, 1948* (Accra: Government Printer, 1950), p. 4. These figures are almost certainly an underestimate.

3. An Anglican spokesman referring to the Gold Coast observed:

> With regard to education, in the opinion of the heads of the missions, the next ten years are of vital importance. If the various missions can rise to the opportunity, nine-tenths of the education in this colony will be under religious auspices. Should they, on the other hand, fail to do so,

The Dynamics of Educational Growth in the Late Colonial Period

the government will be forced to undertake the whole education of the Colony, thereby depriving the missions of what is undoubtedly their most powerful instrument in evangelisation.

Missionary Council of the Church Assembly, *The Call From Africa* (Westminster: Press & Publications Board of the Church Assembly, 1926), p. 118.

4. No attempt was made to regulate the opening of private secondary schools until 1942 when the Education Committee of 1937–41 recommended that these institutions should not be allowed to open without the consent of the Director of Education, subject to registration and inspection. Gold Coast, *Report of the Education Committee, 1937–1941* (Accra: Government Printer, 1942), p. 13. Since that date the provisions have been no more than a formality. The quality of many of these private secondary institutions is a matter for some doubt; in eighteen private secondary institutions which existed in 1948, out of a total staff of 167 only 8 were trained teachers. Gold Coast, *Legislative Council Debates, 1948*, No. 3, p. 43.

5. W. B. Mumford and R. Jackson, 'The Problem of Mass Education in Africa', *Africa*, XI, No. 2 (October 1938), 187–207.

6. It should be noted that rural/urban variations may be heightened by the influx of rural children seeking education in the towns. The extent of this practice is unknown, but it is very unlikely that such a movement could fully explain urban/rural differences.

7. G. Balandier, 'Social Changes and Problems in Negro Africa', *Africa in the Modern World*, ed. Calvin W. Stillman (Chicago: University of Chicago Press, 1955), p. 59. Balandier concludes 'one must . . . emphasize the coincidence which exists between urbanization, modernization, economic expansion and intellectual development which has always characterized the city in all places and all periods of history'.

8. M. Fortes, R. W. Steel, and P. Ady, 'The Ashanti Survey 1945–1946: An Experiment in Social Research', *Geographical Journal*, CX (1947), 161.

9. Ioné Acquah, *Accra Survey* (London: University of London Press, 1958), p. 112.

10. Gabriel A. Almond and James S. Coleman, ed., *The Politics of Developing Areas* (Princeton: Princeton University Press, 1960), p. 281.

11. A glance at the excellent series of statistics produced since 1952, Gold Coast and Ghana, *Statistical Reports*, Series I, Nos. 1–7, 1952–1960 (Accra: Government Printer), indicates that the rate of drop-out in the Northern Territories is still far greater than it is in the south and that wastage is negatively correlated with enrolments in urban areas.

12. I. L. Kandel, 'Problems of Comparative Education', *International Review of Education*, II, No. 1 (1956), 8.

13. Great Britain, *Report of the Commissioners Appointed To Inquire into the State of Popular Education in England* (6 vols.; London: George E. Eyre and William Spottiswoode, 1861), 178.

14. Great Britain, *Census of Population 1851, Education England and Wales. Report and Tables* (London: George E. Eyre and William Spottiswoode, 1854), p. xxxix.

15. During 1960 only 18 per cent of the eligible child population was attending school compared with an average enrolment figure of over 40 per cent for the Western Region.

16. University College of Ghana, 'Surveys of Household Chores' (student manuscripts, Institute of Education, 1960).

17. See also Susan Elkan, 'Primary School Leavers in Uganda', *Comparative Education Review*, IV, No. 2 (October 1960), 108. In her excellent study she

143

observed that there was no evidence that opportunity costs operated in that area as a factor in wastage or non-attendance.

18. The neglect of rural areas was assumed by the Phelps-Stokes Commission to be the primary cause of areal variation, upon what evidence is not very clear. Jesse Jones, *Education in Africa: A Study of West South and Equatorial Africa by the African Education Commission* (New York: Phelps-Stokes Fund, 1922), p. 29.

19. A. E. Southon, *Gold Coast Methodism: The First Hundred Years, 1835–1935* (London: Cargate Press, 1934), p. 149.

20. K. A. Busia, *The Position of the Chief in the Modern Political System of Ashanti* (London: International African Institute; Oxford University Press, 1951), p. 131.

21. Sir Gordon Guggisberg, *A Review of the Events of 1920–1926 and the Prospects for 1927–1928* (Accra: Government Printer, 1927), p. 198.

22. Gold Coast, The Governor's Address, *Legislative Council Debates, 1928–29* (Accra: Government Printer, 1930), p. 15.

23. Missionary Council of the Church Assembly, *op. cit.*, p. 120.

24. Gold Coast, *Economic Survey, 1955* (Accra: Office of the Government Statistician, 1956), p. 55.

25. Gold Coast, *Report of the Education Department, 1920* (Accra: Government Printer), p. 5.

26. See Introduction.

27. F. M. Bourret, *The Gold Coast* (Stanford, 1949), p. 26.

28. By 1952, at the close of the colonial period, Ashanti produced 48·6 per cent of the total crop. During the first decade of the century it had produced virtually nothing. Gold Coast, *Economic Survey, 1955*, p. 25.

29. An interesting comparison here can be made between the districts of Accra and Akwapim-New Juaben. If the 1948 figures for Accra Municipality are removed from those for the Accra District as a whole, the educational level of the latter for Standard VII and above drops to 3·3 per cent of the population, below the average for the Gold Coast. Yet if the figures for Koforidua are removed from those for the whole Akwapim-New Juaben District the level for the rural areas still remains at 10·7 per cent or considerably higher than the Gold Coast average. It is significant that the Accra plain was not suitable for the growth of cocoa and most people outside the municipality remain subsistence farmers while in Akwapim-New Juaben, cocoa cash-cropping was an early development.

30. Busia, *Position of the Chief*, p. 127. In practice, laws relating to land tenure are still in a state of flux, but for a lengthy period there has been an increasing *de facto* recognition of individual claims to cocoa lands.

31. M. Fortes, R. W. Steel, and P. Ady, 'The Ashanti Survey', p. 164.

32. *Ibid.*, p. 165.

33. A. E. Southon, *Gold Coast Methodism*, p. 123.

34. See chap. iii.

35. Gold Coast, *Census of Population, 1901 and 1948*. See also R. W. Steel, 'Africa: The Environmental Setting', *Annals of the American Academy of Political and Social Science*, CCXCVIII (March 1955), 7.

36. Computed from Gold Coast Government, *Census of Population, 1948*. See also Cardinall, *The Gold Coast, 1931* (Accra: Government Printer, 1932), p. 158.

37. In 1960 the population of Accra stood at over 337,000 while that of Kumasi exceeded 180,000. In that year no less than 23·0 per cent of the Ghanaian population lived in towns with a population of 5,000 and above. Ghana, *Population Census of 1960, Advance Report of Volumes III and IV* (Accra: Census Office, 1962), p. 1.

144

38. Gold Coast, *Census of Population, 1948.*

39. *Ibid.* For further details regarding the extent of internal population migration see Cardinall, *The Gold Coast, 1931,* p. 155. Further material is also available in R. B. Davidson, *Migrant Labour in the Gold Coast* (Legon: University College of the Gold Coast, 1954). (Mimeo.) Internal migration into urban areas was by no means confined to British territories but was equally evident in French area. See G. Balandier, 'Approche Sociologique des Brazzavilles Noires; Etude Préliminaire', *Africa,* XXII, No. 1 (January 1952), 22–34.

40. This is not to suggest that lineage and ethnic ties do not persist in the urban environment. Both Rouch and Acquah have pointed to the size and persistence of ethnic associations in the urban areas of Ghana. See Acquah, *op. cit.,* pp. 104–7, and Jean Rouch, 'Migrations au Ghana', *Journal de la Société des Africanistes,* XXVI, Nos. 1–2 (1956), 163–64. Certainly, such associations are particularly strong among recent immigrants, but Rouch's characterization of this as 'supertribalization' seems to confuse short-run and long-run effects. The initial impact of urban centres may lead to the proliferation of ethnic associations in the short run. However, with the growth of a more stabilized urban population it is likely that such ethnic bonds will weaken in the face of other types of association based upon occupational or 'class' lines. At present, urban social structures are still dualistic. For urban citizens, therefore,

le fait que la ville représente une réalité récente, une société dont la structure est en devenir, soumise à de continuelles transformations, explique que le citadin éduqué continue le plus souvent à se situer par rapport à sa société d'origine plutôt que par rapport au milieu urbain . . . , il participie ainsi aux divisions et antagonismes qu'impliquent ses appartenances ethniques et familiales.

G. Balandier, 'Growth of a Middle Class in French West Africa', *Development of a Middle Class in Tropical and Sub-Tropical Areas* (Brussels: International Institute of Differing Civilisations, 1956), p. 413. See also Joan Aldous, 'Urbanization, the Extended Family and Kinship Ties in West Africa', *Social Forces,* XXXXI, No. 1 (October 1962), 6–12, for a very succinct review of the literature concerning the persistence of traditional forms of social organization in urban areas.

41. See Acquah, *op. cit.,* pp. 82–91 and K. A. Busia, *Report on a Social Survey of Sekondi-Takoradi* (London: Crown Agents for the Colonies, 1950), pp. 25–28.

42. *Ibid.,* p. 29.

43. Acquah, *op. cit.,* p. 50.

44. See Ghana, *Population Census of 1960, Advance Report of Volumes III and IV,* p. 77.

45. As late as 1954 just over 33 per cent of all persons employed in government service in Accra were totally unskilled personnel working at a daily rate. Acquah, *op. cit.,* p. 64.

46. Daryll Forde, 'The Conditions of Social Development in West Africa', *Civilisations,* III, No. 4 (October 1953), 471–89.

47. Fortes, *The Ashanti Social Survey: A Preliminary Report. Rhodes-Livingstone Journal* (London, 1948), p. 29, and *The Ashanti Survey, 1945–1946, Geographical Journal,* CX (1947), 161. Unfortunately neither of these articles produces tabular information. Material on the relationship between education and occupation in Jinja, Uganda, in 1949 indicates that a clear relationship exists in this area though there is a degree of 'looseness' in the association as one would expect in new and rapidly expanding townships of this type. Cyril and Rhona Sofer, *Jinja Transformed* (Kampala: East African Institute of Social Research, 1955), p. 44.

145

48. See C. Arnold Anderson, 'The Impact of the Educational System on Technological Change and Modernization', in *Industrialization and Society*, ed. Bert F. Hoselitz and Wilbert E. Moore (UNESCO: Mouton, 1963), pp. 259–76.

49. It is interesting to note with respect to the high correlation between urbanization and education that not only does demand for education develop most strongly in the towns but that its impact on rural youth may produce an increased flow into towns. Fortes observed in Asokore, Ashanti, that 95 per cent of village boys who had passed through the local school had left the area for urban centres. Fortes, *The Ashanti Social Survey: A Preliminary Report*, p. 29. The present writer's research in a Fanti village would confirm this observation. Of all individuals completing ten years of primary education during the preceding ten years, only one remained in the village. The effect of substantial migration of this type would be to increase urban/rural differences even further.

50. Busia, *Position of the Chief*, p. 132.

51. Fortes, *The Ashanti Social Survey*, p. 32.

52. Gold Coast, *Census of Population, 1948*, p. 21.

53. Gold Coast, *Legislative Assembly Debates, 1952*, No. 2, p. 24. A similar situation would also appear to have existed in other parts of Africa during the 1930's. See Scott, *Yearbook of Education, 1938* (London, 1938), pp. 728–30.

54. Gold Coast, *Legislative Assembly Debates, 1952*, No. 2, p. 72.

55. For the degree to which law was still regarded as the most desirable of all careers see an address by Nana Ofori Atta, Gold Coast, *Legislative Council Debates, 1924–1925*, p. 325.

56. By the end of the colonial period the number of Africans in the 'higher professions' of law and medicine must have been extremely small. In a schedule administered to household heads during the 1948 census which gave a return from 195,639 adult males only 102 or 0·05 per cent were in these professional categories. Computed from Gold Coast, *Census of Population, 1948*.

57. Computed from Ghana, *Labour Statistics, 1957* (Accra: Office of the Government Statistician, 1958), p. 3, and Ghana, *Economic Survey, 1958* (Accra: Office of the Government Statistician, 1959), p. 21.

58. Sir Charles Jeffries, 'Recent Social Welfare Developments in British Tropical Africa', *Colonial Review*, III, No. 2 (June 1943), 49. Gold Coast, *Legislative Assembly Debates, 1952*, No. 3, pp. 545–46; Bourret, *op. cit.*, p. 73.

59. Lest the Gold Coast situation appear unique in this respect, Banks commenting on the strength of the English secondary grammar-school tradition and its strong association with white-collar employment remarks:

> Secondary grammar school boys have not entered industrial employment because commercial and other clerical posts seemed to offer them greater prospects of advancement. Moreover, the low social status of much manual work does not, it is suggested, derive from the school, but from its position in the social and especially the economic structure of modern England, and further, the high prestige of the grammar school, far from conferring prestige on the professional and clerical occupations, derives its own prestige from the occupation for which it prepares. . . . It is significant that the technical posts which appear to be attracting grammar school boys since the war are precisely those which offer the greatest financial prospects as well as the highest prestige.

Olive Banks, *Parity and Prestige in English Secondary Education* (London: Routledge & Kegan Paul, 1955), p. 190.

60. C. T. Loram, *The Education of the South African Native* (New York: Columbia University Press, 1915), p. 22.

61. Acquah, *op. cit.*, p. 77.

62. Busia, *Social Survey*, pp. 61–84.

63. There was particularly active discussion of the problem in the twenties.

The Dynamics of Educational Growth in the Late Colonial Period

See Gold Coast Government, *Legislative Council Debates, 1924–1925*, p. 66.

64. A striking independent confirmation of this analysis is contained in a series of recent research findings on unemployment in Nigeria where an analogous position exists. The writer states:

> A second piece of folklore about school-leavers produces the belief that by making massive changes in the curricula of primary schools that school-leavers will be encouraged to remain in villages and work on home farms. . . . The truth is that school-leavers' attitudes toward employment are determined almost exclusively by what is happening outside the schools, in the society and economy. No amount of instruction by itself—whether in primary or post-primary schools—can make modern farmers.

Arch C. Callaway, 'Primary School-Leavers in Nigeria: No. 3', (*West Africa*, 8 April 1961), p. 371.

65. *Ibid.*

66. W. A. Lewis, *Report on Industrialisation and the Gold Coast* (Accra: Government Printer, 1953), p. 2. See also Dudley Seers and C. R. Ross, *Report on the Financial and Physical Problems of Development in the Gold Coast* (Accra: Office of the Government Statistician, 1952).

67. See also Elkan, *op. cit.*, p. 108, and Callaway, 'School Leavers in Nigeria: No. 2', *West Africa* (1 April 1961), p. 353.

68. Apter, *op. cit.*, p. 275.

69. The colonial power was not unaware that the spread of Western education was one of the primary factors behind the development of the Nationalist movement. See Great Britain, Colonial Office No. 231, *Report of the Commission of Enquiry into Disturbances in the Gold Coast* (London: H.M.S.O., 1948).

70. Bourret, *op. cit.*, pp. 54–60.

71. Great Britain, *Colonial Office No. 231*, p. 63.

72. Busia, *Position of the Chief*, p. 108.

73. Guggisberg, *Review of the Events*, p. 17.

74. *Ibid.*, p. 73.

75. Gold Coast Government, *Report of the Committee of Educationalists, 1920.* p. 29.

76. *Ibid.*, p. 82.

V

PROBLEMS OF EDUCATIONAL POLICY IN THE LATE COLONIAL PERIOD

THE last two or three decades of colonial rule were full of controversy regarding the nature and content of African education, decades during which a more coherent policy began to emerge. We may note, however, that it was a programme convincing enough on paper but one that was extraordinarily difficult to translate into reality.

British Policy Regarding Technical Education

Previous chapters have examined in some detail the contention that early administrators in the Gold Coast showed little interest in the development of technical and agricultural education. The rather surprising conclusion was reached that those educational planners were more interested in the provision of such types of education than they were in transplanting substantially academic types of education into Africa. Yet to the superficial observer the neglect of technical education has always appeared to be characteristic of British colonial policy.[1] The observation would seem to be justified by the fact that by 1951 technical institutions in the Gold Coast numbered only twenty-three and enrolled 3,330 pupils or less than 1 per cent of pupils in all types of schools.[2] Yet the limited development of technical schools does not indicate that the administration was disinterested in the provision of technical education. Indeed, up to the end of the colonial period proponents of technical instruction met with the same African indifference as their predecessors had struggled against during the nineteenth century.

In 1908 a committee was appointed by the governor 'to revise educational rules, establish a training institution for teachers, to establish a technical school and to introduce hand and eye, industrial and agricultural training into the schools'.[3] The resulting Education

148

Rules of 1909 attempted to introduce widespread industrial training into the schools beginning with simple crafts and developing progressively advanced instruction. This was to be supplemented by agricultural instruction as a compulsory subject for the purpose of grants-in-aid. Additionally a government technical school was created in Accra to supplement the work of the Basel Mission.[4] Thereafter agricultural and craft courses were to remain parts of primary education within the grant-aided sector. The success of this attempt to counteract a predominantly 'bookish' education is open to some doubt.

The development of a more 'vocationally' oriented education received additional impetus with the appointment by Governor Guggisberg of a new 'Committee of Educationalists' in 1920 to survey education in the Gold Coast. The conclusions of the committee indicated a basic preoccupation with questions of technical and agricultural education at all levels of the school system. The committee strongly advocated a plethora of manual activities such as gardening, woodwork, metal work, and clay work to overcome the 'mere bookishness' of school instruction.[5] Furthermore it suggested the establishment of a new secondary school with a marked technical bias and a great deal of practical work such as gardening and carpentry.[6] In addition, strong recommendations were made for the establishment of junior and senior trade schools providing courses from blacksmithing to net-making.[7] Indeed the whole tenor of the report was to stress technical and agricultural instruction and to develop a type of instruction distinctly different from that provided in academic institutions.

The report of the committee was to receive additional support from the Director of Education himself, largely as a result of a visit to the United States in 1922. With the apparent success of the Tuskegee programme in mind, he observed that 'education should be largely industrial and agricultural so that the people may be trained to make the best use of the natural resources of their country' and went on to suggest not only the importance of practical training in the primary grades but its necessity in the secondary schools as well.[8]

The whole period of the twenties, indeed, was marked by a systematic attempt to alter the basis of primary and secondary education in the direction of technical and agricultural studies. Not only were efforts made to introduce crafts and agricultural instruction in the schools but the recommendations of the 1920 committee were immediately implemented by the opening of four government trade schools in 1922, at Mampong, Kibi, Asuansi, and Yendi. These supplemented the work of the Government Technical School at Accra. Attempts were also made to experiment with special types of agricultural curriculums in rural areas. For example, the Government Boarding School at Tamale devoted ten hours a week to practical farming, with five additional hours of theoretical instruction for pupils specializing in agriculture.[9] This type of curriculum was experimented with in other districts in the hope of effecting substantial changes in curriculums. Governor Guggisberg summarized the policy of the government thus:

> The educational system should, from an early date, provide ample opportunities for technical training in the various vocations incidental to the development of the land, industries and health of the country. This will entail the formation of special schools for mechanics, carpenters, engine-drivers, and other artisans; for nurses, dispensers, midwives, and sanitary inspectors; for electricians and telegraphists; for agriculturalists, foresters, and surveyors; and ultimately for engineers and doctors.[10]

Certainly, Guggisberg's activity in the twenties provided the driving force for the development of technical education and by 1930 (three years after the termination of his governorship), government expenditure on trade and technical schools amounted to just over 55 per cent of expenditure for all government educational institutions.[11] It was with justification that he could observe, 'Government has probably paid more attention to the development of technical and trade training than to any other form of education.'[12]

Yet the overall consequences of the policies that he pursued with energy were by no means rewarding. Legislative Council debates during the period of the thirties contain ample evidence that the technical training programme was once again lagging, and increased demands were made for an extension of schemes for vocational education suited to the 'needs' of the Gold Coast.[13] At the same time the further expansion of the system was discussed, it was recognized that African indifference to such forms of education was the principal obstacle. It was observed that Africans held the 'curious belief' that manual labour was undignified and campaigns were suggested to emphasize 'the dignity of fishing, of digging, of felling trees, of all kinds of manual labour'.[14] How such campaigns could enhance the dignity of these occupations is not clear, but they represented a desperate attempt to swing the educational system away from the academic type of institution to which it was once more drifting.

Yet at the same time that efforts were being made to enlist more widespread support for increasing technical provision there was evidence that unemployment among artisans and technicians was increasing[15] and in 1935 the governor was forced to observe that there might have to be a limitation upon entry into further training to avoid underemployment among trained artisans.[16] Two years before this the Director of Education had stated in reply to a demand for more 'vocational' education that there was just no demand for technical employees on any scale and that the creation of new technical institutions could not *create* employment.[17]

In effect, these discussions regarding the desirability of extending technical education as the key to economic development echoed the deliberations of the Educational Committee of the Privy Council advanced almost one hundred years previously. The same arguments were being given in support of technical provision at the end of the colonial period as at its beginning. As late as 1942, a further Education Committee was recommending the extension of technical education, condemning the curriculums of the schools as too 'bookish', and suggesting the development of agriculture and fishing as core subjects within the curriculum.[18] Apart from the utilization of a somewhat more sophisticated terminology, the proposals of this latter committee showed virtually no advance on the suggestions of earlier committees and got no nearer to understanding the real causes of African indifference to technical or agricultural education.

Preceding chapters have, in fact, indicated why the provision of technical education facilities was not welcomed by Africans. Even though the evidence seemed fairly clear, there seemed little recognition by government that the occupational structure of the Gold Coast limited opportunities for African technicians as against the superior conditions of service and income provided in clerical forms of employment. Technical jobs certainly provided inferior opportunities for social mobility and did not effectively meet African expectations regarding what education should do for *them*, not for the economy in general. In characterizing Africans as having a 'curious belief' that manual labour was undignified there was a blithe disregard of the fact that it was also less well paid. There was, therefore, a constant tendency to overestimate the 'prestige' elements in African vocational expectations. In retrospect, it would be fair to say that had the provision of technical facilities been paralleled by an expanding economy within which the graduates of the technical schools were able to command the income and conditions of service that characterized clerical employment, there most likely would have been no shortage of recruits to them.

Some Contrasts between British and Belgian Attitudes to Technical Studies

An interesting comparison can be made here between Belgian and

British policy in Africa. Of the three major European powers the Belgians were certainly the most 'pragmatic' in their educational approach and were less influenced by general considerations about the role of formal education than were their French or even British counterparts. Belgian efforts in the Congo were directed at the provision of literacy in the vernacular for a large proportion of the population combined with a very restricted development of post-primary schools with a heavy technical and vocational emphasis.[19] Secondary academic provision was virtually non-existent except where schools were connected with seminaries, for the aim of Belgian policy was to restrict the development of a Western-trained elite while concentrating upon the diffusion of technical and manual skills among the population. They strove to closely co-ordinate education with the exploitation of the economic resources of the Congo.

In this respect the Belgian attitude approximated more closely to the French policy of restricting vocational education to those groups who could find employment in the economy, but, unlike the latter, the Belgians only at the last moment adopted an assimilationist policy which would have enabled Africans to enter institutions of professional status. In practice, the Congolese system was a truncated one, virtually without higher institutions but which provided a more developed system of technical and vocational education and enabled trained Africans to move into employment in the lower echelons of the technical sector of employment.[20] This was an essentially utilitarian view of the educational process and it should be conceded that it was successful in preventing the emergence of a large group of unemployed technicians and school products while, at the same time, it provided sufficient numbers of trained recruits to meet the needs of the commercial, industrial, and mining enterprises of the Congo.

It must be conceded that such a utilitarian approach was probably significant in the relatively rapid growth of the Congolese economy, but it would be unwise to ignore the corollaries of the system. Belgian concentration upon technical and agricultural education in the primary and post-primary system was only one element in a co-ordinated programme which implied a rigid control over the curriculum of the schools and the virtual exclusion of alternative types of education. Second, it presupposed a degree of control over the lives of Africans which would have been unthinkable in British or French territories. Thus, Belgian officials tried to control immigration into towns unless specific employment existed for Africans who had been trained for particular types of jobs. A system of pass-laws restricted the internal movement of population and engendered 'paternalism' and rigid control over many aspects of African life. Moreover, it limited the general flexibility of the economy itself and consciously reduced the schools to the role of feeder institutions to the European-dominated sector of that economy.

Admirers of Belgian policy, in practice, seldom realized that these elements of control were the inevitable corollary of such an approach to education. In avoiding the obvious shortcomings of British policy the Belgians had been obliged to extend their control over a whole range of African activities. In summary, therefore, the British, although stressing the need for technical provision, had stopped far short of the ultimate implications of a co-ordinated programme of planning.[21] Such a programme would have necessitated not only restrictions on the development of secondary education but controls over the volume and direction of the labour supply to the exchange sector of the economy. The apparent success of the Belgian system of technical education was achieved through the foregoing of other alternatives, and development in one sector was achieved at the expense of development in another.

Special Problems of Agricultural Education

The position regarding agricultural studies in West Africa was not precisely the same as that in technical education since, in one sense, there were opportunities for individuals within the cash-crop sector of the agricultural economy. If Africans had wished to use them there were income earning opportunities connected with cocoa production (which had become increasingly important since the commencement of the century), but it has already been noted that parents invested money in the education of their children in order to enable the latter to leave farming. What factors, therefore, led these children to ignore cash-cropping as a reasonable alternative to other forms of employment?

Initially, it should be appreciated that cash-crop farming itself was largely restricted to the forest zones which were suitable for the production of cocoa (Fig. 3). Large areas of the Gold Coast could not be utilized for this purpose. In some areas foodstuffs were grown for sale to the urban areas, as in the case of yam production but, generally speaking, cocoa-farming remained the only substantial form of cash-crop production during the colonial period.

Yet cocoa-farming itself suffered from severe disabilities in the face of other opportunities open to the products of the schools. First, it implied taking up permanent residence either in rural areas or in small towns. However difficult the conditions in the larger towns were, the great urban centres still offered amenities which could not

153

be duplicated in the smaller communities of the cocoa districts.

Second, it has been noted that for literates to actively take up agriculture was, to some extent, an admission of failure, since cocoa-farming could be undertaken by illiterates and by its very nature was not a 'progressive' form of agriculture.[22] It involved the clearance of forest areas, planting, and periodic thinning of the bush but was essentially an adaptation of extremely primitive methods of agriculture to a cash crop. The basic operations connected with cocoa-farming could be undertaken by relatively unskilled labour and did not require complex agricultural techniques; it could readily be combined with subsistence farming. Indeed, there was a marked tendency for cocoa-farming operations to be increasingly performed by labourers usually from the Northern Region. Many indigenous farmers in Ashanti, Akim, and Akwapim rely increasingly upon this form of assistance.[23] Where education was regarded as a form of investment, a career as a cocoa farmer would hardly be perceived as constituting the optimal return upon that investment.

Further, cocoa production remained an uncertain form of enterprise. It has been calculated that cocoa farms averaged below 2·2 acres in 1925, while Hill has more recently indicated that in terms of headloads the vast majority of farmers produced less than 100 loads per annum.[24] Cocoa prices were subject to violent fluctuations: between 1908 and 1914 they varied between £38 and £49 per ton; by 1920 they had risen to £129 per ton only to drop in 1933 to £19 per ton.[25] Attempts to stabilize prices received by farmers were not made until the very late colonial period and over most of the twentieth century cocoa production was a risky form of economic enterprise, the disadvantages of which were later enhanced by swollen shoot disease which devastated whole areas of production. Thus, although the crop contributed enormously to the aggregate income of the Gold Coast, the average farmer did not receive a large or even predictable income from it. Total output was determined by the aggregate effort of large numbers of small-scale producers.

The reluctance to enter cash-crop farming was not due only to its limited economic possibilities. To remain within the rural areas was to be subject to traditional pressures that individuals were increasingly reluctant to accept. Thus cocoa-farming frequently involved costly land litigation connected with rights to individual tenure and inheritance, since land was not entirely regarded as a freely transmittable factor of production. Individuals were liable to be burdened with the weight of kin obligations as soon as successful production had enhanced their personal incomes and these factors militated against attempts by them to increase production or improve their methods.

In this sense pressures from traditional society placed checks upon the advance of the progressive farmer and imposed restrictions upon individuals who otherwise might have entered agriculture.

To be sure, the spread of cocoa-farming led to an increasing *de facto* recognition of individual land rights. Such changes were slow, however, and there can be little doubt that cash-crop farming was considered an inferior alternative to full-time wage employment. In this sense, impediments and obstacles arising from the neo-traditional milieu in which farming took place may be regarded as extraordinarily important in precluding the growth of a group of educated and progressive farmers. Tentatively it can be suggested that these factors may be of as much importance as the knowledge of modern agricultural techniques. Such techniques may be known by farmers but they may not be utilized unless an institutional framework exists which provides real incentives for them to improve their methods and utilize the land more effectively.

From this viewpoint, agricultural education was not likely to be successful until marked changes had already occurred in the agricultural sector. As with technical education the success of agricultural studies was largely dependent upon real opportunities being created in the economic and social environment of the Gold Coast.

Technical and agricultural education *by themselves* therefore were no more panaceas for development than any other form of instruction, and African reluctance to undertake such courses of instruction had good foundation. Yet even today there appears to be no clearer recognition of the limitations of such an approach. Thus, the recently published Ashby Report on Nigeria has recommended the compulsory inclusion of manual and agricultural training in all primary and secondary schools, though to what purpose is not quite clear.[26] The success of such schemes will be determined by the real economic and social opportunities offered the products of this type of education. In the words of a particularly shrewd observer of the late colonial period:

> All of us from the Governor and the Director of Education down to the junior education officer, sing the same refrain: 'Be a carpenter; be a peasant farmer; be a motor mechanic. Do not be a clerk, for clerks are parasites. The hoe is more honourable than the pen.' . . . The African, like the European, is more easily attracted by the carrot of self-interest than impelled by the goad of exhortation.[27]

The Phelps Stokes Commission and the Advisory Committee

The period of the 1920's was extraordinarily interesting in terms of the volume of discussion regarding colonial and particularly African education, and it was during this decade that several definitive proposals were made concerning the proposed content and nature of colonial educational practice. Since the very early statement on colonial educational policy made by the Education Committee of the Privy Council in 1847 there had been no general definition of British educational policy in the colonial areas until the Colonial Office established in 1923 an 'Advisory Committee on Education in the Colonies', which two years later published the first general statement on British policies for colonial education in almost one hundred years.[28]

One factor which had led to the creation of the Advisory Committee had come from a rather surprising source. As the result of a proposal of the American Baptist Foreign Missionary Society, the Phelps-Stokes Fund had resolved in 1919 'that a survey of educational conditions and opportunities among the Negroes of Africa, with a special view of finding the type or types of education best adapted to meet the needs of the Natives, be undertaken by the Phelps-Stokes Fund . . .'. The proposal met with a warm response from the British Colonial Office and a commission was appointed to investigate educational conditions in West, South, and Equatorial Africa. It reported in 1922. Two years later, as a result of encouragement by Lord Lugard and the then colonial secretary, a second commission investigated the East African situation and reported in 1925.[29]

So completely were the principles underlying the Phelps-Stokes report accepted by British colonial authorities that the policy statements of the Advisory Committee paralleled in large degree the conclusions of the American organization. Guggisberg saw the first Phelps-Stokes report as 'the book of the century, a combination of sound idealism and practical commonsense', and more than any other colonial governor attempted to model Gold Coast education on the lines suggested by the commission.[30]

In the succeeding years both the Phelps-Stokes reports and the statements of the Advisory Committee have become regarded as generally authoritative statements on colonial education. Thus, it was observed in 1950, that the 1925 memorandum:

> . . . might have given a definite impetus to the study of indigenous methods of education in the African territories themselves. It did, in fact, give rise to several articles in journals, and if these articles had been followed by systematic studies, we should have been in a very different position today, twenty-five years later.[31]

Similarly, Oliver writing in 1952, observed that the Phelps-Stokes Commission:

. . . made detailed suggestions as to how education could be adapted to the needs of African society, so as to promote its development without causing its disruption. In recognising that the education of the masses must be related both to the physical environment in which they lived, and to the social groupings in which they were organised, it forestalled by several years the random criticisms of anthropological scientists.[32]

J. L. Lewis has recently remarked that the principles of the 1925 memorandum are still valid for Africa and only need to be applied to changing circumstances.[33] However, he was forced to observe in an earlier statement that 'the adaptation of education to the needs of different territories has not been pursued satisfactorily. Many attempts have been made to put this concept into practice, but it is doubtful whether any of them can claim to more than ephemeral success'.[34]

Contemporary writers agree on the immense significance of the Phelps-Stokes reports and the work of the Advisory Committee— they also agree that the results stemming from their work have been generally disappointing. It is our purpose here to see why the policies of these two bodies were, under colonial conditions, likely to be sterile and why, in spite of efforts to implement them, achievements fell far short of expectations.

Initially, the Phelps-Stokes Commission made clear the source of its approach by acknowledging the influence of principles developed by Samuel Chapman Armstrong at Hampton and Booker T. Washington at Tuskegee. There was a willingness to equate the position of the African with that of the American Negro, where it was observed that

> though village conditions in Africa differ in many respects from those in America where these activities have had great influence on the improvement of rural life, the resemblances are sufficiently numerous and real to warrant the belief that the plans above described may be adapted to colonial conditions in Africa.[35]

Thus, although the expression 'cultural adaptation' is used frequently in the two Phelps-Stokes reports, it is clear that their recommendations were based on the wholesale transfer of concepts and practices developed with respect to Negro education in the southern United States. From these assumptions the general theses of the two commissions developed as follows:

1. Western educational institutions had been transferred without reflection to the African scene and no effort had been made to modify curricular content in the light of African experience. 'The wholesale transfer of the educational conventions of Europe and America to the

peoples of Africa has certainly not been an act of wisdom however justly it may be defended as a proof of genuine interest in Native people.'[36] In the same vein it was later noted that

> educational slavery has been painfully apparent both in the retention of certain conventional subjects that have excluded others much more applicable to life, and in the teaching of a subject content that should long ago have given way to results of modern research related to the life of the pupils.[37]

2. It was therefore assumed that dysfunctionalities created by Western education (and the commission itself seemed uncertain as to what these were) resulted from wholesale and unthinking transfer of Western educational institutions from the metropole. In consequence the commission advised 'the adaptation of education to the needs of the people . . . as the first requisite of school activities. Much of the indifference and even opposition to education in Africa is due to the failure to adapt school work to African conditions'.[38]

3. It was therefore necessary to undertake a careful sociological investigation of African conditions and upon the basis of this develop a series of specific recommendations on the desired shape of future African education.

It should be noted that the kind of 'sociological' investigations undertaken by the commissions were perfunctory in the extreme and largely consisted of a series of elementary facts concerning the environmental and economic setting of African life. Upon this basis they were able to develop a series of very specific recommendations, the core of which was as follows:

1. The development of an educational system substantially based upon agricultural curriculums—'Even casual observation of educational activities in Africa shows a lamentable neglect of the fundamental needs of the native. The overwhelming majority of the Africans must live on and by the soil, but the schools make very little provision for training in this important element for life.'[39]

2. An agricultural curriculum was to be supplemented by a system of elementary trade schools 'to teach the simpler elements of trades required in Native villages and to prepare for the less skilled occupations in industrial concerns'.[40] It should be noted, however, that although the commissions were primarily concerned with the provision of agricultural and simple technical instruction for the masses, they were conscious of the need for a small number of more academic institutions for the tiny proportion of students who would proceed to further studies and later enter professional or semiprofessional occupations.

3. Tribal languages should be used in the lower elementary stages, while in areas with a degree of linguistic differentiation a *lingua franca* of African origin was to be used in the middle forms. The language of the European nation should be begun in the upper standards only.[41]

4. Other subjects such as history and geography were to be more closely related to the local environment. Thus, in the case of history the Commission remarked that it too

> 'must assume the test of good citizenship. . . . In this spirit recent history is more important than that of ancient times; the history of our own country than that of foreign lands; the record of our own institutions and activities than that of strangers; the labours and plans of the multitude than the pleasures and desires of the few.[42]

These recommendations concerning the history curriculum were followed by similar points concerning instruction in geography and other subjects.

In general, therefore, the aims of the Phelps-Stokes commissions were to develop a more 'practical' and 'functional' education within the African setting and provide more useful instruction for the vast majority of African pupils.

The commissions were not content with merely stating specific proposals for curricular reform. Underlying their whole approach was an implicit theory of the nature of social change. Thus it was observed that educators 'in the careful study of their community needs . . . will find the proportion of Native customs to be continued and the adaptations of European influences that are worthwhile'.[43] It was observed also that

> however perplexing it may be to combine the best elements of primitive life with the adaptable elements of civilization, good statesmanship demands the adoption of the . . . policy, which requires that the colonies and the people shall be ruled and developed according to the best experience of both primitive and civilised society.[44]

As we shall see, it was in this kind of statement that the fundamental weaknesses of the Phelps-Stokes position were most marked. Before turning to this point, however, let us first examine the early memoranda of the Advisory Committee on Education in the Colonies to see how closely they paralleled the conclusions of the Phelps-Stokes commissions. The views of the Advisory Committee as they were embodied in the two major reports of 1925 and 1935 may be summarized as follows: (1) The structure of education was to be based on the continued activities of voluntary agencies but with general direction of policy in the hands of the respective colonial governments.

(2) The schools were to be adapted to native life. (3) Grants-in-aid were to be made on the basis of efficiency. (4) The use of local vernaculars in education, particularly in the lower forms, was to be stressed. (5) There was a growing need for more active supervision of schools by the colonial governments. (6) Great stress was placed on the need for technical, vocational and agricultural training at the expense of more 'traditional' subjects within the curriculum. (7) There was an increasing awareness of the need to expand educational facilities for women and girls.[45]

Clearly, the views of the Committee were generally similar to those of the Phelps-Stokes commissions but amplifications were made concerning the precise application of principles within British colonial areas. Thus, in the light of British practice up to that time, particular attention was paid to policies of grants-in-aid and government supervision. For our purposes the second, fourth, and sixth items are of particular importance. Concerning the adaptation of schools to native life the 1925 report of the Committee observed:

Education should be adapted to the mentality, aptitudes, occupations and the traditions of the various peoples, conserving as far as possible all sound and healthy elements in the fabric of their social life; adapting them where necessary to changed circumstances and progressive ideas, as an agent of natural growth and evolution. Its aims should be to render the individual more efficient in his or her condition of life, whatever it may be, and to promote the advancement of the community as a whole through the improvement of agriculture, the development of native industries, the improvement of health, the training of the people in the management of their own affairs, and the inculcation of true ideals of citizenship and service. . . . The central difficulty in the problem lies in finding ways to improve what is sound in the indigenous tradition. Education should strengthen the feelings of responsibility to the tribal community. . . . Since contact with civilisation and even education itself, must necessarily tend to weaken tribal authority and the sanctions of existing beliefs, and in view of the all prevailing belief in the supernatural which affects the whole life of the African, it is essential that what is good in the old beliefs and sanctions should be strengthened and what is defective should be replaced.[46]

With respect to the provision of agricultural education and the development of rural communities the 1935 report stated:

The basis of African life is, and is likely to remain, agricultural. If this is so, one of the primary tasks of African education must be to assist in the growth of rural communities securely established on the land. . . . The efficiency of the school in promoting the good life of the community depends on the extent to which it is able to co-operate with the moral

160

forces operative in native society and to build on these as a foundation. . . . Economic forces and the onrush of new ideas are tending to
loosen social bonds and weaken traditional restraints and to encourage
an unregulated individualism which is destructive of the best elements
in communal life. Educators have not always been sufficiently alive to
these dangers, and through indifference to the problem education has
even been permitted to assist in the process of social disintegration.[47]

This implied for the Committee a 'radical breach with the traditional, more scholastic system of education' and the development of
far-reaching changes in educational practice and curriculum content.[48]

It will be noted immediately that the views of the Committee concerning the nature of social change and the modification of educational practice that was involved are precisely the same as those of the
Phelps-Stokes commissions. These views were to also receive considerable support from anthropological circles. Thus, writing as late
as 1936 Mair noted:

> Only in one or two African territories has there been an attempt to
> envisage education in its bearing on the needs of native life. . . . At
> present the educational system of the majority of colonies aims at
> rendering the individual superior to his community not at making him
> a more valuable member of that community.[49]

Education had to be adjusted in content to accord more directly with
the needs of society and this implied the replacement of a European
curriculum by more specifically adapted syllabuses.[50] Similar views
were later expressed by Busia when he noted that Gold Coast schools
did not make their pupils 'members of a community' and that this
pointed 'to a need for a change in the content and method of what
is taught in the schools, so as to achieve an integration of the school
with the community'.[51]

It would be impossible to survey adequately the number of educators who have explicitly, or implicitly based their notions about
education in African territories upon the work of the Phelps-Stokes
commissions or the Advisory Committee. Although the emphasis of
writers has varied, it is possible to discern several basic themes that
emerge from their discussion of the educational problem on that
continent.[52] We are now in a position to examine critically some of
the presuppositions of the kind of approach so well demonstrated in
the Phelps-Stokes reports.

First, the economic basis of the arguments presented are clear
enough. Since the basis of the African economies was largely agricultural and likely to remain so, the schools should be developed
along agricultural lines, with a secondary emphasis on technical and

vocational education. This kind of argument should not detain us long in view of our previous comments concerning technical and agricultural education. In effect, the views of the Phelps-Stokes commissions and the Advisory Committee were no more than resuscitations of the far earlier comments of the Education Committee of the Privy Council made in 1847. To be sure, neither body appeared to be conscious of the existence of this earlier document, but one cannot avoid the conclusion that the aim of creating a prosperous agriculture and a 'thriving peasantry' were just as overwhelmingly important to them as to the Committee of the Privy Council.

As we have already seen, however, this was precisely the kind of education that the African did *not* want from the schools. It combined inferior economic opportunities with the notion of tying the bulk of educated Africans to the land—or, at least, it was assumed that this kind of education would have that consequence. There was little or no recognition of the aspirations of Africans so far as education was concerned, nor was the critical role of schooling in processes of social mobility discussed sympathetically or dispassionately.

Although these reports have been frequently seen as extraordinarily 'progressive' documents they were basically reactionary in their implications. To have carried their proposals into effect in the economic sphere would have deprived all but a tiny minority of Africans of the opportunity for effective social advancement in the colonial milieu and the opportunity to achieve social and political parity with the colonial elite. Whether such forms of education would have contributed to the economic development of African territories is a moot point beyond the scope of our present discussion. But it is clear that although the reports made a great deal of the economic needs of Africa, they took very little cognizance of the economic needs of *individual* Africans. Riggs has remarked pertinently in this context:

> By needs we refer to an external observer's estimate of what a person ought to want. The needs are *felt* when the subject consciously wants them, *not felt* when he is not conscious of wanting them. The validity of a need does not depend on its being experienced as felt or not felt, but the practicality of a government program demanded by external clienteles depends on the extent to which the programme meets *felt* needs of the internal clientele.[53]

There was, in fact, a general misunderstanding of African aspirations in this context and no programme based on such an approach was likely to succeed, particularly in the Gold Coast.

Furthermore, in spite of the encomiums heaped upon Tuskegee and Hampton regarding the provision of 'useful education' for the rural American Negro it was equally clear that Negro leadership was divided on this issue. W. E. B. Dubois, in particular, was conscious of the status implications of schooling and foresaw that the development of specific types of instruction appropriate to rural Negro populations could only exacerbate the rigidity of the Negro-white caste structure. For him the question of 'educational parity' was sociologically more significant than the question of educational content. Dubois, understandably, was intensely critical of the work of the Phelps-Stokes Commission in Africa and in this respect was far more attuned to the current of African opinion. Any attempt to provide a useful education for the African could only be interpreted as an attempt to keep him in permanent subservience to a European economic and political elite.

Next let us turn to other aspects of the problem of 'cultural adaptation'. Both the Phelps-Stokes commissions and the Advisory Committee perceived that Western education was one of the factors contributing to the breakdown of traditional African society and the detachment of individuals from the traditional milieu. This had long been recognized and, indeed, in our earlier chapters we have been at great pains to point this out. The important thing about these reports, however, is that they considered that the dysfunctions stemming from Western education could be attributed to *curricular* shortcomings in the schools. Thus it was believed that curricular reform would enable some kind of *modus vivendi* to emerge between traditional and emergent society. Indeed, they went further than this and suggested the incorporation of traditional elements into the schools' curriculums.

Now it is clear that at one level these curricular proposals were timely and sensible. The Phelps-Stokes commissions, in particular, performed a valuable task in drawing attention to some of the kinds of nonsense that went on in African schools at that time. It was appropriate to suggest that more African history be included in the curriculums (though the assumptions of the commissions concerning the motivations to learn one's own local history in preference to that of others were gratuitous and dogmatic). However, a similar problem also existed in the teaching of geography, arithmetic, and other subjects. Few educators would deny the need to develop curriculums based upon the practical problems of everyday life and given in a meaningful context. Since the time of the Phelps-Stokes reports there has been a steady movement to develop appropriate curriculums and textbooks in African schools, and there can be no doubt that this movement does derive in part from the efforts of these earlier bodies. If this was all that 'cultural adaptation' meant, then few educators would find reason to disagree with it, in spite of the fact that there was a great deal of African opposition to these developments throughout the colonial period.

The notion of 'cultural adaptation' went further than this. It was believed that through curricular modifications some sort of 'consensus' could be created between the school and society and that processes of social change could thus proceed smoothly and without disruption of traditional life. In some manner the schools were to operate as a bridge between tradition and change, and this implied that there was a halfway house at which the disintegration of traditional structures could be arrested. The main problem was to find the right proportion of what was 'good' in traditional society and eradicate that which was 'bad'. Thus the schools were seen here as the primary instruments for creating this 'balance'.

It is clear that what we have here is the educational analogue of indirect rule. In the same manner as the colonial elite had believed it possible to utilize traditional political institutions in development, educators considered that it was feasible to adapt the schools more closely to traditional values by using some indigenous educational content as the basis of school curriculums. Underlying this whole approach was the notion that the function of formal education was primarily one of simple cultural transmission with the aim of integrating the individual with his society and not making him superior to it.

The basic weakness of this kind of reasoning lies in presupposing the primacy of curricular problems in the schools. These were real enough to be sure, but it is apparent that the major dysfunctional consequences of formal education would have occurred whether the schools had adapted their curriculums or not. For one of the most important things about formal education is not merely what one learns in school but that one has *been* when the bulk of the population has not. In and of itself, the possession of so many years of formal schooling has status significance which cuts straight across traditional criteria. Within the colonial situation this was inevitably the case, since schools were an alien institution in African society irrespective of what they taught. Rather than being an instrument of social consensus they were bound to become instruments of social differentiation. It was because of this, and not because of the curricular shortcomings of the schools, that the major dysfunctionalities which were attributable to Western education came. In this sense the 'symbolic' or 'legitimating' functions of the schools as they affected an individual's social status or his prospects for upward mobility were largely ignored.

Furthermore, what meaning can really be attached to the notion of

164

'painless' social change or the possibility of combining elements from disparate cultures in such a manner as to obtain the 'best' of both worlds? Quite apart from any ethical problems involved, it is clear that such notions rest upon a 'jig-saw puzzle' theory of culture; that it is possible to manipulate pieces, removing them at will without disturbing other sections and to replace them by new sections. This kind of thinking is completely inappropriate as exponents of indirect rule in the political sphere soon found out. The effects of social change cannot be controlled in such a way as to avoid major disruptions and dysfunctionalities occurring in other areas of social life. Indeed, it would not be too much to suggest that the term 'social change' is almost synonymous with the concept of dysfunctionality, since the former necessarily involves uneven development and consequent disequilibrium between the components of the social structure. Every society exhibits 'pathological' and 'disintegrated' aspects which are the inevitable consequence of social change.[54] In the African case these were to be no more attributed to the unsuitable curriculums of the schools than they were to a host of other factors operating in opposition to traditional society. Social change could not be halted at some 'non-existent half-way station' by any form of manipulation of the curriculums of the schools.[55]

Given the nature of the colonial situation there was little likelihood that the proposals of the Phelps-Stokes commissions or the Advisory Committee could have ever really been translated into reality. African pressure for educational parity could not be denied. It is interesting to reflect what would have resulted if the proposals could have been effectively implemented. It is not too much to say that they would have immeasurably widened the gap between the African masses and the colonial elite. They would have deprived many Africans of the opportunity for occupational and social mobility in the colonial era, and very possibly, they might have deferred the awakening of national political consciousness and the emergence of Ghana as an independent African nation. The motives of these groups were unquestionably honest and sincere, yet their recommendations find more than an echo in the South African Bantu Education Act of 1953. Cultural adaptation viewed as a 'progressive' educational policy can be socially and politically retrograde in its effects, and, in the last resort, African opinion decisively rejected it:

> Intentions and fulfillment are very different things, particularly when those responsible for policy and those for whose benefit it is designed have very different aims and values. . . . The African attitude in those early days was often undervalued, sometimes overlooked; yet like that of Colonial peoples elsewhere, it was always important, and was to

165

become decisive. . . . For western schooling, however thinly spread and rudimentary, had already taken root. African reactions to this new and arresting phenomenon had begun to take shape long before the wisdom of the Advisory Committee or Phelps-Stokes. That having once happened, the fundamental factor in African education generally, is less the policy of government than the attitude of the governed.[56]

Achimota and the Secondary-School System

In spite of attempts to modify the curriculums of the primary schools, perhaps the most dramatic effort to develop a unique institution modelled on African lines was the creation of Achimota school. The development of a government secondary institution had been mooted by the Committee of Educationalists in 1920, and in Guggisberg's Ten Year Development programme for the period 1920–30, a sum of £607,000 was set aside for it. This amount constituted over 85 per cent of proposed education development expenditure during the decade and stressed the government policy of creating an elite institution sufficient for the existing needs of the Gold Coast.[57] It was not envisaged at this period that any rapid expansion of the secondary system was likely and the new school was to constitute a pivot for the whole educational structure, combining as it did a primary section and later a post-secondary component which offered among others, courses at the undergraduate level in engineering.[58]

Achimota was a highly selective, elite, residential institution modelled in some respects on the English boarding school, but it was not in the minds of its founders that the school should duplicate metropolitan institutions. Guggisberg had strongly urged giving an agricultural core to the curriculum to 'assist the gradual spread through the country of improved agricultural methods', while in other areas of the curriculum attempts were made to develop specifically 'African' courses. Gold Coast plants were studied and classified to enable curriculums in botany to accord with Gold Coast conditions.[59] History specialists were required to conduct investigations into traditional sources and develop curriculums based on African experience, while geography teaching was to be developed on similar lines. Courses in vernacular were to be related to the study of native laws and institutions; science and mathematics were to be geared to local life and environment.

A contemporary observer remarked that the students 'will be given a special training, so that instead of flocking into the towns they may go back to their villages, as chiefs, teachers, housewives, farmers, medical assistants, and artisans'.[60] Therefore, although educators were, at the same time, conscious of the necessity for European elements in the curriculum, there was a general consensus that new thought had to be built on African history and background.[61] As a result students were expected to conduct their own investigations into native customs and folklore. At a more practical level they were expected to apply their knowledge of hygiene and agriculture in visits to neighbouring villages.[62] The avowed aim was to integrate the school and the local community in order to produce 'a type of student who is "Western" in his intellectual attitude towards life, with a respect for science and capacity for systematic thought but who remains African in sympathy and desire for preserving and developing what is deserving of respect in tribal life, custom, rule and law'.[63]

It should have been anticipated that a policy based on such conceptions was likely to meet with strong opposition from Africans, who were far less interested in the 'native' content of education than they were in the provision of European-type instruction. Immediately upon the publication of the proposed programme of the new school there was a storm of criticism from the local press and African observers against the compulsory inclusion of vernacular and local studies into a secondary-school curriculum.[64] It was suggested by them that there was a desire for formal studies leading to degrees, not for the study of local languages and customs (which they knew better than the instructors). There was indeed a widespread suspicion that special courses for Africans constituted an attempt to keep them in a subordinate intellectual and social position indefinitely.[65]

This attitude was equally marked in contemporary Legislative Council debates in which clear opposition to the proposals was forthcoming from African members. In this respect both chiefs and members of the 'educated class' were united in their opposition to 'Africanization' of the curriculum. Nana Ofori Attà suggested that it would be an unwise move to restrict studies to the African scene while Casely Hayford characterized as a 'dangerous policy' any attempt to lay down that one class and type of education was necessary for the African as against any other type.[66] The latter was quite specific in suggesting that Achimota should concentrate upon secondary education as commonly understood and that classics should be included as a compulsory part of the curriculum.[67]

The paradoxical situation had arisen, therefore, that while European thought strongly favoured the development of 'African' curriculums, African opinion was equally strongly opposed to it. James Aggrey, the first vice-principal of the institution was, in fact, obliged to recruit scholars for the new school by personal contact in order to prevent its total failure in the opening session.[68] Thereafter the school met with increasing success and gained the support of Casely-Hayford himself.

Yet, the later success of Achimota was less related to its experimental curriculum than it was to its privileged position in the educational system—it was above all an elite institution combining rigorous selection, to some extent from its own attached primary school, with a relatively high scale of fees. It received preferential treatment in the allocation of a trained *European* staff[69] and was almost totally supported from government funds, as against the limited sums available to grant-aided secondary institutions. In every sense Achimota could be regarded as the most favoured institution in the secondary system. Above all, it provided direct access to higher qualifications at professional levels, whether at Achimota itself or at universities in the United Kingdom. It also enjoyed a preferential relationship in terms of access to significant bureaucratic and government positions during the colonial period.[70]

Paradoxically, therefore, Achimota's success was not due to the African components of its curriculum but was rather in spite of them. The school took the same external examinations as other secondary schools but generally achieved better results, not surprisingly, in view of its rigorous selection of students combined with a numerous highly trained staff and exceptional facilities. In practice, the 'African' elements of the curriculum were far less evident as the school developed; by the end of the colonial period the curriculum of the school was virtually indistinguishable from that of its Gold Coast and English counterparts. Achimota has remained one of the myths of Gold Coast education; it was no more a school rooted in African conditions than were Mfantsipim and the other secondary schools, rather was it a secondary institution modelled on English lines but with vastly superior resources.[71]

The influence of Achimota on the development of Gold Coast secondary education as a whole was not marked. Certainly, other schools attempted to emulate its principles of rigorous selection combined with its stress on boarding facilities, but there is no evidence that any other local secondary schools attempted to duplicate Achimota's experiments with curriculum. Most certainly in the new group of unassisted secondary schools which were beginning to develop in the late forties there was a stress on the provision of purely academic courses modelled on English lines.[72] In one other instance a departure from the traditional curriculum was suggested and that was in connection with the development of a new secondary school in Ashanti. Here the aim was to combine a literary education with extensive training in industrial subjects such as shoemaking, blacksmithing, carpentry, and tailoring.[73] It is interesting to note that this school, Prempeh High School, is now in every sense a grammar school with an emphasis on literary subjects and pure science; little trace of industrial subjects remains in the curriculum.[74]

The most notable feature of the later colonial period was not the Achimota experiment but rather the increased pace of development of the whole system of academic secondary schools. We have indicated the accelerated growth of secondary education during the decade 1940–50 and stated that it was largely effected through the non-grant-aided system as a result of the efforts of Africans themselves. The reasons for such a growth are not difficult to determine. Until 1940 the growth of the secondary academic system was extremely slow in spite of early African efforts to create such schools, but between 1940 and 1950 the vastly increased provision in primary education had led to increased pressure on the secondary system. During the last decade of the colonial period the increased output of primary schools had, in effect, lowered the 'currency' of a primary education to such an extent that it could no longer guarantee access to remunerative positions within the European-dominated exchange sector. As the returns to a primary education diminished, direct pressure was exerted for entry to secondary education, which led to higher qualifications and hence to more desirable forms of employment. Since government and missions were unable or unwilling to meet this pressure without lowering standards of secondary education, the demand was met by the growth of an unassisted and partially proprietary system, a feature which had been common in the primary system a few decades earlier. The generation of increased pressure on higher levels of education as a direct result of expansion of the primary system was by no means unique to the Gold Coast, but it points to the impossibility of restricting access to secondary institutions to an elite unless, at the same time, rigid control of the whole educational system is effected. Such a solution would have been antithetical to traditional British policy however much the largely uncontrolled growth of secondary education was deplored. It should be noted that this growth was not paralleled by an equivalent support for the development of higher forms of technical education; had it been so the government attitude might have been more favourable.

A second result of the overall growth of the system was the emergence of increased differentiation within the secondary system. Secondary education was becoming increasingly essential but study at particular schools was equally important. Theoretically all secondary institutions enjoyed parity in so far as their pupils sat for the same examinations but, in practice, the system was highly differentiated.

169

At the apex of the system was Achimota School, closely followed by the older grant-aided institutions such as Mfantsipim and Adisadel; following these were a few institutions which had more recently qualified for grants-in-aid. By 1950 there were thirteen schools in the government and grant-aided system, all of them in the southern half of the country, and these constituted the core of the secondary system. Since these were primarily boarding schools and recruited on the basis of competitive examination irrespective of the regional origin of pupils, they were able to select freely from the increasing supply of senior primary graduates. Parallel with these elite institutions, the remarkable growth of a non-grant-aided system of forty-four schools has been noted. In effect, these latter institutions, virtually all grouped in the larger southern urban areas constituted an inferior alternative to the public system for those individuals who were unable to enter the latter as a result of competitive examination.

In drawing attention to the vigorous development of secondary academic schools it can be seen that educational growth implied not only an overall expansion of the available places in the secondary system but equally led to an increasing differentiation within the system itself. In the following chapters an attempt will be made to examine in more detail this process of internal differentiation of an apparently homogeneous secondary structure. At this stage it is sufficient to observe that such a process was already occurring and that by 1950 the 'strategic' sector of education so far as social mobility was concerned had shifted from the primary to the secondary level.

The Educational Situation at the Close of the Colonial Period

By 1951, which marked the effective end of the colonial period in the Gold Coast, the educational system showed marked structural similarities to that of the metropolitan power. Superimposed upon an expanding primary network were a few highly selective academic secondary schools together with a very limited provision of alternative types of schools offering technical instruction. As in the earlier stages of English educational development, *direct* government provision of schools was negligible, and government action was primarily concerned with offering grants-in-aid to institutions developed by voluntary agencies. Unlike the British system, however, attempts to partially absorb voluntary agency schools into a local authority system had been unsuccessful and local authority schools comprised only an insignificant proportion of the educational structure. The development of such schools would have presupposed the existence of effective local authorities with sufficient fiscal powers to effectively

170

administer district educational systems—a condition that was not present up to the end of the period.

Another difference lay in the nature of the unaided secondary-school system. The existence of a private school system paralleling the state or state-aided structure was apparent in the United Kingdom, but at the secondary level this sector constituted a high-prestige set of institutions recruiting from a relatively narrow segment of British society and enjoying a particularly close relationship with the older universities and with the 'Establishment'. In the Gold Coast, a peculiar reversal of the situation had occurred; the relatively small number of government or government-aided schools constituted the elite sector and provided the most effective access to later professional studies. The private sector remained a low prestige segment of the secondary system competing on unequal terms with the public schools.

In the area of curriculum, certain divergencies had occurred at the primary level from the content of courses available in the metropole, most notably, of course, in the use of vernacular at lower levels of primary education. In spite of attempts at curricular innovation and change, the range of studies was narrow and tended to be influenced by the entrance requirements to secondary institutions. There was, correspondingly, a much greater identity between Gold Coast and metropolitan schools at the secondary level. In spite of the Achimota experiment, the offerings of the secondary schools were substantially the same as those of British secondary institutions. This outcome was a consequence of the pressure for educational parity and also the requirements for entry into institutions of higher learning in the United Kingdom. Generally, all schools at whatever level, had proved remarkably resistant to change and innovation.

By 1950 the Gold Coast had developed a more extensive system of schooling than any other African territory outside the Union of South Africa. In spite of this, functional literacy among the population was well below 20 per cent and vast geographical inequalities existed in the provision of schooling. After 1950 a new African government faced the massive task of expanding educational provision while at the same time attempting to eradicate major inequalities as between areas.

REFERENCES

1. This view is widely held and for a somewhat dogmatic assertion of the point see C. H. Moehlmann, 'Education in Various Cultures', in *Comparative Education*, ed. A. H. Moehlmann and Joseph S. Roucek (New York: Dryden Press, 1953), p. 18.

2. Ghana, *Education Statistics, 1956* (Accra: Office of the Government Statistician, 1957), p. 1.

3. Jesse Jones, *Education in Africa: A Study of West, South and Equatorial Africa by the African Education Commission* (New York: Phelps-Stokes Fund, 1922), p. 141.

4. Gold Coast, *Report of the Committee of Educationalists* (Accra: Government Printer, 1920), pp. 25–28.

5. *Ibid.*, p. 54.

6. *Ibid.*, p. 40.

7. *Ibid.*, p. 52.

8. Gold Coast, *Report of the Director of Education on His Visit to Educational Institutions in the United States* (Accra: Government Printer, 1922), p. 22.

9. 'Vocational Education in the Gold Coast', *Colonial Review*, XI, No. 6 (September 1942), 232.

10. Sir Gordon Guggisberg and A. G. Fraser, *The Future of the Negro* (London: Student Christian Movement, 1929), p. 82.

11. Computed from A. W. Cardinall, *The Gold Coast, 1931* (Accra: Government Printer, 1932), p. 197.

12. Guggisberg, *A Review of the Events of 1920–1926 and the Prospects for 1927–1928* (Accra: Government Printer, 1927), p. 204.

13. See particularly Gold Coast, *Legislative Council Debates, 1933*, p. 94, and *1935*, p. 5.

14. Gold Coast, *Legislative Council Debates, 1933*, p. 5.

15. Gold Coast, *Report of the Education Department, 1935*, par. 332.

16. Gold Coast, *Legislative Council Debates, 1935*, p. 5.

17. Gold Coast, *Legislative Council Debates, 1933*, p. 94.

18. Gold Coast, *Report of the Education Committee 1937–1941* (Accra: Government Printer, 1942), p. 13.

19. The Belgians had always stressed the necessity for a broad basis of elementary instruction in the vernacular and by 1954, for example, the percentage of the total Congolese population in schools was 9·4 per cent as against 4·5 per cent in British territories and 2·7 per cent in French areas. G. Balandier, 'Social Changes and Problems in Negro Africa', *Africa in the Modern World*, ed. Calvin W. Stillman (Chicago: University of Chicago Press, 1955), p. 58. After 1950 the Congo schools had enrolled over 50 per cent of the child population of school age in the schools; a level of primary education hardly equalled in the remainder of Africa. G. Malengreau, 'Recent Developments in Belgian Africa', *Africa Today*, ed. C. Grove Haines (Baltimore: Johns Hopkins Press, 1955), p. 338.

20. For example, the products of the schools were trained as agricultural assistants and medical assistants to perform limited functional roles but were not allowed professional status. Lord Hailey, *An African Survey* (2nd ed., rev., Oxford: Oxford University Press, 1957), p. 1207.

21. It is pertinent to note that the Belgians were ultimately unable to prevent the emergence of political nationalism which they had assumed would be circumvented by economic development and a rise in the economic conditions of the masses. Since the events of 1960, foreign educators who had previously applauded the Belgian stress on technical education have tended to deprecate the absence of an elite education which would have enabled the effective transfer of power.

22. This is not to suggest that many successful educated individuals do not own cocoa farms. Very frequently ownership of a cocoa farm constitutes a valuable subsidiary source of income to individuals otherwise employed.

23. The most adequate account of the cocoa economy is to be found in Polly

Hill, *The Gold Coast Farmer* (London: Oxford University Press, 1956). Forms of payment to labourers range from a type of share-cropping (*Abusa*) to the payment of fixed sums per head load (*Nkoto Kuano*) and annual fixed wages.

24. A 'head load' is assessed at 60 pounds in weight.

25. See Jacques Boyon, *Naissance d'un etat Africain: Le Ghana* (Paris: A. Colin, 1958).

26. Nigeria, *The Report of the Commission on Post-School Certificate and Higher Education in Nigeria, Investment in Education* (Lagos: Federal Ministry of Education, 1960), p. 18.

27. *Oversea Education*, XVIII, No. 1 (January 1946), 390–91.

28. Advisory Committee on Education in the Colonies, *Education Policy in British Tropical Africa*, Cmd. 2374 (London: H.M.S.O., 1925).

29. The conclusions of the two commissions are embodied in the following reports: Jesse Jones, *Education in Africa: A Study of West, South and Equatorial Africa by the African Education Commission* (New York: Phelps-Stokes Fund, 1922), and Jesse Jones, *Education in East Africa* (New York: Phelps-Stokes Fund, 1925).

30. Gold Coast, *Legislative Council Debates, 1923–1924*, p. 56.

31. M. Read, Inaugural Lecture at the University of London Institute of Education, June 1950, reported in the *Colonial Review*, VI, No. 7 (September 1950), 201.

32. Roland Oliver, *The Missionary Factor in East Africa* (London: Longmans, Green, 1952), p. 264.

33. L. J. Lewis, 'The British Contribution to Education in Africa', an address to the Royal Society of Arts quoted in *The Times Educational Supplement*, 11 November 1960, p. 645.

34. L. J. Lewis, *Educational Policy and Practice in British Tropical Areas* (London: Thomas Nelson and Sons, 1954), p. 56.

35. Jesse Jones, *Education in Africa, op. cit.*, p. xxvii.

36. *Ibid.*, p. 16.

37. *Ibid.*, p. 36.

38. *Ibid.*, p. 11.

39. *Ibid.*, p. 20.

40. *Ibid.*, p. 71.

41. *Ibid.*, p. 26.

42. *Ibid.*, p. 67.

43. Jones, *Education in East Africa, op. cit.*, p. 10.

44. Jones, *Education in Africa, op. cit.*, p. 86. It should be noted, however, that the views of the Phelps-Stokes Commission on the importance of vernacular studies and the need for a synthesis of traditional and European elements had already been stressed by the Committee of Educationalists in the Gold Coast two years before the first Phelps-Stokes Report. Gold Coast, *Committee of Educationalists, 1920, op. cit.*, p. 55.

45. The reports are: Great Britain, Advisory Committee on Education in the Colonies, Cmd. 2374, *Memorandum on Education Policy in British Tropical Africa* (London: H.M.S.O., 1925), and Great Britain, Advisory Committee on Education in the Colonies, Colonial No. 103, *Memorandum on the Education of African Communities* (London: H.M.S.O., 1935).

46. Advisory Committee, *Cmd. 2374*, p. 6.

47. Advisory Committee, *Colonial No. 103*, pp. 6–8.

48. *Ibid.*, p. 15.

49. L. P. Mair, *Native Policies in Africa* (London: G. Routledge & Sons, 1936). p. 275.

50. *Ibid.*, p. 137.

51. K. A. Busia, *Report on a Social Survey of Sekondi-Takoradi* (London: Crown Agents for the Colonies, 1950), p. 59. It is interesting to note that although Busia suggests that there was 'widespread dissatisfaction' with the schools the only evidence he gives of this was that parents were unhappy about low standards in the teaching of English!

52. It would not be possible to list all writers whose work stems from a notion of cultural adaptation, but it is particularly clear in the work of Margaret Read, *Education and Social Change in Tropical Areas* (London: Nelson, 1955), and *Children of Their Fathers* (Yale: Yale University Press, 1959). See also Lionel Elvin, 'Social Development', *New Fabian Colonial Essays*, ed. Arthur Creech-Jones (London: Hogarth Press, 1959), and Franklin Parker, 'Some Problems of African Education in Southern Rhodesia', *Oversea Education*, XXXII, No. 1 (April 1960), 20–29.

53. Fred W. Riggs, 'Circular Causation in Development and Local Government: The Philippines as a Test Case', *Economic Development and Cultural Change*, VIII, No. 4, Part I (July 1960), 391.

54. M. Fortes, 'Culture Contact as a Dynamic Process', *Africa*, IX (January 1936), 25. See also Audrey Richards, 'Colonial Problems as a Challenge to the Social Sciences', *Colonial Review*, V, No. 2 (June 1947), 47. It should be added that many educationists and anthropologists have not been able to reconcile themselves to the less desirable but perhaps inevitable consequences of social change and stress the societal tensions created as a result of it. It has recently been observed that

> sociologists and anthropologists appear to be increasingly committed to a hypothesis that culture change increases 'individual anxieties', 'emotional malaise!'. Is this not as dubious as Marxist doctrine of increasing misery under a capitalist economy? And is it not immediately suspect as a possible rationalization of the social scientist, sociologist, or psychologist, resulting from his vested interest in stable phenomena?

Jack Goody, 'Anomie in Ashanti?', *Africa*, XXVII, No. 4 (October 1957), 362.

55. See also A. W. Hoernle and E. Hellmann, Address at the National Conference on the 'Report of the Commission on Native Education in South Africa 1949–1951' held in July 1952 at the University of Witwatersrand.

56. Sir Christopher Cox, 'The Impact of British Education on the Indigenous Peoples of Oversea Territories', an address to the Sheffield Meeting of the British Association on 30 August 1956, reported in the *Colonial Review*, IX, No. 8 (December 1956), 231–32.

57. Guggisberg, *Review of the Events*, p. 17.

58. Guggisberg's views on the nature and function of secondary education in the Gold Coast are summarized in Guggisberg, *The Future of the Negro*, p. 80.

59. *Achimota, 1927–1937* (Achimota: Achimota Press, 1937), p. 16.

60. Raymond Buell, *The Native Problem in Africa* (New York: Macmillan, 1928), II, 848.

61. Alec Fraser, 'My Educational Policy', *Oversea Education*, XXIX, No. 4 (January 1958), 147.

62. Mair, *op. cit.*, p. 168.

63. *Report of the Committee appointed in 1932 by the Governor of the Gold Coast Colony To Inspect the Prince of Wales College and Schools*, Achimota (London: Crown Agents for the Colonies, 1932), p. 21.

64. Edwin W. Smith, *Aggrey of Africa* (London: Student Christian Movement, 1929), pp. 236–40. It is interesting to note that earlier African criticisms of the Basel mission schools had centred about their instruction in vernacular as

opposed to English. See evidence by the Rev. P. G. Djoleto before the *Committee of Educationalists, 1920*, p. 123.

65. M. Musson, *Aggrey of Achimota* (London & Redhill: United Society for Christian Literature, Lutterworth Press), pp. 39–47. See also Buell, *op. cit.*, p. 849, and Hailey, *op. cit.*, p. 1170.

66. Gold Coast Government, *Legislative Council Debates 1928–1929*, p. 286, and *1924–25*, p. 74.

67. Gold Coast Government, *Legislative Council Debates 1928–1929*, p. 172.

68. Musson, *op. cit.*, p. 46. James Aggrey's role in the foundation of Achimota was most interesting. Born in the Gold Coast he resided for over twenty years in the United States as a teacher of classics and theology and only returned to Africa as a member of the Phelps-Stokes commissions. He was later appointed by Guggisberg as the vice-principal of Achimota where he remained only two years before returning to the United States. Aggrey was greatly influenced by ideas of 'cultural adaptation' as developed in the Phelps-Stokes reports yet, though often quoted as 'representative' of African opinion and greatly revered, it seems clear that his influence on the development of Gold Coast education was negligible. In effect, he completely misunderstood the motivation of his Gold Coast contemporaries and seemed oblivious to the political and social consequences of formal education. In practice, though Aggrey has been regarded as a great African educator, his contemporaries in the Gold Coast seemed to have a far shrewder perception of the significance of Western schooling.

69. Fraser, *op. cit.*, p. 148.

70. Coleman has pointed to the significance of such highly selective schools as Achimota in the process of elite formation. See Gabriel Almond and James A. Coleman, *The Politics of Developing Areas* (Princeton: Princeton University Press, 1960), p. 353.

71. See also Cox, *op. cit.*, p. 232, for a similar analysis of the position of Achimota.

72. That new schools within a secondary system should largely model themselves closely upon existing institutions is a very general phenomenon. In the case of England particularly, the newer public schools created about the middle of the nineteenth century and deriving their support from the 'new' middle classes, modelled themselves closely upon the established 'great schools'. Similarly, the state provided secondary grammar institutions have attempted, as far as possible, to emulate the independent schools in terms of organization and curriculum content.

73. *Colonial Review*, I, No. 7 (December 1940), 237.

74. It should be noted that the French met with no more success in their efforts to adapt education to 'African needs' than did the British. Far from being entirely assimilationist in their policies the French since 1903 had attempted to develop locally devised curricula with a stress on agriculture, a system that was substantially enlarged in 1936. See H. Labouret, 'L'Education des Masses en A.O.F.', *Africa*, VIII, No. 1 (January 1935), 98–102. However, such attempts were strongly opposed by local populations and in 1947 at the unanimous request of elected African representatives these curricula were abolished. V. M. Thompson and R. Adloff, *French West Africa* (London: George Allen & Unwin, 1959), pp. 519, 529.

PART TWO

The Contemporary Scene

VI

SELF-GOVERNMENT AND INDEPENDENCE
—THE FIRST DECADE

THE election of a new Legislative Assembly which took its seat in Accra on 20 February 1951, symbolized the passing of the colonial era. From that date, the effective control of internal policy in the Gold Coast lay in African hands. Although formal independence was not granted until 6 May 1957, self-government was achieved long before, and educational policy in particular, reflected the aims of the new African leadership. 'The Gold Coast Revolution' was as much an educational as a political one.

The Gold Coast situation in 1951 represented the optimal conditions for the transfer of effective political authority, conditions which have hardly been duplicated in those other areas of Africa which have been granted independence since that date. The financial position of the Gold Coast in 1951 was sound, and a substantial financial reserve existed as a result of the activities of the Cocoa Marketing Board. This organization had been founded in an attempt to stabilize the prices paid to cocoa farmers, but wartime conditions and the relatively high prices paid for cocoa in the immediate post-war years had enabled the accumulation of reserves, which in 1946 amounted to over £20 million and which by 1951 had reached a level of almost £200 million. This 'forced saving', which was effected by the payment to cocoa farmers of prices considerably below world market levels, became the financial basis of post-independence schemes for social and economic development.

Besides this satisfactory financial position the Gold Coast had developed a small but relatively efficient administrative structure and a limited group of professionally trained individuals who could increasingly assume posts of greater administrative responsibility.

British policy had been remiss in training any large number of Africans to assume higher administrative posts but, in practice, a small core existed and was rapidly enlarged. Such action guaranteed the continued existence of an efficient administration.[1]

Finally, a period of long contact plus the absence of any large number of permanent European settlers had led to independence being achieved with a minimum of rancour and bitterness. This enabled the new nation to utilize remaining expatriate officers effectively and indeed increase their number. The continued use of expatriate administrative, technical, and educational staff was vital to the new government and enabled the transition to be made comparatively smoothly.

The Economy since 1951

Nevertheless, in delineating some of the factors that were favourable to the achievement of independence and to a degree of political and financial stability thereafter, some less satisfactory aspects of the post-1951 period cannot be ignored. Predominant among these was the continuous underfunctioning of the economy which, as we noted, was a feature of the colonial period. The apparent post-war prosperity of the Gold Coast was largely based on the export of cocoa and relatively few other primary products; during the period since 1951 the basis of the economy has not undergone marked transformation. The economy during the colonial period may be characterized as fragile and rigid in the extreme, depending as it did almost totally upon cocoa exports, with the danger that fluctuations in the world price of that commodity affected the general prosperity of the country. The post-colonial period has been characterized not by any remarkable increase in flexibility and diversity within the economy but rather by its continuing rigidity. Thus the essential dependence of the country upon cocoa is amply illustrated by the fact that between 1952 and 1958, cocoa exports as a percentage of total exports varied between 56 and 75 per cent. The overwhelming importance of this crop to the exchange economy is clear. In 1958 gold, the second largest export, accounted for only 10·2 per cent of the value of domestic exports. The total value of exports shows no marked upward trend and yearly fluctuations are primarily a reflection of fluctuations in the world price of cocoa.

Contemporary Ghana is thus characterized by those features delineated in the colonial period; a relatively high rate of income per capita of approximately $200 per annum,[2] which is ultimately dependent upon a relatively fragile economy based on the production of cocoa. So far, there is little indication of any substantial industrial development, nor is any likely to occur until marked changes occur in agriculture itself.[3]

Additional light can be shed upon the present condition of the Ghanaian economy by examining the distribution of the adult labour force—a factor of considerable significance so far as this study is concerned. In 1960 this labour force amounted to 3·73 million out of a total population of 6·72 million. However, only 2·56 million of the labour force was actually classified as employed at the time of the 1960 Population Census.[4]

Of this employed group just over 60 per cent were occupied in farming, fishing, forestry, and hunting, thus indicating the continuing overwhelming importance of subsistence and cash-crop activities to the economy. A further 13 per cent of the employed category were engaged in small-scale trading activities, as contrasted with only 4·5 per cent occupied in professional, administrative, technical, and clerical roles. Even allowing for the inadequacies of the 1948 Census it would appear that no very marked changes have yet occurred in the composition and characteristics of the Ghanaian labour force.

Another way of looking at the problem is to consider the employment status of the occupied portion of the labour force. Over 78 per cent are characterized as employers, self-employed, or 'family workers'—this becomes an indirect index of the importance of small-scale traditional and cash-cropping activities. Correspondingly, only a little over 21 per cent are actually classified as paid employees or apprentices. It is this latter group which is of particular importance in this study, since schools graduates normally seek employment within this 'modern' sector. It is the relationship between the volume of output of the schools and the extent of actual employment opportunities within the 'modern' sector of the economy which is crucial.

Clearly, the 'employee' sector is still relatively small. In 1960 only just over 542 thousand persons were so classified and about one-quarter of these employees were occupied in farming, fishing and hunting, etc., while an unknown but probably substantial number were engaged in traditional activities of a craft nature. As a very rough estimate the actual number of employees engaged in essentially 'modern-type' occupations of all kinds either with government or private industry is somewhere between 300 and 350 thousand.

This estimate seems to find support in previous partial returns systematically collected from government agencies and the larger and more established private employers. At the end of 1957 the figure for total employment of this nature stood at just over 277 thousand.[5] These figures are almost certainly an underestimate but would tend

181

to confirm the limited extent of the employment sector specifically important to schools graduates.

Of course, the major problem is to ascertain the rate of growth in employment in the 'modern' sector of the economy. In 1958 this was calculated to be something over 4 per cent per annum so far as *recorded* employment was concerned.[6] This would indicate a very low absolute growth in new jobs per annum of approximately 20 thousand. More recent census figures would tend to suggest that the rate is higher than this, but it would seem fairly safe to assert that the absolute increase per year is not above 30 thousand and is more likely to be nearer 20 thousand. It should be noted that this does not include merely occupations of a clerical or administrative nature only but *all* levels of occupation that can be legitimately described as 'modern'.

This occupational sector is, therefore, relatively small in relation to the whole volume of employment and at the same time is not expanding very rapidly. Another factor of considerable importance is also apparent. This is the extraordinary role of government and other public agencies as employers of labour. No less than 38 per cent of all recorded employees are employed by public authorities of one variety or another. It should be clear, however, that so far as the most modern sector of the economy is concerned government activity is even more impressive. It was calculated in 1958 that over 50 per cent of all employment of this nature was with government, and this would seem to be well substantiated by more recent materials in the 1960 census. Furthermore, the rate of growth in the public sector of employment is markedly higher than in the private sector. Indeed one of the initial consequences of self-government and independence has been the proliferation of government activities, the substantial enlargement of existing government agencies and departments and the creation of new public organizations of various kinds. It would seem probable that government controls no less than 60 per cent of the employment outlets to which the schools graduates are oriented. We shall see that this combination of relatively limited occupational opportunities and the highly important role of government itself has had considerable implications for the educational system.

Educational Policy since 1951

Against this economic background we may now consider some of the main features of government educational policy in the last decade and contrast them with policies in the colonial period. We have already seen that by 1951 the school system comprised a relatively small group of highly selective secondary schools superimposed upon an expanding but still very limited primary school sector. Further, marked ecological inequalities existed within the system in terms of the urban-rural distribution of schools and also in the differential access of various ethnic groups into the system. Two other features were also apparent; first, the increasing tempo of secondary-school expansion *outside* the state-aided sector and second, the rapidly growing volume of unemployment among primary school-leavers.

It should be stated that educational policy since 1951 has not shown any radical change of approach from that of the earlier period but has been rather a reinforcement of earlier objectives. There is little doubt that expansion has been undertaken with far more vigour and with far greater results in terms of the proportion of the child population in school, but structural and curricular change has been a more difficult problem.

One of the most outstanding features of African leadership in the newly independent states has been the overwhelming emphasis placed upon programmes of educational expansion, often at the expense of other alternatives foregone, reflecting the belief that formal education is the pre-eminent instrument for promoting desirable social and economic change. The reasons for this remarkable preoccupation with education are not difficult to discover.

First, formal education was probably one of the most clear-cut manifestations of European power during the colonial period, and, for persons who were able to obtain it, there were tangible advantages in terms of individual wealth and prestige. Yet belief in the advantages of formal education went further than this, resting upon a noncritical faith in its supposed benefits. It has been remarked that formal education has become regarded almost as a 'juju' the possession of which confers almost certain success upon its possessor. It is not, therefore, surprising that the populations of the new states have increasingly demanded access to the schools.[7]

Second, the new states have interpreted high levels of literacy as being one of the primary indices of 'modern' or 'developed' nations (however we may define these terms). There is a desire on their part to be judged on some of those standards that the West itself has stressed; education, therefore, possesses a symbolic function of overwhelming importance to them. The possession of universal literacy enables them to perceive themselves as the equals of the older nations and no longer as 'backward' or 'underdeveloped' areas.

Third, the vigour with which educational systems have been expanded reflects the exigencies of the political situation itself. There is no doubt that in the Gold Coast, for example, the demand for education had far outstripped its provision in the southern areas by the end of the colonial period. The new government was elected to a large extent upon its promises to extend education to a wider proportion of the population. One of the most marked pressures upon the governments of the new nations has been the necessity to demonstrate that they are maintaining a rate of growth and development which is far greater than that effected under the colonial regime. Education is above all the area in which tangible manifestations of progress can be demonstrated to the population. The percentage of children enrolled in school, the number of schools built, the amount of money spent on education, or the level of literacy among the population serve the political end of convincing the masses that real efforts are being made.

Apart from these immediate political pressures there is no doubt that the naïve and uncritical belief in the power of education to effect radical transformations in the well-being of the population is also a reflection of Western ideology and belief. The new nations in their desire to emulate or surpass the achievements of the Western world merely reflect the climate of Western educational opinion which has rarely attempted to explore the consequences of massive educational programmes in primarily subsistence economies.

Essentially, the aim of the new Gold Coast government in 1951 was to emphasize the development of the primary and middle-school system and to obtain the maximum enrolment of children at that level.[8] To this end, fees were abolished in all primary schools and special provision made for the emergency training of teachers. The secondary-school system, however, was to undergo more limited expansion with the creation of a number of 'day secondary schools' to supplement the existing boarding institutions. It is clear that the intentions of the government were not to undertake immediately any massive increases in secondary-school provision.[9]

> From experience in the United Kingdom and elsewhere it is likely that no more than thirty per cent of the pupils will have the ability and aptitude to enter a secondary or secondary technical school. The majority, perhaps 75 per cent, will be more suited to a less academic type of education in a middle school where the course will be designed to prepare children to grapple with the practical problems of living. Schools must be related to the interests and environment of these pupils, all but the few required to fill positions demanding a high degree of specialist training and education will derive most benefit from a liberal type of course, with a wide range covering the practical as well as the literary aspects of life, rather than from a bookish type of grammar school course.[10]

To this end, the former senior primary schools were renamed

'middle schools' and offered a four-year sequence after the completion of a six-year primary course. These new middle schools were, in effect, to perform the dual function of providing a terminal course for the bulk of scholars while supplying recruits for highly selective five-year secondary schools.[11] They were, therefore, to constitute the intermediate link between the primary and secondary schools, as well as being terminal institutions. The consequences of this 'dual' function have been disastrous to the programme of the middle schools themselves.

Apart from this innovation in nomenclature, such a policy was a continuation of that carried out in the colonial period. Emphasis was largely upon the primary and senior primary (now middle-school) system while secondary provision was to be limited. Increased interest was manifested in the perennial problem of technical education. The 'dual' system of control was substantially retained.[12] Even more important, few restrictions were placed upon the opening of private or proprietary secondary schools, though such institutions could not qualify for grants without meeting certain minimal standards.[13] It would not be unfair to characterize the Accelerated Development Plan of 1951 as one seeking to retain virtually every structural element of colonial education but attempting to provide 'more of everything', particularly at the primary-school level.

The proposed massive changes in the extent of educational provision were not paralleled, however, by any immediate proposals to radically restructure curriculums. Quite the reverse, deviations from the colonial curriculum were regarded often with suspicion. For example, the proposed establishment of a West African Examinations Council in 1951 which would be responsible for the administration of the School Certificate Examinations in Nigeria, Sierra Leone, and the Gold Coast was strongly resisted in the Legislative Assembly on the grounds that such qualifications would be 'as worthless as those of Ceylon and India' and have no educational currency. Similarly, the decision to retain the General School Certificate Examination in West Africa rather than adopt the new General Certificate of Education regulations current in England was construed as an attempt to continue an inferior system of education abandoned by the metropole.[14] Certainly, until very recently there was some reluctance to accept curricular innovation or 'Africanization' at the expense of 'standards'.[15]

In one area at least, the curriculum approximated even more closely to that of the metropole. During the last decades of colonial rule the British had stressed the necessity for conducting the early years of education in the local vernaculars to enable children to enjoy their early learning experiences within a familiar linguistic framework. In this sense the vernacular problem was regarded as an essentially 'educational' one resting upon the supposed needs of the children. One of the first actions of the new government, however, was to stress the necessity for instruction in English from the earliest grades.[16] In spite of an unfavourable report from a ministerial committee appointed in 1956 there has been every attempt to systematically increase the percentage of time devoted to English.[17] The reason for such stress on English is not difficult to discover; political requirements necessitated the development of one national language for the Gold Coast in a situation where no single indigenous vernacular could have been introduced in the schools without inducing serious conflict among major ethnic groups.[18] In stressing instruction in the local languages as part of a policy of cultural adaptation the British had ignored the political concomitants of vernacular instruction. The new African leadership has perceived the overriding necessity for a programme of linguistic unification. African political sagacity has enabled Ghana to avoid the 'linguistic pandemonium' that has characterized post-independence India.[19]

A peculiar ambivalence characterizes educational development in the post-1951 Gold Coast and Ghana. At one level, political leadership has stressed the necessity for an educational system which would reflect 'African nature and substance',[20] while at the same time there has been some reluctance to allow either the structure or content of the educational programme to deviate very markedly from that prevailing in England. The European 'image' does not disappear with the achievement of independence, and such radical changes in educational structure and content as have been broached since 1951 normally reflect immediate political goals.

The Expansion of the Primary and Middle-School System, 1952–59

The most notable achievement of the Accelerated Development Plan was a vast expansion in the provision of primary and middle-school education over the period 1952 to 1960. This growth was certainly accompanied by progressive 'dilution' of the teaching force by untrained teachers, but we should regard this lowering of standards as a secondary factor of limited importance, in contradistinction to the remarkable overall growth of the system itself (tables 9 and 10).

TABLE 9

THE GROWTH OF THE PRIMARY-SCHOOL SYSTEM, 1952-53—1959*

Year	THE COLONY†		ASHANTI		TRANS-VOLTA TOGOLAND		NORTHERN REGION		TOTAL	
	Schools	*Pupils* ‡	*Schools*	*Pupils*	*Schools*	*Pupils*	*Schools*	*Pupils*	*Schools*	*Pupils*
1952–53	1,575	183	901	90	543	58	96	7	3,115	338
1954	1,610	216	960	105	578	72	123	10	3,271	403
1955	1,655	228	988	112	613	76	138	13	3,394	429
1956	1,717	237	997	114	599	77	165	18	3,478	446
1957	1,775	250	1,000	120	605	78	191	20	3,571	468
1958	1,805	250	1,008	121	606	77	215	24	3,644	472
1959	1,800	253	1,023	128	644	76	246	27	3,713	484

* Computed from the Gold Coast and Ghana, *Reports of the Education Department and Ministry of Education*, 1950-1956, and *Education Statistics*, 1952-53–1959.

† Since 1951 regional boundaries have been changed and the term 'Colony' is no longer used with respect to the southern regions. However in this table we have adhered to earlier usage for purposes of comparison with earlier periods.

‡ Given in thousands.

TABLE 10

THE GROWTH OF THE MIDDLE-SCHOOL SYSTEM, 1952-53—1959*

Year	THE COLONY		ASHANTI		TRANS-VOLTA TOGOLAND		NORTHERN REGION		TOTAL	
	Schools	*Pupils*	*Schools*	*Pupils*	*Schools*	*Pupils*	*Schools*	*Pupils*	*Schools*	*Pupils*
1952-53	398	51	195	26	114	14	11	1	718	92
1954	464	57	234	28	152	17	14	2	864	104
1955	517	63	246	30	194	19	17	2	974	114
1956	545	64	258	31	166	18	21	3	990	116
1957	621	71	266	32	216	21	28	3	1,131	127
1958	729	78	287	35	233	23	38	5	1,287	141
1959	763	82	327	42	260	25	44	5	1,394	154

* Computed from the Gold Coast and Ghana, *Education Statistics*, 1952-53–1959.

Total enrolment in both primary and middle schools was increased by one-half in a seven-year period, with the middle schools showing a slightly greater overall rate of expansion (67·0 as against 43·0 per cent). The rate of middle-school growth was, as we should expect, faster in the second half of the period when the rate of primary growth began to decline as a result of the growing saturation of demand for primary-school facilities. An increasing pressure on the middle-school sector was generated directly by the earlier growth of the primary system. Throughout the history of the Gold Coast, expansion at lower levels has always exerted a direct influence on education at intermediate or higher levels; the system tends to react reflexively to such pressures.

A factor of even greater significance apparent from the tables is the persistence of ecological variations in the provision of schools and in the access of the population to them. For example, although the Northern Region shows a more rapid *rate* of growth in school provision, its starting base is so small as to render this statistic relatively meaningless. In practice, the major growth has occurred within the southern areas (notably in the former Colony), where the creation of new primary and middle schools amounted to 590 with an increased enrolment of 101 thousand, as against respective increases of 183 and 24 thousand in the Northern Region. It is in the southern half of the country particularly that the main increase in schools provision is apparent. This conclusion can be further illustrated by reference to Table 11 which indicates the position in 1960.

It is apparent that variations still exist as between the major regions of Ghana. As might be expected, Accra Capital District which includes Accra Municipality itself, is distinctly ahead of all other regions, but, for the most part, there is not too great a difference between the southern areas of the country. Ashanti has now caught up with most parts of the south but the Western Region tends to lag as the result of very low levels of development in the relatively isolated areas of the far southwest. Very clearly, however, the new region of Brong-Ahafo which lies to the north of Ashanti is far behind the average for the southern part of the country, and in the Northern Region itself only about one in ten of the child population actually attends school. Thus, although it is likely that there has been a smoothing out of patterns of inequality as between the south and Ashanti, the northern problem still remains and perhaps is even more acute than before.

In similar fashion distinct urban-rural differences in levels of enrolment have persisted in spite of energetic government attempts to diffuse schooling more evenly.[21] Thus within all urban areas an average of 55·4 per cent of all children of school-going age are at present in regular attendance at schools—this figure drops to only

TABLE 11

PERCENTAGE OF CHILD POPULATION, BY REGIONS, NOW ATTENDING
SCHOOL*

Region†	Number of Children of School Age‡	Number of Children of School Age at Present in School	Percentage of School-Age Children in Attendance
Western	327,620	132,660	40·5
Accra, C.D.	105,970	63,170	59·6
Eastern	273,160	136,010	49·8
Volta	194,850	89,630	45·9
Ashanti	270,940	132,000	48·7
Brong-Ahafo	140,440	44,700	31·8
Northern	276,760	32,380	11·7

* Ghana, *Census of Population 1960, Advance Report of Volumes III and IV*
(Accra: Census Office, 1962).

† This division is in conformity with the new regional boundaries as used in
the census of 1960.

‡ This has been defined as the proportion of population aged between six
years and fifteen years. In practice, Ghana has no legal maximum or minimum
age for schooling and a proportion of children attend school after the age of
fifteen though very few attend before the age of six.

35·2 per cent for all rural localities. As we might expect, the distinction between urban and rural localities is less marked within regions
with overall higher levels of enrolment. Thus in Accra Capital District, enrolment within the urban section of the area stands at 65·1
per cent of the potential school-going population and this only drops
to 43·3 per cent in rural areas. Conversely, the distinction in the north
is very sharp indeed. Here an enrolment ratio of 36·8 per cent for
urban areas drops to only 9·8 per cent for rural localities. Thus, given
marked differences for the country as a whole, each region shows its
own distinctive pattern of internal variation which is associated both
with the extent of urbanization and the proportion of the population
engaged in other than farming activities.

It seems quite evident that geographic differentials in the diffusion
of schooling are remarkably stubborn and difficult to eradicate since
they are so intimately related to other aspects of social change. The
real acceleration in educational development in Ghana actually began
before 1951 and was very marked from 1945 onwards. Thus, in spite
of about fifteen years of considerable effort the government can only

189

point to limited success in this direction, and it can be anticipated that areas like the north are likely to lag behind the rest of the country for another decade or longer. The most disturbing thing about regional and district differentials, however, as we shall see in later pages, is that they tend to coincide with ethnic divisions and become foci for political conflict.

Some Consequences of Educational Growth

The Accelerated Development Plan of 1951 was not without its local critics who characterized it as an 'ill-digested series of proposals based on political expediency'.[22] The primary criticisms of the plan, however, were based upon the necessity for maintaining high academic standards. Objections mainly centred upon the dilution of the teaching force in the primary and middle schools by untrained or partially trained teachers. Such criticisms reflected an earlier British preoccupation with the maintenance of standards, but the objections were directed at what was, in effect, a transitional state of affairs. In 1956 the proportion of trained teachers in the assisted primary and middle schools constituted only 35·3 and 84·6 per cent respectively of the total; only three years later these percentages had risen to 46·2 and 91·2 per cent. There is little doubt that the period of rapid expansion did lead to a lowering of academic standards within the primary and middle schools, but it is equally true that the emergency teacher-training schemes could enable the system to 'recover' at a rapid rate once the initial peak of enrolments was past.[23] The opponents of the plan, in reiterating criticisms which had formerly led the British administration to proceed cautiously in the diffusion of educational facilities, ignored more significant consequences of mass educational expansion.

The Expansion of Academic Secondary Schools

It has been a central thesis of this study that increased enrolments at lower levels of an educational structure generate direct pressure on higher institutions. Where this is combined with what we have typified as the 'free market' approach in education (minimal restrictions on the opening of new institutions), the growth of the system is likely to proceed by the proliferation of private or proprietary schools which reflect quite closely the prevailing state of mass demand for particular types of education. Within French and Belgian territories more definite restrictions were placed upon expansion of the secondary system. The reverse was the case on the Gold Coast; the government

190

adopted a typically British policy in allowing the relatively un-controlled growth of the system while extending aid on as wide a basis as possible to formerly proprietary institutions. The results of the policy may be seen in Table 12.

TABLE 12

THE GROWTH OF THE SECONDARY-SCHOOL SYSTEM 1951–1960*

Year	Government and Approved Schools		Private Schools		Total	
	Institu-tions	Enrol-ment	Institu-tions	Enrol-ment	Institu-tions	Enrol-ment
1951	13	2,937	49	3,964	62	6,901
1952	26	5,033	27	2,709	53	7,742
1953	30	6,066	28	2,337	58	8,403
1954	31	6,936	19	1,666	50	8,602
1955	31	7,711	28	2,306	59	10,107
1956	35	8,908	23	2,157	58	11,065
1957	38	9,860	22	2,259	60	12,119
1958	39	10,423	24	2,773	63	13,196
1959	39	11,111	30	4,206	69	15,317
1960	59	14,000+†	52	6,000	101	20,000+†

* Computed from Ghana, *Education Statistics, 1959*, pp. 1–2.
† These are fairly close approximations based on the 1960 Census.

In 1951 a relatively small group of thirteen highly selective Govern-ment and Assisted schools plus forty-nine private institutions ac-counted for all secondary enrolments. By 1960 total enrolment had more than tripled and the number of institutions in both sectors had almost doubled.

Certain other features in the table must be noted. We have pre-viously shown the very sharp upswing that occurred in secondary-school provision in the last decade of colonial rule. The period after 1951 indicates rather a steady but not phenomenal growth in the secondary-school system. Indeed, although total enrolment rose, the number of private secondary schools dropped to only nineteen in 1954, though there was again a steady growth in their numbers up to 1959. This temporary decline was a result of government policy. It was not the aim of government in the 1951 plan to greatly increase secondary-school provision except by the creation of a limited number of day secondary schools, which were theoretically to cater to local pupils only.[24] Further, there was an attempt to extend limited finan-cial aid to *existing* private institutions which could satisfy the government as to certain minimal standards of instruction and accommodation.[25] These institutions which received government aid after 1951 were designated Encouraged schools. Thus the drop in the number of private institutions between 1951 and 1954 was actually due to the transfer of private institutions to the public sector while, correspondingly, the growth in the public sector was a reflection of this transfer. It was not primarily a result of the creation of new institutions.

The year 1960, however, was crucial for the secondary-school system. At this point, after a period of steady expansion, the first tremendous pressures were exerted on the academic secondary system through the increased output of the primary and middle schools. In that year, twenty new schools were added to the public sector and, more significant, twenty to the private list, while enrolment jumped by at least 5,000. After the eight-year lag between primary or middle, and secondary school expansion, Ghana is now faced with the problem of an unprecedented demand for secondary-school education. It can be confidently expected that in spite of considerable government efforts to meet this demand, a proportion of it will once again be met through private secondary institutions, which may later be incorporated into the public system.

It is to be noted that this demand is generally for an academic type of education modelled closely upon that provided by the elite Government and Assisted schools, which themselves reflect a primarily British stereotype. In contradistinction to this, in spite of government efforts to promote technical education, enrolments in all technical and trade institutions numbered only just over 4,500 in 1959, and there were only 1,781 students in private technical establishments most of which could certainly claim no secondary status.

The preoccupation with academic secondary education is amply confirmed by examination of Legislative Assembly Debates since 1951. Paradoxically, at the very period in which the primary and middle schools were undergoing expansion, members' questions to the representatives of the Ministry of Education in the House were more generally concerned with the provision of secondary schools. There has been less debate on the primary and middle-school system. Thus as early as 1951, Magnus J. Sampson was to observe, 'Secondary education should be given priority over primary education because students from secondary schools will feed the two ends of the stick— the primary and university.'[26] Similarly another member in addressing the minister remarked that 'the people are telling you they want secondary schools; they do not want two year Teacher Training Colleges'.[27] These remarks, indicating the general tenor of debate in the House since 1951, are not unconnected with ethnic rivalries. They represent a basic demand for secondary academic education, that has its roots in the very earliest periods of colonial educational development.

This pressure for secondary education received recognition by the government in the 'Second Development Plan' for 1959–64. It was noted that it had become increasingly necessary to expand the secondary system with the aim of providing places for 10 per cent of the pupils in each region who were potentially eligible to enter.[28] Such a programme was to include expansion of existing schools and the building of new ones by the Ghana Educational Trust, a body endowed with £2·5 million from Cocoa Marketing Board funds.[29]

Such a policy has, therefore, added yet another category of secondary school to the existing system. Thus at the commencement of 1961, the types of secondary schools were as follows:

(*a*) Government Secondary schools of which there were only two: the Government Secondary School at Tamale and the Government Secondary Technical School at Takoradi. These institutions were totally financed from government revenues.

(*b*) Thirteen Assisted Secondary schools. These, with the two government schools, formed the high-status section of the secondary system; the 'Great Schools' of Ghana are all to be found within this sector. Most of these schools received government aid for staff salaries and capital costs before 1951.

(*c*) Six Assisted Day Secondary schools. It will be recalled that although the creation of such schools, recruiting their pupils from local districts, was one of the aims of the Accelerated Development Plan, increasing pressure for selection into the schools has obliged some of these institutions to provide boarding facilities.

(*d*) Encouraged Secondary schools. This large group of twenty-two schools is a recent innovation since 1951. All these institutions were formerly non-aided private schools which since that date have received limited aid from the government in the form of payment of staff salaries.

(*e*) Sixteen Ghana Educational Trust schools. These are largely new institutions most of which have not developed senior forms. Most date from 1958 and depend almost entirely upon funds from the Trust.

(*f*) The Private Secondary schools, of which there were fifty-two, depend entirely upon their own resources and upon student fees. In practice, this group may be dichotomized into schools run by the voluntary agencies and purely proprietary or profit-making institutions run by individual entrepreneurs. The former are usually new institutions which are hoping ultimately to obtain government aid and enter the Encouraged sector. The latter are, more frequently than not, institutions offering the lowest standards of instruction and often 'going out of business'. The rapid turnover in such institutions does not affect their overall numerical growth.

This elaborate classification of secondary schools is of great functional significance. Theoretically all schools within the public sector (i.e. those from *a* to *e*) enjoy parity of status; their pupils take the same courses and prepare for the same public examinations. Most important, entry into schools within this public sector is most often obtained through success in a Common Entrance Examination held annually throughout Ghana for all middle-school students aspiring to secondary-school entry. This examination is uniform and centrally administered by the West African Examinations Council. At the same time that students apply to sit for it they are also obliged to list three secondary schools in order of their personal preference. Selection for secondary education is on a national competitive basis, and it is theoretically possible for any middle-school student to choose any secondary school in Ghana. Usually, able students tend to make the older Assisted schools their first choice, and the principals of these schools are then able to select freely from the limited number of highly placed students. The remaining schools within the public system must accept the less highly ranked examinees and their enrolment includes many second and third preference scholars.[30]

Thus the expansion of the secondary system has involved not only an overall growth in the number of schools. It has also led to the internal differentiation of that system itself. Later we shall demonstrate how this internal differentiation is partially reflected in the backgrounds of students within the component parts of the secondary-school system. In practical terms, the main axis of differentiation is between the thirteen Government and Assisted schools and the forty-six Assisted Day, Encouraged, and Ghana Educational Trust institutions that form the low-status segment of the secondary system. Increasingly in contemporary Ghana, acceptance at such schools as Mfantsipim or Achimota is far more significant than attendance at any other secondary institution.

The fierceness of competition for entry into secondary schools is borne out by the fact that in 1950 out of 7,000 candidates who sat for the Common Entrance Examination only 800 were accepted by any secondary institution.[31] In July 1959, 14,500 candidates from the second and third years of the middle-school courses sat for the examination. To this latter figure must be added 26,500 candidates from Middle Form IV who sat for the Middle School Leaving Certificate, the first part of which was also used as a temporary selective device for secondary-school entry.[32] Thus the rate of selection from the middle schools has declined from 11·4 per cent to 5·3 per cent during the decade—a clear indication of the pressures exerted on the secondary schools by middle-school expansion.

The decision taken in 1959 to allow only middle-school pupils in their second or third year to sit for the Common Entrance Examination while using the Middle School Leaving Examination for Middle Form IV pupils reflects the policy first outlined in the Accelerated Development Plan. Progressively a larger proportion of the entry into the secondary schools will be from the lower forms of the middle schools while Middle Form IV will constitute a terminal class for the bulk of non-successful students.[33] This development is of profound significance since it suggests the emergence of a classical 'dual' system of secondary schools on a European pattern from an initially single-track structure. Throughout the colonial period, entry into secondary school could only be achieved after completion of a six-year primary course and a four-year senior primary sequence. The attempt to select secondary pupils from lower segments of the system suggests that the ultimate development is likely to be a six-year primary system topped by a group of highly selective secondary schools providing a basic five-year course with sixth-form studies leading to entry into higher institutions.[34] A parallel group of non-selective middle-school institutions will offer terminal courses for the bulk of non-successful candidates for secondary-school entry.

If it is borne in mind that the present educational administration also envisages the development of secondary-technical schools, of which there is at present only one, then it seems possible that there will grow up a tripartite system of post-primary education very much on the British model. The three sets of institutions may enjoy a theoretical 'parity of esteem', but they will prepare for occupations enjoying markedly different social prestige and income.[35] In effect, the post-colonial period has not diverged from metropolitan precedent but is approximating increasingly closely to that model. Ghana represents, in fact, a classical study in the emergence of a complex, highly differentiated secondary structure from a simple unilineal system.

The sociological significance of such a trend is considerable. One of the primary aims of the preceding pages of this study has been to indicate that formal education has been a contributing factor, though not the only factor, leading to the emergence of 'nascent' class structures in West Africa. As we shall indicate in later pages, recruitment into the secondary schools does not accurately reflect occupational or educational groupings within the Ghanaian population as a whole. If this is the case, then the selectivity of the system, which is likely to consistently favour urban groups and also individuals whose parents come from certain occupational categories, may tend to reinforce the process of class formation in contemporary Ghana. By themselves the schools cannot *create* class differentiation on the basis of occupational criteria, but they can reinforce class boundaries, and increasing differentiation within an educational system may become an indirect index of the process of class formation. Numerous studies both in Europe and the United States have indicated how educational 'success' and access to higher institutions is correlated with class origin. If then patterns of recruitment into the Ghanaian secondary schools show similar features we might construe this as constituting an indirect index of the emergence of social classes as we understand them. These factors, however, are additionally complicated by differential rates of ethnic access into the schools.

It is not surprising, therefore, that one of the main functional consequences of the expansion of primary and middle schools has been to increase the importance of the academic secondary school. Even by 1950, the secondary school dominated access into significant status positions within the 'modern' social structure. The widening of opportunities at lower levels has increasingly lowered the occupational currency of a primary and middle-school education since employment opportunities within the exchange sector are so limited. It has become increasingly necessary to obtain a secondary education for a limited number of prestigeful and relatively well-paid posts, and this has generated the increasingly powerful demand for secondary education paradoxically at a period when government has been extending the provision of primary, middle, and technical facilities.

Another significant factor has emerged which reinforces this trend. During the colonial period the two primary modes of social mobility had been through politics and education. The former career was not necessarily correlated with the possession of high educational qualifications. It perhaps functioned in the same manner as did small-business enterprise in nineteenth-century Europe and the United States by providing mobility opportunities for those with limited educational backgrounds.[36] With the stabilization of the existing regime and its political elite, it seems fairly certain that politics as a profession is likely to be of diminishing importance in Ghana for aspiring individuals.[37]

Coincident with the decline in politics as an alternative avenue for mobility there has been a marked expansion in public as opposed to private employment within the limited wage-employment sector until by 1960 the former constituted about 60 per cent of the total. Occu-

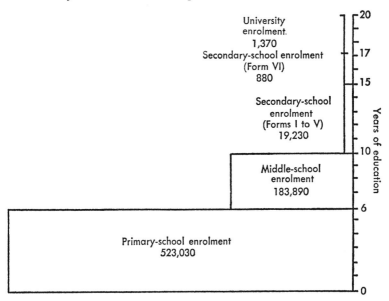

University
enrolment.
1,370
Secondary-school enrolment
(Form VI)
880

Secondary-school
enrolment
(Forms I to V)
19,230

Middle-school
enrolment
183,890

Primary-school enrolment
523,030

Years of education

20
17
15
10
6
0

Explanation: The year 1960 represents the last for which complete statistics were available. It should be noted that completion of five years of secondary study involves anything between twelve and fifteen years of schooling.

Some eleven thousand students in Arabic schools have been included in the primary-school total; over nine thousand students in teacher training colleges or commercial and technical institutions are not shown in the diagram.

Fig. 4. The Profile of the Ghanaian Educational System, 1960.

pations within the public service uniformly require more formal educational criteria for selection than any other form of employment. Indeed, one of the features of public bureaucracies is the degree to which their recruitment policies are based on rational or achievement criteria and specifically on formal educational qualifications.[38] Thus, increasing growth within public employment as against relatively limited opportunities within other sectors has led to an exaggerated concern with the possession of 'pieces of paper'. It may well be that the continuance of this trend will lead to an increasing closeness in the relationship between educational and occupational criteria.

Accordingly, the academic secondary school has become increasingly vital for social mobility, since it commands entry to nearly all significant roles within the public service or even into the larger commercial companies as well as access into higher institutions such as the University of Ghana or the Kwame Nkrumah University.[39]

This 'strategic' position of secondary schools is clearly illustrated in Figure 4. It will be readily observed that the two points of most rigorous selectivity within the system both occur at the secondary level: (*a*) at entry into the secondary system and (*b*) at the point of selection for the sixth form (after completion of the five-year basic secondary course). Once a student has obtained entry into secondary school he is very likely to continue with his studies into the fifth form, since wastage within the public secondary sector is very low.[40] The next major selective point occurs at the transition from fifth-form to sixth-form studies, only a small proportion of school-certificate holders entering the higher level. It is to be noted that all the sixth forms are now to be found in eleven schools which form the core of the Government and Assisted sector of the public secondary-school system. Though it is possible for students from Encouraged, Assisted Day, or Ghana Educational Trust schools to enter the Assisted schools at this level, discussions with school principals indicate that sixth-form students are more often drawn from the fifteen Government and Assisted schools and far less frequently from other categories of institutions within the public sector. Virtually no candidates ever enter sixth-form studies from the private sector.[41]

Completion of sixth-form studies in turn, virtually guarantees entry into higher institutions. In 1959 when sixth-form numbers stood at 630, with an annual graduation of approximately 300, the total output of the sixth forms could be absorbed by the University College of Ghana and the Kumasi College of Technology (now the Kwame Nkrumah University of Science and Technology). By 1961 total sixth-form numbers stood at approximately 800, which still implied virtual certainty of entry into higher institutions. Even with a projected increase in sixth-form pupils, their chances of entering university are likely to remain extraordinarily high and certainly will not drop below the 75 per cent level during the next five years, assuming that sixth forms continue to exist. However, since these sixth-form students are drawn mainly from a very limited segment of the secondary system, it is to be inferred that opportunities for higher education vary markedly as between segments of that system, producing marked inequalities in educational access to higher institutions.

To summarize our general argument, it seems clear that Ghanaian educational policy, though aiming primarily at an expansion of the primary and middle-school system, has created an expanding demand for secondary education and has enhanced the role of the latter as one of the most crucial components in the whole process of social mobility. Far more than in the late colonial period, the academic secondary school dominates the educational system which has increasingly taken on some of the structural characteristics of those of Western

198

Europe. This growth, however, has been accompanied by the internal differentiation of the secondary system itself. We must now take a look at the other side of the picture.

The Eclipse of the Middle Schools

It will be recalled that the policy of the Accelerated Development Plan which had converted the old four-year senior-primary schools into middle schools had left the latter in an ambiguous position. Not only were they to provide terminal courses for the bulk of students; they were also to act as feeder schools to the secondary institutions and ultimately become terminal institutions.

It was further intended that the middle schools should develop a wide range of non-academic courses suitable to the bulk of their students, and to this end the colonial government had abolished the old Senior Primary School Leaving Examination in 1950. It was hoped that the absence of this essentially academic hurdle would enable the schools to experiment freely with their curriculums without being subject to competitive examination pressures. The Department of Education observed at the time:

> The public which has grown to recognize success in this examination as a passport to 'respectable' employment will mourn its departure. Headteachers will in the future award a certificate testifying to the satisfactory arrangement of the senior primary course, but this substitute arrangement will not be immediately welcomed by all.[42]

This remark may be regarded as perhaps the greatest understatement in the educational history of the Gold Coast. Throughout the next five years there was a mounting body of popular opinion in favour of the restoration of a formal national examination leading to the award of a Middle School Leaving Certificate. Supporters of its restoration argued on the basis of the incentives that such an examination provided, but there is little doubt that the agitation among the public for its reintroduction stemmed from that reason noted by the department, its use as an occupational passport.[43]

However intrinsically desirable the aims of the department were, they clearly conflicted with the aspirations of the bulk of the Gold Coast population and rested on a misapprehension of the purposes for which the senior-primary and later the middle schools were being used. Popular pressure was once again discounted, but once again it was ultimately decisive; in 1955 as a result of general demand the examination was reinstated and in 1957 the West African Examinations Council was entrusted with its administration. The annual num-

199

ber of entries in this examination has exceeded 25,000 in all years since that date.[44]

In failing to perceive the social and economic function of the examination system or at least in discounting it, educationists had once again found it impossible to effect an intrinsically desirable reform. In one sense both the Department of Education and the public were incorrect in assuming that the certificate did, in fact, constitute a passport to employment. The previous chapter has indicated that even before 1950 there was considerable unemployment among Senior Primary School Leaving Certificate holders and that as a result their role in political developments in the Gold Coast was quite decisive. Nonetheless, the pressure for 'legitimating' educational symbols which were believed to provide access into the world of jobs was effective in reimposing on the middle schools an essentially academic curriculum terminated by an examination in which only 55–65 per cent of annual candidates are successful.

Pressure on the middle schools was to come from another direction, and this stemmed from their role as feeder institutions to the secondary schools. Although it had been hoped that a terminal curriculum could be developed alongside this recruitment function, it seems quite clear that there was no possibility of success so long as pupils thought mainly in terms of access to the secondary schools. This latter view was clearly shared by teachers whose reputation to some extent was determined by their success in training children for the Common Entrance Examination. As a result, although the present middle-school curriculum theoretically comprises a wide diversity of subjects, there is a definite stress on English and mathematics which are the crucial subjects on the Common Entrance Examination and, accordingly, some neglect of other areas within the curriculum.[45] Though this trend may be undesirable it might be considered inevitable; it was certainly predictable if the articulation of the system had been examined more closely. The government has, indeed, been forced to recognize the failure of the middle school to provide an alternative to secondary education:

> In these circumstances the reformation of the middle-school course in the direction of practical activities and as an introduction to living has proved almost impossible of achievement. Middle schools at present tend to be judged by their success in the Common Entrance Examination to secondary schools.[46]

In effect, the middle schools have been depressed to the status of feeder institutions to the secondary-school segment and have been progressively obliged to give a heavily academic bias to the curriculum. We have tried to show that this is a very old story in Ghana and the solution to the problem does not lie in successive attempts at curricular reform. The root cause of the phenomenon is to be found in the nature of the social structure of contemporary Ghana and to problems of social mobility within the system. The schools do not exist in a curricular vacuum and must generally respond to social pressures imposed upon them.

The prognosis for the middle schools is a very uncertain one, and it is probable that their ultimate emergence as purely terminal institutions which are not responsible for supplying recruits to the secondary schools will not alleviate the problem. British experience is pertinent here, since one of the aims of creating the secondary modern school was to provide a distinct set of non-academic courses for students without these schools being involved in processes of selection for the secondary grammar sector. In practice, the result has been that the secondary modern schools have increasingly provided academic courses and entered candidates for public examinations normally entered for by the secondary grammar-school students.[47] This 'blurring' of the distinction between segments of the post-primary system is an inevitable consequence of the differential prestige accorded to the types of occupation for which they prepare. Public examination plays a significant role in this occupational selection process and there is little doubt that the approximation of the secondary modern to the secondary grammar schools is likely to continue. It would seem that the Ghanaian middle schools are in the same unhappy position. Two largely incompatible functions have been thrust upon them and, if British precedent is any guide, it is likely that they will continue as alternative academic institutions providing generally inferior offerings to a non-selective student body.

The Growth of Unemployment

A far more serious consequence of massive increases in the outflow from primary and middle schools has been the dramatic growth in unemployment among primary and middle school-leavers. Since 1951 the situation has been vastly exacerbated and has become a crucial problem for government not only because of its fear of a rapid rise in the rate of juvenile delinquency in the towns but also because the presence of large numbers of unemployed youth is not without political implications.[48]

The precise extent of this unemployment is difficult to estimate in the absence of accurate statistics, but there is no doubt in official circles that it has reached large proportions despite the considerable efforts made by government to alleviate it. As late as 1953 the government was denying the existence of unemployment on any scale, and the ministerial secretary to the Ministry of Labour in reply to questions about what was to be done with respect to this serious problem observed:

> According to the information available no significant real unemployment exists in the Gold Coast at present, and what appears to be unemployment arises either from unwillingness on the part of the workers to accept employment offered to them, which may involve moving to another area, or from lack of the necessary qualifications and experience by persons who seek employment in skilled occupations.[49]

The attempt to deny the existence of unemployment was combined, therefore, with the statement that what unemployment existed was largely of a 'frictional' variety in which the ancient arguments of white-collar unemployment and geographical immobility were invoked. The previous chapter has indicated the unsoundness of the white-collar argument and similarly indicated that geographical mobility within Ghana is remarkably high, many individuals being prepared to travel long distances to obtain work. If unemployment was an 'optical illusion' it appears to be a remarkably constant one to which observers have continually made reference and to the alarming extent of which Busia drew attention in his survey of Sekondi-Takoradi.[50] More dramatic statistical illustration of the problem was finally afforded in April 1961, when a survey by the Office of the Government Statistician and the Ministry of Labour reported that there were over 31,000 unemployed individuals within the Accra Municipality of whom a majority were recent middle-school-leavers. This represented almost 10 per cent of the total population of Accra and a far higher proportion of the actual available labour force.

Certainly unemployment is more observable in the urban areas and it is not unreasonable to suggest that the conditions in Accra and Sekondi-Takoradi exist also in most of the larger Ghanaian towns; the problem is exacerbated in all cities by the urban movement of school-leavers. Though unemployment strictly speaking may not exist within the rural areas, it is highly likely that concealed underemployment does exist in the sense that school-leavers do virtually nothing except for an occasional stint on the farm while waiting for a job to come along or preparatory to moving to the towns.[51]

An equally revealing indication of the extent of the problem has been the growing volume of discussion in the popular press over the last few years and the increasing number of public appeals addressed on behalf of unemployed middle-school-leavers. A recent statement is worth quoting in entirety since it typifies the nature of the problem.

> *Give Us a Chance to earn a Living:* I write to appeal to the government,
> public corporations, firms and all employers, of labour to consider
> holders of Middle School Leaving Certificates for employment in their
> establishment. There are certainly some holders of the Middle School
> Leaving Certificate who can do better in the offices than some of the
> holders of the School Certificate. It is disheartening to observe that
> whenever vacancies are advertised in the newspapers the qualification
> required from the prospective applicants is either School Certificate at
> the ordinary or the higher level, or their equivalents. This situation is
> very discouraging to middle school leavers and parents who cannot
> afford to send their children into higher institutions to continue their
> education beyond the middle school level. Looking at the issue another
> way round, it is quite logical to state that the holders of the Higher
> School Certificate can do better on the farms of Ghana than the middle
> school leavers. My anxious plea on behalf of all middle school leavers
> and myself is: Employers, consider middle school leavers too and give
> them a chance.[52]

The statement indicates the extent to which the School Certificate
has become the gateway to certain forms of employment, but we
shall indicate later that the writer is perhaps incorrect in assuming
that it is 'clerical' employment alone that is at question.

During recent years the government has been obliged to take cognizance of the problem and attempts at its partial solution have been
three-fold. All have been largely unsuccessful and the first two have
rested on the assumption that unemployment is largely frictional.

Initially, there has been a large-scale attempt within the middle
schools to persuade school-leavers to return to the land, a variant of
a very old theme. The previous chapter has shown, however, that the
obstacle to the return to the land may lie in the nature of traditional
farming itself and the limitations of the institutional framework in
which such individuals would be obliged to function. The success of
any scheme to persuade individuals to return to the land is, therefore,
almost entirely contingent upon changes already having taken place
in the rural areas themselves. There is among school-leavers no intrinsic objection to farming so long as the conditions favour modern
or progressive cultivation.[53] Since little effort has been made, so far,
in Ghana to tackle the problems of land tenure, marketing, and
onerous kinship obligations, where the root of the problem seems to
lie, the campaign has been largely unsuccessful.

In the last two years, the government has attempted to develop
vocational guidance schemes through liaison with the schools and by
setting up a vocational guidance division within the Ministry of

Labour. To a great extent this policy reflects some misunderstanding of what vocational guidance actually means. There appears to be a general impression that vocational guidance can actually create jobs for school-leavers whereas the essential function of this type of activity is to develop appropriate techniques for the optimal selection of personnel for occupations within the existing structure. Such a service is crucial in areas with manpower shortages where maximization of labour efficiency can be effected by careful selection techniques. It is certainly far less significant in Ghana except that appropriate instruments might be able to select the most promising candidates from large numbers of applicants for a very restricted number of jobs. Similarly, branches of the Ministry of Labour can help in limited cases where real frictional unemployment exists by providing applicants with information about existing job opportunities in alternative areas. But the combined efforts of vocational guidance teams and labour offices can make little impression on the overall volume of unemployment among school-leavers.

The third approach of the government has perhaps been more realistic since it implicitly recognizes the true nature of the problem. This has been the creation of a Workers' Brigade involving the large-scale recruitment on a voluntary basis of workers for public works projects in agriculture and construction. Volunteers serve within the brigade for specific periods, receive subsistence and modest pay, and may be drafted to any part of Ghana. In practice, the organization is run on para-military lines.[54]

Theoretically, at least, the aims of the organization are promising. The Brigade has been responsible for the creation of three large-scale experimental farms where chances to develop progressive methods of joint farming do exist. It is hoped that agricultural instruction over a two-year period will enable ex-members to become progressive agriculturalists within their own areas. However, success here depends on whether they can utilize newly acquired techniques in the traditional rural areas. Similarly, the Brigade has performed useful service in projects connected with airfield construction and other public works and it is hoped to provide on-the-job instruction in basic trades to be utilized after discharge from the organization.

The limitations of the scheme, which bears some resemblance to the Civilian Conservation Corps of the U.S.A. during the depression years, should be apparent. It can do nothing about the supply side of the problem and the government, for political reasons, can do little to exert direct control over the output of the school system. Second, membership is voluntary and many do not wish to enter a body of this nature. Thus, although the organization grew from just over

8,000 in 1958 to over 15,000 in 1961 and applications for entry vastly exceeded the possible intake, only about 25 per cent of the force was composed of middle-school-leavers.[55] Since the annual output of the middle schools alone is now just under 40,000, the Brigade can only deal with an insignificant proportion of ex-middle-school pupils.

During the last two years there has been considerable pressure to make membership of the Brigade compulsory and draft all middle-school-leavers into an 'agricultural army'.[56] In this case the government is liable to be defeated by the sheer logistics of the problem. There is already an acute shortage of supervisory personnel within the Brigade and problems of accommodation, supervision, and administration for an annual output of 40,000 middle-school-leavers per year are already certainly beyond the present capacities of the government.

In short, the actions of government to check the problem of unemployment are likely to be unsuccessful. The first two elements of policy are ineffective since they are remedies suggested by an inaccurate diagnosis and the third, though useful as a temporary measure, is unlikely to have much effect on the overall position.

Although the urgency of the problem is realized there is still a widespread belief that unemployment is due to the unwillingness of school-leavers to accept anything other than white-collar work and to their reluctance to work with their hands, as a result of the kind of educational process to which they have been exposed. Unemployment is thereby attributed to idleness, and the general notion that literates consider manual work beneath their dignity still prevails.[57] We have noted that this view has been set forth often since the earliest periods and has acquired the authenticity that derives from repetition with little empirical evidence to support it. We have pointed to the reasons why clerical employment was originally favoured and concluded that it was not prestige motivations alone that were significant. In the present period there is little justification for making inferences about the clerical orientations of school graduates. What Callaway has observed in the case of Nigeria is equally true in Ghana:

> Present day school-leavers *do* work with their hands and many may be classified as general labourers. They compete first to work on town building sites rather than on up-country roads. Their pay is between four and five shillings a day. Some harbour thoughts of becoming labour clerks or eventually rising to positions as headmen of gangs. But even jobs as general labourers are not plentiful and employers often prefer more mature, stronger people, who, as it happens, are illiterate. And there is an immense surplus of this kind of labour.[58]

In addition to direct observation in Nigeria and Ghana some systematic evidence is now forthcoming on the fallacy of the white-collar thesis. In a study by Barnard of 416 middle-school boys in the Accra area, it was noted that no less than 44 per cent of the sample wished to enter technical employment in trades, such as motor-car mechanics, electricians, carpenters, masons, etc.[59] A further 9 per cent were most interested in obtaining posts which were primarily manual in nature ranging from farming, the police force, and lorry driving to petty trading. A further 47 per cent preferred work in the white-collar sector, ranging from professional work (28 per cent) to ordinary clerical employment (19 per cent).

In practice, therefore, the majority of boys (53 per cent) preferred actual manual and technical employment to white-collar jobs.

It is sometimes suggested that African children's aspirations are unreal, and it might be agreed that the group who preferred professional jobs were in this category. But it should be realized that the response is largely a function of how the question is put. If children are asked what job they would prefer when they leave school they are likely to respond in terms of jobs that they may not be able to obtain but which they would like to enter. In a society where emergent status concepts are increasingly being based on occupational criteria what is surprising in the result is that the majority of children still opted for technical, artisan, and manual employment. Barnard's type of question was, therefore, ambivalent and liable to be interpreted by children in terms of what they would most prefer or alternatively, what they *expected* to obtain.

In order to further examine this problem the present writer conducted a survey of 210 boys in nine randomly selected middle schools in the Accra area in December 1959. In this case all the sample comprised students who were due to leave middle school that month, the majority of whom would not be entering secondary school. Care was taken to elicit differential responses on the basis of 'What kind of job would you really like to get if you could *freely* choose what you wanted to do?' and 'What kind of job do you *expect* to obtain, in fact, when you leave school?' Here an attempt was made to clarify differences between what may be regarded as fantasy or optimal choices and the responses when children were actually faced by the realities of their own situation and of the job market (Table 13).

TABLE 13

OCCUPATIONAL CHOICES OF MIDDLE FORM IV CHILDREN (N = 210)

Occupational Category	(1) Free Choice Response (Percentage)		(2) Job Expectation Response (Percentage)	
I Higher Professional*	11·0	(23)	5·2	(11)
II Lower Professional†	10·0	(21)	1·9	(4)
III Teacher‡	0·9	(2)	3·8	(8)
IV Clerical and Allied§	8·1	(17)	10·0	(21)
V Artisans and Skilled Workers¶	51·0	(107)	22·4	(47)
VI Commercial**	1·9	(4)	9·5	(20)
VII Semi-skilled and Unskilled††	3·3	(7)	35·2	(74)
VIII Uniformed Services‡‡	2·4	(5)	4·8	(10)
IX Fishermen and Farmers	10·5	(22)	6·7	(14)
X Miscellaneous and Unclassified §§	0·9	(2)	0·0	(0)
No Answer	0·0	(0)	0·5	(1)
Total	100·0	(210)	100·0	(210)

* Doctor, lawyer, minister of religion, etc.

† Nurse, dispenser, draughtsman, journalist, agricultural officer, surveyor, etc.

‡ All teaching roles within the primary, middle, secondary, or technical institutions.

§ Clerk (unspecified), cashier, bookkeeper, typist, bank clerk, librarian, letter writer, etc.

¶ Electrician, motor mechanic, plumber, carpenter, mason, printer, painter, shoemaker, locomotive engineer, tailor, etc.

** Petty trade and small-scale shopkeepers.

†† Labourer (various), messenger, bus conductor, watchman, steward, quarryman, miner, cook, etc.

‡‡ Police, Army, Workers Brigade.

§§ Musician, boxer, artist, jockey, etc.

It is quite apparent from column (1) that rather than indicating any marked preference for the white-collar cluster (I–IV) there is an overwhelming interest in skilled trades involving distinct manual activity. There is also, interestingly enough, a substantial minority who express a preference for entering farming and fishing. Teaching, however, remains a most undesirable occupation which tends to confirm the writer's opinion that the number of middle-school scholars entering the Teacher Training Colleges do so *faute de mieux* and that the status of the Ghanaian primary and middle-school teacher has declined rapidly in recent years. Generally speaking, even where middle-school children are given the opportunity to fantasy and express optimal preferences these aspirations are very moderate and only those expressing preferences in categories I and II could be considered to be carrying their aspirations far beyond actual possibilities.

Direct comparison between columns (1) and (2), however, yield the most striking data. As we should expect, the overall percentage of white-collar responses drops from 30 to 21 per cent with an increase in categories III and IV but a very marked drop in categories I and II. Teaching emerges rather more clearly as an occupation that is not preferred but expected by a proportion of children. The most radical drop is in category V, from 51 to 22 per cent with a corresponding rise in category VII from 3 to 35 per cent. Although the majority of children would prefer skilled manual work, they are reconciled to seeking semiskilled and unskilled employment. A similar phenomenon is apparent in the commercial category of small-scale trading.[60] Though trading is not highly preferred there is a substantial rise of almost 8 per cent in this category, and it is clear that children reconcile themselves to undertaking this activity which is, in fact, open to them. Category IX shows a slight fall which illustrates to some extent that, although farming itself is not as unpopular as some other activities, there are factors operating that militate against children actually taking it up.

These results by no means substantiate the view that middle-school literates desire or expect white-collar employment. Rather do they indicate the remarkably moderate level of aspirations and expectations and the eminently realistic view of the occupational structure that these children have. Although both studies mentioned have been conducted on limited samples and cannot be regarded as conclusive, the evidence is sufficiently striking to be noted. Indeed, since both these studies were conducted in large urban areas it is not unreasonable to suppose that the aspirations of these children will, if anything, be higher than the aspirations of the bulk of the Ghanaian middle-school population.

The tragedy is that, in one sense, most of these aspirations are unrealistic. In practice, a high proportion of these pupils will be unable to find any sort of paid employment however humble it may be. We have previously analysed in some detail the causes of unemployment and explained why students are reluctant to re-enter the subsistence-traditional sector of the economy. This situation is likely to remain a feature of Ghanaian society for some years to come and proposals for the alleviation of the problem can be no more than partial solutions. It might be suggested that the devolution of educational costs from the central government to the local authorities might result in checks being placed upon the rate of growth of the system.[61] Attempts of this nature to place limitations upon the supply position would be politically difficult for the government and reasonably enough would conflict with other legitimate national aims. Similarly compulsory drafting of school-leavers and the provision of work for them would be extraordinarily hazardous from a political point of view.

In the last resort the solution lies in Ghana reaching a level of development leading to a rise in national income and a considerable enlargement in the size of the exchange structure. It is beyond the scope of this study to discuss factors leading to such growth but it does indicate that the schools might have less role in the process than the growth of an entrepreneurial class in a milieu in which these entrepreneurial talents can be effectively utilized. Recent studies on human capital formation through education frequently ignore the fact that training in skills alone will have little effect unless an occupational structure exists in which these skills can be effectively utilized.[62] Little can be expected, for example, from technical education, since there are already some signs that the market for certain technical skills is becoming saturated. It might be reasonably suggested that education will act as a multiplier in an economy which has already reached the take-off point and is beginning a period of expansion, but to have a surplus of unemployed technicians is no more advantageous than to have a surplus of clerks. Ghana represents a classic situation where the pursuit of educational goals has produced an unanticipated consequence of serious proportions.

Ethnicity and the Schools

It has already been noted that differential rates of economic and social change plus European penetration from the coast had resulted in an uneven spread of schools and, in consequence, marked inequalities among ethnic groups in terms of their access to them. These inequalities were, in fact, closely related to differential levels of demand for formal education and, for example, low early enrolments in Ashanti and the North generally reflected indifference or even hostility to the schools on the part of local populations. We have seen how early Ashanti interest in education arose partially from a need to compete on equal terms in trade with the coastal peoples. Though the colonial power tended to govern the Colony, Ashanti, and the Northern Territories separately, at the same time, it relied heavily upon local traditional political structures, thus minimizing ethnic conflict throughout the colonial period. Since 1951 this policy has been generally reversed as part of a greater movement towards a unitary form of political structure. There has been a consequent diminution of regional functions and a consistent attempt to destroy the foundations of localized traditional political structures and replace them with conciliar forms of secular authority.

Thus, for example, the Coussey Commission on Constitutional Reform of 1950 made an attempt to perpetuate the institution of chiefship within the central government structure, and these proposals were put into effect in the new constitution of that year.[63] They provided for a degree of territorial representation which was not based on popular election but upon the election of representatives by regional councils of chiefs. However, the proposals for a new constitution (published on 19 June 1953, and promulgated in 1954) specifically recommended a unicameral legislature elected on a popular basis with no provision for specific regional interests to be represented.[64] The Constitution of 1957 did provide for Regional Assemblies and Houses of Chiefs but, in practice, these bodies have never been effectively constituted.[65] In general, therefore, there has been a steady trend away from regionalism and parallel with this a systematic attempt to destroy the vestigial power of the chiefly office.[66] At the local level this has entailed the creation of overwhelmingly secular local councils and the abolition of the Native Authorities system thus sweeping away the remnants of indirect rule.[67] In 1955 Apter was able to conclude that 'the structure of Gold Coast Government more and more resembles its formal British counterpart'.[68]

This trend towards centralization and secularization of authority, involving as it did the underplaying of distinct ethnic interests as manifested in regional or district structures, was not accomplished without intense opposition. The separatist movements in Ashanti and Togoland and the opposition of the National Liberation Movement (later the United Party) to the government have been exhaustively described elsewhere.[69] However, political defeat of regionalist or separatist movements which express the interests of diverse ethnic groups, shifts the ethnic rivalries to a new level. The incorporation of these elements into a more universalistic structure and the defeat of regionalist groups at the polls implies that conflict will largely occur between ethnic minorities for the limited number of strategic status roles within the new polity. Since education and particularly secondary and higher education is of crucial importance in access to these roles, rivalry will now manifest itself in competition between ethnic groups for school facilities and marked suspicion of minorities who appear to be getting 'more than their share'.[70] It is to be further noted that members representing the majority party in the Legislative Assembly are similarly constrained to press for the educational interests of their local constituencies.

The question of the allocation of government secondary-school scholarships affords an example of this process. In a general debate on government education policy in 1952, representatives from the Northern Territories, Ashanti, and Western Province suggested that conditions of award favoured the Eastern Province and that most scholarships in fact went there. It was therefore suggested that the allocation of such assistance should be effected on a purely regional basis.[71]

Government spokesmen, however, strongly supported the idea of allocation on the basis of merit alone (as expressed in competitive examination), while suggesting that 100 out of the 300 scholarships then available could be allocated on a regional basis. In answer to the critics the then ministerial secretary, Mr. Erzuah stated:

> It has been suggested by some regional interests . . . that there has been discrimination in the award of scholarships. This, of course, is wholly untrue. The reason for apparent inequality is neither discrimination, nor difference in mental capacity; it is merely the accident of history and it is paralleled in many other countries. The development of facilities for, and the growth of interest in, education has been uneven and the story has been one of slow penetration northwards from the seaboard. In secondary education, in particular, the main concentration has been on the coast—notably in Cape Coast. Although entry to the assisted secondary schools is by competition through the Common Entrance Examination and is thus open to all regardless of geographical origin, it is possible to argue that lack of facilities in the past in inland areas has operated in some way to the disadvantage of the hinterland.[72]

Such a reasoned response would be hardly likely to satisfy the diverse ethnic groups representing the critics but, in practice, Erzuah's reply conceded the general thesis that inequalities in access did reflect differential levels of demand, a situation that government policy since 1951 has only modified. Since that date ethnic rivalry has not only taken the form of direct requests by members for secondary schools within their own districts but has gone on to impute gross inequalities in the regional allocation of overseas scholarships.[73] Further, competing groups have been moved to demand special educational and occupational privileges within the system; thus, it was suggested that northerners should be allowed to enter clerical service on the basis of lower standards than in the south.[74]

The government, therefore, finds itself in a dilemma in that attempts to recruit into the public secondary schools or grant scholar-

P   211

ships on the basis of merit alone, i.e. the adoption of achievement criteria of selection, run counter to regional and ethnic interests which cannot be totally ignored for political reasons. Critics of 'merit selection' are correct in assuming that it might tend to favour certain areas; selective devices which place a high premium on literary skills are likely to favour the urbanized segment of the southern population.

Rather than concede to the demands of regional interests the government has maintained its position on selection by merit while attempting to rectify the situation within recent years by increased construction of Ghana Educational Trust Secondary schools mainly in rural districts in Ashanti, the Northern Region, and Western Region.

However, the growth in the number of secondary schools produces another side effect which tends to cut across the idea of free selection into any secondary school; this is the tendency for the schools to become ethnic institutions. It was a cardinal principal of British educational policy that highly selective secondary schools with boarding facilities enabled recruitment to rest on a wide ethnic basis and that the experience of living and learning together would be instrumental in reducing ethnic loyalties. This thesis has not been empirically demonstrable so far, and its proof would require longitudinal sociometric studies of patterns of friendship formation and association in multi-ethnic boarding institutions.[75] However, whether this thesis is justified or not, it would seem equally clear that schools which recruit from limited ethnic groups would do little to assist the development of sentiments of interethnic solidarity. In practice, the growth in number of secondary schools is likely to lead them increasingly to recruit students from local populations.

With the increase in the number of secondary schools it will be possible to recruit locally and, in effect, there may emerge two conflicting processes. First, the tendency of exceptional students will be to opt for the Assisted and Government schools irrespective of their location, and, second, there will be a tendency for an increasing number of students to choose schools within their own regions and districts as soon as facilities become available. We shall indicate in the following chapter that this trend is clearly evident in the secondary schools at present. Although each of these institutions contains a number of ethnic groups, most pupils come from the local region, and in a large number of cases, the largest single tribe represented is the predominant tribe in the immediate district.

In general, therefore, partly as a consequence of the emergence of more centralized secular structures and the decline of regionalism as an effective political issue, the schools have become increasingly a focus for ethnic rivalry and conflict. For obvious reasons, however, it is access to secondary and higher education that is really vital, since primary and middle schools' facilities are of far more limited importance. Paradoxically, the very growth of the secondary-school system leading to an increased number of purely ethnic institutions serving local populations may reinforce interethnic rivalries. Although Ghana exhibits few of the marked tendencies to regional fission so apparent in Nigeria, it seems equally clear that, even within the framework of a unitary state, opportunities exist for the continuance of powerful regional and ethnic loyalties which do not find expression in active political opposition but in the struggle for the 'commanding heights' of the new polity.

Some General Conclusions

The post-independence period has not been characterized by any overwhelmingly divergence of the Ghanaian educational system from that of the former metropole. Sometimes the opposite has occurred in that some aspects of the system have continued to approximate more closely to the English prototype.

Attempts to diffuse primary and middle-school education more widely have led to a series of unanticipated consequences. Sharp regional irregularities in educational provision still persist. The social significance of the academic secondary school has been enhanced; large-scale unemployment has emerged among the products of primary and middle institutions, and, finally, the schools have played some role in rivalries between ethnic minorities. Most of these side effects might be considered unsought as well as unanticipated, but they might have been predicted if the mobility functions of the schools had been examined and if more attention had been paid to the economic and occupational structure of contemporary Ghana. In practice, nearly all of these elements were evident in the Gold Coast before 1951.

It must not be assumed that the consequences of educational expansion are uniformly so depressing. It is rather that this type of consequence is more readily observable and demonstrable. It is not suggested here that literacy, for example, is not essential in attempting to promote sensible political judgment or in assisting the process of breaking down insularity and local sentiment.[76] Similarly literacy may be vital in economic development not only in the narrow sense of 'human capital' formation but also through its ability to generate new consumption needs which are reflected in higher levels of economic activity. These consequences are long-run, however, and empirically

213

difficult to demonstrate in the absence of significant changes in the Ghanaian economy. All we do suggest here is that attempts at reform produce many consequences, some of which are non-desired side effects and which may, in the short run, figure more largely than the achievement of the formal goals themselves.

REFERENCES

1. It is difficult to exaggerate the importance of the bureaucracy since 1951 with respect to its role in maintaining administrative efficiency and effectively carrying out development schemes. See also E. A. Shils, 'Political Developments in the New States', *Comparative Studies in Society and History*, II, No. 3 (April 1960), p. 290. Perhaps one of the most serious features in Ghana during the last three years, has been the progressive erosion of the powers of this administrative elite and the concentration of their functions into quasi-political structures.

2. United Nations, *Economic Survey of Africa since 1950* (New York: United Nations, 1959).

3. It seems likely that industrial development does in many cases presuppose vigorous agricultural growth as a prerequisite. See W. A. Lewis, *Report on Industrialisation and the Gold Coast* (Accra: Gold Coast Government, 1953), p. 2.

4. Ghana, *Population Census of 1960, Advance Report of Volumes III and IV*.

5. Ghana, *Quarterly Digest of Statistics* (Accra: Office of the Government Statistician, 1959), p. vi, and Ghana, *Economic Survey, 1958* (Accra: Office of the Government Statistician, 1959), p. 21.

6. *Ibid.*

7. Wallerstein, *The Emergence of Two West African Nations: Ghana and the Ivory Coast* (New York: Columbia University Press, 1959), p. 136.

8. Gold Coast, *Accelerated Development Plan for Education, 1951* (Accra: Government Printing Department, 1951), p. 1.

9. *Ibid.*, pp. 4–5.

10. *Ibid.*, p. 3.

11. It is to be noted that the long-run aim was to reduce the age of entry into the secondary schools and eventually recruit students directly from the last form of the primary schools, thus making the middle schools purely terminal institutions. *Ibid.*, p. 4.

12. *Ibid.*, p. 7.

13. *Ibid.*, p. 5.

14. Gold Coast, *Legislative Assembly Debates, 1951*, No. 4, II, 612–15.

15. It should be noted that so far as Ghana is concerned Legislative Assembly debates are a far more valuable source of data than articles published in educational journals. These latter rarely reflect mass feeling; speeches of representatives in the House reflect far more accurately the state of popular opinion regarding education.

16. Gold Coast, *Accelerated Development Plan for Education*, p. 1.

17. Ghana, *Education Report for the Year 1956* (Accra: Government Printer, 1957), p. 1.

18. It is somewhat surprising that professional educators in Africa have rarely paid attention to the political pressures imposed on educational systems. In general, decisions regarding language policy are far more likely to be based on political expediency than on the needs of children. Since the schools command

access to positions of power and status and are of central importance to the polity, it is probable that no educational system could ever allow the content of its curriculums to be determined by the psychological needs of children. In Ghana this has implied that political leadership has effectively pressed for the development of English instruction and this policy has only been resisted by a very limited and relatively ineffective minority among the intellectuals who advocated a return to African tongues. Paradoxically, this latter group is by far the most 'acculturated' minority in the Gold Coast. See also Wallerstein, *op. cit.*, p. 138.

19. See Selig S. Harrison, *India: The Most Dangerous Decade* (Princeton: University Press, 1960), pp. 68–70.

20. Statement by the Permanent Commission on Educational Policy for Africa at a meeting in Kampala, Uganda, in June 1960, reported in *The Times Educational Supplement*, 24 June 1960.

21. Ghana, *Census of Population 1960, Advance Report of Volumes III and IV*. The census differentiates urban and rural localities upon the basis of populations above and below 5,000. This is a relatively crude distinction and unfortunately census data does not yet allow us to examine levels of educational enrolment within the larger towns.

22. K. A. Busia in Gold Coast, *Legislative Assembly Debates, 1952*, No. 1, I, 23.

23. For an account of the modes by which the trained teaching force was rapidly enlarged see E. D. Roberts, 'Emergency Teacher Training in the Gold Coast', *Oversea Education*, XXVII, No. 2 (July 1956), 75–80.

24. Gold Coast, *Accelerated Development Plan, 1951*, p. 4. Some of these have become partially boarding schools since that date. Competitive entry into secondary schools has become so intense that day secondary schools serving genuinely local populations cannot be successful and prospective students move into areas to obtain 'residential' qualifications for entry into day schools. Further, the schools themselves are reluctant to recruit from limited local populations, since this greatly narrows the selection pool with possible adverse effects in later examination results. Thus the day schools have found themselves at a competitive disadvantage in relation to boarding institutions which can recruit from the whole national Middle School population. As a result the day schools have occasionally created their own boarding facilities.

25. Gold Coast, *Accelerated Development Plan, 1951*, p. 5.

26. Gold Coast, *Legislative Assembly Debates*, 1951, I, 181.

27. Mr. Kodzo, a representative from Volta. Ghana, *Legislative Assembly Debates*, No. 3, 1954, p. 275.

28. Ghana, *Second Development Plan, 1959–64* (Accra: Government Printer, 1959), p. 37.

29. *Ibid.*

30. There was one notable exception to this. The Government Secondary School at Tamale was specifically designed for entry by students from the Northern Region. Therefore, particular conditions of entry prevailed for this school which was essentially a 'northern' institution. It would appear that this school, however, is now open completely to southern applicants.

31. Gold Coast, *Legislative Assembly Debates, 1951*, I, 180.

32. West African Examinations Council, *Annual Report for the Year Ending 31 March 1960* (Oxford: Oxford University Press, 1961), pp. 13–14.

33. As a result of the survey reported in the following chapter, it was discovered that two-thirds of the sample of fifth-form students were drawn from the lower forms of the middle schools.

34. These predictions may have to be modified in the light of very recent government proposals to change the structure of the system. See Ghana, *Seven Year Development Plan 1963-64 to 1967-70* (Accra: Office of the Planning Commission, 1963), pp. 141–72. Present plans envisage the abolition of the four-year middle schools and their replacement by two-year 'continuing schools' with a vocational emphasis. Thus the total period of elementary education will be reduced from ten to eight years. At the same time, the secondary schools will be expanded to cope with about 25 per cent of the most able pupils. It would seem that these reforms will increase the gulf between the secondary schools and other forms of post-primary education. However, there have been so many changes proposed in the education system since 1951, virtually none of which has ever been adopted, that it would be premature to assume that these recent plans will be effectively implemented.

35. See Ghana, *Second Development Plan 1959–64*, pp. 37–39. It is interesting to note that at a Teachers' Conference summoned by the Ministry of Education in December 1959, and attended by the present writer, the main proposal from the teaching body was that there should be the development of a tripartite system of secondary grammar, secondary modern, and secondary technical schools. It should be noted also that the government of Western Region in Nigeria has already gone so far as to christen its non-selective senior primary institutions 'secondary modern' schools.

36. It is not inappropriate to regard the role of politics in West Africa as being somewhat similar to the role of small business enterprise in the mobility process in Western Europe and the U.S.A. Thus in the Gold Coast Legislative Assembly for 1954 only 14 per cent of members had a university education, 42 per cent had reached secondary-school level, while 44 per cent of the membership had some primary or senior-primary education only. H. H. Price, 'The Gold Coast's Legislators', *West Africa* (26 May 1956), p. 34. See also Gustav Jahoda, 'The Social Background of a West African Student Population', *British Journal of Sociology*, V, No. 2, 355, for a further account of the significance of politics in West Africa.

37. Thus it is quite clear that levels of political activity in the University of Ghana have remained low since 1951 while later pages in this study will indicate a similar disinterest in political activities among secondary-school pupils. This phenomenon of reluctance to enter the political arena is typical of a wider process that E. A. Shils has described as a form of retreatism. Shils, *op. cit.*, pp. 274–77.

38. The administration advertises widely in current Ghanaian newspapers and journals, since most public appointments must be formally advertised and application invited. It is significant that virtually all these posts require minimal educational qualifications such as the General School Certificate. Access to training schemes in the technical and agricultural fields similarly require formal academic qualifications as a condition of entry.

39. A small proportion (less than 5 per cent) of middle-school-leavers can enter certain types of teacher training college for preparation in primary and middle-school teaching. It is possible, after considerable teaching experience and the grant of a further 'A' Certificate, to enter the University of Ghana for a one-year associateship course in education. The number of such students, however, is rarely more than twenty per annum. It is also possible for some middle-school-leavers to ultimately enter University through training in junior technical institutes followed by senior craft or senior technical courses. Ghana, *Second Development Plan, 1959–64*, pp. 38–40. It is yet too early to assess the success of this plan, but in view of the length of training it is unlikely that many

216

school-leavers will achieve this level. Indeed personal communication with some principals of technical institutes would indicate that as the secondary system expands these schools will tend to recruit progressively from secondary-school-leavers. In practice, though theoretical opportunities exist, it is almost certain that the middle school will become essentially a terminal institution and recruits into the field of higher education or technical studies will largely come from the secondary-school stream.

40. This is not quite so true of the private secondary sector but, within the public sector wastage over the five-year course is below 5 per cent.

41. This conclusion is confirmed by examination of a sample of 336 sixth-form students obtained in 1961 by the present writer, a group comprising 43 per cent of all sixth-form students. Of these, 71 per cent were from Government or Assisted schools, 14 per cent from Encouraged institutions, and 0·6 per cent from private schools. A further 12 per cent gave no answer. It is also significant that 55 per cent of these students were undertaking sixth-form studies in the same schools in which they had previously completed courses up to the fifth-form level. This stresses the great importance of not only attempting to enter Government or Assisted schools but in entering the eleven schools within that group which offer sixth-form courses.

42. Gold Coast, *Report of the Education Department for the Year 1950–1951*, p. 20.

43. For an interesting exchange of views on this point, see Gold Coast, *Legislative Assembly Debates, 1952*, No. 3, pp. 586–91.

44. Ghana, *Report of the Ministry of Education, 1956*, p. 1, and West African Examinations Council, *Annual Report for the Year Ending 31 March 1956*, p. 18.

45. The 'Suggested Time-Table for Middle Schools' published by the Ministry of Education includes English, mathematics, religious instruction, geography, history and civics, physical education, housecraft and woodwork, Ghana language, arts and crafts, music, hygiene, gardening, and library work.

46. Gold Coast, *Progress in Education in the Gold Coast* (Accra: Government Printing Department, 1953), p. 15.

47. Olive Banks, *Parity and Prestige in English Secondary Education* (London: Routledge and Kegan Paul, 1955), pp. 210–19.

48. This concern with juvenile delinquency is not confined to Ghana. See Susan Elkan, 'Primary School Leavers in Uganda', *Comparative Education Review*, IV, No. 2 (October 1960), 108, for the situation in Uganda. The French areas of Africa are similarly concerned with the problem. See Centre International De L'Enfance, *Étude des conditions de vie de l'enfant Africain en milieu urbain et de leur influence sur la déliquance juvénile* (Paris: Centre International de l'Enfance, 1959), *passim*.

49. Gold Coast, *Legislative Assembly Debates, 1953*, I, 424.

50. K. A. Busia, *Report on a Social Survey of Sekondi-Takoradi* (London: Crown Agents for the Colonies, 1950), pp. 61–84.

51. This situation is well documented by Elkan, *op. cit.*, p. 108, and the writer's observations would confirm that the few representatives of youth who have terminated their education make only sporadic contributions to the village economy. See also Arch. C. Callaway, 'School Leavers in Nigeria: No. 3', *West Africa* (8 April 1961), p. 371.

52. *Daily Graphic*, 1 May 1961, p. 7. See also the *Ghanaian Times*, 3 May 1961, p. 4.

53. This point has been most cogently argued by Callaway in the case of Nigeria and he has suggested modes by which a limited number of school-

leavers might be induced to undertake farming. Needless to say these proposals have no relation to programmes of curriculum reform within the schools, since this factor is irrelevant to the problem. Callaway, *op. cit.*, p. 371.

54. The movement, of course, is not free of political overtones and members of the Workers' Brigade are not infrequently employed in the creation of 'spontaneous' mass demonstrations and act as 'rowdy boys' at political rallies.

55. Ghana, *Economic Survey*, 1958, p. 23. A very detailed account of the development of the Brigade is now available in Peter Hodge, 'The Ghana Workers Brigade: a Project for Unemployed Youth', *The British Journal of Sociology*, XV, No. 2 (June 1964), 113–27. Hodge indicates that the proportion of former middle-school pupils in the Brigade is now rising.

56. A speech actually announcing this intention of the government was made by Mr. N. A. Welbeck, Minister of State in November 1959. *Daily Graphic*, 15 November 1959, p. 4.

57. See Welbeck, *ibid.*, also Ioné Acquah, *Accra Survey* (London: University of London Press, 1958), p. 77. Furthermore the *Economic Survey* for 1958 concludes that 'the preference for clerical work does not appear to have changed in spite of limited employment prospects in that field.' Ghana, *Economic Survey, 1958*, p. 24.

58. Callaway, 'School Leavers in Nigeria: No. 3', p. 371.

59. G. L. Barnard, 'Gold Coast Children Out of School', *Oversea Education*, XXIII, No. 4 (January 1957), 170.

60. This category is traditionally significant in Ghana but is usually carried out by women, most of whom are illiterate.

61. The Accelerated Development Plan did make proposals for local authorities to make increased contributions to educational expenditure particularly at the middle school level. Ghana, *Accelerated Development Plan for Education, 1951*, pp. 1–3. Local authorities, however, have made little effort to meet their share of costs and the central government has been obliged to meet the burden of teachers' salaries and many construction costs.

62. It can be suggested that formal education may lead to a more efficient labour force in terms of product per capita, but national programmes of mass educational expansion may go far beyond the diffusion of formal education required for initial economic development. By this we mean that the marginal returns to successive increments of education drop so sharply that it would be far more advisable to divert much expenditure to other more directly productive activities, e.g., development of the communication network. It seems wasteful from a purely economic point of view to achieve 80 per cent literacy to perform tasks that could be effectively done by a population that is only 30 per cent literate. Here the question of timing and relative allocation of resources is vital. However, mass educational programmes may *indirectly* affect the rate of economic growth by creating new consumption needs among the population and thus generating a more intense level of economic activity.

63. Gold Coast, *Report to His Excellency the Governor by the Committee on Constitutional Reform, 1949*, Colonial No. 248 (The Coussey Report), pp. 4–5.

64. See Great Britain, *Despatches on the Gold Coast Government's Proposals for Constitutional Reform* (London: H.M.S.O., 1954), Colonial No. 302.

65. Ghana, *Proposed Constitution of Ghana* (Accra: Government Printer, 1957).

66. This policy reached its climax in 1959 with a series of acts making it possible for the government to withdraw recognition from chiefs or eject them and also seize stool property and state revenues. See Leo M. Snowiss, 'Demo-

cracy and Control in a Changing Society: The Case of Ghana' (Master's disserta-
tation, University of Chicago, 1960), p. 62.

67. Gold Coast, *Local Government Ordinance of 1951* (Accra: Government
Printer, 1951). The movement away from regional and traditionalistic structures
has been well described in D. E. Apter, *The Gold Coast in Transition* (Princeton:
Princeton University Press, 1955), pp. 175–98, and J. G. Amamoo, *The New
Ghana* (London: Pan Books Ltd., 1958).

68. Apter, *op. cit.*, p. 198.

69. *Ibid.*, pp. 314–15, and Amamoo, *op. cit.*, pp. 80–106.

70. It is surprising that in spite of the systematic examination of regionalist
movements in the new states, political scientists have been little concerned to
examine the role of the schools in this process. However, the projected development of what will be in fact ethnic universities in Nigeria is receiving some
recognition.

71. Gold Coast, *Legislative Assembly Debates, 1952,* No. 1, I, 499–508.

72. *Ibid.*, p. 507.

73. *Ibid.*, No. 2, I, 267.

74. *Ibid.*, No. 1, III, 1202. We have already noted that the government secondary school in the North has hitherto enjoyed special privileges as regards
recruitment.

75. It is possible that under certain conditions ethnic conflict might be heightened in such institutions where the few representatives of a lowly rated ethnic
group are subjected to isolation and even contempt by a majority of students.
The present writer is aware of several such cases in Uganda. It is also pertinent
that during the empirical investigation of secondary schools (which we shall discuss in the following chapter) the students, who were allowed to sit wherever
they pleased during the investigation, almost invariably grouped themselves into
ethnic 'blocs'.

76. Shils, *op. cit.*, pp. 272–73.

VII

ACHIEVEMENT, SELECTION, AND RECRUITMENT IN GHANAIAN SECONDARY SCHOOLS

THROUGHOUT the previous chapters we have frequently drawn attention to the focal role of secondary schools in the Ghanaian educational system. Their position merits special attention within the context of this study. A detailed examination of this type of school will enable us to illustrate some of the general processes that we have noted in previous discussion. We will draw upon empirical data collected in the field, in contrast with earlier discussion where we have been obliged to rely heavily upon documentary materials and existing statistical sources. The succeeding materials are drawn from a large-scale empirical survey of Ghanaian secondary schools which was carried out in 1961, and they serve to justify some of the conclusions which we have reached in previous chapters concerning the relationship between the schools and the contemporary social and occupational structure in Ghana. In this sense we are using the secondary schools as a paradigm for empirical research, since their small numbers and great selectivity might be presumed to highlight certain processes and relationships which we have already considered in historical perspective.

In 1961 there were 59 secondary schools in the Ghanaian educational system which were either totally or partially supported by government funds. Of these public institutions no less than thirteen were very new schools which had not yet been built up to the fifth-form level. The remaining forty-six schools were established institutions with a full complement of grades. These became the basis for our study and from them twenty-three schools were selected on a random basis. Information regarding the principal characteristics of these institutions was gathered and a questionnaire was administered

220

to all scholars in their fifth forms. Details of the method of sampling and a specimen of the questionnaire used are to be found in Appendices I and II to this volume, but it is sufficient to say at this juncture that a very adequate representation of schools was obtained in terms of both geographical location and type. In all, individual questionnaires were completed by 775 boys and 188 girls who represented, respectively, 45·4 and 47·9 per cent of the fifth-form student population in all public secondary schools.

TABLE 14

THE SAMPLED SECONDARY SCHOOLS

Name	Student Body	Type	Date of Original Foundation*	Date of First Extension of Public Aid†
Elite School	Co-educational	Assisted	1927	1927
Fanti College	Boys	Assisted	1876	1923
Ashanti College	Boys	Assisted	1952	1952
Kumasi School	Boys	Assisted	1949	1949
St. Benedict's	Boys	Assisted	1930	1937
State School	Co-educational	Government	1909	1952
Government College	Boys	Government	1909	1952
Cape Coast Academy	Co-educational	Encouraged	1940	1952
Cardinal's School	Boys	Encouraged	1952	1956
Volta College	Boys	Encouraged	1952	1955
Town School	Co-educational	Encouraged	1941	1952
Akwapim College	Co-educational	Encouraged	1946	1952
Eastern Academy	Co-educational	Encouraged	1936	1953
Capital School	Co-educational	Encouraged	1925	1952
St. Joseph's	Boys	Encouraged	1952	1956
Mission College	Boys	Encouraged	1952	1958
Ewe College	Co-educational	Encouraged	1937	1952
Central Academy	Co-educational	Assisted Day	1953	1953
Southwestern School	Co-educational	Assisted Day	1951	1951
Coast College	Co-educational	G.E.T.	1949	1960
Ridge School	Girls	Assisted	1858	1946
St. Margaret's	Girls	Assisted	1946	1946
St. Theresa's	Girls	Assisted	1946	1946

* In a few cases institutions were begun as primary schools or teacher-training colleges and later emerged as secondary institutions.

† This gives the date on which schools first received state support as recognized *secondary* schools.

It is interesting to note that nine of the sampled schools were for boys only, three were girls' schools, while the other eleven were co-educational institutions. The term 'co-educational', however, may be regarded rather lightly, since places in such schools are overwhelmingly taken by boys. In fact, only 38·5 per cent of the female sampled students were drawn from the eleven 'co-educational' schools; the remainder came from three large girls' institutions. Such a situation indicates not only the considerable lag in female enrolments at this level of education but reflects in some degree an existing widespread antipathy to co-education in what, for the most part, are boarding institutions.

With respect to type of school, we have previously noted the elaborate classification of Ghanaian public secondary schools based largely upon the nature of government assistance to them. In practice, the sample contained eight Assisted schools, two Assisted Day schools, ten Encouraged schools, two Government schools and one Ghana Educational Trust institution. All of the schools for girls only were in the Assisted category.

The final list of sampled institutions is given in Table 14. Clearly, the names of the schools are fictitious and every effort has been made to ensure that individual institutions are not readily identifiable.

The Purpose of the Survey

It has been made clear that the growth of the secondary-school system in Ghana has involved increasing internal differentiation of that system. The Government and Assisted schools form a 'high status' sector while the Encouraged, Assisted Day and Ghana Educational Trust schools form a 'low-status' group. What justification do we have for this designation? It has already been shown that Assisted and Government schools enjoy a dominant position with respect to entry into the pre-university sixth forms. Here we shall attempt to show also that they vary markedly from the low-status schools with respect to other variables, most notably in the levels of academic achievement of their students. We are not dealing with a unitary secondary-school system but rather with two systems which enjoy ostensible 'parity of esteem' and are structurally similar but which are at the same time, functionally heterogeneous.

If markedly different levels of academic achievement occur in the two sectors of the system then the question arises as to what extent such variations are correlated with differences in the social composition of the student bodies? Thus we are faced with two general sorts of selectivity: overall patterns of social recruitment into all secondary schools and the examination of internal variations in recruitment patterns between schools.

One of the impacts of Western education in Ghana has been the partial emergence of 'social strata' which, in some respects, might seem to parallel Western models. If this assessment is correct then the examination of access to highly selective educational institutions becomes an indirect index of the emergence of quasi-class structures. We must discover whether we are confronted by familiar patterns of 'self-selectivity' into the educational system in terms of occupational and educational background and if there is a consistent relationship between urban origin and secondary-school access. Besides the delineation of familiar features, however, there is the equally important task of ascertaining in what respects patterns of recruitment do not conform to Western models. In this sense the study springs not only from an intrinsic interest in secondary schools themselves but constitutes an attempt to verify some of our previous generalizations.

One other factor of considerable importance is ethnic origin, since inequalities in ethnic access to education in Ghana have been historically very marked and politically significant. Our task here must be first to obtain some indications of overall ethnic inequalities in secondary-school access; second, to ascertain whether particular ethnic groups obtain preferential access into high-status institutions and third, to illustrate the degree to which there is a tendency to the 'ethnicization' of particular schools. This latter relationship would be sure to exist if Ghanaian secondary schools were institutions which explicitly drew their student bodies from local school districts. In fact, we have observed that they are not 'district' but 'national' institutions drawing upon a national middle-school reservoir. Thus there is no necessity that there should be a close relationship between individual schools and local ethnic groupings.

The Hierarchy of Secondary Schools

Here we shall attempt to justify our dichotomy of the public secondary-school system into 'low' and 'high' status sectors. We shall exclude the three sampled girls' schools from this aspect of the study, since they really form a separate segment of the secondary system and are hardly competitive with boys' or co-educational schools. We are justified in including the latter institutions since the enrolment of girls in them is less than 7 per cent, and, for all practical purposes, they may be regarded as boys' schools. Of the twenty schools which concern us here, one Assisted school was unwilling to provide certain

223

TABLE 15

SCORES AND RANKING OF NINETEEN SAMPLED SECONDARY SCHOOLS WITH RESPECT TO FIVE SETS OF VARIABLES

Name of School	(i) Size of Enrolment		(ii) Size of Entry for External Examinations (Last 5 years)		(iii) Mean Weighted Score for Examination Success		(iv) Teacher-Pupil Ratio		(v) Proportion of Graduate Staff		(vi) Proportion of European Staff	
	Size	Rank	Size	Rank	Score	Rank	Ratio	Rank	Proportion	Rank	Proportion	Rank
Elite School	665	1	483	1	2·10	2	12·5	1	73·6	3	50·9	4
Kumasi School	584	2	356	3	2·57	4	16·6	6·5	71·4	4	42·9	6
Fanti College	542	3	375	2	2·15	3	17·4	11·5	90·3	1	54·8	2
State School	451	4	206	7	2·82	7	15·0	5	60·0	9	16·7	9
Ashanti College	450	5	339	4	2·58	5	17·3	9·5	84·6	2	53·8	3
Southwestern School	382	6	236	5	2·97	8	20·1	18	63·4	6	15·8	10
Volta College	332	7	99	12	2·75	6	17·4	11·5	26·3	17	26·3	8
Cape Coast Academy	317	8	233	6	3·44	16·5	17·6	13	61·1	8	00·0	16
Central Academy	281	9	80	13	3·16	12	20·1	18	42·8	13	00·0	16
Ewe College	268	10	199	8	3·15	10·5	14·8	4	16·7	19	00·0	16
St. Joseph's	265	11	149	10	3·44	16·5	18·9	16	64·4	5	57·1	1
Coast College	261	12	38	19	3·29	15	20·1	18	23·1	18	00·0	16
Government College	258	13	152	9	2·00	1	12·9	2	45·0	11	15·0	11
Akwapim College	243	14	79	14	3·57	19	17·3	9·5	35·7	14	00·0	16
Eastern Academy	225	15	71	15	3·18	13·5	18·7	15	33·3	15	00·0	16
Cardinal's School	217	16	121	11	3·15	10·5	16·6	6·5	61·5	7	38·5	7
Capital School	216	17	69	16	3·18	13·5	18·0	14	58·3	10	8·3	12
Town School	187	18	50	18	3·56	18	17·0	8	27·3	16	00·0	16
Mission College	129	19	62	17	3·03	9	14·3	3	44·4	12	46·7	5

basic data; therefore, our final examination of the secondary-school hierarchy rests upon a sample of nineteen schools.

We may initially differentiate our two main clusters of schools in terms of relatively simple objective criteria: (1) enrolment, (2) size of entry for public examinations, (3) success in such examinations, and (4) teaching staff characteristics. A summary of scores and rank orders for these nineteen schools with respect to these variables is given in Table 15.

Academic Achievement

Initially, it is quite obvious that the six Government and Assisted schools which we have designated as high-status institutions are far larger than schools of other types. Their mean enrolment is just over 491, as against a mean of 255 for all other institutions; when schools are ranked on the basis of their total enrolments the five largest schools are in the Government and Assisted category. 'Government College' is the only school in this cluster which approximates to the mean size of the other thirteen institutions with an enrolment of 258. The greater size of the Government and Assisted schools reflects in some degree the established nature of these institutions compared with the newer schools.

As we should expect, the largest schools also provide the greatest number of candidates for the West African General School Certificate Examination given at the end of the five-year secondary course. In fact, four out of the six Government and Assisted schools emerge as among the first five schools in order of examination entry, and these six schools account for 56 per cent of the total entry over the last five years.

Far more important from our viewpoint is the fact that the high-status schools dominate the examination system qualitatively as well as quantitatively. A satisfactory pass in the General School Certificate Examination is overwhelmingly important to an individual student's educational and occupational future, and we shall assert that overall examination results are the most important single factor in determining the position of an individual school in the secondary-school hierarchy.

In order to be able to rank schools in terms of their general record of examination success, recourse was had to a device based on a simple weighted mean. All candidates for the School Certificate Examination are assessed by the examiners on an overall basis of first class, second class, and third class passes or failures. It is possible, thereby, to compute a percentage distribution of various grades of pass for each school with respect to its total examination results over the last five years. In addition, an arbitrary score is assigned to each category of pass: a first-class pass is given a score of one, a second-class pass a score of two, and so on. The percentage distributions are then multiplied by the weighted scores and divided by 100. In this manner a simple mean weighted score was obtained for each school. Thus a school with a record of 100 per cent first-class passes received a score of one and an institution with a record of 100 per cent failures received a score of four. It was then possible to rank sampled schools in terms of their examination success. This ranking appears in column (iii) of Table 15.

On this basis scores ranged from 2·0 to 3·57 but, most strikingly, the rank order shows the immense superiority of Government and Assisted schools in levels of academic achievement. The five leading schools are all in this category and one additional school is ranked seventh. In only one case does a school drawn from the remaining thirteen institutions approach the level of the six Government and Assisted schools. In general, the mean weighted score for 'high-status' institutions is 2·3 as against a mean score for Encouraged, Assisted and Ghana Educational Trust schools of 3·2. It is clear, therefore, that the larger 'high-status' institutions dominate satisfactory examination statistics and are responsible for producing the vast majority of students obtaining high-level passes in the public examination system.

The Composition of the Teaching Force

Markedly distinct levels in academic achievement are, however, not the only critical difference between 'high-status' and 'low-status' institutions. An equally important variable concerns the size and training of the teaching force at these various types of school, and it is in this area that we may find an indication of one of the factors influencing levels of pupil-achievement.

There are no great differences between high and low-status schools in terms of simple pupil-teacher ratios as defined by the number of pupils per teacher irrespective of the latter's qualifications (col. iv). In Government schools this ratio is 14·2; in Assisted schools 15·5; in Encouraged schools 17·1; in Assisted Day schools 20·9 and in the Ghana Educational Trust school 20·8. In practice, the mean pupil-teacher ratio for high-status schools is 15·1, and for the other thirteen schools it is 17·9. This is not a striking difference and if schools are ranked on the basis of their pupil-teacher ratios as against their rank in terms of external examination success only a moderate rank order correlation of 0·48 is obtained. Although we cannot disregard gross pupil-teacher ratio as being one factor related to examination success we consider that it is of rather less significance than the composition of the teaching force in different types of school.

There are wide differences in the proportions of actual university graduates on the teaching staffs of these schools as there are also in the number of partially qualified or non-graduate staff. Thus in Government and Assisted schools, university graduates comprise 72·3 per cent of all staff as against 43·0 per cent in all the other schools. In fact the pupil-*graduate* teacher ratio is 20·9 in the Government and Assisted sector as against 41·5 in the remaining schools taken together. When schools are ranked in terms of their proportion of graduate staff, four of the first five schools are once again to be found among the six Government and Assisted schools. If this ranking is contrasted with their success in examinations a coefficient of 0·76 is obtained: pupils from schools which have a preponderantly university trained staff do consistently better in the examinations. The only school which achieves consistently good results in examinations with a low proportion of graduate staff is Government College, which ranks first in examination results but only eleventh in its proportion of graduate teachers. The reasons for this are fairly clear in that Government College is the only secondary school in Ghana with a technical orientation; a high proportion of its staff lack formal university degrees but have obtained specialist technical diplomas or certificates.

Finally we must examine these teaching staffs in terms of their origin as well as their qualifications. In Government and Assisted schools no less than 41·5 per cent of the staff is European, while in all other institutions their representation drops to 14 per cent of the teaching force. In this case there is little point in differentiating between European graduate and non-graduate staff since all but three of 107 are graduates of universities. Once again, if schools are ranked on the basis of their proportion of European staff, four out of the first six schools are in the Government and Assisted category.

This relationship is worth exploring further; apparently there are particular advantages in possessing a high proportion of European staff at the schools. We may hazard the suggestion that a great deal of the importance of European teachers lies in the area of instruction in English. Unlike any other subject in the School Certificate Examination, a failure in the English paper results in total failure in the whole examination, and there is no doubt that fluency in written English counts for something in papers set in most other subjects consisting as they do largely of essay-type questions. It is not un-

Q   227

reasonable to suppose that a proportion of native English speakers on the staff is a marked asset to any school in terms of its pupils' examination performance.

In summary, we can say that the high-status Government and Assisted schools vary markedly in terms of simple objective criteria from all other sampled institutions. They are typically larger.They are long established schools. They have a record of pronounced examination success and command highly qualified teaching staffs, with a sizable proportion of expatriate personnel. In this sense we are justified in speaking of a secondary-school hierarchy and in concluding that the overall growth of secondary education in Ghana has been paralleled by a progressive functional differentiation of the system. Though in principle all schools enjoy 'parity of esteem', in practice a centralized and apparently homogeneous structure masks a pattern of internal variation which has emerged largely since 1951.

It is not sufficient, however, to assess the secondary-school hierarchy in terms of objective criteria alone. It would seem equally important to indicate whether students within the schools are aware of the existence of such a hierarchy and whether this significantly influences their choices of schools. In the following section we report the preferences of our male sample among the nineteen selected schools and examine the impact of examination results in affecting student perceptions of the status of schools.

Student Perceptions of the School Hierarchy

In previous chapters we have constantly drawn attention to the 'instrumental' context in which education has been viewed in West Africa and how people have evaluated Western education in terms of the financial and status rewards that it can provide. This is not to the discredit of the West African. It can hardly be expected that people living near a subsistence level will invest their limited funds in the education of their children without view to a tangible return. Indeed, the conception of formal education as an end in itself, to be enjoyed for its own sake, has been rare in history and confined to small elite groups whose monopolization of power and wealth permits them this luxury. Whatever the putative benefits of education, there is little doubt that people are more likely to be impressed by its tangible rewards, and the West African has always had this aspect presented to him in dramatic fashion. If secondary-school children are therefore asked, 'What is the most important reason for choosing a secondary school?' their answers are likely to be quite hard-headed.

It is clear that students are overwhelmingly concerned with the

228

examination results of a school and understandably so, since it is this which, to a great extent, determines their scholastic and occupational futures (Table 16). Low fees are another but far less important con-

TABLE 16

STUDENT RESPONSES TO THE QUESTION, 'WHAT DO YOU
THINK IS THE BEST REASON FOR CHOOSING A SECONDARY SCHOOL?'

Reason	Proportion of Responses (Percentages)	
Good Examination Results	76·7	(594)
Low Fees	11·7	(91)
Same Religion as Student	6·0	(47)
Proximity to Home	3·9	(30)
Not Difficult Scholastically	0·6	(5)
No Answer	1·0	(8)
Total	100·0	(775)

sideration. Most of these schools were founded by religious groups and are still nominally regarded as Methodist, Roman Catholic, Anglican, or other denominational schools. But students seem not to be particularly influenced by this factor in their choices; all of the sampled schools contain nominal or practicing adherents to a wide variety of churches, though there is a tendency for Roman Catholic schools to draw more heavily from Catholic families. Students do not appear to attach much importance to how far they have to travel for their education. They are indifferent to the lure of easy courses. Since all schools must take the School Certificate Examination, it could hardly be said that any offer 'soft' courses, though some schools do have the reputation of setting exceptionally rigorous standards. This writer's experience suggests that these standards of excellence probably make these schools *more* attractive to pupils who feel that they are deriving extra benefit from such instruction. These students are academically and vocationally oriented and do not attend school for their own comfort or amusement.

When students apply to take the Common Entrance Examination they are entitled, you will recall, to submit the names of three schools to which they would wish to be admitted in the order of their choice. In this study, in order to obtain a ranking of schools by the students, a similar procedure was followed, and boys were further allowed to

229

enter the names of private secondary schools if they wished. The students' choices were scored for each separate school on the basis of three points for a first choice, two points for a second choice, and one point for a third choice. In this manner each school could be given a total score and ranked accordingly (Table 17, col. i). It was to be

TABLE 17

STUDENT CHOICES OF SECONDARY SCHOOLS

Name of School	Category	(i) ALL CHOICES		(ii) CHOICES EXCLUDING STUDENTS' OWN SCHOOLS	
		Score	Rank Order	Score	Rank Order
Elite School	Assisted	1,265	1	1,078	1
Fanti College	Assisted	1,052	2	846	2
Kumasi School	Assisted	569	3	353	3
St. Benedict's	Assisted	369	4	245	4
Ashanti College	Assisted	254	5	176	6
Episcopal College	Assisted	225	6	225	5
Government College	Government	199	7	77	8
Ho College	Assisted	113	8	113	7
State School	Government	107	9	32	10
Southwestern School	Assisted Day	88	10	11	13·5
Anum College	Assisted	61	11	61	9
St. Joseph's	Encouraged	46	12	—	—
Cape Coast Academy	Encouraged	43	13	—	—
Volta College	Encouraged	36	14	—	—
Central Academy	Assisted Day	34	15	1	19
Akwapim College	Encouraged	26	16	—	—
Accra School	Assisted	22	17	22	11
Coast College	G.E.T.	19	18	—	—
Eastern Academy	Encouraged	17	19	—	—
Capital School	Encouraged	16	21	—	—
Hayford Academy	Encouraged	16	21	16	12
Ewe College	Encouraged	16	21	6	15
Independence School	Encouraged	11	23	11	13·5
Mission College	Encouraged	6	24	—	—
Sarbah College	G.E.T.	5	25	5	16
Cardinal's School	Encouraged	4	26	—	—
Forest School	G.E.T.	2	27·5	2	17
Town School	Encouraged	2	27·5	—	—
Ofori Atta College	Encouraged	1	29·5	1	19
President's School	Encouraged	1	29·5	1	19

expected that some students, out of a sense of loyalty to their present schools would cast votes for those schools; in the case of large institutions this might have seriously affected the rank order. Thus column (ii) of the table gives the scores and rank order of schools when choices made by students for their *own* schools were excluded. It was believed that this 'impartial' assessment would give a more accurate picture of the pattern of choice.

It will be noted from column (i) of the table that out of the fifty schools within the public system which boys are eligible to enter, only thirty receive any choices whatsoever, and no private secondary schools receive any ballots.[1] The first nine choices, in fact, are all for Government and Assisted schools and the scores for 'Elite School' and 'Fanti College' are far higher than for any other institutions. The rank order alone does not do justice to the tremendous gap between Assisted or Government schools and other schools of all types, but this is clear from the fact that the mean score for the former group is 385 as against a mean score of 21 for all the remaining schools.

Column (ii) of the table reveals an even more striking picture since, when student choices for their present schools are not counted, ten schools disappear altogether from the list. In this column the first eleven schools are in the Assisted or Government category and the highest rankings are virtually unchanged. Indeed the major change is the exclusion or downgrading of schools whose position in column (i) is entirely due to votes cast for them by their own pupils. As is to be expected, the mean score for both main categories of schools decreases, but it remains as high as 294 for Government or Assisted schools and drops to only 6·0 for all other institutions.

It is apparent that children have a very realistic perception of the school hierarchy which corresponds remarkably with our ranking of schools on the basis of objective criteria. Pupils are perfectly aware of the status differences among institutions, and their choices reflect a very accurate knowledge of the practical workings of the system. This is confirmed if we look at the relationship between our ranking of schools based on examination results and the children's ranking of schools based on total choices. Using column (ii) of Table 17 we note that ten of our nineteen sampled schools receive no choices whatsoever. If we take the nine remaining schools and compute a rank order correlation between examination success and total student choices we obtain a coefficient of 0·83 indicating that children not only state that examination results influence their choices but seem to act in this manner when it comes to actually choosing schools. The scores and rank orders for these nine schools are given in Table 18.

Name of School	External Examinations		Students' Choices	
	Mean Score	Rank	Score	Rank
Elite School	2·10	2	1,078	1
Fanti College	2·15	3	846	2
Kumasi School	2·57	4	353	3
Ashanti College	2·58	5	176	4
Government College	2·00	1	77	5
State School	2·82	6	32	6
Southwestern School	2·97	7	11	7
Ewe College	3·15	8	6	8
Central Academy	3·16	9	1	9

It is to be noted in this case that the sole deviation from a perfect correlation is attributable to the presence of Government College in the list. This school rates first in examination results but only fifth in student choices. In this case we are faced with the presence of a special kind of institution with a technical emphasis whose course of study will appeal only to a more limited group of students, even though its examination ranking is high.

The functional hierarchy of the schools is, therefore, reflected in the evaluations of students, and examination results appear to be the primary factor in determining pupil ratings. The degree to which pupils have knowledge of the system is, indeed, remarkable but to be expected in a situation where the choice of secondary school is of overwhelming significance in the future careers of these young people.

In general, therefore, it is fairly easy to demonstrate that a functional hierarchy of secondary schools does exist in Ghana both in terms of levels of student achievement and student expectations. A question that immediately arises concerns the social composition of the student bodies of these schools. From what groups of the Ghanaian population are they drawn and to what extent are variable levels in academic achievement associated with differential patterns of student recruitment into the system?

Recruitment into the Secondary-School System

We have seen in previous chapters of this study that recruitment into Ghanaian schools has been markedly uneven throughout the period of expansion of Western education. Circumstances have favoured the enrolment of the southern, more urbanized ethnic groups; it has also been suggested that the social background of pupils diverges considerably from educational and occupational distributions within the Ghanaian population as a whole. Our secondary-school sample gives us an opportunity to examine these propositions in empirical detail. This analysis initially entails a study of patterns of selection in the secondary-school system taken as a whole. Later we shall try to indicate how recruitment patterns vary significantly as between high-status and low-status schools. Certainly the marked differences in the schools' levels of academic achievement might lead us to suppose that they have quite different patterns of recruitment. Finally, we must attempt some analysis of the relationship between our main sets of variables so far as access into secondary schools is concerned. In the following pages, in contrast with our examination of the secondary-school hierarchy, we shall include all twenty-three sampled schools and give particular attention to the characteristics of female students.

The Ethnic Composition of the School Population

The general profile of ethnicity is given in Table 19 and these data confirm our previous generalizations concerning ethnic recruitment. No less than 42 distinct tribes are represented in the twenty-three schools. We have first divided tribes into four major groupings in terms of their proximity to the coastal zone. As we have previously observed, geographical location has been historically very significant in determining access to formal education and these data enable us to perceive the broad pattern of variation as between southern, central, and northern peoples.

In addition, these groups have been further subdivided into individual ethnic minorities in order to examine in more detail the internal patterns of variation within the major areal divisions. In the case of the northern peoples, however, the smallness of the sample and the fact that no less than twelve tribes were represented in it made this procedure impossible.

Figures for male and female students are compared through the use of 'selectivity indices'. These are simply the ratios between sample representation and known ethnic proportions within the general

233

TABLE 19

THE ETHNIC ORIGINS OF SAMPLED STUDENTS COMPARED WITH THE
ETHNIC COMPOSITION OF THE GHANAIAN POPULATION (PERCENTAGES)

(i) Ethnic Group by Area	(ii) Percentage in Sample			(iii) Distribution of Ethnic Groups in Total Population (1948)*	(iv) Selectivity Indices		
	Boys	Girls	Total		Boys	Girls	Total
Southern	64·2 (498)	77·1 (145)	66·8 (643)	47·0	1·4	1·6	1·4
Akwapim	5·0 (39)	10·6 (20)	6·1 (59)	2·2	2·3	4·8	2·8
Fanti	17·5 (135)	25·0 (47)	18·9 (182)	11·3	1·5	2·2	1·7
Other Akan†	9·9 (77)	5·3 (10)	9·0 (87)	10·0	0·9	0·5	0·9
Ewe	16·7 (130)	11·7 (22)	15·8 (152)	12·5	1·3	0·9	1·3
Ga-Adangame	10·9 (85)	21·3 (40)	13·0 (125)	8·9	1·2	2·2	1·5
Guan	2·1 (16)	1·1 (2)	1·9 (18)	1·0	2·1	1·1	1·9
Nigerian	2·1 (16)	2·1 (4)	2·1 (20)	1·1	1·9	1·9	1·9
Central	28·2 (218)	19·1 (36)	26·4 (254)	20·7	1·4	0·9	1·3
Akim	3·2 (25)	5·8 (11)	3·7 (36)	3·2	1·0	1·8	1·2
Ashanti	21·9 (169)	12·2 (23)	20·0 (192)	14·1	1·6	0·9	1·4
Brong.	3·1 (24)	1·1 (2)	2·7 (26)	3·4	0·9	0·3	0·8
Northern	6·3 (49)	2·1 (4)	5·5 (53)	30·7	0·2	0·06	0·2
Other‡	1·2 (9)	1·1 (2)	1·1 (11)	1·6	0·8	0·6	0·7
No Answer	0·1 (1)	0·6 (1)	0·2 (2)	—	—	—	—
Total	100·0 (775)	100·0 (188)	100·0 (963)	100·0	—	—	—

* Derived from the Gold Coast, *Census of Population, 1948.* Unfortunately material on ethnic origin is not yet available from the 1960 Census.

† This includes a number of smaller Akan groups such as the Ahanta, Nzima, Wassaw, and Aowin who largely hail from the southwestern portion of Ghana.

‡ This comprises a number of peoples drawn from the 'Volta remnant' group whose geographical position between the Ewe and the Gur-speaking peoples of the North justifies their being placed in a separate category.

population and they merely provide a general indication of how far various ethnic groups stand above or fall below their 'quota' within the schools. To be sure, this is a crude device, since ethnic proportions derived from the Population Census of 1948 are subject to some error and, furthermore, cannot be broken down by sex and age. In spite of these limitations, the table does give an overall picture of ethnic recruitment and gives us some indication of inequalities in selectivity patterns.

An examination of the selectivity indices for students as a whole reveals, as we might anticipate, a decreasing ratio of enrolment to population as we move from south to north. Differences are minimal as between southern and central groups. It would seem that the increased provision of public secondary education, combined as it has been with a 'national' system of selection, has tended to minimize ethnic variations as between the southern and central portions of Ghana. The tendency to parity in ethnic recruitment is far less in the case of the North where the selectivity index drops to only 0·2. Indeed, there is good reason to suppose that our sample exaggerates the proportion of northern pupils in secondary institutions, since it includes one school which has, until very recently, admitted northern students on a preferential basis. If this school is excluded, the proportion of northern pupils in the total student body drops to only 1 per cent and the overall selectivity ratio declines to 0·03. Now that this school has opened its doors to competitive entry through the Common Entrance Examination it will be interesting to see whether patterns of northern recruitment will suffer still further when northerners are obliged to compete directly with southern students.

The pattern of individual variation within distinct ethnic groups is generally in an expected direction. The Akwapim, Fanti, and Ga-Adangme, all coming from the immediate coastal zone are well represented in the schools as are the Guan; the Guan are largely composed of coastal Efutu and Guan minorities from the Akwapim ridge area. The peoples of central Ghana can hardly be said to be much underrepresented and, indeed, Ashanti representation compares very favourably with that of several southern groups. The Brong, however, who lie in the zone between Ashanti and the Northern Region are, as we might anticipate, somewhat underrepresented.

When a separate analysis is made of male and female recruitment, it is clear that patterns of ethnic inequality are much sharper for girls than for boys. This is precisely what we should expect. Since the enrolment of girls in Ghanaian schools has always lagged well behind that of boys, it can be anticipated that female representation in secondary institutions will be drawn to a great degree from the

235

southern, more urbanized ethnic groups. To put it another way, variations in female enrolment parallel but lag behind patterns of male recruitment, and the situation for girls probably is rather similar to that which prevailed for boys a decade or more ago. Thus, for example, almost 57 per cent of the girls are drawn from three groups: the Akwapim, the Fanti, and the Ga-Adangme, while these three peoples together only account for 22 per cent of the Ghanaian population. Correspondingly, Ashanti, Brong, and Northern representation is far more limited. As we shall indicate in later pages these apparent ethnic inequalities in female representation are associated with contrasts in parental occupation and education.

What conclusions can we draw from this overall picture of ethnic representation? First, it is clear that ethnic inequalities do exist and they tend to be in the expected direction, with a gradation from south to north. However, it is equally apparent that, with the exception of the northern cluster, ethnic differentials are far less than is commonly supposed. There is little doubt in view of these findings that the secondary-school system is moving towards greater ethnic parity. Indeed, given the present system of secondary-school selection based upon a national Common Entrance Examination, it is possible to infer that patterns of ethnic recruitment into the public secondary-school system are rather less uneven than they are in the primary and middle schools. We have previously shown that there are marked regional inequalities in the provision of these latter institutions which serve local populations. In this case geographical inequalities can produce marked ethnic variation. However, although most of the secondary schools still lie in the coastal zone their method of selection minimizes geographical inequalities. It can only be concluded that present methods of selection have worked effectively to lessen ethnic inequalities in a situation where very limited secondary-school provision is combined with a very uneven internal geographical distribution of schools.

Although ethnic parity is greater than one might have expected, this does not imply that ethnic origin is unrelated to the particular schools students attend. Conceivably present methods of selection could obliterate any association between area of origin and school attendance. But, in fact, there is a marked relationship between tribal origin and particular schools (Table 20). The pattern of recruitment is really the outcome of two sets of rather contradictory forces. On the one hand is the tendency to recruit on the basis of merit irrespective of tribal origin. On the other hand particularistic patterns in school recruitment persist, producing trends towards the 'ethnicization' of individual schools.

236

TABLE 20

THE REPRESENTATION OF ETHNIC GROUPS IN SAMPLED SCHOOLS

(i) Name of School	(ii) Size of the Fifth-Form Sample	(iii) Total Number of Ethnic Groups represented in the Sample	(iv) Principal Ethnic Group in the District	(v) Largest Ethnic Group in the Fifth-Form Sample	(vi) Percentage of Fifth-Form Sample	(vii) Percentage of Sampled Students drawn from the District	(viii) Percentage of Sampled Students drawn from the Region
Volta College	38	5	Ewe	Ewe	86·8 (33)	94·7 (36)	94·7 (36)
Ewe College	29	3	Ewe	Ewe	93·1 (27)	93·1 (27)	93·1 (27)
State School	51	16	Dagomba	Dagati	23·5 (12)	13·7 (7)	88·2 (45)
Eastern Academy	17	4	GaAdangme	GaAdangme	64·7 (11)	64·7 (11)	76·5 (13)
Ridge School	50	11	Akwapim	Akwapim	30·0 (15)	30·0 (15)	74·0 (37)
Central Academy	22	6	Fanti	Fanti	68·2 (15)	72·7 (16)	72·7 (16)
Southwestern School	56	7	Fanti	Fanti	50·0 (28)	64·3 (36)	71·4 (40)
Mission College	13	5	Ashanti	Ashanti	69·2 (9)	69·2 (9)	69·2 (9)
Ashanti College	67	10	Ashanti	Ashanti	67·2 (45)	67·2 (45)	67·2 (45)
St. Joseph's	37	8	Fanti	Fanti	29·7 (11)	51·4 (19)	59·5 (22)
Akwapim College	28	10	Akwapim	Kwahu	21·4 (6)	17·9 (5)	57·1 (16)
Kumasi School	80	11	Ashanti	Ashanti	56·3 (45)	56·3 (45)	56·3 (45)
Cape Coast Academy	42	10	Fanti	Fanti	52·4 (22)	52·4 (22)	54·8 (23)
Elite School	97	13	GaAdangme	GaAdangme	19·6 (19)	19·6 (19)	47·4 (46)
St. Margaret's	52	9	Fanti	Fanti	40·4 (21)	40·4 (21)	46·2 (24)
Capital School	22	5	GaAdangme	GaAdangme	31·8 (7)	31·8 (7)	45·5 (10)
Fanti College	84	12	Fanti	Fanti	33·3 (28)	33·3 (28)	45·2 (38)
St. Benedict's	49	16	Fanti	Fanti	28·6 (14)	28·6 (14)	44·9 (20)
Coast College	14	6	Fanti	Fanti	35·7 (5)	35·7 (5)	42·8 (6)
Cardinal's School	20	7	GaAdangme	GaAdangme	35·0 (7)	35·0 (7)	35·0 (7)
Town School	19	7	GaAdangme	Ashanti	31·6 (6)	21·1 (4)	26·3 (5)
St. Theresa's	28	7	Ashanti	GaAdangme	35·7 (10)	17·9 (5)	17·9 (5)
Government College	48	14	Fanti	Ewe	50·0 (24)	10·4 (5)	14·6 (7)

First, all schools are interethnic in character, ranging from a representation of sixteen tribes in two schools to a lower limit of three in one institution. There is a general tendency for schools to largely recruit from their own tribal hinterland. Thus, in no less than eighteen schools the largest tribe represented in fifth-form enrolments is also the largest tribe within the immediate district in which the school is located. Furthermore, in ten schools the predominant local tribe constitutes at least 50 per cent of the fifth-form enrolment. The relationship is, of course, even more striking when the regional pattern of recruitment is considered. In spite then of a system of selection which places a high premium upon academic merit as the principal criterion for allocation of students as between schools, there is little doubt that particularistic factors influence patterns of selection.

More striking, however, are the distinct differences between high-status and low-status institutions in this connexion. It was observed in the previous chapter that the newer public secondary schools have tended to become increasingly 'ethnicized' and parochial in their recruitment patterns. This generalization is clearly confirmed by these data. Thus, in the ten high-status institutions the mean number of ethnic groups represented stands at twelve; conversely, with low-status schools this figure drops to six. Only two Government and Assisted schools out of ten draw over half of their fifth-form pupils from the immediate district of the school while of the remaining thirteen low-status schools no less than eight conform to this pattern.

This establishes another significant difference between high-status and low-status institutions. The tendency to 'ethnicization' of student bodies is most marked among newer secondary institutions which serve essentially local populations. The older elite institutions rely upon their higher academic standards to draw upon far wider segments of the population and downgrade ethnicity as a factor in recruitment. It is possible that as the secondary-school system expands the tendency to local recruitment will increase, and we are likely to find an increasing approximation to the usual Western practice where secondary institutions serve local populations. The situation in Ghana is complicated by the fact that local district boundaries often coincide with ethnic divisions. One great advantage of the Common Entrance Examination has been that it minimizes ethnic inequalities despite geographical mal-distribution in the availability of schools. At present, there is some discussion as to whether this method of selection should be replaced by district examinations. If this occurs, given present shortages in the provision of secondary education, the obvious result will be the acceleration of 'ethnicization' in the schools

238

and the exacerbation of tribal inequalities. Such a move would not be without political consequences.

An equally significant question concerns the degree to which certain ethnic groups appear to obtain preferential entry into high-status schools in the system. It is possible to argue that even if ethnic parity existed in Ghanaian secondary schools in purely quantitative terms, there would still be certain ethnic groups who were overrepresented in the very best schools and who might thus obtain a disproportionate share of sixth form and university places. It is commonly believed in Ghana, for example, that the Fanti, Akwapim, and Ga are considerably overrepresented in the best schools and that other tribes have to be content with inferior institutions.

TABLE 21

THE DISTRIBUTION OF ETHNIC GROUPS AMONG CATEGORIES
OF SCHOOL (PERCENTAGES)

Ethnic Group	Category of School		
	High Status Schools	*Low Status Schools*	*Total*
Akim	60·0 (15)	40·0 (10)	100·0 (25)
Akwapim	71·8 (28)	28·2 (11)	100·0 (39)
Ashanti	73·9 (125)	26·1 (44)	100·0 (169)
Brong	87·5 (21)	12·5 (44)	100·0 (24)
Fanti	42·2 (57)	47·8 (78)	100·0 (135)
Other Akan	51·9 (40)	48·1 (37)	100·0 (77)
Ewe	38·4 (50)	61·6 (80)	100·0 (130)
Ga-Adangme	50·6 (43)	49·4 (42)	100·0 (85)
Guan	56·2 (9)	43·8 (7)	100·0 (16)
Northern	100·0 (49)	—	100·0 (49)
Nigerian	12·5 (2)	87·5 (14)	100·0 (16)
Other	55·5 (5)	44·5 (4)	100·0 (9)
No Answer	100·0 (1)	—	100·0 (1)
Total	— 445	— 330	— 775

Some indication of the actual state of affairs is given in Table 21. (We have only considered our male sample—we have previously noted the inadvisability of considering the girls' schools as part of the secondary-school hierarchy.) The table does not indicate any substantial differences in the access of various ethnic groups into different types of school. In only one case is a tribal group not represented in a category of school and this is the northern cluster which, as we have

239

already observed, is almost entirely confined to 'State School' with its conditions of preferential entry for northern pupils. For the most part, the distribution is markedly even. Certainly the Akwapim are well represented in high-status schools but so also are the Ashanti. The Fanti and Ga-Adangme are split very evenly between high-status and low-status institutions. From these data it would be difficult to identify any clear patterns of preferential access; all major ethnic groups achieve some degree of parity in their recruitment to both superior and inferior institutions.

The Socioeconomic Background of the School Population

Although there is some ethnic selection into Ghanaian secondary schools, other social characteristics of students are of greater apparent importance in determining access into these institutions. Perhaps one of the most significant characteristics of selective secondary schools in the Western world has been the persistence of a degree of 'self-selectivity' in the composition of their student bodies. To a greater or lesser extent, secondary-school entry has been correlated with parental characteristics such as occupation and education. Although within recent years, patterns of recruitment have shown greater fluidity, there is no evidence that groups recruited from the lower levels of the occupational and educational hierarchy have achieved parity commensurate with their population proportions. Selective secondary schools, therefore, give a picture of persistent inequalities in recruitment. In spite of efforts to broaden the range of social representation of their student bodies they exhibit a degree of 'stickiness' in this matter and continue to draw disproportionately upon limited segments of the population. This kind of pattern is one of the corollaries of Western-type systems of social stratification, and it is important to see to what extent this phenomenon operates in Ghanaian schools. Are there marked social inequalities in patterns of recruitment to secondary schooling in contemporary Ghana?

TABLE 22

PATERNAL OCCUPATIONS OF SAMPLED STUDENTS AS COMPARED WITH THE OCCUPATIONAL CHARACTERISTICS OF THE GHANAIAN ADULT MALE POPULATION (PERCENTAGES)

Occupational Group	Distribution of the Adult Male Labour Force*	MALE STUDENTS		FEMALE STUDENTS		TOTAL	
		Paternal Occupation	Selectivity Index	Paternal Occupation	Selectivity Index	Paternal Occupation	Selectivity Index
Professional, Higher Technical, Administrative and Clerical Workers	6·9	34·3 (265)	4·9	65·5 (123)	9·5	40·3 (388)	5·8
Private Traders and Businessmen	3·8	10·9 (85)	2·9	7·4 (14)	1·9	10·3 (99)	2·7
Skilled Workers and Artisans	11·8	12·8 (99)	1·1	9·5 (18)	0·8	12·1 (117)	1·0
Semiskilled and Unskilled Workers	13·4	1·5 (12)	0·1	1·1 (2)	0·1	1·5 (14)	0·1
Farmers and Fishermen	62·8	37·4 (290)	0·6	12·2 (23)	0·2	32·5 (313)	0·5
Other (including Police and Uniformed Services)	1·3	0·6 (5)	0·5	1·1 (2)	0·8	0·7 (7)	0·5
No Answer and Don't Know	—	2·5 (19)	—	3·2 (6)	—	2·6 (25)	—
Total	100·0	100·0 (775)	—	100·0 (188)	—	100·0 (963)	—

241

* This distribution has been computed from the *Ghana Population Census of 1960, Advance Report of Volumes III and IV* (Accra: Census Office, 1962). The occupational categories used in the census, however, have been regrouped for our present purposes. Percentages refer to all employed males of fifteen years and above.

Table 22 indicates that there is a definite association between paternal occupational characteristics and access to secondary-school education which is even more striking for girls than it is for boys. Although professional, higher technical, and clerical workers constitute only 7 per cent of the Ghana adult male labour force, they supply 34 per cent of our male students and no less than 66 per cent of the female students. Whereas farmers and fishermen, who account for over 62 per cent of the employed adult male population, provide only 37 and 12 per cent of these respective samples. The selectivity indices provide a clearer comparative picture of inequalities in recruitment and they show very clearly the greater spread among paternal occupational characteristics of the male sample as compared with female students.

These data are substantially paralleled by those relating to education background (Table 23). It will be noted that educational gradients are somewhat steeper than those for paternal occupation, which suggests the somewhat greater importance of paternal education in influencing secondary-school selection processes. Once again the female profile is far more constricted and uneven than that for boys.

One extraordinarily interesting feature is evident both in the 1960 census figures for the Ghanaian adult male population and among the fathers of secondary-school pupils: There is no continuous gradation between primary and middle-school experience. Thus only 6·2 per cent of the adult male population has a level of education up to six years of primary school, while no less than 12·1 per cent have had some middle school. This is a marked deviation from the usual educational pyramid, and we would suggest as a partial explanation that once individuals obtain a minimal level of primary education they are then likely to persist into middle school. It would seem from existing statistics for the present adult generation that this critical level is reached at about the third year of primary education.[2] Before that year drop-outs are very high; attrition between the fourth and sixth year of primary education is quite low. This would suggest that we are confronted with an educational commitment to further schooling that does not become evident until basic literacy has been obtained after about three years of schooling.

One other factor needs to be considered in the context of this discussion and this is the proportion of students drawn from either urban or rural backgrounds. Of course, classification by size of locality of origin is a very imperfect measure of urban background, since size is only one index of a complex of factors that determine the extent of urbanization. In the absence of more adequate data this can

Table 23

Paternal Education of Sampled Students Compared with the Educational Characteristics of the Ghanaian Adult Male Population (Percentages)

Educational Level	Adult Male* Population	Male Students		Female Students		Total	
		Paternal Education	Selectivity Index	Paternal Education	Selectivity Index	Paternal Education	Selectivity Index
No Formal Education	78·8	32·4 (251)	0·4	7·9 (15)	0·1	27·6 (266)	0·4
Primary School 1 to 6†	6·3	9·4 (73)	1·5	4·7 (9)	0·7	8·5 (82)	1·4
Middle School I to IV‡	12·1	29·9 (232)	2·5	29·1 (55)	2·4	29·8 (287)	2·5
Secondary School I to VI	1·4	9·6 (74)	6·9	20·7 (39)	14·8	11·8 (113)	8·4
Teacher Training College	0·7	7·3 (57)	10·4	14·8 (28)	21·1	8·8 (85)	12·6
University or Equivalent	0·3	3·9 (30)	13·0	11·7 (21)	39·0	5·3 (51)	17·7
Commercial and Technical School	0·4	2·2 (17)	5·5	2·6 (5)	6·5	2·3 (22)	5·8
Don't Know and No Answer	—	5·3 (41)	—	8·5 (16)	—	5·9 (57)	—
Total	100·0	100·0 (775)	—	100·0 (188)	—	100·0 (963)	—

* This distribution has been computed from the *Ghana Population Census of 1960, Advance Report of Volumes III and IV* (Accra: 1962). In this case figures relate to the adult male population of twenty-five years and above and include just less than 0·2 per cent at present engaged in full-time study.

† This includes a small proportion of adult males who attended Arabic schools.

‡ The term 'Middle School' is used here but refers also to graduates of the former Senior Primary Schools.

be used as a rough measure. Once again it is clear that there is a fairly consistent pattern of relationship between secondary-school access and urban origin, though gradients are less steep than they are with respect to educational variables (Table 24). Marked differences are apparent once again between male and female students. It should be noted, however, that this is, in many respects, a minimal statement of the relationship between recruitment and urban background since we have here categorized students by the size of their place of birth. If we use 'present residence' of sampled students as the basis for comparison with the whole Ghanaian population the relationship becomes much sharper, particularly as it influences movement away from settlements with a population of below 5,000 to towns with a population of over 50,000. Thus, only 19 per cent of male students were born in centres with populations of over 50,000 though no less than 33 per cent are now resident in such towns. Similarly, although 38 per cent of boys were born in small rural communities only 27 per cent are still resident in these villages. This picture is equally clear among girls and indicates a strong and consistent drift into the urban areas. It should be noted that an examination of data relating to residence and geographical mobility does not indicate a simple movement from the very smallest to the largest localities but also shows a complex pattern of migration as between towns of slightly different or equivalent size. No more than 40 per cent of sampled students are at present resident in their place of birth.

The preceding materials on student social background speak eloquently for themselves. In one sense they convey a picture of self-recruitment into an academic secondary-school system with which sociologists who have worked in Western societies are reasonably familiar. The offspring of educated parents with urban patterns of residence appear to have greater chances of obtaining access to secondary education than other groups within Ghanaian society. Given present methods of selection there can be little doubt that such patterns are likely to persist. In these circumstances we might be justified in stating that some of the educational concomitants of Western systems of social stratification are characteristic of Ghana also.

However, a caveat must be entered at this point. While findings show a degree of constriction in patterns of selectivity, they also indicate a remarkable degree of fluidity in access into the schools. For example, although it has been shown that 34 per cent of our male sample is drawn from a group who constitute less than 7 per cent of the Ghanaian adult male population, it is equally important to note that over one-third of them are the offspring of farmers and fishermen,

TABLE 24

BIRTHPLACE OF SAMPLED STUDENTS COMPARED WITH THE RESIDENTIAL CHARACTERISTICS OF THE GHANAIAN POPULATION (PERCENTAGES)

Size of Population of Locality	Size of place of residence* of the Ghanaian Population	Male Students		Female Students		Total	
		Percentage	Selectivity Index	Percentage	Selectivity Index	Percentage	Selectivity Index
Below 5,000	77·0	38·1 (295)	0·5	20·7 (39)	0·3	34·7 (334)	0·5
5,000–9,999	6·0	14·3 (111)	2·4	9·6 (18)	1·6	13·4 (129)	2·2
10,000–19,999	5·4	10·3 (80)	1·9	11·2 (21)	2·1	10·5 (101)	1·9
20,000–49,999	3·9	14·1 (109)	3·6	18·6 (35)	4·8	15·0 (144)	3·8
50,000 and over	7·7	19·4 (151)	2·5	36·7 (69)	4·8	22·8 (220)	2·9
No Answer or not born in Ghana	—	3·8 (29)	—	3·2 (6)	—	3·6 (35)	—
Total	100·0	100·0 (775)	—	100·0 (188)	—	100·0 (963)	—

* Computed from the *Ghana Population Census of 1960, Advance Report of Volumes III and IV* (Accra, 1962).

245

only one-third of whom have had any formal education whatsoever. Even in the two most exclusive secondary institutions in Ghana, Elite School and Fanti College, just under one-fifth of the boys had totally uneducated rural parents. If we examine the three preceding tables in this light and even include the far more selective patterns of female recruitment, then our most striking finding is not the extent of self-selectivity into the system. It is the remarkable degree to which youth from rural backgrounds and markedly low levels of parental education and occupation are successful in entering these highly selective academic schools. If it is borne in mind that probably no more than 2 per cent of any cohort of 100 Ghanaian children finally achieve secondary-school entry, then the success of the schools in drawing upon a relatively wide segment of the Ghanaian population testifies to a clear mobility function for these schools.

It may be contended that this kind of pattern is to be expected in a society where the vast bulk of the population is composed of illiterate farmers. Such wide recruitment probably did not prevail, however, at earlier stages in European development when the occupational structure was not entirely dissimilar to that of contemporary Ghana and when secondary education was in roughly comparable supply.[3] Materials relating to the social composition of secondary-school populations in earlier stages of Western history are difficult to come by, but it is probable that the Ghanaian picture would not be duplicated in studies of nineteenth-century German gymnasia, French lycées, or British grammar schools. Given that the Ghanaian secondary-school system shows some characteristics of a 'social class' nature there is enough of a divergent pattern to show that we are not dealing with a 'typical' situation.

Some conjecture can be made concerning the nature of recruitment patterns into these schools in contradistinction to Western experience. Perhaps one of the characteristics of highly selective academic secondary schools in the Western world has been their slowness in reflecting changes in the social composition of their student bodies even when various barriers to competitive access into them have been progressively removed. Thus, although the number of children of lower-class origin entering this type of European school has gradually risen, their proportion within the secondary-school population has been considerably less than most reformers originally anticipated. Research tends to indicate that the most important factor that inhibits greater fluidity of access has been the persistence of class correlated norms and values relating to education. This is one of the educational corollaries of a class structure; levels of educational motivation and aspiration diverge considerably from one social class to another. This is another way of saying that social classes in the Western world have constituted distinctive subcultures which markedly influence levels of educational and vocational aspiration. The persistence of values which stress that particular types of academic education are 'not for the likes of us' or which are deemed useless in the acquisition of status within certain class subcultures, have been crucial in determining the remarkably slow rate at which the demand for secondary education has developed in parts of the Western world.

Secondly, it is appropriate to note that Western nations also developed quite early a number of alternative mechanisms for mobility outside the acquisition of formal educational qualifications. The greater complexity of the economic structure afforded this. Systems of apprenticeship and opportunities to develop small business all tended to provide alternate mobility mechanisms which were often more acceptable to the mobile individual and certainly more accessible to him. This also provides a reason why academic secondary schools have appeared rather 'monolithic' in terms of the composition of their student bodies.

In Ghana, and probably most African territories, both these factors are less operative. Although Western education has been introduced, class correlated values which limit the educational aspirations of subgroups do not appear to have emerged. In Europe the selective secondary school has been and still is, in some degree, a 'middle-class' institution. In Ghana, it is not subjectively regarded as essentially the preserve of any social subgroup. Levels of educational motivation are less structured along class lines and the 'social distance' between the secondary school and substantial segments of the population is not great. This is to suggest that we are not dealing in Ghana with typical social class subcultures. The reason for this is probably that ties based on lineage and descent still cut across occupational and educational strata and, in consequence, the degree of cultural differentiation between strata is not so great as it is in the West. To put it another way, although great differences in income, occupation, and educational level may occur among segments of the Ghanaian population, there has been a fundamental cultural egalitarianism in the education field reflected in a rapid diffusion of educational demand at all levels of society.

Furthermore, the relative absence of alternative mechanisms for mobility has placed a greater premium on the possession of formal educational qualifications in contemporary Ghana than they did up till very recently in the Western world. As we have seen, one of the reasons for the exaggerated concern with such qualifications is the control of the majority of employment opportunities by government, which invariably tends to stress formal educational criteria for occupational recruitment. The rather paradoxical result has been that the educational qualifications for obtaining a variety of posts are as high if not higher in Ghana than they are in some Western nations, in spite of the limited diffusion of formal education among the population as a whole.

In the light of these general comments it is not, perhaps, surprising that Ghanaian secondary schools should manifest this broad spectrum of social recruitment, with students of 'humble' origin being quite well represented. Whether this fluidity in recruitment patterns will persist is another question. Perhaps we are only looking at a stage in the development of social classes as we understand the term. If secondary education remains highly selective, then perhaps a much more restrictive pattern in the social composition of student bodies will ensue. This view is perhaps somewhat premature in that it posits the emergence of systems of social stratification in Ghana which will duplicate Western and particularly Western European models. There may be no inevitability about this process; perhaps fundamentally 'populistic' attitudes to formal education will persist even where systems of status differentiation tend progressively to duplicate Western models in other respects.

It should be noted that our material does not imply that rates of social mobility in contemporary Ghana are high.[4] Some observers, impressed by dramatic instances of individual mobility in Africa and by the humble origins of so many contemporary leaders have concluded that what characterizes much of this continent is an extraordinarily high rate of social mobility.[5] Occupational mobility is a reasonably good proxy variable in the Ghanaian context for social mobility, but educational mobility by no means serves equally well or does so only so long as education is relatively scarce.[6] In view of our remarks on the strategic position of secondary education and the substantial proportion of students with very limited educational and occupational backgrounds in these schools, it might be assumed that our data lend credence to this view concerning high mobility rates. In fact, of course, they do not. The principal characteristic of the Ghanaian occupational structure is the very limited number of high-status occupational roles open to individuals, in the sense that only a very tiny proportion of the population can achieve them. In practice therefore, overall rates of mobility in Ghana and probably in most African societies are quite low. Our conclusion would be that there is considerable fluidity in terms of access into strategic educational institutions combined with relatively low rates of occupational mobility in the society in general.

Ethnicity and Socioeconomic Status

We are now in a position to examine the ethnic composition of our students as they relate to other social variables, since it has been contended previously that apparent ethnic differentials really reflect the presence of more crucial determinants. How closely, in fact, are ethnic inequalities explainable by significant differences in other characteristics such as paternal education or occupation and urban origin?

In order to obtain some partial insight into this problem all sampled students were grouped into the twelve ethnic categories used in Table 19. These ethnic divisions were then regrouped into three major categories on the basis of their selectivity indices. Thus, Group 1 comprised all peoples having a selectivity index of 1·5 and above; this category included all groups who were very well represented in the sample. Group 2 comprised all tribes having a selectivity index ranging from 1·0 to 1·4, while Group 3 included all tribes having a selectivity index of below 1·0. These three major divisions were then systematically compared with respect to their other social characteristics. The results of this operation are given in Tables 25, 26, and 27.

TABLE 25

THE RELATION BETWEEN ETHNICITY AND THE PATERNAL EDUCATION
OF SAMPLED STUDENTS (PERCENTAGES)

Paternal Level of Education	ETHNIC GROUP		
	Group 1 (Selectivity) Index above 1·5)	*Group 2* (Selectivity) Index 1·0 to 1·4)	*Group 3* (Selectivity) Index below 1·0)
No formal education	10·1 (41)	32·8 (124)	56·4 (101)
Primary School 1 to 6	5·2 (21)	12·2 (46)	8·4 (15)
Middle School I to IV	33·7 (136)	28·9 (110)	22·8 (41)
Secondary School I to VI	20·3 (82)	7·4 (28)	1·7 (3)
Teacher Training College	14·1 (57)	5·8 (22)	3·4 (6)
University or Equivalent	6·2 (25)	5·8 (22)	2·2 (4)
Commercial and Technical Schools	3·2 (13)	2·2 (8)	0·6 (1)
Don't Know and No Answer	7·2 (29)	4·9 (20)	4·5 (8)
Total	100·0 (404)	100·0 (380)	100·0 (179)

TABLE 26

THE RELATION BETWEEN ETHNICITY AND THE PATERNAL OCCUPATION
OF SAMPLED STUDENTS (PERCENTAGES)

	ETHNIC GROUP		
Paternal Occupation	*Group 1 (Selectivity Index above 1·5)*	*Group 2 (Selectivity Index 1·0 to 1·4)*	*Group 3 (Selectivity Index below 1·0)*
Professional, Higher Technical, Administrative and Clerical Workers	60·2 (243)	30·8 (117)	21·2 (38)
Private Traders and Businessmen	9·4 (38)	10·3 (39)	12·3 (22)
Skilled Workers and Artisans	12·6 (51)	11·6 (44)	6·7 (12)
Semiskilled and Unskilled Workers	1·2 (5)	1·3 (5)	2·2 (4)
Farmers and Fishermen	11·9 (48)	44·5 (169)	53·6 (96)
Other (including Police and Uniformed Services)	0·8 (3)	0·8 (3)	0·6 (1)
No Answer and Don't Know	3·9 (16)	0·7 (3)	3·4 (7)
Total	100·0 (404)	100·0 (380)	100·0 (179)

TABLE 27

THE RELATION BETWEEN ETHNICITY AND URBAN OR RURAL
ORIGIN (PERCENTAGES)

	ETHNIC GROUP		
Size of Population of Locality of Birth	*Group 1 (Selectivity Index above 1·5)*	*Group 2 (Selectivity Index 1·0 to 1·4)*	*Group 3 (Selectivity Index below 1·0)*
0 to 9,999	30·2 (122)	58·2 (221)	67·1 (120)
10,000 to 19,999	6·7 (22)	11·0 (42)	17·9 (32)
20,000 to 49,999	26·7 (108)	5·3 (20)	8·9 (16)
50,000 and over	34·2 (138)	19·7 (75)	3·9 (7)
No Answer and Not Born in Ghana	2·2 (9)	5·8 (22)	2·2 (4)
Total	100·0 (404)	100·0 (380)	100·0 (179)

It is clear that a marked relationship exists between ethnicity and other social variables. In the case of education, for example, no less than 44 per cent of the fathers of students in Group 1 had a formal education of no less than Secondary 1 standard as compared with 8 per cent for Group 3 students. At the other extreme, only 10 per cent of the fathers of Group 1 students had no formal education contrasting with a figure of 56 per cent for Group 3 students. Comparison on occupational variables reveals a similar pattern; 60 per cent of all students in Group 1 have fathers involved in professional and clerical occupations while this figure drops to 21 per cent for all Group 3 students. Conversely, only 12 per cent of the fathers of Group 1 students are farmers and fishermen as against 54 per cent in the case of Group 3 students. Table 27 also shows a rather similar relationship prevailing between urban or rural origin and ethnicity; only just over 30 per cent of Group 1 students come from the smallest rural communities as against over 67 per cent of Group 3 students. On the other hand, 34 per cent of Group 1 students derive from towns with populations of 50 thousand and above, as opposed to only 4 per cent of Group 3 pupils.

The relationship between ethnicity and other social variables is, therefore, remarkably clear and consistent, and it is difficult to avoid the conclusion that apparent ethnic differentials really conceal the operation of other factors which are more critical in influencing the social composition of student bodies. When individual tribes are ranked on the basis of their selectivity index and then examined in terms of their other social characteristics, the relationships indicated above stand out even more clearly. The Fanti, Ga, and Akwapim, for example, are markedly different from other groups in terms of paternal education and occupation, and with respect to their distinctively urban background.

If we now bear in mind our materials relating to differences in male and female recruitment patterns, then it would seem that we are justified in concluding that apparent ethnic inequalities stem largely from differential internal rates of social and economic change in Ghana and are not attributable to the operation of ethnic factors *per se.* These inequalities can partially trace their origin to the differential pattern of European contact as between the coast and the interior which we have been previously at such pains to describe. The educational advantages which particular ethnic groups have historically enjoyed tend to persist, though in modified form, and the data would suggest that those advantages will continue to persist and to reflect a pattern of uneven socioeconomic development within Ghana.

The Contemporary Scene

Socioeconomic Status and the School Hierarchy

A final task arises in connexion with our study of recruitment patterns. The existence of marked differentials in levels of academic achievement as between most of the schools might lead us to expect that these are associated with distinctive differences in the social composition of different student bodies. We have noted that no clear relationship exists between ethnicity and varying types of secondary school, except in the sense that low-status institutions do tend to be somewhat more ethnicized. Similarly, it is difficult to point to any overall relationship between the academic standards of different schools and other social characteristics of their student bodies.

Thus, when the sampled male and co-educational schools were simply dichotomized into 'high-status' and 'low-status' institutions and their student bodies examined in terms of the education and occupation of their parents and urban or rural origin, the differences between the two sets of schools were very slight. For example, high-status schools do not recruit more markedly from professional or clerical groups, nor do they attract students whose fathers show distinctively higher levels of formal education. They also present a similar distribution of students in terms of urban and rural origin. Even when all schools were ranked in order of examination achievement, it was difficult to perceive any systematic pattern of variation in the social composition of student bodies except for two notable cases. These exceptions were Elite School and Fanti College, the two most eminent secondary institutions in Ghana. Rather than present tabular materials concerning all the dimensions of difference, we summarize in Table 28 the critical divergences between these two schools and all other institutions in the public secondary system with respect to paternal occupational differences. Data on parental education and urban origin essentially parallel these materials. Once again we have restricted the table to male patterns of recruitment.

Taken collectively, the two major sectors of the secondary system show minimal divergences in the composition of their student bodies. If anything, the high-status schools (indicated in column i) display slightly more fluid recruitment patterns than those prevailing in low-status institutions. The former are no more socially restrictive in the kinds of students that they attract than are inferior schools. This is even more strikingly confirmed if we realize that the schools listed in column (i) of the table include Elite School and Fanti College. If the figures for these two institutions (given in column iii) are deducted from column (i), it is immediately apparent that all other Government and Assisted schools show a consistently broader pattern of recruit-

252

TABLE 28

THE PATERNAL OCCUPATIONS OF SAMPLED STUDENTS IN RELATION
TO THE CATEGORY OF SCHOOL NOW ATTENDED (PERCENTAGES)

Paternal Occupation	*Category of School*		
	(i) *High Status Schools*	(ii) *Low Status Schools*	(iii) *Elite School and Fanti College*
Professional, Higher Tech- nical, Administrative and Clerical Workers	33·8 (150)	34·7 (115)	50·4 (75)
Private Traders and Businessmen	10·6 (47)	11·5 (38)	11·4 (17)
Skilled Workers and Artisans	11·7 (52)	14·2 (47)	14·1 (21)
Semiskilled and Unskilled Workers	2·0 (9)	0·9 (3)	1·3 (2)
Farmers and Fishermen	38·3 (170)	36·3 (120)	18·1 (27)
Other (including Police and Uniformed Services)	0·7 (3)	0·6 (2)	—
No Answer and Don't Know	2·9 (13)	1·8 (6)	4·7 (7)
Total	100·0 (444)	100·0 (331)	100·0 (149)

ment than the newer and less reputable establishments. This is a rather surprising conclusion, since it tends to reverse any *a priori* judgments that might have been made regarding the relation between academic achievement and social origin. Achievement levels are consistently higher in the Government and Assisted sector, but this is certainly not attributable merely to the presence of Elite School and Fanti College in the group. In the case of these two latter institutions (which rank second and third respectively in achievement) a rather different pattern arises (Table 28, column iii). These schools offer a picture completely divergent from all other public secondary institutions in Ghana. The number of students from professional or clerical families is far higher, while recruitment from the ranks of farmers and fishermen is just about half that for other schools. Students in these schools also show markedly superior backgrounds in terms of paternal levels of education; over 46 per cent of their fathers had a secondary education or above as against 12 per cent in other Government and Assisted schools and 17 per cent in all other public secondary institutions. Similarly, 32 per cent of their students hail from the two largest urban centres in Ghana (Accra and Kumasi), as

253

. against 18 per cent for other high-status schools and 13 per cent for low-status institutions. Elite School and Fanti College constitute a special elite sector within the general range of high-status schools, and they display a very specific and constricted pattern of recruitment which sets them apart from all other institutions.

Apart from these two schools, however, it would seem that there is virtually no association between the overall ranking of institutions on the basis of academic achievement and the social composition of their student bodies. This does not preclude the possibility that levels of achievement of individual students are related to their social characteristics, but the absence of adequate measures of individual student achievement make it impossible to test such a proposition. For our purposes, however, the study of the secondary-school system as a collectivity is most important and our data suggest that most secondary institutions are by no means restrictive in terms of their recruitment profiles. Academically outstanding schools are not, for the most part, socially exclusive—even students with the humblest origins can and do enter the most exclusive secondary schools in Ghana in appreciable numbers.

The students of high-status and low-status schools do differ very markedly, however, with respect to age and point of entry into the secondary-school system. The mean age of fifth-form students in high-status schools is only 18·7 years while in the low-status sector it rises to 19·8 years. In the latter schools 64 per cent of the male pupils are aged twenty and over, while this figure drops to 21 per cent in the better institutions.

Further, there is a clear tendency for high-status institutions to recruit from the lower forms of middle schools. No less than 75 per cent of male students in low-status schools were recruited from Middle Form IV as against only 4 per cent in the high-status schools. Thus the better schools consistently recruit their students at an earlier age and from a lower segment of the middle-school system. The older and initially less successful students find their way into the low-status sector. This factor is certainly much more pronounced than differences related to the social background of students. The better schools are able to select the most talented pupils not only by checking examination results for a given year but also by identifying capable candidates at an early age. In this respect their policies conform most closely to the intentions of the Accelerated Development Plan of 1951 by lowering the age of entry into secondary schools. In effect, the low-status schools are obliged to accept the rejects of the high-status system.

Some Observations on Educational Selection and Occupational Mobility in Ghana

In this chapter we have shifted the emphasis of our study from a macroscopic investigation of formal education in Ghana to a more detailed study of a segment of the system. We can now view our specific findings in terms of the more general questions pertaining to the relation between formal education and social mobility in contemporary Ghana. More particularly we are interested in seeing to what extent Ghanaian patterns conform or deviate from more familiar Western models.

What we observe is the co-existence of a complex and highly selective system of formal education and an economy which is still to a large extent subsistence in nature. From the earliest period a high premium has been placed upon the possession of formal education for effective access into the 'emergent' modern component of the social and economic structure. At present, the secondary schools probably constitute the most crucial selecting and sorting agency for new-type occupational roles in Ghana, and it would seem, given the present characteristics of the economy, that their importance will increase rather than diminish for some time to come. Through their doors will pass an overwhelming proportion of the potential Ghanaian elite. It is probable too that there will be an increasingly close association between the educational and occupational characteristics of the population as a whole. At present we have no overall picture of the nature of this relationship but a very partial indication is given in Table 29 in which we examine the relationship between the occupational and educational backgrounds of the fathers of our sampled students.

Although it is clear enough that a consistent relationship obtains between paternal occupation and education, it is equally apparent that, so far, many individuals have been able to achieve relatively high-status occupational roles with quite low levels of schooling. Thus over one-sixth of fathers in professional, higher technical, or administrative vocations have a middle-school education or less, while just over one-third have no more than a secondary education. The data illustrate, in fact, the considerable rewards accruing to even limited levels of formal education so far as this older generation is concerned.

But this kind of pattern is not likely to persist. Given a relatively slow rate of expansion in employment opportunities, plus the fact that the majority of these new opportunities are likely to be available in the public sector, it would follow that minimal educational require-

TABLE 29

The Relationship between the Educational and Occupational Characteristics of the Fathers of Sampled Students

Paternal Occupation	Paternal Education							
	No Formal Education	Primary School 1 to 6	Middle School I to IV	Secondary School I to VI or Teacher Training College	University or Equivalent	Commercial and Technical Schools	Don't Know and No Answer	Total
Professional, Higher Technical, and Administrative Workers	2·2 (3)	1·5 (2)	12·7 (17)	35·8 (48)	37·3 (50)	6·0 (8)	4·5 (6)	100·0 (134)
Clerical Workers	0·8 (2)	1·6 (4)	48·8 (124)	41·7 (106)	—	1·2 (3)	5·9 (15)	100·0 (254)
Private Traders and Businessmen	22·2 (22)	9·1 (9)	38·4 (38)	18·2 (18)	—	3·0 (3)	9·1 (9)	100·0 (99)
Skilled Workers and Artisans	21·4 (25)	12·8 (15)	41·9 (49)	12·8 (15)	—	6·8 (8)	4·3 (5)	100·0 (117)
Semiskilled and Unskilled Workers	50·0 (7)	—	42·9 (6)	—	—	—	7·1 (1)	100·0 (14)
Farmers and Fishermen	64·6 (202)	16·6 (52)	13·7 (43)	1·6 (5)	—	—	3·5 (11)	100·0 (313)
Other (including Police and Uniformed Services)	14·3 (1)	—	71·4 (5)	—	4·0 (1)	—	14·3 (1)	100·0 (7)
Don't Know and No Answer	16·0 (4)	—	20·0 (5)	24·0 (6)	—	—	36·0 (9)	100·0 (25)
Total	— (266)	— (82)	— (287)	— (198)	— (51)	— (22)	— (57)	

256

ments for entry to white-collar employment may rise very sharply in a relatively short period. At least a secondary education is likely to be needed for all white-collar occupations, while it is possible that secondary schooling will become increasingly a prerequisite for even some types of technical and artisan training. Thus, there will be a probable tightening of the fit between occupational and educational characteristics, accompanied at the same time by a rapid rise in the minimal educational levels required for all occupations outside the subsistence sector.

It should be clear that this kind of development presupposes three conditions: a very low rate of economic growth with consequently limited occupational opportunities, the dominance by government of these opportunities, and a very limited secondary-school provision. Conversely, increased economic expansion, a lessening of government control over employment, or a radical expansion in the provision of secondary education would make for a much looser fit between occupational and educational characteristics. It seems likely that Ghana in the immediate future will approximate to the first model for some time to come. Clearly, it is easier to expand secondary-school places than it is to ensure continued economic growth or a lessening of the extent of government employment, but even under present conditions the schools recruit from a surprisingly broad spectrum of the Ghanaian population and, in this context, it is worth summarizing our principal conclusions.

The Ghanaian secondary-school system has not only expanded numerically during the last decade, but this expansion has been accompanied by an internal differentiation of the system on the basis of several objective criteria, notably in levels of academic achievement as measured by success in public examinations. This differentiation has created a dichotomy in the system which is clearly recognized even by secondary-school pupils themselves. The principal consequence of this development is that a minority of secondary schools within the system operate increasingly as feeder institutions to higher education through the medium of the sixth forms, while a larger number of schools provide essentially terminal education for their pupils. Except in the case of two very elite schools, however, there is little difference in the social characteristics of the student bodies throughout the system. Neither in terms of ethnic background nor with respect to other social characteristics do student bodies at high-status and low-status schools vary in any major respect. This does not preclude the possibility of greater differentiation occurring in the future but, so far, recruitment shows distinct differences from those characteristic of the Western world, where internal differentiation of

257

secondary-school systems has largely been paralleled by marked variations in the social composition of student bodies as between types of secondary school.

Looking at the system as a whole there is no doubt that familial background is important in entry to secondary school—though children coming from essentially rural backgrounds with illiterate parentage still enter these highly academic schools in substantial numbers. European-type academic secondary systems have often been regarded as checks on social and occupational mobility in the past, and they have tended to perpetuate high social status for already privileged minorities. It has even been stated that this has been one of their principal characteristics in underdeveloped areas. So far as the present data are concerned there is no justification for such a conclusion, and there can be no doubt that the schools operate as extraordinarily effective channels for occupational and social mobility. To be sure, various subgroups in the population fall below their 'quotas' within the student population, but this is equally true of societies where access to secondary education is far less restricted. Thus, in Ghana at present we find a low rate of overall occupational mobility but, at the same time, note the existence of a very selective system of academic secondary education, recruitment into which is on a very broad basis. The chances for an individual to be occupationally mobile in Ghanaian society are very slight, but such chances as there are seem to be more evenly diffused than in some Western societies. Only in the case of the Northern Region have historical factors tended to provide distinctively less favourable opportunities.

Ethnic differentials, the extent of which has been a topic of political dissension, are less than has sometimes been supposed. Very clearly, a gradation does exist as between the northern, central, and southern portions of Ghana, and though slight differences occur as between the former two areas there is no doubt that the northern groups still lag behind. These ethnic differentials, however, seem to be consistently related to other distinctive variations such as paternal occupational and educational characteristics. This suggests that such ethnic inequalities as exist are largely attributable to the greater rate of urbanization and economic change in the southern portion of Ghana. Educational demand follows such developments rather than precedes them. The North will continue to trail other areas until such time as it begins to share more effectively in other aspects of social and economic development in Ghana.

The greatest inequalities are apparent, however, in patterns of female recruitment. Here particular ethnic groups are very highly represented in secondary schools, while other minorities are correspondingly hardly represented at all. Once again these differences are paralleled by very sharp inequalities in terms of other student characteristics and it is apparent that girls are drawn from relatively restricted segments of the Ghanaian population. This is precisely because girls are far less likely to be sent to secondary schools than boys, and, when they do enter these institutions, they are most likely to come from families with educational and occupational backgrounds that are well above the average. In this respect, Ghanaian experience parallels that of most Western societies. Notwithstanding these restrictions and inequalities one can only conclude that the Ghanaian secondary schools perform a remarkable job in terms of their selective and allocative functions. Underlying this is, perhaps, the existence of a set of values which makes secondary education a 'popular' institution in spite of its restricted provision and highly academic content. The secondary school in Ghana is not, so far, the prerogative of any social minority; it is believed to be open to *all* individuals of talent, irrespective of their origins. The very existence of such a belief tends to ensure that the secondary schools do operate as real channels of mobility.

REFERENCES

1. Needless to say, the table contains a number of schools not included in our sample.
2. See *Ghana, Educational Statistics, 1959* (Accra: Government Printer, 1960), p. 11.
3. In practice, the present distribution of secondary schooling in Ghana is very similar to that prevailing in England in the 1890's. At that time there were 3·5 pupils in endowed grammar schools per thousand population. In 1960 in Ghana there were 3·0 pupils per thousand population.
4. See also Seymour Martin Lipset and Reinhard Bendix, *Social Mobility in Industrial Society* (Berkeley and Los Angeles: The University of California Press, 1959), p. 27 *et passim.*
5. For example see Gabriel A. Almond, and James A. Coleman, *The Politics of Developing Areas* (Princeton: Princeton University Press, 1960), p. 279.
6. See C. Arnold Anderson, 'A Skeptical Note on the Relation of Vertical Mobility to Education', *American Journal of Sociology*, LXVI, No. 6 (May 1961), 560.

VIII

THE ASPIRATIONS OF SECONDARY SCHOOL PUPILS

OUR account of the functions of secondary education in Ghana would not be complete without an attempt to discern what aspirations and expectations students hold with regard to their future occupational roles within Ghanaian society. We now have a picture of the kinds of students who obtain secondary education but no evidence concerning what they expect to do with it. Yet one of the themes of this present study has been the delineation of the changing characteristics of the Ghanaian occupational structure. How far, indeed, do the aspirations of these students conform to or reflect the realities of that occupational structure? Or do they rather indicate that African students have highly unrealistic views about the occupational characteristics of the world into which they will enter?—a situation that will increasingly make for disappointment and frustration among them. Previous evidence concerning middle-school students would suggest that these latter are more realistic than many observers have believed, but in the following pages we shall be dealing with a far more tightly selected student body with correspondingly higher levels of aspiration. It must be remembered that the very expansion of formal schooling in Ghana has led to a decline in the occupational returns to a given level of education and it is important to see how far student ambitions reflect a re-evaluation of their occupational opportunities.

Finally, we should point out that our study of these ambitions provides only a partial answer concerning the determinants of such expectations. It has often been held that the vocational aspirations of students are largely governed by the kind of education that they receive. There is little evidence in the following pages to indicate that this is the case. Students are likely to obtain some image of what occupations are most desirable from a variety of sources, of which the school may be only one. Indeed, it is possible that the school is the least important source of perceptions of the desirability of various occupations. Whatever the determinants of occupational choice we cannot concede that there is a close causal relationship between curriculum content and vocational aspirations—a fact that will become more evident as we proceed.

The Scholastic Ambitions of Secondary-School Pupils

Clearly, the aspirations of students and the perception that they have of their own potential roles in Ghanaian society are related to their educational ambitions and the extent to which they believe they will be able to proceed with their studies after completing the basic five-year secondary course. Entry to professional occupations is obviously associated with access to higher education and most student ambitions are dependent to some extent upon their obtaining further full-time schooling.

Initially, the most outstanding characteristic of our students is that the vast majority of them do not regard their secondary education as the terminal point of their full-time education. Thus 97 per cent of pupils hoped to continue with full-time schooling after the completion of their present fifth-form course. Differences between male and female students were minimal in this respect: 97 per cent of boys hoped to continue as against 94 per cent of girls. This uniformity is all the more striking if we consider how recently girls have entered the secondary schools. Furthermore, the whole picture presents something of a contrast with Western European experience, where markedly different levels of desire to continue with further studies occur among secondary-school students. It would appear that once Ghanaian students have been fortunate enough to gain access to the selective secondary schools they become committed to a continuous programme of full-time studies beyond the secondary level.

Equally striking are student expectations of being able to continue with their full-time education. On this point pupils were required to be somewhat more 'realistic' about their chances of being able to continue in view of the restrictions, both scholastic and financial, that might limit their opportunities for further study. So far as boys were concerned, no less than 37 per cent felt that they would certainly be able to continue while a further 48 per cent felt that they had a good chance of continuing. Only 15 per cent felt it unlikely or impossible that they would be able to carry on with their studies. Rather surprisingly, the expectations of girls were even higher. Thus 42 per cent felt certain of continuing, while another 49 per cent believed that they had a good chance; only 7 per cent of girls felt pessimistic about their future educational opportunities. This last finding would, at first, seem surprising in view of the more limited opportunities for education that girls have traditionally enjoyed. The girls' replies become more meaningful if we relate educational expectations to socioeconomic background.

So far as educational hopes are concerned, there is little variation among our students—nearly all aspire to continue with their education. *Expectations* do vary, however, in relation to parental characteristics. Thus, using the criterion of paternal education alone, only 77 per cent of all students whose fathers did not go to school felt certain or felt they had a good chance of continuing their education. In the case of students whose fathers went to primary or middle school this figure rises to 84 per cent and to 91 per cent for students whose fathers had had a secondary education or above. Of this latter group only 8 per cent felt that it was impossible or unlikely that they would be able to proceed, as against 22 per cent of those whose fathers had had no formal schooling. These figures are paralleled by those relating to paternal occupational characteristics, and it is clear that there is a relationship between socioeconomic status and educational expectations. There is, however, no difference whatsoever between boys and girls with similar educational and occupational background, and it seems safe to conclude that the slightly higher expectations of girls reflect their superior socioeconomic background as contrasted with that of boys.

Given the existence of such a pattern it should be clear at the same time that the relationship is a limited one. After all, about three-quarters of the students from the lowest socioeconomic categories still felt optimistic about their educational chances, underlining once again the fairly loose relationships that were so observable in the analysis of educational recruitment. The dependence of educational expectations upon socioeconomic status was to be expected. The surprising fact is how slight it is.

These generally high levels of educational aspiration and expectation are perhaps not so startling in a country where the narrow diffusion of higher education has made its rewards in terms of income and prestige so great. Nonetheless, the hopes and expectations of students are by no means realistic in terms of the actual educational opportunities open to them. In practice, the expansion of the secondary-school system has lessened the possibility of students proceeding to further studies, since at present access to higher education is generally attained through the sixth forms of secondary schools. To be sure, government has considered the possibility of abolishing the latter and enabling students to proceed directly to university from the fifth forms. Such a programme has yet to be carried into effect. When this survey was undertaken, the annual intake into the sixth forms was about 400 pupils as against an annual fifth-form output of approximately 2,500: the chances of a student proceeding to the sixth form were less than one in six. To be sure, other opportunities for further study exist. Students may enter teaching training colleges direct from the fifth form, and a number of additional training schools accept graduates from this level. Many of our students, however, as we shall indicate later, expect to enter the University of Ghana or the Kwame Nkrumah University of Science and Technology, where hitherto successful completion of sixth-form studies has been most frequently required. Student chances for continuing with any type of further schooling probably stood at about one in four in 1961.

In this context it would seem clear that pupils' educational expectations do not reflect accurately the actual possibilities open to them. With a rapidly growing secondary-school system, it would seem that secondary education will become increasingly terminal for most students unless a radical change occurs in admission to higher education. During the early 1950's, a student's chances of continuing with his schooling after having completed his fifth-form studies were relatively good—indeed for a period, direct access could be obtained to the University of Ghana with a General School Certificate, but with the growth of sixth forms this has been made more difficult. It is likely that student expectations still tend to reflect the realities of an earlier period. Adjustment of expectations to reality is likely to be a lengthy process unless imaginative planning modifies restrictive recruitment procedures into higher institutions in the face of mounting pressure from the secondary level.

Student Preferences Concerning Post-Secondary Education

Granted that the majority of students do not regard their secondary studies as terminal in nature, it is still necessary for us to examine the kinds of institutions they wish to enter and the types of courses that they wish to follow there. It should be noted that since all our students were in the final year of their basic secondary studies, the question of their scholastic and occupational futures loomed very large. Their responses showed a considerable degree of clarity and indicated that most had given a great deal of thought to these questions. To be sure, many will not achieve their ambitions, while others will shift in their preferences. The profile that follows gives us an overall picture of the general trend of student educational aspirations.

The Contemporary Scene

TABLE 30

STUDENT CHOICES OF POST-SECONDARY INSTITUTIONS*

Institution	Proportion of Choices (Percentages)		Total
	Males	Females	
The University of Ghana	35·3 (266)	27·1 (48)	33·8 (314)
Kwame Nkrumah University†	27·0 (203)	10·2 (18)	23·8 (221)
Universities and other Higher Institutions Overseas	14·3 (108)	5·6 (10)	12·7 (118)
Teacher Training Colleges	9·3 (70)	17·0 (30)	10·7 (100)
Commercial Colleges‡ and Secretarial Training Schools	8·6 (65)	15·8 (28)	10·0 (93)
Nursing School	0·0 (—)	19·2 (34)	3·6 (34)
Technical Institutes§	3·1 (23)	2·8 (5)	3·0 (28)
Ghana Military Academy¶ and Nautical College	1·9 (14)	0·0 (—)	1·5 (4)
Not Decided and No Answer	0·5 (4)	2·3 (4)	0·9 (8)
Total	100·0 (753)	100·0 (177)	100·0 (930)

* Totals represent only those students who expressed a wish to continue with their studies.

† Formerly the Kumasi College of Technology, this institution has now had full university status conferred upon it and has been renamed the Kwame Nkrumah University of Science and Technology.

‡ These colleges are not degree granting institutions and for the most part offer shorter courses in the secretarial and commercial field.

§ Technical Institutes in Ghana are a recent development and provide opportunities for both craft and technological training at a level below that afforded in the Kwame Nkrumah University.

¶ These relatively new institutions prepare candidates for commissioned rank in the Ghanaian army and merchant marine. Access to them normally requires a very satisfactory pass in the West African School Certificate Examination.

Table 30 indicates the types of post-secondary institution that students wish to enter. It is apparent that the University of Ghana and the Kwame Nkrumah University of Science and Technology account for a high proportion of both male and female choices. For the most part, entry to these high prestige institutions is through the sixth form and this necessitates two or more years extra secondary-school study. A very interesting group are the students who wish to study overseas at institutions of university status. Needless to say, overseas study has a long tradition behind it in Ghana, but it seems clear that foreign institutions (particularly those in the United King-

264

dom and the United States) have a considerable attraction for students even when courses of a similar nature are available in Ghanaian Universities. Overseas study has attractions far beyond the immediate advantages of training as narrowly defined.

All other types of institutions mentioned in Table 30 do not normally require an education to sixth-form level for entry; thus 23 per cent of boys and 55 per cent of girls prefer courses, access to which can be gained directly through the fifth forms. This is a significant sex difference and indicates that although more girls than boys expect to continue their studies they, at the same time, opt for training courses requiring lower standards of entry. They do not anticipate undergoing the rigours of sixth-form work to such an extent as male students. Girls, in fact, consistently tend to be oriented toward post-secondary courses of a more narrowly defined vocational and professional nature, while boys are more directly drawn to institutions offering more general courses of study at a somewhat higher level.

This becomes clearer if we examine the actual choice of courses that students make. Here very marked sex differences occur (Table 31). To be sure, general arts courses constitute the largest single

TABLE 31

STUDENT CHOICES OF POST-SECONDARY COURSES

Preferred Courses	Proportion of Choices (Percentages)		Total
	Males	*Females*	
Arts (including languages, history, geography, classics etc.)	21·1 (159)	23·2 (41)	21·5 (200)
Law or Medicine	20·3 (153)	9·6 (17)	18·3 (170)
Engineering and Technology	16·2 (122)	—	13·1 (122)
Education	9·2 (69)	16·4 (29)	10·5 (98)
Commercial and Business Subjects	7·9 (60)	15·8 (28)	9·5 (88)
Science or Mathematics	9·9 (75)	5·7 (10)	9·1 (85)
Agricultural Science or Forestry	8·3 (62)	2·8 (5)	7·2 (67)
Nursing or Pharmacy	2·5 (19)	21·5 (38)	6·1 (57)
Social Science	2·4 (18)	1·1 (2)	2·2 (20)
Other	1·1 (8)	1·1 (2)	1·1 (10)
Not Decided and No Answer	1·1 (8)	2·8 (5)	1·4 (13)
Total	100·0 (753)	100·0 (177)	100·0 (930)

category of choice for both sexes. Yet this percentage of choices is outweighed by *total* choices in scientific, technical and specifically professional fields. Thus no less than 37 per cent of boys opt for courses in science and mathematics, engineering and technology, agricultural science and pharmacy. Similarly, 33 per cent of girls favour the occupations in this group, though, in practice, almost two-thirds of female students are oriented towards one occupation only—that of nursing.

Girls, however, show far greater interest in areas of study such as education and commercial or business subjects; 32 per cent of girls favour such fields as against only 17 per cent of boys. This kind of distribution is to be expected and reflects to a considerable degree the very real occupational opportunities open to the sexes in contemporary Ghana, a point to which we shall return in greater detail in later pages of this chapter.

Law and medicine, of course, figure very extensively in the plans of boys and to a considerable if lesser degree among girls. This is not surprising since these two occupations have traditionally been the 'great professions' of Ghana. It is worth mentioning at this point that as between these two great professions both male and female students are oriented to medicine and not law. We shall examine the reasons for the decline of interest in law when we consider actual vocational aspirations in more detail. Clearly, these two occupations do not have the degree of fascination for students that we might have supposed. To be sure, they are still very important, but students of both sexes are more oriented to other scientific, technical, and professional training courses.

The most striking feature of this whole profile of educational aspirations, however, is that these students do not conform to the stereotype of an educated elite primarily concerned with the arts, the humanities, and the literary skills. Some observers, upon what evidence is not clear, have so characterized the products of African secondary schools[1] attributing this proclivity to the students' previous schooling. The plain fact of the matter is that these students are, for the most part, oriented to professional and technical courses of various types and, in this respect, are not unlike secondary-school students in other nations. To be sure, although many are oriented to technical courses, few are interested in craft training as indicated by the very low level of choices for entry to technical institutes. It is too much to expect that in any country an educational cohort which comprises a tiny minority will orient itself to artisan training. In terms of selectivity, for instance, our sample is more to be compared with American college graduates than American high-school students and, in this context, much of the criticism of the literary and non-manual educational orientation of the graduates of selective secondary schools is partially inaccurate and very inappropriate. What is significant here is that although most students are oriented to various forms of professional and subprofessional training a large minority of them have chosen technical and scientific studies.

It would appear from these data that sex generally accounts for the majority of differences in the educational interests of students. Conversely, socioeconomic origin seems to be a much less significant factor in predicting educational aspirations. If, for example, sex and paternal level of education are held constant, there are few differences between subgroups with one exception. Teacher training is much more important among students of both sexes who come from the least educated segments of the population. Thus 14 per cent of boys and 29 per cent of girls whose fathers had had no formal education proposed to enter teacher training colleges and pursue courses in education. By contrast, only 6 per cent of boys and 14 per cent of girls whose fathers had received a secondary education or more were interested in this field of preparation. This pattern of choice is to be expected. Though teacher-training courses are of relatively low status as compared with many alternative types of post-secondary education they would appear to be a significant channel of occupational mobility for students from more humble families.

Precisely the reverse relationship appears with regard to the fields of law and medicine. It is evident that these courses are not often chosen by girls, but so far as boys are concerned, preferences for law and medicine are almost twice as high for students coming from superior educational backgrounds as they are for students where fathers did not attend school (27 per cent as against 15 per cent). This, needless to say, is correlated with a substantially higher preference for overseas study in the field of medicine. Similarly, nursing emerges as a much more favoured form of training among girls drawn from the higher educational levels; no less than 25 per cent of females whose fathers had received a secondary education or above favoured this type of study as against none whose fathers lacked formal education. Conversely agricultural science and training was more consistently favoured by male students who came from non-literate rural homes as against those with substantial educational backgrounds (12 per cent as against 5 per cent).

In summary, educational or agricultural training appear to be rather more related to lower socioeconomic origin while law, medicine, and nursing are more significantly associated with recruitment from higher status groups. None of these differences is very great, however, and for the most part, preferences for particular institutions or types of study are not markedly associated with educational and occupational origins. As in our previous examples, it is not the presence of these relationships that is surprising but their limited incidence and magnitude. For the most part, choices of students from even the most humble origins do not differ very much from individuals with considerably superior backgrounds. Whether we use paternal education, occupation, or urban-rural background, no clear-cut pattern of association between these variables and educational preference emerges. We are not dealing with a typically 'Western' set of characteristics. For the most part students see their educational futures as fairly 'open' with few limitations on their choices. This constellation of features seems to fit very well with the picture of relatively open recruitment into the secondary-school system that we described in the previous chapter.

Student Perceptions of the Occupational Hierarchy

Before proceeding to a more detailed examination of student vocational aspirations we shall attempt to gain some impression of how students themselves view different occupations in terms of the social prestige which is accorded to them in contemporary Ghana. It has been a central theme of previous chapters that the emergence of conceptions of social status based principally upon occupational criteria has been overwhelmingly a result of European contact. It follows from this that African perceptions of the occupational hierarchy are likely to conform very closely to Western patterns since the colonial elite itself provided the model from which new African conceptions of social status emerged. We may test this proposition by asking students to rank a variety of occupations in terms of their perceived differential 'prestige'. This approach is not a new one and has been used previously in Africa by both Mitchell and Epstein and Xydias.[2]

Partially following Mitchell and Epstein's procedures, Ghanaian students were asked to rank twenty-five occupations on a five-point scale ranging from 'very high prestige' to 'very low prestige'. The results of this ranking are given in Table 32, where it will be noted that virtually all the jobs listed were essentially modern or 'new type' occupational roles. Two listed occupations do not conform to these criteria; those of 'chief' and 'chief's counsellor'. Justifiable criticism could be made concerning the inclusion of these two items. Strictly speaking, neither is an occupation in the same sense as the others. Most chiefs do not receive formal income *qua* chief though some paramount chiefs do receive government stipends besides the less

TABLE 32

STUDENT RANKINGS OF TWENTY-FIVE OCCUPATIONS IN ORDER
OF THEIR PERCEIVED PRESTIGE

Occupation	Rank Order					
	Males			Females		
	Mean Score	S.D.	Rank	Mean Score	S.D.	Rank
Doctor	1·12	0·31	1	1·21	0·54	1
University Lecturer	1·16	0·31	2	1·22	0·53	2
Lawyer	1·45	0·64	3	1·47	0·59	3
Chief	1·89	0·78	4	1·94	0·77	5
Author	1·97	0·80	5	1·86	0·86	4
Secondary-School Teacher	2·05	0·51	6	1·97	0·53	6
Clergyman	2·06	0·84	7	2·14	0·82	7
Businessman	2·50	0·73	8	2·45	0·70	9
Nurse	2·60	0·64	9	2·49	0·78	10
Political Party Worker	2·70	0·93	10	2·36	0·79	8
Government Clerk	2·71	0·59	11	2·76	0·54	11
Soldier	2·78	0·81	12	2·84	0·76	15
Actor	2·81	0·90	13	2·79	1·01	12
Chief's Counsellor	2·82	0·74	14	2·83	0·73	14
Policeman	2·94	0·73	15	3·00	0·62	17
Farmer	2·95	0·96	16	3·05	0·96	18
Office Worker	2·96	0·60	17	2·81	0·54	13
Middle-School Teacher	3·00	0·50	18	2·96	0·50	16
Primary-School Teacher	3·25	0·67	19	3·27	0·69	19
Motor Car Mechanic	3·59	0·73	20	3·55	0·77	20
Petty Trader	3·62	0·75	21	3·55	0·87	20
Shop Assistant	3·80	0·66	22	3·63	0·64	22
Carpenter	3·84	0·73	23	3·77	0·69	23
Farm Labourer	4·47	0·70	24	4·26	0·81	24
Street Cleaner	4·74	0·56	25	4·62	0·70	25

formal perquisites of office; certainly chiefs' counsellors do not receive formal stipends. Furthermore, it could be asked how meaningful such concepts are for students coming from ethnic groups where formal chiefship has not traditionally existed? It would have been easy enough to select a number of more specific traditional roles if the students had hailed from one ethnic group but, under the circumstances, more general terms had to be used even if precise meaning was sacrificed. These two occupations, therefore, were inserted to indicate in a very general and perhaps rather unsatisfactory way, to what extent traditional office still commands prestige even among secondary-school students.

Most of the post-traditional occupations in the list were well known to students, but it was decided to include one or two occupations with which they might be less familiar in the Ghanaian context. Such an occupation was that of 'actor', where it was anticipated that a relatively high standard deviation of scores would indicate that conceptions of occupational prestige had not yet fully crystallized. In practice, in those cases where a high standard deviation of scores was observed, it was found either in association with *very* new type occupations such as actor, author, or political party worker or with general occupational groups having a considerable degree of variation in their characteristics. This was the case with the 'farmer' category, for example, which was not given a high mean ranking. Farmers in Ghana, however, are a very heterogeneous group ranging from a small group of more wealthy cocoa farmers to very marginal subsistence cultivators.

The findings generally confirm those of Xydias and Mitchell in that occupational prestige rankings conform closely to the Western pattern from which they are apparently derived. At the top are concentrated the various professions, followed by clerical and skilled technical workers with minor artisans, petty traders and unskilled workers ranged at the bottom. To be sure, the table tells us nothing about the relative 'distance' between occupations but at least in order of ranking this is a very familiar picture.

Cross-cultural comparisons of occupational prestige rankings are a somewhat hazardous undertaking owing to the difficulty of really equating occupations from various cultures. Some previous studies have attempted this and a recent effort has shown a remarkably high correlation of 0·80 as between the occupational prestige rankings made by a sample of Japanese and American high-school students.[3] In this present study it was possible to select seventeen occupations which were included in this latter study and compare them with the American and Japanese results. There is a correlation of 0·83 between the Ghanaian and Japanese rankings with an even higher correlation of 0·88 as between American and Ghanaian rankings. There is considerable consensus between two relatively industrialized areas and a society whose occupational structure is markedly less differentiated.

When we examine the Ghanaian prestige rankings in more detail, we see that the traditional role of chief still commands considerable prestige even among this minority of 'modernized' and educated youth. 'Chief' ranks along with the 'professional' occupations as an activity with considerable status in Ghanaian society in spite of the fact that recent government policy has tended to strip the chiefs of the real powers that they once possessed and has left them with essentially vestigial ceremonial roles. Even the more limited role of 'chief's counsellor' is far from the bottom of the rank order in spite of the fact that this kind of function is often performed by older lineage heads or subchiefs with very limited educational backgrounds. These facts would certainly suggest that social change in contemporary Ghana may have lessened but has by no means obliterated the dignity of traditional office.

If we examine the position of 'contemporary' occupations we observe, first, the low ranking accorded primary and middle-school teachers. Male students place them just above the level of motor-car fitter and petty trader while female students are hardly more generous. This low ranking is to be expected, since rapid expansion of this segment of the teaching force has led to lowered standards of entry and training. As a result, the position of these teachers is totally different from those in secondary schools who are accorded something like professional standing. It is probable, in fact, that recent developments in Ghanaian education have broadened the gap between secondary and other forms of teaching and have induced a dramatic decline in the status of an occupational group of primary and middle-school instructors who were formerly highly rated. These findings underline the danger of treating teachers as a group enjoying a homogeneous occupational status.

Contrary, perhaps, to common impressions, the Ghanaian farmer is by no means at the bottom of the prestige hierarchy. In terms of the rubrics employed, he ranks above his Japanese counterpart and at about the same position as the American farmer. He also ranks above primary and middle-school teachers and some skilled artisans. In the light of many jeremiads concerning the contempt for agriculture among secondary-school pupils, it is refreshing to find how highly they esteem the status of the farmer. Similarly, the category of 'businessman' receives a far higher rating from students than might have been expected. On the other hand the 'government clerk' ranks higher than the 'office worker', who is defined as any clerical worker outside government employment. This, interestingly enough, is one of the few occupations for which marked deviation occurred between male and female ratings. Apart from this, however, there is a high correlation between the rankings of the sexes.

Given the fact that the prestige hierarchy is similar in general conformation to those found in other and quite distinct cultures it was decided to take the matter a little further and to see whether students associated occupational prestige with perceived income.

271

Following the precedent of the earlier Japanese-American study, students were asked to rate the same occupations on the basis of what level of income they thought these various types of worker commanded. Once again a simple five-point scale ranging from 'very high' income to 'very low' income was used (Table 33).

TABLE 33

STUDENT RANKINGS OF TWENTY-FIVE OCCUPATIONS IN ORDER
OF THEIR PERCEIVED INCOME

Occupation	Rank Order					
	Males			Females		
	Mean Score	S.D.	Rank	Mean Score	S.D.	Rank
Doctor	1·24	0·47	1	1·27	0·55	2
University Lecturer	1·28	0·51	2	1·19	0·41	1
Lawyer	1·40	0·55	3	1·31	0·53	3
Chief	2·47	0·80	8	2·36	0·84	9
Author	2·25	0·86	6	2·00	0·77	4
Secondary-School Teacher	2·23	0·58	5	2·10	0·54	5
Clergyman	3·10	0·95	15	3·26	0·80	19
Businessman	1·92	0·79	4	2·11	0·77	6
Nurse	3·01	0·57	13	3·17	0·65	17
Political Party Worker	2·38	0·90	7	2·11	0·83	6
Government Clerk	2·78	0·58	11	2·81	0·48	11
Soldier	3·00	0·64	12	3·10	0·63	14
Actor	2·47	0·94	8	2·16	0·91	8
Chief's Counsellor	3·21	0·79	16	3·09	0·77	13
Policeman	3·21	0·55	16	3·15	0·57	15
Farmer	2·75	1·06	10	2·70	1·07	10
Office Worker	3·03	0·56	14	2·92	0·53	12
Middle-School Teacher	3·21	0·51	16	3·15	0·47	15
Primary-School Teacher	3·53	0·65	21	3·53	0·63	21
Motor Car Mechanic	3·35	0·77	19	3·26	0·92	19
Petty Trader	3·36	0·82	20	3·20	0·88	18
Shop Assistant	3·84	0·64	23	3·63	0·68	22
Carpenter	3·73	0·75	22	3·70	0·79	23
Farm Labourer	4·51	0·63	24	4·33	0·75	24
Street Cleaner	4·73	0·53	25	4·70	0·56	25

The most striking feature to emerge from the analysis is the extraordinarily high correlation between perceived prestige and perceived income rankings; for male students this is 0·92 and for girls it is 0·87. These correlations may be contrasted with a correlation of 0·65 for

Japanese and 0·52 for American students. One cannot avoid observing that the United States has often been characterized as a society in which occupational prestige has been very consistently correlated with income variables. In practice, the correlation is far below that obtaining for our Ghanaian sample.

It can be contended that an association of this type is spurious in the sense that it is merely the result of students' automatically believing that any prestigeful occupation *must* by definition command a high income. Even if this were the case it would still be significant in a society where, traditionally, variations in income have not been great. A closer inspection of the two sets of tables leads us to conclude that students have a very shrewd perception of actual variations in income. Thus, in virtually every case where a marked deviation between prestige and income ratings appears, student ratings can be justified by examination of actual incomes accruing to an occupation. The two clearest cases are, of course, clergyman and chief. The former do, in fact, command relatively low levels of income, while there can be little doubt that the income of many chiefs is not substantial.

What is the general significance of these findings? To a considerable degree they throw doubt upon the frequent observation that 'prestige' factors largely govern the assessment of jobs by educated Africans. It is sometimes assumed that they ignore income factors and, of course, this contention constitutes another version of the white-collar argument that we have discussed in previous chapters. No doubt Africans, like most other groups, do attach considerable importance to occupational prestige in job choice, but it is clear that prestige and income factors do not operate independently. They are very highly associated and this strengthens our contention that when Africans prefer white-collar employment they do so with the knowledge that these jobs are more highly paid. This finding contrasts very markedly with a study in Ceylon; there, prestige and income factors appeared to be very loosely associated and changes in income seemed hardly to be reflected in vocational preferences.[4]

Our conclusions here have far more than academic significance. If we assume that levels of income are normally related to conditions of supply and demand for particular categories of labour, then it is logical to conclude that shortages of particular types of skill will be reflected in the income levels of individuals possessing those skills. To be sure, one must enter the caveat in the case of Ghana that the predominance of government employment may act as a very serious obstacle to the workings of the market. Bureaucratic structures are notorious for regulating rates of remuneration in their own interest and maintaining incomes above an 'equilibrium price'. In spite of this there is likely to be, as in most exchange economies, a rough correspondence between income levels and market demand. In this sense, wage levels tend to reflect economic realities and although, strictly speaking, an association between income and occupational prestige does not imply a causal relationship, our evidence would certainly lead us to suggest that an increase in the real income of an occupational group will be reflected fairly promptly in the prestige of that group vis-à-vis other occupations.

What we are implying here is that vocational aspirations more often than not in the Ghanaian situation, are based upon perceptions of the occupational structure itself in which income perceptions play a salient part. In this sense, changes in the demand and supply position for various types of labour which reflect themselves in real income terms, will in turn be reflected in the prestige rankings of occupations and probably ultimately in the vocational aspirations of students. From this viewpoint the argument that certain types of academic education lead to certain types of attitude to occupations is a doubtful proposition; on the contrary, we suggest here that vocational aspirations are, to a large extent, derived from people's perceptions of the rewards of the occupational structure itself. Admittedly these perceptions may reflect misinformation but, in the case of these students, one is impressed by the accuracy of their assessments.

Clearly, in any society we are unlikely to obtain a perfect relationship between income and prestige factors, but a high association between these two as indicated by people's responses is a healthy sign. It does imply that aspirations will respond to the realities of the market instead of creating only the type of situation that Ryan has depicted in Ceylon where individuals preferred to enter 'high-status' jobs on minimal pay or even remain unemployed rather than accept more lucrative manual work.[5]

The argument that vocational aspirations reflect to a great extent the market situation for trained labour in Ghana applies equally well to the schools themselves. We have reiterated that the academic secondary school maintains its dominant position not because of the prestige of academic studies but because its pupils have heretofore obtained access to the most lucrative employment. Should any changes within the Ghanaian economy lead to any real shortage in the supply of technically trained people one would expect an increased demand for technical instruction to manifest itself first in the private school sector, which has always been the most sensitive indicator of public demand. Any attempt to force the growth of technical instruction in the face of public disinterest is likely to be quite ineffective and economically wasteful. Similarly, I question any belief that curricular change will have any great effect on children's vocational intentions. Bearing these facts in mind we are now in a position to examine the vocational ambitions of our sampled students in greater detail.

The Vocational Aspirations of Secondary-School Pupils

To some extent, examination of the educational aspirations of students has pointed to their vocational ambitions. This is clear, for example, in cases where students opt for rather specific vocational courses such as nursing or teacher training. The pattern is less clear, however, where students indicate preferences for general arts courses and it is necessary that we examine their actual vocational aspirations and expectations in greater detail.

It is important to differentiate between pupils' aspirations and expectations; failure to make this differentiation in earlier studies has sometimes resulted in ambivalent responses. The procedure adopted resembled that followed in the earlier middle-school study to which we have made reference in chapter VI. Students were asked first what kind of job they would most prefer if they were absolutely free to choose any occupation. They were told that they were not being asked to be realistic about their choices in terms of their own rating of their scholastic ability, actual job opportunities, or financial resources. They were, therefore, allowed to fantasy as much as they wished, and in this manner what might be termed an 'optimum' distribution of responses was obtained (Table 34). This profile of responses, therefore, represents the pattern of what Ghanaian secondary pupils consider to be the most desirable occupations in their society. These responses can be meaningfully compared with the income and prestige ratings. Once again male and female responses have been tabulated separately, since distinct variations do occur as between the sexes.

As we might expect, the pupils manifest a consistent preference for highly ranked occupations of a professional or semiprofessional nature. It was to be anticipated that no students would choose artisan-type employment which is relatively lowly ranked and lowly paid on our occupational ratings. However, among boys the largest single block of preferences is for scientific and technical occupations of various kinds. To be sure, this is a very broad category ranging from professional engineering to laboratory assistant or agricultural demonstrator. Just over two-thirds of this group are oriented towards the natural sciences and their related technology in physics, chemistry,

T   275

The Contemporary Scene

TABLE 34

THE VOCATIONAL ASPIRATIONS OF SECONDARY-SCHOOL STUDENTS

Occupation*	Proportion of Choices (Percentages)		Total
	Males	Females	
Medicine	17·3 (134)	11·2 (21)	16·1 (155)
Law	3·7 (29)	3·7 (7)	3·7 (36)
Ministry	0·1 (1)	—	0·1 (1)
Other Professional†	1·0 (7)	0·5 (1)	0·8 (8)
Higher Administrative‡	6·8 (53)	4·3 (8)	6·3 (61)
Higher Commercial§	7·2 (56)	3·7 (7)	6·6 (63)
Politics	1·5 (12)	0·5 (1)	1·4 (13)
Clerical (Government)¶	1·0 (7)	3·7 (7)	1·5 (14)
Other Clerical**	3·6 (27)	16·5 (31)	6·0 (58)
Scientific and Technical††	26·2 (203)	3·2 (6)	21·7 (209)
Nursing and Pharmacy	2·4 (19)	18·1 (34)	5·5 (53)
University Teaching	2·6 (20)	1·1 (2)	2·3 (22)
Secondary School Teaching	14·8 (115)	22·9 (43)	16·4 (158)
Primary or Middle School Teaching	4·3 (33)	6·4 (12)	4·7 (45)
Teaching at other Institutions‡‡	0·8 (6)	—	0·6 (6)
Police and Uniformed Services	4·6 (36)	—	3·7 (36)
Minor Commercial§§	—	—	—
Farming and Fishing	1·0 (8)	2·1 (4)	1·3 (12)
Miscellaneous¶¶	0·6 (5)	0·5 (1)	0·6 (6)
No Answer	0·5 (4)	1·6 (3)	0·7 (7)
Total	100·0 (775)	100·0 (188)	100·0 (963)

* Occupational categories which are not self-explanatory are as follows:
† Economist, Statistician, Sociologist.
‡ Senior Civil Servants, Chief Secretaries, Directors of Public Corporations, District and Regional Commissioners, etc.
§ Accountants and Auditors, Bank Managers, Business Executives, etc.
¶ All choices specifying clerical work which indicated a specific preference for government employment.
** All choices specifying clerical work which indicated a specific preference for private employment.
†† Including engineering of all types, surveying, agricultural research, veterinary activities, laboratory assistantships and work in the field of the physical or biological sciences, etc.
‡‡ Primarily at Technical Institutes or Commercial Schools.
§§ Small Shopkeepers and Petty Traders.
¶¶ Actor, Dramatist, etc.

276

meteorology, and engineering, while the remainder indicate preferences in the fields of biology and agricultural science. Girls show
considerably less orientation towards these fields but, correspondingly, there is a marked emphasis among them upon nursing
which can be legitimately regarded as a quasi-professional field
of a primarily technical variety. In general the relatively high
level of responses within these categories show that these students
are not oriented towards purely administrative and bureaucratic
roles.

The next highest group of choices is for medicine, and it is apparent
here that this is a far more popular choice than the other 'great
profession' of Ghana, law. The high preference for medicine is readily
explainable if we look at the income and prestige ratings accorded to
doctors by students. Lawyers are also given extraordinarily high
ratings in terms of both these variables and law has traditionally been
one of the most desirable occupations in Ghana.[6] What would account for this relative disinterest in an occupation which is so highly
ranked and which has been historically so significant? We may only
speculate that law in contemporary Ghana has come to carry certain
risks specific to that occupation. Frequently, it has been a prelude to
other political activities and even normal practice in the courts may
involve advocates in disputes with political authority. The same complex of features is apparent in the sphere of politics. It is probable
that a few years ago a relatively high proportion of students would
have seen politics as a promising vocational outlet. It is apparent
that this is not so today. With the greater stabilization of the present
regime, political opportunity has probably diminished for younger
individuals, moreover, such activities are not without certain professional hazards. Political party workers are not highly ranked on
either prestige or income, and this combined with the uncertainties of
politics as a career may account for the relative apathy towards the
occupation. Certainly, this limited finding would confirm the view
that initially high levels of political commitment during the earlier
struggle for independence are followed by a gradual political retreatism among the educated elite. This does not signify a lack of political
concern but rather withdrawal from the active political arena and
orientation to 'professional' careers.

Our evidence does not, it should be noted, support the contention
that students are markedly oriented to high-level government administrative roles or posts in the senior civil service. Somehow, it has
always been assumed that this kind of career has had particular
appeal for African students. In practice, these occupations tend to be
no more popular than those comprised within the 'higher com-

mercial' group. These latter occupations lie predominantly in the private sector and many students, in fact, stressed their preference for working with the larger commercial companies.

One thing is very clear. African male students at least, do not want to become clerks either in government or private employ. Only 5 per cent of all boys would prefer this kind of activity if they were free to choose. This accords well with our contention in previous chapters that the products of the schools have entered clerical employment in large numbers not by preference but because this was the kind of post most accessible to them and which guaranteed a reasonable level of income. To be sure, just over 20 per cent of girls would prefer clerical employment which underlines the fact that throughout, the vocational aspirations of female students are less 'ambitious' than those of boys. This is in spite of the fact that their socioeconomic background is substantially higher. As elsewhere, fewer vocational outlets are open to women in contemporary Ghana. Even where they expressed free choices regarding their occupational future it was difficult for them to move away from a group of activities generally regarded as appropriate for women. Thus, just over 67 per cent of the girls were interested in teaching, nursing, or clerical work as against only 26 per cent of the boys.

One feature does, however, arise from an examination of the clerical preferences of both boys and girls. A government clerk tends to be rated more highly by both sexes than a clerk in private employment in terms of occupational prestige and income. Yet there is a marked preference, particularly among girls, for clerical employment with private commercial companies and, as we shall see, this becomes even more marked when we examine patterns of vocational expectation. It should be noted, however, that the vast majority of students who prefer clerical work in the private sector perceive this mainly in terms of employment with relatively large commercial concerns such as the banks and insurance companies whose conditions of service are at least equivalent to those in many government departments. Interest in clerical work with small-scale private companies hardly appears in student responses.

Finally, a word concerning teaching as a profession. It goes without saying that teaching is significantly more popular among girls than boys, but there is a fairly high preference for secondary-school teaching among both sexes. This occupation is very highly ranked in Ghana and enjoys a degree of truly professional status. Traditionally at least, entry into this level of teaching has normally been gained via university studies, though the recent expansion of secondary schools has led to some dilution of standards. It would be interesting to see how far this dilution will have an effect upon the future status of this profession.

Preferences for primary and middle-school teaching, however, are markedly low for both sexes, and a glance at the occupational and prestige ratings for this class of teachers confirms the relatively low esteem in which this job is held. To be sure, teaching in these schools has been one of the most important occupational outlets for educated youth for a long period; it has not, however, usually been a significant destination for *secondary*-school pupils. The bulk of primary and middle-school teachers have been drawn from the ranks of senior primary, and middle-school graduates who have then undergone a further period of instruction in teacher training colleges. Indeed, in 1959 less than 5 per cent of the whole primary and middle-school teaching force had completed secondary school, and it is safe to say that up to comparatively recently, secondary-school students did not enter this level of teaching unless they had failed their School Certificate Examination or obtained very mediocre results.

What conclusions can we draw from this brief picture of vocational aspirations? Quite obviously these students do not conform to the familiar stereotype of a group oriented primarily to administrative, clerical, or bureaucratic-type occupations. Boys certainly show a marked interest in scientific and technological fields and their occupational ambitions are by no means limited to the traditional twin pillars of law and medicine. Girls show a narrower range of aspirations, but one can hardly feel that their pattern of responses is very different from the profile among female secondary students in Western countries. Furthermore, although pupils were given the opportunity to express 'optimum' choices, the pattern of responses is not an entirely unrealistic one. To be sure, the majority will not be able to continue with full-time studies long enough to enable them to enter many of these professions. Yet, in numerical terms they are a highly selected educational elite with potential access to all these occupations. Some of these listed occupations do not necessarily require full university training. Ghanaian secondary students do enter the kinds of occupations portrayed here and one is impressed by the moderate levels of aspiration of many of these young people.

Finally, it should be added that there is very little relationship between vocational aspirations and the social backgrounds of students whether these are examined in terms of paternal occupation, paternal level of education, ethnicity or urban-rural origin. The sole exception to this has been noted previously; there is a significantly greater preference for medicine among students of superior socio-economic background and a rather greater emphasis upon teaching,

279

both primary and secondary, among groups of lower socioeconomic status. Aside from this no significant differences arise and overwhelmingly, sex remains the factor generally associated with statistically significant differences.

The Vocational Expectations of Secondary-School Pupils

Optimum aspirations and vocational expectations are, of course, very different things. Considerable practical difficulties can result from attempts to differentiate them empirically. We are aware that most sampled students not only hope but expect to continue with their full-time studies after completing fifth-form work. If, therefore, they are asked to differentiate between what occupations they would most like to enter and what occupations they *expect* to enter there is likely to be some confusion and parallelism in responses. This was clearly evident in earlier preliminary interviews conducted with a small sample of students. Thus it was essential in this study for expectations to be related to *a given level of formal education.* Consequently, the final form of the question to students concerned their expectations if they were *unable* to proceed with their full-time studies beyond the fifth-form level in which they were then enrolled.

This was a perfectly legitimate device, since it is apparent that most students do not continue their studies. Indeed, within three months after this study was undertaken it was possible to predict that 75 per cent of the sampled students would be involved in a search for employment. It was vitally important, therefore, to obtain some impression of what students thought they could achieve with a fifth-form education. Here a totally different pattern of responses emerges from that reported above and it is quite evident that students have few illusions as to the character of occupations open to them given this level of formal schooling (Table 35).

Virtually no students believe that it will be possible for them to enter professional or semiprofessional employment. The number who anticipate entering scientific and technical fields drops to just over 7 per cent among boys. Even here the vast majority expect to obtain relatively low-level technical jobs such as laboratory assistant or agricultural demonstrator.

The proportion of pupils expecting to enter clerical employment within the public or private sector rises to over 51 per cent of the total student body; over 60 per cent for female students and 49 per cent for males. Thus, though there is a considerable disparity between the sexes regarding their aspirations for clerical employment, this differential tends to narrow markedly so far as expectations are con-

TABLE 35

THE VOCATIONAL EXPECTATIONS OF SECONDARY-SCHOOL STUDENTS

Occupation	Proportion of Choices (Percentages)		Total
	Males	*Females*	
Medicine	—	—	—
Law	—	—	—
Ministry	—	—	—
Other Professional	0·1 (1)	—	0·1 (1)
Higher Administrative	—	—	—
Higher Commercial	0·1 (1)	—	0·1 (1)
Politics	—	—	—
Clerical (Government)	18·3 (142)	20·7 (39)	18·8 (181)
Other Clerical	31·3 (243)	40·5 (76)	33·1 (319)
Scientific and Technical	7·4 (57)	1·1 (2)	6·1 (59)
Nursing and Pharmacy	0·8 (6)	10·1 (19)	2·6 (25)
University Teaching	—	—	—
Secondary School Teaching	1·4 (11)	0·5 (1)	1·3 (12)
Primary or Middle School Teaching	34·1 (264)	23·9 (45)	32·1 (309)
Teaching at other Institutions	0·4 (3)	—	0·3 (3)
Police and Uniformed Services	4·5 (35)	—	3·6 (35)
Minor Commercial	0·1 (1)	—	0·1 (1)
Farming and Fishing	1·0 (7)	1·1 (2)	1·0 (9)
Miscellaneous	—	0·5 (1)	0·1 (1)
No Answer	0·5 (4)	1·6 (3)	0·7 (7)
Total	100·0 (775)	100·0 (188)	100·0 (963)

cerned. Boys may be far less inclined to enter clerical work than girls but, in practice feel to an almost equal extent that they will be obliged to enter this occupation. There is also a much greater expectation of entering the private sector of clerical employment among both sexes and we might add that almost half this group expect employment with the larger commercial banks.

Similarly, almost one-third of the students of both sexes feel that poorly paid teaching posts in the primary or middle schools are their most likely occupational destination. Even the small number who expect to teach in secondary schools specify teaching in *private* secondary institutions which, as we have seen, are hardly more than middle schools. Interestingly enough, a rather higher proportion of boys

281

than girls expect to enter primary and middle-school teaching, though this is somewhat less popular among boys so far as patterns of aspiration are concerned. Girls do, of course, have nursing as an alternative and realistic vocational outlet.

These data indicate, in fact that over 84 per cent of all students expect to enter low-level clerical employment or primary and middle-school teaching if they are unable to continue with their studies beyond the fifth form. At this level the relative difference between male and female students, so marked at the aspiration level, tends to disappear, and there is a greater degree of conformity between the sexes so far as actual expectations are concerned. Furthermore, patterns of expectation do not vary significantly in relation to social background except in one respect. There is a distinct tendency for both boys and girls with superior levels of paternal education to prefer clerical forms of employment, while students from more limited educational backgrounds expect to enter primary and middle-school teaching to a greater degree. Just over 38 per cent of students whose fathers have received no formal education expect to enter clerical employment as against 58 per cent of students whose fathers had at least a secondary-school education. Almost 47 per cent of the former group expect to enter primary or middle-school teaching, as against just over 25 per cent of students coming from superior educational backgrounds. To the extent that clerical work is rated slightly more highly in terms of prestige and income, it is clear that students from somewhat superior socioeconomic backgrounds do have slightly higher vocational expectations. The difference, however, in overall levels of expectation is not very striking. There can be little doubt that each student perceives his own level of educational achievement as being the overwhelming factor determining his occupational future. The urban child of superior socioeconomic origin does not anticipate a very different career from his rural counterpart with a more limited background. It is evident, however, that the rather higher preference for teaching among groups with lower socioeconomic origins is consistent enough at both levels of vocational preference. While teaching still remains attractive for this group, its importance has already declined for other students. This kind of evidence supports a general contention that teaching in Ghana as in most countries constitutes the principal mode of occupational mobility for lower-status groups and may constitute a 'staging post' in general patterns of upward mobility.

Our evidence suggests that critics who have implied that African students are unrealistic in their vocational expectations or wish to enter only clerical and white-collar employment are generally incorrect. They have not realized what these students appear to perceive, that there are few openings in the occupational structure apart from this kind of employment. Up to the present, clerical and teaching opportunities have expanded relatively more rapidly than other occupational alternatives and no one is more aware of this than the students themselves. Even after a formal education of anything between twelve and fifteen years the expectations of students are limited enough. To be sure, many nourish rather unjustifiable hopes of being able to continue with their studies, but for a given level of education their expectations are remarkably realistic. It is very probable, indeed, that their expectations are diminishing; for example, a decade ago very few secondary students would have anticipated entering primary or middle-school teaching—such an occupation was largely for the senior primary, or middle-school graduate. Quite obviously the reverse is the case at present, and it would seem that students do lower their expectations in the face of an occupational reality, which is determined by a relatively slow growth in employment opportunities coupled with an accelerating output from the schools.

In examining the relationship between the schools and the occupational structure not a few observers have been led into a rather elementary error. Since a majority of secondary-school graduates have entered clerical employment in past years it has been inferred that clerical employment figures very largely in the vocational preferences of students. Ultimate occupational destination may, of course, be partly influenced by vocational preferences but, in the last resort, it is determined by the structure of job opportunities in the economy. By a process of *post-hoc* reasoning it has been assumed that vocational destinations reflect the real aspiration patterns of students. It has been our task here, however, to indicate that more often than not people are obliged to accept jobs that do not figure very highly in their plans. Put in this manner, the point seems quite obvious—so obvious, in fact, that it has been frequently ignored and unjustifiable assumptions made about the characteristics of the African secondary-school graduate.

Clearly, our conclusions here are at variance with a great deal of current opinion. Rather than suggest that there is an insatiable demand for technically trained individuals, we have suggested that at present the actual structure of job opportunities may favour clerical employment. Proponents of the view that the demand for technical skills is almost unlimited in the developing nations seem to imply that in some manner this demand operates independently of the actual market for skills and that certain types of training automatically generate their own demand. This is highly questionable to say the least, and it is perhaps one of the marked characteristics of less developed economies that the demand for technically trained individuals is likely to remain low for some period. Certainly, many of the new nations are initially characterized by a quicker expansion of their bureaucratic and administrative structures rather than by a formidable increase in the demand for alternative occupational skills. In the light of these remarks the patterns of preference and expectation among students seem to make a good deal of sense. In large measure, their aspirations appear closely related to their perception of various occupations in terms of prestige and income factors, whereas patterns of expectation appear to be meaningfully linked to the characteristics of the contemporary occupational structure.

The Occupational Destinations of Students

So far, our comments concerning the occupations that secondary-school graduates do, in fact, enter have been derived from a variety of sources. The comments of school principals and employers give us some evidence, but it must be confessed that detailed census data do not yet exist which would reveal the relationship between secondary schooling and occupation. A partial picture can be obtained, however, through an attempt to follow-up post secondary-school graduates and to find out what occupations they do enter. An effort was made in this direction using a sample of past students drawn from our twenty-three secondary schools.

It should be noted at the outset that such a procedure was fraught with difficulty. Although school records are probably maintained in better order in Ghana than in virtually any other African nation, they are still very inadequate by most standards. It was finally possible to draw a random sample of 1,012 students who had graduated from the selected schools between the years 1956 and 1960. This sample did not include school drop-outs but comprised a group of both sexes who had completed the full five-year course of secondary studies and who had sat for the West African School Certificate Examination (whether they had actually passed it or not).

It was possible to complete a partial record of present occupational activities through a variety of methods. In some cases head teachers' records were available, and this was particularly true for the very recent graduates of high-status schools, many of whom were still engaged in sixth-form studies. In consequence, there can be no doubt that the final results exaggerate the actual proportion of secondary graduates who proceed with full-time studies after completing the fifth form.

284

In other cases where adequate forwarding addresses were available, an attempt was made to contact ex-students by mail. It was anticipated that such a procedure would yield sparse results but, as it turned out, the return was far more satisfactory than was expected. Altogether, 742 short questionnaires were sent, out of which 333 or 45 per cent were returned by graduates and completed in such a manner as to give adequate and detailed information on present employment. Once again, however, these returns tended to be biased towards more recent graduates of schools.

In the final analysis, out of the initial group of 1,012 students it was possible to obtain definite information on the present occupation or courses of study of 49 per cent of them, amounting to some 491 cases. To be sure, biases exist in the returns. There is a skew to the more recent graduates of some of the better secondary schools, while it is apparent that the returns exaggerate the proportion of students who proceed to further studies. It can be safely assumed, for example, that the overwhelming majority of the 526 cases that proved absolutely untraceable proceeded direct from school into employment—otherwise many of them could have been traced. Granted these difficulties, however, the returns provide a more adequate picture of the occupational destinations of secondary-school-leavers than has yet been available in this or any other African country.

Out of the 491 cases no less than 264 or 54 per cent were still engaged in pursuing some course of full-time training. However, it is the other group of 223 ex-pupils who were actually employed at the time of the survey that mainly concerns us here.[7] Only just over 20 per cent of this group had undergone any further training since leaving the fifth form, and the vast majority of these were concentrated in primary and middle-school teaching, agriculture and forestry, or nursing. The bulk of the graduates had obtained only a basic secondary education before entering the labour market.

The profile of occupations of graduates who were actually in employment at the time of this study is given in Table 36. Its most striking feature is the extent to which the occupations entered conform to the expectations of students given in Table 35. Overwhelmingly, the graduates of secondary schools find employment at the clerical level in both the private and public sectors, with a slightly smaller number in primary and middle-school teaching. As we have seen, just over 32 per cent of all fifth-form pupils expect to enter primary and middle-school teaching while, in fact, 31 per cent of employed graduates are actually so occupied. There is, however, a reversal in the sex position here; more male students expect to enter teaching, while in practice a higher proportion of female students are

TABLE 36

PRESENT EMPLOYMENT OF SECONDARY SCHOOL GRADUATES
(PERCENTAGES)

Occupation	Males		Females		Total	
Managerial and Executive	3·8	(7)	4·6	(2)	3·9	(9)
Clerical	46·7	(85)	34·1	(15)	44·4	(100)
Primary and Middle-School Teaching*	29·7	(54)	38·6	(17)	31·3	(71)
Nursing	—		6·8	(3)	1·3	(3)
Minor Technical†	6·0	(11)	6·8	(3)	6·2	(14)
Agricultural and Forestry‡	2·7	(5)	2·3	(1)	2·7	(6)
Semiskilled and Unskilled	1·2	(2)	—		0·9	(2)
Unemployed	6·1	(11)	6·8	(3)	6·2	(14)
Not Classifiable and No Answer	3·8	(7)	—		3·1	(7)
Total	100·0	(182)	100·0	(44)	100·0	(226)

* For purpose of convenience we have included four individuals teaching temporarily in secondary schools. These four had completed sixth-form studies and were waiting to enter a higher institution.

† Includes Laboratory Assistants, Assistant Surveyors, Geological Survey Assistants, etc.

‡ These workers were employed by government as agricultural or forestry assistants and demonstrators. None was a farmer.

so occupied. On the other hand 6 per cent of fifth-form students expect to enter some form of technical employment, while the actual figure for school graduates is 9 per cent. In practice, nearly all this latter group are employed as agricultural or forestry assistants or as low-level laboratory assistants.

By far the bulk of graduates, however, are employed in clerical duties in both the public and private sector. Here 52 per cent of students expect to enter such employment, as against 44 per cent of graduates so employed. In fact, the only significant divergence is that a far higher proportion of graduates obtain clerical employment in the public sector than students anticipate. This is readily understandable, for although conditions of employment with the larger commercial companies may be equivalent or even superior to those in government, there is no doubt that opportunities in the public sector are relatively more numerous.

This partial and not entirely satisfactory comparison can only lead us to conclude that student expectations relative to a given level of education are realistic. Graduates tend to obtain precisely those jobs

they expect, and, for the most part, these occupations are not particularly highly rated. Students are under no illusions as to the occupational currency of a formal education which has lasted from anywhere between 12 and 15 years. The fact of the matter is that pupils
do adjust their expectations to the realities of the occupational structure. The very expansion of secondary schools obliges them to continually modify their perceptions of their occupational future in the
light of a more limited horizon of opportunities.

TABLE 37

CURRENT COURSES OF STUDY OF SECONDARY-SCHOOL GRADUATES
STILL IN FULL-TIME TRAINING (PERCENTAGES)

Institutions	Males		Females		Total	
University after completing						
sixth-form studies*	15·5	(32)	1·8	(1)	12·5	(33)
Sixth Forms	44·4	(92)	29·8	(17)	41·3	(109)
Military Academy and						
Nautical College	7·7	(16)	—		6·1	(16)
The College of Administra-						
tion and the School of						
Social Welfare	3·4	(7)	1·8	(1)	3·0	(8)
Schools of Agriculture and						
Forestry	10·6	(22)	1·8	(1)	8·7	(23)
Nursing Training	1·0	(2)	17·5	(10)	4·6	(12)
Teacher Training Colleges	5·3	(11)	21·0	(12)	8·7	(23)
Study Overseas	6·3	(13)	24·5	(14)	10·2	(27)
Other†	5·8	(12)	1·8	(1)	4·9	(13)
Total	100·0	(207)	100·0	(57)	100·0	(264)

* All such students were attending the University of Ghana and the Kwame
Nkrumah University of Technology.

† This largely includes students in Technical Institutes and a few undergoing
commercial training in private institutions.

We can now briefly examine the other group of school graduates
who were still continuing with their studies at the time of the survey.
Table 37 provides some picture of their present courses of training,
but it is apparent that it vastly overestimates the proportion of students who enter the sixth form, since these were mostly recent graduates of the fifth forms who were comparatively easy to trace. Of
course it would have been more meaningful to divide the total group
into cohorts according to the year in which they completed fifth-form

work, but the smallness of the sample precluded such a possibility. At best we can only suggest that the table provides a very rough picture of the kinds of training that secondary-school pupils enter.

Very marked sex differences occur so far as further training is concerned. As we might expect, boys are more highly represented in the sixth forms, the universities, schools of agriculture and forestry, and military training establishments. Girls are much more involved in nursing training and primary or middle-school teacher-training. The wider range of boys' training suggests the relatively greater number of post-secondary training opportunities open to them, and girls seem confined in some degree to precisely those types of training that they anticipate entering (see Table 31).

The number of graduates studying abroad is rather high, though overseas study has had a long history in Ghana and a small proportion of students annually make their way to other countries for further education. A very interesting difference arises between the sexes within this group of overseas scholars. All the male students are in receipt of Ghanaian or overseas scholarships and are pursuing courses of study at the university level in engineering or medicine in a variety of countries. All the female students are privately supported (indicating for the most part a markedly superior socioeconomic background) and have undertaken studies only in the United Kingdom. Furthermore, they are training in only two fields—nursing and secretarial work. The irony is that this kind of training is available in Ghana and one can only conjecture that the attractiveness of the former metropole is most important for those coming from markedly superior social backgrounds. The significant thing is that one goes overseas for further studies whether the training is available in Ghana or not.

Some General Observations

We have tried to indicate in this chapter that the aspirations and expectations of African secondary-school children hardly conform to popular stereotypes. Perhaps no less than their overseas counterparts, they are interested in entering a wide range of occupations and notably are far more oriented to various technological-type jobs than might have been believed. Their perceptions of the occupational value of a secondary-school education taken alone, however, leads to a totally different pattern of responses. Here the nature of the occupational structure itself tends to become one of the principal determinants of levels of expectation.

Students are both realistic and unrealistic in their responses. They are most unrealistic in assessing their own chances of obtaining further education and thus entering the most desirable occupations in contemporary Ghana. This is understandable if it is realized that the expansion of the secondary-school population has not yet been paralleled by a looser policy concerning access into higher institutions. In this sense there would appear to be a lag between student expectations and educational realities. For the bulk of students a secondary education must become increasingly terminal unless some break is made with the traditional notion of what constitutes 'true' university or higher studies. There is some indication indeed that this may be the case if plans to abolish the present sixth forms reach fruition.

Students are at their most realistic, however, in assessing the kinds of jobs that will be available to them with a given level of education (notably the General School Certificate). Here their expectations are relatively limited and few expect to obtain more than 'middle-level' jobs. One can only conclude that there is a downward trend in expectations and the secondary-school pupil no longer enjoys the kinds of opportunities that were available to him a few years ago. This levelling down of expectations is not an unhealthy sign in so far as it signifies that students do adjust themselves to changes in occupational opportunities.

A further point might be made along these lines concerning the possible incidence of actual unemployment among secondary-school graduates. This is certainly very evident among the products of the middle schools, but it was rather striking during the survey how many school principals suggested that unemployment was beginning to occur among secondary-school graduates. Their evidence for this was fragmentary and impressionistic, but they suggested that it was becoming a very real problem for the graduates of poor quality secondary schools who had either failed the General School Certificate Examination or obtained a low-level pass. Our own evidence on this matter does not support their opinions. To be sure, 6 per cent of our sample did indicate that they were unemployed at the time the survey was taken, but most had been unemployed for less than three months and were in the process of changing occupations. It is true, however, that the vast majority of respondents indicated that they had experienced difficulty in obtaining employment after leaving school. Certainly, no adequate evidence exists concerning the nature and extent of unemployment among the products of secondary institutions, and its incidence is probably still very low. Given a relatively low rate in the expansion of job opportunities, it is not unlikely to occur among some sections of the secondary-school graduate population in spite of the fact that there is a downward trend in their levels of expectation.

Returning to the problem of vocational aspirations our evidence would lead us to conclude that income expectation is an extraordinarily important factor in influencing preferences. Contrary perhaps, to previous impressions, Ghanaian children correlate occupational prestige and perceived income very highly—more highly, for example, than do students in the United States. This merely reinforces an argument that we have constantly presented in earlier chapters, that it is the income accruing to various types of occupation that has been so important to the products of the schools. One can only guess at the reason for the startlingly high correlation between income and prestige factors. Very possibly it may be itself a reflection of the fundamentally egalitarian nature of African traditional society. The historical absence of a 'high culture', with its accompanying group of literati to whom deference was customarily paid, may have made all the difference to contemporary African societies and led to a rapid equating of wealth and status so far as new type occupational roles are concerned. Certainly, some divergences between India and Africa would suggest the importance of this factor, but whatever its cause there is little doubt that it is to Africa's advantage so far as economic development is concerned.[8]

Finally, and perhaps partly connected with these observations, is another factor of considerable significance. This concerns the looseness of the relationships between vocational ambitions and the social origins of pupils. Apart from relatively minor examples, socioeconomic background seems to exert a very minor influence on the aspirations and expectations of students. The absence of such a relationship is in itself extraordinarily significant and parallels in some degree our data concerning recruitment. Here it was found that considerable 'fluidity' existed in recruitment patterns and, similarly, marked fluidity occurs in vocational ambitions. Students from the humblest social origins share the ambitions of more favoured individuals to a considerable degree. This may well be a characteristic of the new nations of Africa—the emergence of patterns of social differentiation which, in some respects, resemble or appear to resemble some Western-type 'class' societies, but where the corollaries of class as they are reflected in patterns of recruitment and vocational ambitions appear in extremely attenuated form. We shall return to this topic in our concluding chapter.

The Aspirations of Secondary School Pupils

REFERENCES

1. For Example, see Judson T. Shaplin, 'A Sea of Faces', *Bulletin of the Harvard Graduate School of Education*, VI, No. 2 (Summer 1961), 4.

2. See J. Clyde Mitchell and A. L. Epstein, 'Occupational Prestige and Social Status Among Urban Africans in Northern Rhodesia', *Africa*, XXIX, No. 1 (January 1959), 22–39. Also N. Xydias, 'Prestige of Occupations', *Social implications of Technological Change and Urbanisation in Africa South of the Sahara*, ed. Daryll Forde (London: International African Institute for UNESCO, 1955), pp. 458–69; and N. Xydias, 'Les Africains du Congo-Belge: Aptitudes, Attitudes vis-à-vis du Travail', *Le promotion humaine dans les pays sous-developpes* (Paris: Presses Universitaires de France, 1960), pp. 39–52. However, the method followed in this section is not identical with those of Mitchell or Xydias.

3. See Charles E. Ramsey and Robert J. Smith, 'Japanese and American Perceptions of Occupations', *American Journal of Sociology*, LXV, No. 5 (March 1960), 475–82. Ramsey and Smith were further able to make comparisons with an earlier study in the Philippines, see Edward A. Tiryakian, 'The Prestige Evaluation of Occupations in an Undeverdeloped Country: The Philippines, *American Journal of Sociology*, LXII, No. 1 (January 1958), 390–99.

4. See Bryce Ryan, 'The Dilemmas of Education in Ceylon', *Comparative Education Review*, IV, No. 2 (October 1960), 86.

5. *Ibid.*

6. It will also be noted that university teaching is another occupation which is very highly rated but attracts few students. It is not possible to give any reason why this should be the case. At the time this survey was taken, the University of Ghana was going through an extraordinarily difficult period and was subject to intense newspaper criticism. It seems unlikely, however, that students were very conscious of this.

7. One proxy return completed with respect to a recently deceased student was omitted.

8. In this case, we are merely reiterating the opinions of those observers who have felt that the presence of a traditional Indian high culture has interfered with processes of economic development. However, the regional and cultural diversity of the Indian sub-continent should make us very cautious of this kind of judgment.

IX

SOME COMMENTS ON PRESENT AND FUTURE DEVELOPMENTS

IN this study we have attempted to assess the social impact of Western education upon the cluster of traditional societies which are now being welded into the newly independent nation of Ghana. This has necessarily involved a broad sweep of discussion ranging from the story of the struggling coastal schools in the eighteenth century to an examination of the characteristics of the contemporary student population of the Ghanaian secondary-school system. Yet one is impressed not by the apparent discontinuities of this story but by the persistence of similar problems, similar discussions, and similar educational consequences throughout the entire colonial and post-colonial period. To many observers independence seems to mark a tremendous watershed in the history of African peoples; the growth of independent African polities and experiments with new forms of political control appear exciting and unique. Yet this kind of ferment is not yet so apparent in the educational field. Although Western-type schools have been one of the principal agents of modernization and political change in contemporary Africa, they themselves have been perhaps less responsive to change and innovation than have other political and social institutions. The fact is that educational systems are rather monolithic in nature, slow to manifest any rapid response to a desire for reform and, in consequence, current controversy in Ghana merely re-echoes almost two hundred years of identical argument about the nature and content of the educational process.

Rather than pursue an unfruitful discussion as to the course that future development should take, it is perhaps more to the point to examine the objective consequences of formal education and thus be in a position to indicate the probable consequences of present developments. If precedent is a worthwhile guide, it seems fairly clear that future major decisions concerning educational development in Ghana will not be made in accord with the rubrics of professional educationists but will be rather formulated in response to a balance of political and economic pressures.

Historically, of course, the development of schooling in Ghana has been intimately linked with economic changes generated by colonial overrule. The demand for Western schooling was mainly a consequence of the growth of new economic opportunities created by the transition from a subsistence to an exchange economy. But the schools also contributed directly to the steady if slow growth of that economy. A very significant development for the schools was that rates of economic change within Ghana itself were highly differentiated and uneven. The corollary of this was that sharp and persistent inequalities arose in the extent and quality of formal schooling as between parts of the country. This kind of outcome is not unique— it is a common pattern throughout most of Africa. Indeed, it can be argued that such inequalities are likely to exist in most areas in the initial stages of economic growth and may not, in themselves, be detrimental to early development. Their existence, however, is politically embarrassing to new African leadership pledged as it is to notions of 'equity' in educational provision.

Although it is easy enough to demonstrate in the Ghanaian case that the kind of educational system that developed has been intimately linked to the realities of the colonial and post-colonial occupational structure, it is equally true that the schools have been consistently criticized from the earliest period as being obstructive of economic growth. It is customary in contemporary Ghana for African administrators to bemoan the absence of widespread technical and agricultural education and to attribute this to the sinister designs of former colonial officials. Nothing could be further from the truth; we have shown at numerous points in previous pages how African opinion was almost uniformly opposed to earlier proposals for the development of technical and agricultural education. This opposition was not based upon an uncritical desire for a 'prestige' education but was, in large measure, the result of a very canny calculation of the alternative rewards accruing to different kinds of schooling. A great deal has been made of the lack of response by Africans to economic incentives, yet the history of the Gold Coast tells a different story. Whether one considers the development of cocoa production, largely a result of the efforts of African entrepreneurs, or examines attitudes vis-à-vis different types of formal education, one is impressed by the shrewdness and economic sagacity of the citizens of Ghana. That shrewdness and realism was fully apparent in the early historical period; it remains no less evident in the vocational aspirations and expectations of contemporary schoolchildren.

In this context, a number of present efforts to develop technical and agricultural education on a large scale in Ghana are likely to be no more successful than their numerous predecessors unless such endeavours are paralleled by changes in the economic structure. Technical and agricultural education failed in the colonial period because it was manifestly an inferior alternative to academic schooling. Unfortunately, the post-independence period has not as yet shown any marked change in the characteristics of the occupational structure and the rate of economic growth has been disappointing over the last decade. It would seem that technical or vocational education is the cart rather than the horse in initial stages of economic growth. Such instruction is unlikely to be successful unless economic growth provides real opportunities for the products of vocational schools. For example, the success of agricultural education may depend largely upon crucial changes occurring in land tenure, the development of lucrative cash-crop possibilities outside cocoa, and the knowledge of marketing opportunities. In view of the fact that Ghanaian schoolchildren rank farming a long way from the bottom of the occupational list, it would appear that the factors which inhibit the development of a group of educated and 'progressive' farmers lie in the neo-traditional institutional complex in which agriculture is embedded. From our point of view no amount of exhortation to 'return to the land' and no amount of curricular change in the schools will have much effect on the loss of schoolchildren to the rural economy. The tragedy is that a great deal of present policy precisely parallels the former efforts of colonial educators; there is little sign that contemporary administrators have profited much from the example of previous failures.

Similar problems still attend the development of technical education. This was a relative failure in colonial times, and there was a low correlation between technical schooling and the later employment of individuals in the skills in which they had been trained. This was simply because opportunities were superior in other sectors of the economy. At present Ghana faces the same problem, although to be sure, the successful development of the Volta project and the creation of small new industrial enterprises may act as a stimulus to the demand for technical schooling. It needs to be pointed out, however, that one of the characteristics of an underdeveloped economy is that the market demand for technical skills is small. This conflicts with the conception that there is an insatiable need for technically trained people in underdeveloped areas. One may suggest that this is more likely to be one of the characteristics of a developed economy than one of the Ghanaian type. Proponents of massive technical schooling in the underdeveloped areas implicitly assume that such education is the primary factor behind economic growth. Although we may concede that technical skills must play a partial role in early development, it is hardly likely that they are the primary necessary conditions of growth.

Furthermore, we may even question whether formal schools are the best institutions for the dissemination of those technical skills necessary to economic development in the early stages. Western experience has something to say in this context; it would seem fairly clear that the bulk of technical training which was conducted in many Western nations at earlier stages of development went on outside the schools. Western nations very early developed systems of apprenticeship and on-the-job training which were of crucial importance in their development. The standard rejoinder to this argument is that Ghana and other African nations lack such ancillary institutions and, *faute de mieux*, new functions must be incorporated into the system of formal education. In the case of Ghana, however, this is not entirely true. There is already in existence a rapidly growing system of apprenticeship supported also by a number of training schemes incorporated within various government departments such as Railways and Harbours and Agriculture.[1] These programmes are not comprised within the formal educational structure, but they may make a far greater contribution to training than the schools could. Such developments can take place without forcing on the schools a range of vocational and agricultural functions that they are eminently unfitted to perform.

Behind the current controversy over 'practical' and vocational education, however, lies a deeper commitment to formal education, of whatever type, as the most important single factor in economic development. Perhaps the unqualified belief that widespread schooling is the primary instrument of economic transformation characterizes the new African states more fully than those in any other area of the world. In some measure this belief may have been strengthened by economists' recent tentative conclusions concerning the role of education in contemporary Western economic growth.[2] African leadership has not been slow to utilize the concept of 'human capital' as a justification for massive programmes of educational development. Yet it must be contended that limited findings concerning the role of investment in education in economically developed nations do not provide very good prescriptions for economies that are still relatively undifferentiated and which contain a large subsistence sector. Much

295

more investigation is needed before even tentative conclusions can be reached concerning the role of education in very early stages of economic growth.

It may well be, indeed, that the principal role of formal education in early stages of economic development does not lie in the creation of human skills as narrowly defined. It may lie rather in the expectations that it generates, the new consumption needs to which it leads, and the emergence of a general dissatisfaction with the restrictions of traditional society. If such dissatisfaction provides personal incentives and, at the same time, institutionalized means exist to meet new aspirations, then the schools will have contributed indirectly to economic growth. From this viewpoint 'general' or 'academic' education may make more of an ultimate contribution than narrow forms of vocational and technical training, in the same way that the former has contributed far more to rising aspirations for political independence.

In this sense the most important function of education may be precisely one of 'detachment' from the traditional environment—a consequence of education which seems to be generally bemoaned but which may be a necessary prelude to economic growth. Not infrequently, it is suggested that too much is being spent on education relative to other forms of investment. Final events may justify current rates of expenditure, not in the sense that returns to educational investment are direct and immediate (as perhaps present Ghanaian leadership supposes) but that, in the long run, formal schooling creates a cultural environment in which innovation can take place. Thus it may well be that the considerable expenditure on education by the present Ghanaian government will, in the long run, be justified by ultimate and indirect returns.

Whatever the long-term consequences of educational growth may be it seems clear that serious short-run dysfunctionalities are inescapable. Principal among these is the growth of unemployment among schools graduates. Although this is an old problem in Ghana it has reached disturbing proportions in recent years. It is hoped that in previous pages we have done enough to dispose of the tenacious belief that this unemployment is due to the white-collar aspirations of African students and the parallel belief that curricular change can alter that situation. The plain fact is that it is easier to expand schooling than it is to expand employment opportunities in the exchange economy. It would seem that Ghana is likely to be faced with this problem for some years to come until the economy has expanded sufficiently to provide opportunities for school-graduates. This will entail a difficult period of transition not without its political concomitants. It must be added that Ghana is not alone in facing the problem. Indeed, the greater development of education in Ghana than in most other African territories points to the probable consequences of educational expansion in other independent nations. For example, unemployment of a similar nature is becoming increasingly evident in both Kenya and Uganda. It is something of a tragedy that programmes for the expansion of education which have been pursued with vigour and imagination should carry with them such a depressing consequence. The schools should not be improperly blamed for this situation, and their graduates should not be condemned for holding unrealistic expectations as to their futures. Our empirical findings would in no sense justify such a conclusion.

This brings us directly to the political consequences of Western education in Ghana. It is clear that the growth of schools, paralleled as it was by limited occupational opportunities for Africans, gave a powerful impetus to Nationalist movements. At first, frustration was confined to a relatively small group of African intellectuals deprived (partially as a result of defective colonial policy) of opportunities to assume political and occupational roles commensurate with their training and educational background. Before 1940, this created an incipient Nationalist movement without mass support. Broad popular support did not emerge until a quickening rate of educational development after 1940 created, particularly in the urban areas, a reservoir of unemployed youth who could effectively be mobilized for direct political action. This process of mobilization resulted in the departure of older Nationalist leaders from the scene and their replacement by new, dynamic leadership more directly in tune with the demands of the urban masses.

Although there is little doubt that unemployment fostered the growth of urban nationalism after 1945, we do not wish to ignore other consequences of education. After all, Western-type schools were essential for the diffusion of political ideas of independence and self-determination. This ideological commitment was Western in its source and reflected the nominal values of the colonial power. Concepts of democracy, self-government, and the rights of man are more likely to emerge in the context of academic schooling than in institutions designed to 'fit' the African environment. Bearing this in mind, it was unlikely during the colonial era that Africans could be fobbed off with alternative educational experiments at 'Africanization'.

African opposition to 'educational adaptation' in colonial times had, therefore, a strongly rational basis, supported as it was by a very realistic perception of the social functions of schooling. This places present political authority in Ghana in an extraordinarily painful

dilemma. Committed on the one hand to a programme of modernization and economic development the government feels at the same
time compelled to extol the virtues of traditional African society and
assert that Western schooling in the colonial context robbed Africans
of their traditional cultural heritage. Now it is clear enough that this
was hardly the case, since such experiments in Africanization as were
made were regarded with suspicion. Indeed, sometimes one feels that
no one was more anxious to be robbed of his traditional culture than
the educated African. Furthermore, since 1951 the present government has probably done more to destroy the basis of traditional
social organization than did the colonial regime. This is manifest in
its attacks on traditional political organization. Indirect rule with its
manifold inconsistencies did attempt to give some place in the polity
to traditional forms of office; there is little room for this in contemporary Ghana. The use of traditional symbols in the current political
context no more suggests a basic commitment to traditional organization than the custom of the 'King's Champion' at the British
coronation indicates the persistence of feudalism in the United
Kingdom.

Yet the formal commitment to the 'resuscitation' of African culture, inconsistent as it may be, reflects perhaps a reaction to the most
basic evil of colonialism. Apart from the disgraceful period of the
slave trade, the colonial era in the Gold Coast was one of steady, if
not startling development. Furthermore, racial antagonism was relatively slight and African culture was by no means without its warm
protagonists among the colonial elite. Yet however non-repressive it
may have been, the colonial context was inevitably one of basic
humiliation wherein such rights as were possessed by Africans were
proffered by the hand of an alien minority. Small wonder that since
independence there has been an attempt to diffuse a sense of national
dignity and purpose and to create, if necessary, unifying cultural
myths. Whether couched in the vague terms of 'African Personality'
or in the somewhat mystical and suspect concept of 'Négritude',
these efforts serve a valuable purpose and meet the need for a sense
of national identity and cultural self-respect.

In consequence we see in contemporary Ghana a demand for the
'Africanization' of the schools and the eradication of 'European'
education although these demands are frequently made by individuals
who are themselves the most acculturated and 'deracinated' among
the Ghanaian population. To be sure, some of these pressures have
been reflected in the rewriting of African history books for the
schools and some attempts have been made to modify other curriculums. Yet the surprising thing is how little effect 'Africanization'

has upon the educational system. We have seen how since 1951, in some respects, that system has grown more like that of the former metropole. Apart from the vigour with which the educational system has been expanded, there has been a surprising degree of timidity in effecting any other major changes.

The reason for such caution stems from a basic ambivalence in the values held by the new elite. The influence of the former metropole persists long after the achievement of independence. The normative reference-group functions of the ex-colonial elite manifest themselves even after overt rejection of the colonial heritage. Conceptions of what constitutes a 'good' education are still derived in large measure from the metropole, and African leadership is understandably cautious in innovation. The startling thing about Ghana is not the radical break with the colonial past but the persistence of neo-colonial values and practices among a political elite which ostensibly rejects them. It must be clearly understood that while asserting its new status as an African nation, Ghana is, at the same time, understandably anxious to be recognized as a progressive and modern polity by the larger powers. In this kind of situation there is a reluctance to move too far from the educational standards and practices prevalent in the more developed areas of the world for fear of criticism of its educational endeavours. This clinging to colonial practice and precedent has indeed been characteristic of virtually every ex-colonial territory in Africa or elsewhere. The break with certain colonial conditions is made even more difficult in Ghana by the greater duration and intensity of Afro-European contact in the southern half of the country as compared with most other African areas.

We now turn to a consideration of the role that the schools have played and will continue to play in the emergence of new types of social differentiation in Ghanaian society. In our opening chapter we saw that in spite of certain variations in their degree of complexity the group of traditional social structures that now comprise Ghana shared certain marked structural attributes. These societies lacked clearly defined social strata; social and political rights and their concomitant duties and obligations were largely defined by age, sex, and lineage membership. Although these societies permitted social mobility for groups and individuals, the crucial thing was that such mobility was not overtly considered desirable. To put it another way, no ideological charter existed which formally sanctioned or extolled processes of mobility.

But perhaps the most striking feature of these societies was their fundamental 'egalitarianism'. By this we do not imply that there was an even distribution of authority or even wealth within them. In spite

299

of the fact that political authority was subject to elaborate checks upon the exercise of despotic power, it is clear that in terms of the uneven distribution of high-status roles these societies were far from being egalitarian. In what sense then is the term at all meaningful? Following Fallers superb analysis of Kiganda society, we may suggest that this egalitarianism lay essentially in the absence of subgroups possessing distinctive subcultures, with their own particular styles of life, and possessing a degree of self-consciousness concerning their common rights and duties.[3] We find an absence of 'status groups' in Weber's use of the term in traditional Ghanaian society. We do find the existence of 'social classes' in the Weberian sense in that we can discern subgroups possessing common *objective* characteristics in terms of equivalent political power or economic status. The important thing, however, is the relative absence of cultural differentiation within these societies and the lack of distinct subcultural identity among the individuals possessing equivalent social prestige. As we have seen, this is precisely the characteristic of 'social classes' in the Western world; they are not only social classes but 'status groups' possessing their own distinctive cultures and styles of life. Indeed, the emergence of such status groups within African traditional societies was further checked by slight actual differences in wealth and by the existence of informal educational processes whose content did not vary significantly as between various social subgroups.

In some respects, Kiganda traditional society and traditional Ghanaian forms were very dissimilar. They differed greatly in their degree of centralization of political authority and in their recruitment to traditional office. Both groups, however, were very much alike in terms of the relative absence of traditional status cultures. This combination of convergence and divergence has led to extraordinarily different results so far as Western education is concerned. Ghanaian structures, resting as they ultimately did upon a segmentary lineage organization, were at first highly resistant to Western education. After an initial period of non-assimilation, however, there was a constantly accelerating level of demand. Basically, the diffusion of Western education was antithetical to the persistence of traditional social structures and led to a conflict between traditional authority and the emergent educated minority which was perhaps sharper than anywhere else in Africa. The opposite was the case in Buganda where Western schooling was very rapidly incorporated but the traditional social hierarchy remained basically intact. Paradoxically, contemporary Ghanaian social structure (at least in the south) seems in many respects more 'modern' than does Kiganda society, in spite of an initially slower rate of educational growth. In Ghana, so far as 'modernity' is concerned, it is clear enough that formal education, income, and occupation are significant determinants of social status. Our empirical findings demonstrate, for example, a clear hierarchy of occupations of a Western type which is more closely associated with income variables than it is in some other nations. Similarly, we have advanced reasons to suggest that at present, education plays a more crucial role in relation to social status and social mobility than it did at comparable stages in Western development. At the same time a considerable body of evidence points to the persistence of elements of traditional social structure even within the most 'modern' sectors of Ghanaian society. Ethnic background, kinship affiliation, and traditional residence patterns still play a role even within the urban context and indeed may provide the basis for organizations which appear at first sight to be essentially Western in nature. For example, voluntary self-help associations, trade unions, and political parties all contain components based upon traditional patterns of association and affiliation.

It is the persistence of these traditional patterns of affiliation which cross-cut 'objective' strata based upon occupation, education, and income that has militated against the emergence of clearly defined status groups in Ghanaian society. One might have thought, for example, that the emergence of a small educated minority in the Gold Coast in the nineteenth century which modelled itself very consciously upon the European minority might have presaged the development of an elite subculture. Yet this was not the case and the group never solidified. On the one hand the symbols of modernity never became a monopoly of these few, while on the other hand the educated minority never entirely separated itself from traditional society and its obligations.

This absence of 'subjective' lines of cleavage between segments of the Ghanaian population has had significant implications for formal education. Although the structural characteristics of British education have been substantially reproduced in and incorporated into Ghanaian society, there is little evidence that the norms and values underlying the educational process were also effectively transferred. In Britain, for example, selective academic secondary schools were traditionally not 'popular' forms of education in the sense that they were in close 'psychological' proximity to the lower classes. In Ghana, on the contrary, they are essentially popular institutions, not in the sense that most children enter them but that they are seen to be accessible to all segments of society. They are not conceived to be primarily the preserve of any particular status group. In this sense the functional incorporation of such schools has rendered them 'non-elitist' in character. Although the demand for Western education was slow to take in the initial period of Afro-European contact, once it had become diffused more widely it was accompanied by a general belief in the accessibility of all schools to all sections of the community. To be sure, sharp inequalities still exist as we have been at pains to point out, yet there is a basic commitment to make education accessible to all those who demand it.

Interestingly enough this kind of picture finds substantial parallels in one major Western country—the United States. Here it would appear that after an initial period, when educational practice was still dominated by metropolitan precedent, there was a progressive abandonment of 'elitist' forms of schooling in favour of an emphasis upon the wider diffusion of popular education with a less conscious attempt to 'maintain standards'.[4] Progressively, European models based upon rigorous selection procedures were abandoned in the face of a mounting pressure of popular demand. There can be little doubt that American secondary and higher education has been much more responsive to such pressures than European institutions, basically because the norms and values underpinning the educational system are fundamentally 'populist' in orientation. Although inequalities of access to education exist, they are perhaps less than in most European nations and basically, there is a commitment to a fundamental liberalization of the educational system.

We would submit that this kind of 'ethos' underpins the educational system in Ghana, in spite of the fact that the latter's structure is still essentially British. This tends to explain some of our empirical findings. Thus, social patterns of access into the school exhibit some features in common with Western experience but at the same time the relatively broad basis of recruitment finds little parallel in earlier European development. In a similar manner the relationship between socioeconomic background (defined in terms of objective criteria) and the educational or vocational aspirations and expectations of pupils is very loose to say the least. There is very little difference in this respect between pupils of very humble socioeconomic origin and those from markedly superior backgrounds. These features we would suggest are the educational correlates of a social structure which is not characterized by the existence of clearly defined status subcultures and at the same time where a general commitment to popular education is becoming widely diffused.

So far, there has been an understandable reluctance to move too far from colonial educational models, but if our general thesis is correct it may well be that within the next decade Ghana may move rapidly from its present educational position. The most dramatic developments will not occur in the 'Africanization' of the curriculum (though some innovations in this direction is inevitable), nor will it occur in the growth of highly specific forms of vocational and technical education.[5] They will rather be manifest in an enormous expansion of education at the secondary and higher level with a progressive de-emphasis of conventional European standards of achievement and rigid standards for entry to selective institutions. This is precisely the kind of development that has already occurred in the United States. Such a situation is frequently deprecated by European scholars in view of their emphasis upon minimal standards and the use of uniform external examinations. It can be rejoined, however, that far wider patterns of access to secondary and higher education can be combined with high standards for a minority through the internal differentiation of the educational system and the proliferation of institutions of variable quality. This is clearly evident in American higher education where high levels of achievement in certain schools are paralleled by less rigorous standards in a host of others. This variability enables maximal access for a variety of groups into alternative types of schooling. It should be clear that this is precisely what has already happened in Ghanaian *secondary* education—a small group of elite institutions has now been supplemented by a range of poorer secondary schools. To be sure, the latter are 'inferior' institutions, but they meet a growing public demand and enable a larger clientele to profit from additional years of education. Correspondingly, while standards of achievement in the better schools still remain high, those schools are not markedly more restrictive in terms of the social backgrounds of their student bodies.

The drive for a wider diffusion of education at the expense of standards is already characteristic of Ghanaian secondary education. Furthermore, this pressure is beginning to be felt at the university level where proposals for the abolition of the sixth forms and a consequent lowering of rigid standards of entry to university education are already being considered. There is little doubt that the observer can detect a great deal of parallelism between American attitudes to public education and a growing body of Ghanaian opinion.

Whatever the outcome of these developments it is clear that Western schooling has been one of the major factors operating in the transformation of the new African nations. In Ghana, the schools have rarely functioned in the manner anticipated by educationists or officials and the story of their development is largely one of the unplanned consequences of educational growth. Perhaps the story of the schools provides less exciting fare for the reader than the saga of political development in West Africa. Yet without Western schools there would have been no Nationalist movement, no independence, and no Ghana. Most important, for Ghanaians themselves, education has meant one thing above all—they are no longer driving the horse but are riding it!

REFERENCES

1. In 1960 in Ghana, there were just over 48,000 apprentices among employed persons aged 15 years and over. Ghana, *1960 Census of Population, Advance Report of Volumes III and IV*, p. 51.

2. The liteiature on this subject has now reached considerable proportions, but for a recent summary see Theodore W. Schultz, *The Economic Value of Education* (New York: Columbia University Press, 1963).

3. L. A. Fallers, 'Despotism, Status Culture and Social Mobility in an African Kingdom', *Comparative Studies in Society and History*, II, No. 1 (October 1959), 11–32, and Reinhard Bendix, *Max Weber: An Intellectual Portrait* (New York: Doubleday & Co., 1962), pp. 85–87.

4. For a fine discussion of the situation as it manifests itself in American higher education, see Martin Trow, 'The Democratization of Higher Education in America', *European Journal of Sociology*, III, No. 2 (1962), 231–62.

5. In this context it is interesting to note that American educationists seem to persistently delude themselves that what characterizes American as contrasted with European education is the high emphasis upon vocational and technical subjects in the schools as opposed to an 'academic' emphasis. In practice, at least at the secondary level, American education has a less developed vocational and technical sector than do many European systems. Generally, the American high school offers an essentially academic curriculum of a 'watered down variety', This kind of development may well typify Ghanaian schools as secondary education becomes more widely diffused.

APPENDIX 1

STUDY OF GHANAIAN SECONDARY SCHOOLS
INSTITUTE OF EDUCATION, UNIVERSITY
COLLEGE OF GHANA, LEGON

THE following questions are part of a study being made by the Institute of Education of the University College of Ghana. It is an attempt to learn about the various interests which the students of Secondary Schools in Ghana have. We should like to know particularly about your dreams for the future after you leave school and what you hope to be doing in a few years' time. This will be of great help to us all because your views will enable us to see how we may improve our schools. By answering the questions as truthfully and as accurately as you can you may be sure that you will be helping us to plan better things for students in the Secondary Schools who will come after you.

Now this is *not* a test so there are no right and wrong answers and nobody can fail it, so we are anxious that you answer the questions as carefully as you can. As you will see we shall not ask you for your name and we promise you that no one in the school will see your answers. They will be absolutely private. Try to answer the questions in the order in which they appear so that you will not forget any and do not copy answers from your neighbour because we want *your* views and not his or hers.

Most of the answers do not require a great deal of writing and in most questions you can indicate your choice by putting a little tick in the box (like this: ☐) or by putting a number on a short line. If you have any difficulties just raise your hand and we shall come to help you. Do not hurry, you will have time to finish, and try not to miss any questions out.

Above all do not answer questions in the way that you think *other* people will want you to answer them. As you know, your name will not be placed on the question sheet so answer what *you* truly think.

1. Interview Number ....

2. Name of School ....

3. Category ....

4. Sex   1   ☐   Male

            2   ☐   Female

Appendix I

5. What is your form?

       6 ☐ Fourth

       7 ☐ Fifth

       8 ☐ Sixth

6. What is your age? ....

7. Are you a boarder or a day scholar?

       4 ☐ Boarder

       5 ☐ Day Scholar

8. What is your tribe or people? ....

9. Do you hope to continue your full-time education after you have completed your secondary school course?

       1 ☐ Yes

       2 ☐ No

10. Looking *realistically* at your future, how would you regard your chances of continuing your education after secondary school?
Put a tick in the box which expresses your view.

       1 ☐ Will be certain to continue my education

       2 ☐ Have a good chance of continuing my education

       3 ☐ Will not really be likely to continue my education

       4 ☐ Will certainly not be able to continue

11. If you do have the chance to continue your education, what kind of college do you hope to go to?

       1 ☐ A Teacher Training College

       2 ☐ The University College of Ghana

       3 ☐ The Kumasi College of Technology

       4 ☐ A Commercial College

       5 ☐ A Technical Institute

       6 ☐ Nursing School (girls only)

       7 ☐ Another Institution which we have not mentioned (if so, what?) ....

What kind of course do you hope to study there?

       0 ☐ An Arts course (by this we mean such subjects as English, foreign languages, history or geography)

       1 ☐ Science or mathematics courses

       2 ☐ Engineering (boys only)

306

    3 ☐ Nursing (girls only)

    4 ☐ Professional courses (such as Law or Medicine)

    5 ☐ Teacher Training courses

    6 ☐ Agricultural science

    7 ☐ Other courses we may not have mentioned (if so, what?) ....

    8 ☐ Not yet decided

13. If you were free to choose *any* job that you wished, what kind of job would you like to have more than another? Explain the job fully

    ....

    ....

    ....

14. Of course, we cannot always choose the kind of job we should like best of all. From your experience and that of your friends who have left secondary school already, what kind of job do you think you are most likely to get *in fact* if you leave school after you have completed work in the Fifth Form?

    ....

    ....

    ....

15. What was the last form in Middle School that you completed before coming to Secondary School?

    1 ☐ M.1   3 ☐ M.3

    2 ☐ M.2   4 ☐ M.4

16. What is your religion?

    1 ☐ Methodist   5 ☐ Other Christian denomination

    2 ☐ Presbyterian   6 ☐ Moslem

    3 ☐ Roman Catholic   7 ☐ Other (if so,

    4 ☐ Anglican   what?)

                                                ....

17. If you were free to choose whatever Secondary School in Ghana that you wished to go to, what three schools would you choose?

    1st Choice ....

    2nd Choice ....

    3rd Choice ....

18. What do you think is the *best* reason for choosing a Secondary School among these?

     1   ☐   It is near my home
     2   ☐   It is a school with good examination results
     3   ☐   It is not expensive to go to
     4   ☐   It is of the same religion as myself
     5   ☐   The courses given are not hard

19. Where were you born? If you were born in Ghana write down

     the Town or Village ....
     the District ....
     the Region ....

If you were not born in Ghana just write down the country in which you were born.

     ....

20. Where do you live now?

     Town or Village ....
     District ....
     Region ....

21. How much education did your father have? Just put a tick in the box opposite the highest level that he reached.

     Y   ☐   Did not go to school
     X   ☐   Had some primary school
     0   ☐   Finished primary school
     1   ☐   Had some senior primary or middle school
     2   ☐   Finished senior primary or middle school
     3   ☐   Had some secondary school
     4   ☐   Finished secondary school
     5   ☐   Attended Teacher Training College
     6   ☐   Went to a University (if so, where?)

     ....

     7   ☐   Finished at another kind of school (if so, what?)

     ....

     8   ☐   Don't know

22. What is his present occupation? Be very careful to explain the work he does exactly. Tell us who he works for and the kind of thing he does there. If he is dead, then write in what he used to do, if you know.

....
....
....

23. For whom does he work?

    1 ☐ For himself

    2 ☐ For a government department

    3 ☐ For someone else

24. Here is a list of different types of jobs that people in Ghana have. Read the list carefully and against each job indicate the prestige and respect in which this job is held. As you see against each job we have put five squares showing whether the job is held in *very* high respect, *high* respect, *average* respect, *low* respect and *very* low respect. Against each job put a tick in the box which describes the job most exactly.

Job	Very High Prestige	High Prestige	Average Prestige	Low Prestige	Very Low Prestige
Clergyman	☐	☐	☐	☐	☐
Lawyer	☐	☐	☐	☐	☐
Policeman	☐	☐	☐	☐	☐
Primary Schoolteacher	☐	☐	☐	☐	☐
Shop Assistant	☐	☐	☐	☐	☐
Carpenter	☐	☐	☐	☐	☐
Government Clerk	☐	☐	☐	☐	☐
Chief	☐	☐	☐	☐	☐
Farmer	☐	☐	☐	☐	☐
Author	☐	☐	☐	☐	☐
Street Cleaner	☐	☐	☐	☐	☐
Actor	☐	☐	☐	☐	☐
Motor Car Fitter	☐	☐	☐	☐	☐
University Teacher	☐	☐	☐	☐	☐
Soldier	☐	☐	☐	☐	☐
Petty Trader	☐	☐	☐	☐	☐
Secondary Schoolteacher	☐	☐	☐	☐	☐
Political Party Worker	☐	☐	☐	☐	☐
Nurse	☐	☐	☐	☐	☐
Farm Labourer	☐	☐	☐	☐	☐
Middle Schoolteacher	☐	☐	☐	☐	☐
Chief's Counsellor	☐	☐	☐	☐	☐
Businessman or Merchant	☐	☐	☐	☐	☐
Medical Doctor	☐	☐	☐	☐	☐
Office Worker	☐	☐	☐	☐	☐

25. Here are the same jobs again. This time we want you to give us your view on the money these people earn. Once again we have put down five squares showing whether you think their income is *very* high, high, average, low and *very* low. Put a tick in the box opposite the job that you think best describes the incomes these people earn.

Job	Very High Income	High Income	Average Income	Low Income	Very Low Income
Clergyman	☐	☐	☐	☐	☐
Lawyer	☐	☐	☐	☐	☐
Policeman	☐	☐	☐	☐	☐
Primary Schoolteacher ..	☐	☐	☐	☐	☐
Shop Assistant	☐	☐	☐	☐	☐
Carpenter	☐	☐	☐	☐	☐
Government Clerk ..	☐	☐	☐	☐	☐
Chief	☐	☐	☐	☐	☐
Farmer	☐	☐	☐	☐	☐
Author	☐	☐	☐	☐	☐
Street Cleaner	☐	☐	☐	☐	☐
Actor	☐	☐	☐	☐	☐
Motor Car Fitter ..	☐	☐	☐	☐	☐
University Teacher ..	☐	☐	☐	☐	☐
Soldier	☐	☐	☐	☐	☐
Petty Trader	☐	☐	☐	☐	☐
Secondary Schoolteacher	☐	☐	☐	☐	☐
Political Party Worker ..	☐	☐	☐	☐	☐
Nurse	☐	☐	☐	☐	☐
Farm Labourer	☐	☐	☐	☐	☐
Middle Schoolteacher ..	☐	☐	☐	☐	☐
Chief's Counsellor ..	☐	☐	☐	☐	☐
Businessman or Merchant	☐	☐	☐	☐	☐
Medical Doctor	☐	☐	☐	☐	☐
Office Worker	☐	☐	☐	☐	☐

APPENDIX 2

A NOTE ON SAMPLING

THE final selection of a sample for the study of Ghanaian secondary schools was partially determined by the characteristics of the Ghanaian student body itself. It was necessary that any instrument or questionnaire used should be in English because of the range of vernaculars spoken by Ghanaian students. Although the questionnaire administered in this study utilized simple English forms this implied that only the senior classes of secondary schools should be included in the investigation. Students at the senior level have a good command of English and their responses were likely to be far more reliable and clearly made.

Furthermore, although it might have been desirable to randomly select students from *different* forms in a sample of schools, this procedure was not agreeable to the school authorities, since it involved dislocating a whole range of institutional activities from the first form onwards. Any investigation, therefore, had to concentrate on one form per sampled school. The fifth forms were the obvious ones to choose in view of their facility in English and the fact that this group was in the terminal year of its basic secondary-school course. Problems of job selection and the possibility of being able to continue with their studies were salient for these pupils.

Having decided that the fifth forms of Ghanaian secondary schools would constitute the universe, it became clear that the number of schools to be investigated could be reduced. In March 1961 there were fifty-nine secondary schools of all types in the public system and fifty-two in the private system. In practice, forty-six schools in the public system had built up to the fifth-form level and only three in the private system. It would have been very desirable to include these three private secondary schools in the universe, but since they were not enthusiastic in their response to the suggestion, it was deemed inadvisable to conduct any investigation in them. In effect, we were left with forty-six public secondary schools; these schools, however, included the bulk of the Ghanaian secondary-school population.

It would have been impossible to visit all these schools in the time available, yet it was very desirable to take as wide a range of institutions as possible. In view of limitations of time and the necessity for considerable travel it was decided to take a 50 per cent sample of these institutions. This sample was drawn by listing the forty-six schools in rank order of their fifth-form size, dividing this list into pairs of schools and selecting randomly from each pair. Thus twenty-three institutions were selected for investigation.

The total fifth-form population in public secondary schools as indicated in government returns stood at 2,101 in March 1961. The number of expected responses was 1,107 or 52·7 per cent of that population. In practice, due to absences, the actual responses consisted of 963 cases or 45·8 per cent of all enrolled fifth-form students. This included 47·9 per cent of all male fifth-form students and 45·4 per cent of the females.

It is interesting to note how the twenty-three selected schools were related to all schools having fifth forms by region and type. So far as the number of schools is concerned, the sample over-represented schools in the Western Region and under-represented those in the Eastern Region. However, in general the sample provided a reasonable regional dispersion of schools.

TABLE A

THE RELATION BETWEEN THE REGIONAL DISTRIBUTION OF SAMPLED SCHOOLS AND THE TOTAL REGIONAL DISTRIBUTION OF SECONDARY SCHOOLS IN THE PUBLIC SYSTEM

	Eastern Region	*Western Region*	*Ashanti Region*	*Volta Region*	*Brong Ahafo*	*Northern Region*	*Total*
Number of sampled institutions	7	9	4	2	—	1	23
Total number of institutions with Fifth Forms	17	13	7	7	1	1	46

So far as type of school is concerned, Table B indicates that the distribution in the sample was a fairly good reflection of the distribution in the system as a whole.

A Note on Sampling

The Relation between Types of Secondary School within the
Sample and Types of Secondary School within the
Public System

	Assisted Schools	Assisted Day Schools	Encouraged Schools	Government Schools	Ghana Educ. Trust School	Total
Number of sampled institutions	8	2	10	2	1	23
Total number of institutions with Fifth Forms	13	6	22	2	3	46

The relationship between enrolments in public secondary schools and in the sample distribution is given in Table C.

Table C

The Relationship between Total Fifth-Form Enrolments
and the Distribution in the Sample (Percentages)

Enrolments	Type of School					
	Assisted	Assisted Day	Encouraged	Government	G.E.T.	Total
In all schools	42·9 (901)	10·6 (222)	35·6 (748)	4·9 (104)	6·0 (126)	100·0 (2,101)
Expected response	49·9 (552)	9·8 (109)	29·4 (325)	9·4 (104)	1·5 (17)	100·0 (1,107)
Actual response	52·6 (507)	8·1 (78)	27·5 (265)	10·3 (99)	1·5 (14)	100·0 (963)

Clearly, the sample as drawn tended to exaggerate the proportion of students in Government and Assisted schools and correspondingly it under-represented students in other types of institutions. This tendency was further exaggerated in the level of actual responses which amounted to 86·9 per cent of those anticipated.

INDEX

Aborigines Rights Protection Society, 96

Academic schools, 8, 53–4, 56–8, 65, 87–8, 101–3, 105, 108 n., 115–16, 133–7, 148–51, 160, 168–9, 184, 296–7

Accelerated Development Plan of 1951, 185–6, 190, 193, 195, 199, 218 n., 254

Access to schooling: by ethnic group, 119–21, 209–13, 233–40, 249–51
  by Region, 46–7, 116–19, 187–9, 235–6, 239–40, 258
  by socio-economic background, 240–54
  urban/rural differentials, 89, 118–23, 128, 143 n., 144 n., 146 n., 183, 188–9, 242, 244

Accra, 18, 50–1, 88, 90, 92, 102, 118–19, 124, 128–30, 149, 179, 188–9, 202, 206, 253

Accra, British, 48–9; *see also* James Fort

Accra Technical School, 149

Achimota School, 135–6, 166–71, 175 n., 194

Acquah, Ioné, 120, 129, 143 n., 145 n., 146 n., 218 n.

Adisadel School, 102, 170

Adloff, R., 175 n.

Advisory Committee on Education in the Colonies, 155–65

Ady, P., 143 n., 144 n.

African attitudes to Western schooling, 52, 58–65, 68, 70, 125–6, 136, 150–1, 155, 167, 209, 228, 300

African Company of Merchants, 41, 44–5, 47, 49

Africanization of education, 185–6, 297–9, 303

Aggrey, James, 110 n., 167, 175 n.

Agricultural education, 8, 53–4, 56–8, 65–6, 87–90, 101, 104–6, 108 n., 116, 124, 133, 137–8, 148–51, 153–5, 158, 160–2, 166, 293–5

Akan peoples: definition of, 18
  influence on the Ewe, 29–30
  influence on Northern peoples, 31
  land tenure, 25
  migration of, 18–19, 35 n.
  religion of, 25
  traditional organization among, 20–5, 31, 33; *see also* Ashanti; Fanti

Akim, 16, 42, 126, 142, 154, 234, 239; *see also* Akan

Akwapim, 42, 79, 120, 126, 144 n., 154, 234–7, 239–40, 251; *see also* Akan

Aldous, Joan, 145 n.

Almond, Gabriel A., 107 n., 109 n., 110 n., 143 n., 175 n., 259 n.

Amamoo, J. G., 219 n.

American Baptist Foreign Missionary Society, 156

314

Index

Education of women and girls, 49, 51, 88, 101, 110 n., 160, 222, 261–2

Efutu, 19, 235

Elkan, Susan, 143 n., 144 n., 147 n., 217 n.

Elmina, 39, 43–5, 50

Elvin, Lionel, 174 n.

Emerson, Rupert, 94, 109 n.

Emirates of Northern Nigeria, 121

Encouraged schools, 193–4, 198, 217 n., 222, 226

Enrolments, 124, 143 n., 209
  in middle schools, 187–8
  opposition to, 124
  and poverty, 122–3
  in primary schools, 187–8
  in secondary schools, 191–2, 225
  in trade and technical schools, 192
  urban-rural variations 122–3, 188

Environment, physical, 13

Epstein, A. L., 110 n., 268, 291 n.

Erzuah, Hon. J. B., 211

Ethnic groupings, 16–20

European settlements, early, 39–41, 44–6, 75, 94

Ewe: annexation of territory, 75
  location and migration, 16–18
  representation in schools, 120, 234, 237, 239
  traditional social organization, 29–30

Examinations: Common Entrance Examination, 194–5, 200, 211, 229, 235, 238
  Middle School Leaving Certificate, 194–5, 199, 203
  Senior Primary School Leaving Examination, 199–200
  Teacher's 'A' Certificate, 216 n.
  West African Higher School Certificate, 203
  West African School Certificate, 185, 216 n., 225–7, 229, 263, 284, 289

Expenditures on education, 122, 150, 166, 218 n., 296

Faidherbe, L. L. C., 61, 72 n.

Fallers, L. A., 36 n., 300, 304 n.

Fanti, 120, 122, 235–6, 239–40, 251
  annexation of, 75
  early European contacts with, 40–1, 46–8
  Fanti Bible Group, 50
  Fanti Confederation, 62, 94–6, 100–1
  location and migration, 18
  representation in schools, 120, 234, 237, 239
  role in coastal trade, 42–3
  traditional organization among, 20–5, 31, 33; *see also* Akan

Fanti Confederacy, 94–6, 100–1

Fanti National Education Scheme, 102

Fanti Public Schools Company and National Education Fund, 102

Field, M. J., 35 n., 36 n., 37 n., 109 n.

Findlay, G. G., 72 n.

Floud, J. E., 6, 10 n.

Forde, Daryll, 145 n.

Forest zone, 16

Fortes, M., 10 n., 37, 63, 73 n., 119–20, 130, 132, 143 n., 144 n., 145 n., 146 n., 174 n.

Fourah Bay College, 68, 93

Fraser, A. G., 172 n., 174 n., 175 n.

Freeman, Thomas Birch, 50, 52, 54, 59–60, 87

Ga-Adangme: annexation of territory of, 75
  creation of 'chiefships' among, 92
  location and migration, 17–18
  representation in schools, 120, 234, 237, 239
  traditional social organization, 27–9

Gbanya; *see* Gonja

Ghana Educational Trust schools, 193–4, 198, 212, 222, 226

Index

Vocational opportunities open to Africans, 65–7, 89–92, 104, 129, 133–7, 139–40
in agriculture, 172 n., 173 n.
in administration, 93, 132, 134–5, 140
as artisans, 90, 98, 134
as clerks, 64, 86–90, 98, 105
as cocoa farmers, 153–5, 172 n., 173 n.
in commerce, 132–5
in law and medicine, 93, 134, 139, 146 n., 172 n.
in teaching, 238
as technicians, 133–5, 138, 151, 283–4, 294
Volta Region, 16
Volta River, 18

Wallerstein, I. M., 89, 108 n., 109 n., 111 n., 214 n., 215 n.
Ward, W. E. F., 35 n., 108 n.
Wartemberg, J. S., 70 n.
Washington, Booker T., 157
Weber, Max, 300

Welbeck, N. A., 218 n.
Wesleyan Methodist Missionary Society schools, 48, 50, 52–4, 58–9, 78, 80, 85–8, 90–1, 100, 102, 104, 107 n., 110 n., 124
West African Examinations Council, 185, 194, 199–200
Westermann, D., 35 n.
Western Province, 211
Western Region, 188
education in, 188, 212
Wilkie, A. W., 71 n.
Wiltgren, R. M., 70 n.
Winneba (Winnebah), 19, 50
Winniett, Governor, 54, 65, 94, 109 n.
Wise, C. G., 10 n., 70 n., 71 n., 72 n.
Wolfson, F., 71 n., 73 n.
Wolseley, Sir Garnet, 75
Workers' Brigade, 204–5, 218
Wright, F., 107 n., 110 n.

Xydias, N., 268, 270, 291 n.

Yeld, E. R., 109 n.